# JOEY

## HAROLD HORWOOD

First published in 1989 by
Stoddart Publishing Co. Limited
34 Lesmill Road
Toronto, Canada
M3B 2T6

---

**CANADIAN CATALOGUING IN PUBLICATION DATA**

Horwood, Harold, 1923–
  Joey

ISBN 0-7737-2293-9

1. Smallwood, Joseph R., 1900–    . 2. Prime
ministers—Newfoundland—Biography.
3. Newfoundland—Politics and government–20th
century.  I. Title.

FC2175.1.S63H67 1989    971.8′04′0924    C89-094420-2
F1123.S63H67 1989

---

Cover Design: Leslie Styles

All photographs, unless otherwise noted, are used by permission of the *Evening Telegram*.

Printed in the United States of America

# Contents

# Preface

I UNDERTOOK THIS BIOGRAPHY OF J.R. SMALLWOOD ONLY AFTER thinking about itfor many years, and only because no other writer in Canada was equipped to do it by such a long personal association with him. It is now almost forty-five years since he and I became associated in the Newfoundland confederate movement, in which I was one of his three closest collaborators. Later, I was also his most active public critic, at a time when he was premier and I was columnist and editorial writer for Newfoundland's largest newspaper.

This book, consequently, is based on my personal knowledge of Smallwood, supplemented by documentary research, and is full of personal judgments about his character, his motives, and his personality. I believe it is sympathetic, but not flattering. He was a great man, as well as a great politician, but I have not tried to hide his weaknesses, his failures, or the tragic changes in his personality brought about by the prolonged experience of near-absolute power.

The anecdotes included here come mainly from three sources: stories told me by Smallwood of his experiences as a young journalist and international socialist; incidents in which I was personally involved; and, in later years, stories from his colleagues and associates. The published memoirs of J.W. Pickersgill and Lester B. Pearson have also been useful.

I must acknowledge the generous co-operation of Greg Power, Ed Roberts, Dale Russell Fitzpatrick, Dick O'Brien, Steve Herder, Evelyn Power, John O'Dea, Harry Cuff, and Mrs. Mary O'Keefe, a volunteer worker at the archives of the Newfoundland Historical Society, as well as that of the regular staff of the Newfoundland Archives and Gosling Memorial Library. *The Evening Telegram* loaned negatives and prints from its picture file, and gave permission for the use of its copyright materials. Gosling Memorial Library and the Newfoundland Archives provided me with photocopies of documents.

I must also acknowledge Smallwood's own work. Even more important than his published memoirs was the great series of reminiscences by other politicians which he collected and published in *The Book of Newfoundland*. The first two volumes of his *Encyclopedia of Newfoundland and Labrador* provided a ready source of reference materials, especially the tabulated results of all elections held in Newfoundland from 1832 to 1979.

H.H.
Annapolis Royal, N.S.
1989

# A St. John's Corner Boy

JOEY SMALLWOOD, THE MOST LOVED, FEARED, AND HATED OF Newfoundlanders, was a superb politician who changed his country's history and held power continuously, almost unchallenged, for twenty-two years and eight months. He was a man who, in his time, played many parts: a union organizer who eventually became a strike breaker, a journalist who carried on a running battle with the press, an agnostic with a passion for collecting materials on the life and teachings of the English evangelist John Wesley. Smallwood was also a self-proclaimed socialist whose private friends included the right-wing premier of Quebec, Maurice Duplessis; the Portugese dictator Antonio Salazar; and the most controversial president of the United States, Richard Nixon. I once asked him why he was so pally with the political boss of Quebec's Union Nationale. He looked at me and grinned. "Well...," he said, "Duplessis is the only politician in Canada who's an inch shorter than me."

Even at the height of his power and respectability Joey did quirky things. He and Nixon, tourists in Moscow, went prowling off at night, guided by a CBC journalist, knocking on the door of Nikita Khrushchev, hoping for a private chat with the former chief of the Politburo, who had by then become the Soviet Union's most famous "nonperson." While on an official tour of European capitals he flew off in the private airliner owned by mining promoter John C. Doyle, with its famous perfume bottles and cut-glass chandeliers, to see the holy city of Isfahan, Iran, where Moslem mobs even then might have lynched an unbeliever. When he quarrelled with his wife (very privately and quietly) he left her stranded in New York City until a friend of hers appeared and bought her a ticket home.

The only card game Joey ever played was solitaire. The only exercise he took was behind the wheel of a car, which he drove himself for most of his political career, sometimes at speeds in excess of a hundred miles an hour. Yet, in Newfoundland's first Oxfam walk, he not only went the symbolic mile like other Canadian premiers, but finished the full twenty miles, and then walked on for one mile more, just to show those city kids what a genuine outport boy could do.

Actually, Joey was no outport boy (though all his life he pretended to be) and his people were not outport people. It is true that he was born in a lumber camp near Gambo, Bonavista Bay, where his father had a temporary job surveying wood, but he was only five months old when the family returned to St. John's. Except for one brief childhood visit to Renews he never remembered laying eyes on an outport until he went to Flat Islands as a newspaper reporter from the city where he had grown up poison poor beside the docks, a typical St. John's corner boy except for one thing: his conviction that he was different, an outsider with a thirst for greatness. He could not recall when he conceived the single-minded intention to become prime minister of his country, and to be knighted by the king of England, but it was some time before the age of fourteen.

By instinct Joey was neither a bayman nor a townie, but a farmer, as the Smallwoods of Prince Edward Island had been for countless generations. Unlike Newfoundlanders, they came not from the fishing ports of western England and Ireland and the Channel Islands, but from the sheep-raising country of the Cotswolds. The first Joseph Smallwood on record in Canada was the inheritor of an early land grant made by the British Crown after Île Royale was ceded to Britain by the French. He was landowner of lot number 38, near Charlotte-town, in 1798. He farmed there, and had six children; three sons and three daughters. Joey's grandfather, David Smallwood, was born on that farm in 1838, but was never more than a part-time farmer. As a youth he was apprenticed to a master carpenter, became a journey-man, and practised his trade in Prince Edward Island before moving to Newfoundland at the age of twenty-three to take advantage of a building boom in St. John's. He worked there at only one job before starting out in business for himself.

Joey always believed that he inherited his ambition and his nearly inexhaustible energy from his grandfather David. Late in Joey's life his government opened the David Smallwood Provincial Park near Gambo, named for his grandfather, who had built the first sawmill in that part of the country about a hundred years earlier. David moved from St. John's to Bonavista Bay in the 1860s, and set up a wide-ranging merchant business centred at Greenspond. Joey loved to tell the story about his grandfather raising the Confederate flag at Greenspond in 1869 during the general election when Newfoundland rejected confederation with Canada so decisively. His grandfather, he said, had threatened to defend the flag at gunpoint when his neighbours gathered to tear it down. He was one of the few pro-confederate voters in Bonavista Bay until Joey himself came along, eighty years later, with his consummate powers of persuasion.

Like many another outport merchant, David Smallwood was bankrupted by repeated fish failures. Even the sawmill went to pay his debts, but continued to operate under new owners and managers. Undaunted, he moved back to St. John's, bought an old boot factory, and proceeded to change it into a national institution. Attached to the factory was a retail store selling footwear.

It was mere coincidence that Joey's father happened to be surveying lumber for what had once been his father's mill when Joey was born. Charles Smallwood had inherited none of David's vigour and drive. He was shiftless, almost without skills, and something of a wastrel. He drifted from business to business and from job to job while he struggled vainly against compulsive drinking. He was the kind of alcoholic who disappears into a drunken stupor for a week or two at a time, then goes on the wagon for a month, only to repeat the cycle again. At one point in his career he owned a carting business with eight to ten horses. It failed. He tried, unsuccessfully, to run a dairy farm. As he went from one paid job to another, his family struggled with poverty that never quite reached the level of destitution.

Charles was married in St. John's to Mary Ellen (Minnie-May) DeVanna, the daughter of a British army sergeant who had served at Halifax, then settled at St. John's. DeVannah is the usual spelling of this French-Hugenot name, but Joey spelled it Devanna, and it is spelled DeVana in the records at St. John's.

The circumstances of Joey's birth were unusual. According to the records of the Division of Vital Statistics, Charles William Smallwood was married on December 21, 1900, to Mary DeVana, the marriage ceremony performed by Reverend H. P. Coperthwaite, a Methodist minister. The marriage was registered on March 31, 1901.

The Return of Births for 1900 has this entry under Mint Brook, Bonavista Bay:

> Dec. 24, 1900. To Chas. W., Minnie Smallwood
> Name: Joseph Robt.
> Baptised May 24, 1901 by Rev. Chas. Lench.
> Registered Jan. 8 by H. J. Creasy.

Mint Brook is a small river that flows into Gambo Pond, about five miles west of Dark Cove, Gambo, the place where Joey is usually said to have been born. There was a mill on the river, and it appears that Joey was born there in a lumber camp, baptised five months later because there was no resident minister in the area, and that the minister then forwarded the return of birth and baptism to St. John's, where it was entered in longhand in the birth book for 1900. If the marriage certificate is correct, Joey escaped by a whisker being born on the train or in a horse cart between Gambo Station and Mint Brook. His parents must have arrived at the Mint Brook mill only a day or so before his birth.

By the spring of 1901 Charles, Minnie-May, and the baby were back in St. John's, where Charles worked for a while in his father's boot factory. The family lived in two rooms over a corner store at LeMarchant Road and Lime Street—at that time a poor neighbourhood near the northern outskirts of the city. The next year they moved to a flat in a three-storey house on Bond Street, and were still there when Joey started school. This could hardly have been earlier than 1905, though Joey thought that he may have started school at about the age of three. On the other hand, his family reported that he was almost three before he uttered his first word, and that his mother was afraid he might be a deaf-mute. At any rate, he started school at the Church of England's British Hall, but was there for perhaps only a few weeks before the family moved once again—this time to Coronation Street near the centre of the city's west end. Here Joey went to the neighbourhood Centenary School, run by the Methodists.

Much more important to the child than the school he attended was the fact that he was now in his grandfather's neighbourhood, and able to help the old man on his "farm"—a large vacant lot, perhaps about an acre, that David rented to grow cabbages, turnips, and potatoes. He also kept a couple of carriage horses, one of which Joey's grandmother drove in style about the town. So the boy began to learn how to feed and curry a horse, and how to hoe and hill potatoes. It must have been pleasant work because, like his grandfather, Joey always wanted to be a farmer, among many other things. He never ceased trying to run a farm, even when he was a successful radio personality and later a powerful politician—and even though, time after time, his farming ventures failed. When, at the height of his political career, he built his dream house, he did something that Newfoundlanders found hard to believe: he built it far back in the woods, many miles from the sight and sound of the sea, and there, with borrowed machinery, he created what he called a ranch. When he chose a site for Confederation Building, to house the government and its offices in St. John's, he contrived to put that back in the woods, too, with a nice ridge of land hiding it from the ocean.

Both acts were highly symbolic. Apart from my paternal grand-mother, who lost her two brothers in a shipwreck, Joey was the only Newfoundlander I knew who had a genuine, deep-seated mistrust of the sea. His whole political career was coloured by the belief that Newfoundlanders only went to sea out of necessity, that they would quit fishing and flock to the production lines to earn "good cash wages" in factories at the first opportunity.

The St. John's in which he grew from infancy to manhood tended to reinforce this attitude. Though it had a couple of captive fishing villages, at Quidi Vidi and the Batteries, it was less a fishing centre than an old mercantile town with worldwide connections, a town filled with traders who tended to think of fish in terms of investment, and of the sea as an intercontinental trade route. Ships were tools of com-merce, fish something to be exchanged for rum and molasses, Spanish salt, Smyrna figs, and above all for British leather goods and textiles. The infant Joey drank in this attitude with his bottle of Pet Milk, consumed it with his "lassy bread," and never once questioned it. From his early days the budding socialist was also a trader, a dealer, and a small-time businessman.

St. John's had been a trading port since the beginning of the sixteenth century. It is the only city in Canada whose origins cannot be traced. It was never "founded" or "colonized". It simply grew of its own accord when the European fishery established it as its New World headquarters around the year 1500 A.D.—more than a century before the founding of Port-Royal or Quebec. No matter who claimed sovereignty, St. John's was always an international port, accommodating ships and traders from France, Spain, Portugal, and England. For more than a hundred years it was also a favourite resort of pirates, who went there to repair their ships and recruit crews from the thousands of fishermen who came and went through St. John's during the summer. It is a well-known jest in St. John's taverns that the pirates never left, but settled on Merchant's Row along Water Street, and in the Colonial Building, the seat of government.

In 1541 Jean-François de La Roque, Sieur de Roberval, stopped at St. John's on his way to the St. Lawrence to try to establish the first French colony in Canada (it failed that winter). There were seventeen European fishing crews in the harbour when he arrived, and he found he was able to buy supplies, and materials for ship repairs. He lingered at St. John's for several weeks, and there met two of Jacques Cartier's ships returning from the French explorer's last voyage of discovery in Canada.

By the middle of the sixteenth century, Spain was sending six thousand men annually to the Newfoundland fisheries—most of them Spanish Basques. By 1578 ten thousand fishermen and whalers from England, France, Portugal and Spain were working in Newfoundland, using St. John's as their trading and outfitting centre, though many of them made direct voyages from Europe to the Strait of Belle Isle. In 1583, when Sir Humphrey Gilbert took possession of Newfoundland for Queen Elizabeth I, proclaimed English law, and made land grants at St. John's, two rows of merchant houses paralleled the harbour-front—one along the Lower Path and the other along the Upper Path, which were later to become Water Street and Duckworth Street.

Although the English and French fought over St. John's for more than a century (the French were not finally dislodged until three years after the fall of Quebec), its international character, flavour, and outlook were set, and remained unchanged right through Joey's boyhood and early manhood.

By the time he was growing up in St. John's, the town had expanded to become a city of forty thousand people, with mayor and city council, and a few imposing buildings, including the huge Roman Catholic Basilica, the Court House rising five storeys above Water Street and looking rather like a stone fort, the splendid Anglican Cathedral of St. John the Baptist, designed by the famous English architect Sir George Gilbert Scott, and the Colonial Building, with a front like a Greek temple in the neoclassical style of the time. This building, where the two houses of government met, became the major shrine of Joey's boyhood.

The little city rose, a semicircular amphitheatre, along a ridge on the north side of the harbour. Some streets were so steep that they had flights of steps instead of sidewalks. About half a mile from the waterfront the land levelled out, then dipped into small river valleys, where the woods and fields and berry barrens began. West and north were many small farms, most owned by Irish settlers, and a few large commercial farms hemmed in by dense forests of spruce and fir.

The merchants had their homes on the outskirts of the city, and their businesses on the waterfront. Most of them lived beyond the crest of the harbour ridge, and westward along Waterford Valley. Their houses were imposing wooden buildings with many rooms, large servants' quarters, coach houses, and stables, surrounded by horse-chestnut trees, sycamore maples, and English hawthorns.

The centre of the city had been totally gutted by the great fire of 1892, and much of it had been rebuilt cheaply and hastily with "ranges" of wooden buildings—the town houses of their time—run up by developers to provide shelter for the homeless and quick profits for themselves. Flimsy and draughty, they were practically instant slums, and by Joey's time had degenerated from their original sorry state to a state yet sorrier. Only good luck and good firefighting prevented yet another holocaust, and preserved the slums until the coming of the bulldozers a generation later.

During Joey's youth, horses were everywhere: huge draught animals hitched in teams hauling slovens (the transport trucks of the time), smaller cart horses hauling coals and cattle feed and fishery salt, light delivery horses distributing meat and groceries, smart carriage horses trotting through the streets with the merchants and their families on business and social calls, and the Victorias, equivalents of taxicabs, running passengers to and from the railway station.

Horse fountains in red-painted cast iron stood at major intersections spewing water from the mouths of lions into shell-shaped reservoirs where teams could pause for a drink, and small boys could climb to the rim to slurp the splashing water. Often a public cistern stood close by, for only the main streets had a piped water supply. People on side streets usually had to carry water to their houses from the "pumps" as the cisterns were called.

Except for two arteries running east and west—one asphalted and the other covered with paving stone—the streets were dust in summer, mud in spring and autumn, packed frozen snow in winter, all of it liberally mixed with horse droppings. Great flocks of house sparrows fed upon the semi-digested oats, and pigeons were everywhere. In many places the sidewalks were covered with coal dust, and the air was heavily polluted with smoke and soot, for all the houses, rich and poor, were heated with coal stoves, coal-burning fireplaces, and in a few of the big houses, coal-burning furnaces. Anyone who wanted to know which way the wind was blowing just had to glance out a window at the forest of fuming chimney-pots.

In addition to the mercantile establishments along Water Street and the small civil service, the main business of the city was light manufacturing. Iron foundries, clothing factories, boot and shoe plants, tanneries, small shipyards, a paint and varnish factory, wood finishing operations, carriage and furniture factories, soft drink and tobacco factories, bread and biscuit bakeries, a margarine plant, and a rope factory all flourished in St. John's, all powered by coal furnaces, all contributing to the air pollution and the respiratory diseases from which hardly anyone escaped.

Apart from the merchant estates and the middle-class suburbs, St. John's was a grimy little city where bedraggled chickens and the occasional pig rooted along the gutters among harried women, bare-foot kids, and mongrel dogs. It was dusty below and smoggy above. Underfoot, St. John's pedestrians sometimes had the benefit of a stone crosswalk, permitting dry-shod and dust-free travel from one street corner to another, assisted by the crossing sweepers—boys with brooms who were rewarded with copper coins dropped into grimy palms by wealthy citizens in top hats or bowlers, carrying gold-headed or ivory-headed walking canes, their ankles sheathed in spats.

It was a European city, built by displaced Europeans, with a European outlook. Its trade was with Europe, the West Indies, the Mediterranean, South America, and the United States. It had little to do with Canada, which was at its back door. Many people regarded the British Isles as home, and to everyone England was the mother country. If you had asked Joey's young companions about their nationality, many of them, even those whose grandparents had been born in St. John's, would have replied, "I'm English." But Joey would have said without equivocation, "I'm a Newfoundlander."

The Charles Smallwoods did not remain on Coronation Street. Their next move was to a small house on a piece of wooded land on the lower slope of the Southside Hill near Kilbride, a couple of miles west of the city. Joey, now about nine years old, at first walked to and from St. Mary's school, near the Long Bridge at the west end of St. John's harbour—a lot of tramping for a small boy, so when school opened the following September he went to the one-room Roman Catholic day school run by the nuns from Littledale Convent at Kilbride.

While living on the Southside, he tended his father's horses, and learned to harness and drive them. He hauled firewood down from the hill and sawed it with a crosscut into lengths suitable for the kitchen cookstove—the only source of heat in the house. He helped to fence the land, and helped to clear an acre of it. Besides horses, the family raised a pig each year for meat, and kept a dozen laying hens.

Joey sometimes went trouting with his father and one of his father's drinking companions at The Goulds—a chain of lakes about ten miles west of St. John's. Later he took his young brothers there fishing. They would start the journey by horse cart before dawn, and arrive home after sunset with a string of trout. Between subsistence farming and casual work the family eked out a living, sometimes scraping the bottom of the flour barrel, but on the whole leading a fairly happy life while their fortunes went from bad to worse. Despite the poverty, the lack of proper sanitation, and the prevalence of such diseases as tuberculosis, pneumonia, and typhoid fever—all of them virtually incurable at that time—the thirteen little Smallwoods born to Minnie-May between 1900 and 1925 all lived to become adults, and most of them lived into old age.

If Joey lacked a stable family background, he also lacked the stability of a religious tradition. His father was a nominal Methodist, and his mother a nominal Catholic, but oddly, for the time, neither of them ever went to church, and if Joey went during his first ten years it would have been only out of sheer curiosity. He grew up with no religious belief or teaching whatsoever, and went through life without the consolations of either religion or philosophy.

Like other boys from downtown St. John's, he spent many hours hanging around the docks, which in those days consisted of a ring of wooden wharves projecting into the harbour for two hundred feet or so, wooden schooners moored on either side. There freight from Europe, America, and the Caribbean came ashore to be stored in the merchants' sheds, to be loaded later into the holds of smaller ships, mostly fifty- to one-hundred-ton coasting schooners, which carried goods to the little outports along the coasts of Newfoundland and

Labrador. At the outports the goods would be delivered to the merchants' branch stores, or stores owned by their dealers—the outport shopkeepers who, like David Smallwood a generation earlier, were trying their luck as independent businessmen.

Whatever young Joey knew of the sea, he learned on the docks. Now and then he may have bummed a ride across the harbour on a boat, but it is unlikely that he ever took even the shortest voyage outside The Narrows. In April he saw the stinking seal pelts with their thick layers of rancid fat being unloaded from the big sealing ships, and in October he saw fishery salt being hoisted from the holds of foreign-going vessels. He heard the men speak of Pernambuco, of Demerara, of Gibraltar and Naples and Oporto, all of them distant cities to which the ships delivered their dried cod, returning with salt and rum and the mixed cargoes of foodstuffs and drygoods and hardware that had been the lifeblood of St. John's from the days of Sir Richard Whitbourne and Sir Humphrey Gilbert.

During Joey's childhood the harbour water was already polluted, but boys swam there just the same. Sometimes a pair of nude swimmers would arrive on the Water Street docks from the Southside, and would then have no choice but to dive in and swim back again. Joey went skinny dipping too, but not in the harbour. He and a dozen other boys would hike inland to Rennie's River, to a place just under the hill where he would later build Confederation Building, to swim in Sliding Rock Pool, and then would hike home again, two or three miles each way.

Joey remembered the harbour as a "paradise of excitement" for boys. There were parrots and sugar cane on the docks, brought by sailors from British Guiana and the West Indies. There were puncheons of molasses lying in the sun, their bungs open to allow gases to escape. He and other urchins would stick their fingers into the bung holes, then lick off the molasses, and keep doing it until a watchman spotted them and kicked them off the wharf, sometimes literally giving them a boot in the behind if he could get near enough.

Except for swimming and running (and perhaps boxing) Joey had no talent for athletics. He sometimes kicked a soccer ball around a field, but really cared nothing for competitive sports. Despite such an unpopular attitude, he never lacked friends. The picture of the lonely, withdrawn little boy, huddled off by himself on the edge of school life, is totally false. He was cocky, self-assertive, and self-confident, and always the centre of a group of young scamps, most of them older than himself. Friends flocked around him when he was a boy just as they did when he became an adult. He had the one thing a leader really needs— more brains than his followers.

At home Minnie-May did her best to hold the growing family together and keep them clothed and fed. Often there was just bread and potatoes, and not too much of that. Joey acquired a great taste for bread and molasses, the treat of his youth, sometimes with butter as well. In middle age he still enjoyed this primitive concoction, and sang its praises in the House of Assembly.

"But if you put butter on the bread, the molasses will run off!" the leader of the Opposition objected one time. (He was from a well-heeled merchant family, and had been educated at Oxford.)

"Oh no!" Joey explained. "The Honourable Leader of the Opposition obviously knows nothing about lassy bread. You put the molasses on *first*, then spread the butter on top."

Minnie-May made and baked the bread herself, and fetched the molasses from the nearest store, where it was pumped out of a huge puncheon barrel into her quart milk bottle. Occasionally the store owner would give her an extra special treat for her hungry taggle of youngsters—molasses sugar scraped out of the bottom of a puncheon, rich with all the sediment that had collected there since the barrel had been filled in Barbados.

But the real centre of Joey's childhood was not the nuclear family. It was Grandfather David. The old man loved to tell stories, and Joey loved to listen. Together they pottered about the boot factory and the store, now managed by Joey's Uncle Fred. Smallwood's boots were a respected institution, well-known to all Newfoundlanders, their memories assisted by bits of crude doggerel:

Smallwood's boots for lads and lasses,
Smallwood's boots they suit all classes,
Smallwood's boots they are so grand,
They are the best in Newfoundland.

The principal customers were fishermen, for whom the rubber boot was still a thing of the future—oiled leather was the universal footwear of the fishery. Every time a fisherman sailed in or out through The Narrows, he would see a huge black boot hanging from an iron bar fixed into the cliff, with "Buy Smallwood's Boots" inscribed on it in white letters.

Like Grandfather David, Uncle Fred managed the small business well, made a modest profit, and had a few dollars to spread around among the poorer members of the extended family. It was through Uncle Fred that Joey got three years or so of what we would now call junior high school in one of the three really good schools in the city.

After Joey had attended four small neighbourhood schools, run by teachers with little more than high school education themselves, Uncle Fred—presumably influenced by Grandfather David—came to the rescue. The boy was obviously bright. He should get at least enough schooling to enter the family business and go on to become a manager. In time, the Smallwoods might even be accepted into the St. John's business aristocracy. For this the right kind of old school tie was important.

At that time the only schools in Newfoundland equipped to prepare students for advanced education were the "colleges" in St. John's run by boards from the three principal religious denominations. Bishop Feild, the school to which Joey was to go, was an Anglican institution that took only boys, mostly the sons of merchants and professional people. Like the other colleges, it took boarders from out of town, as well as day students. Joey, Uncle Fred decided, should be a boarder. He lived more than four miles from the school, without easy transportation. Besides, boarding there would take the boy away from the influence of his drunken father, and put him in respectable surroundings where he might learn some of the social graces, as well as how to write up a bill of sale and keep an account book.

The cost was not extreme, even by the standards of the times: $41 for each school year. Uncle Fred also provided the school uniform, smartly got up in light and dark blue. (At other times Joey was dressed in made-over hand-me-downs, and he continued through life to wear odd socks and unmatched parts of suits.) There was also supposed to be a ten-cent weekly allowance, but most of it was held back by the school for misbehaviour. That was the limit of Uncle Fred's generosity. Of the extra spending money that the day scholars received at home he had never a sniff—nothing for such luxuries as candy, bottles of porter, and the illegal cigarettes that every highschool boy consumed when the teachers' backs were turned.

He overcame this financial handicap by opening his first business—a lending library of juvenile literature which he purchased from Sammy Garland's Bookstore in downtown St. John's. All the English journals—*Chums*, *Boy's Own*, and the like—he bought as they arrived, rented them out to his schoolmates at a cent each, and used the proceeds to buy all the penny dreadfuls on the shelves.

His original capital came not only from the remains of his weekly ten-cent allowances, but also from summer gardening work. Neighbours in Kilbride hired him at fifty cents a day to cut grass with a reaping hook, and to weed their gardens. Most of the money he earned in this way had to go to the family, but he hoarded what he could, to spend on books and magazines. According to his own account, he never spent the money from his lending library on anything else. It was strictly a rotating fund for more reading material.

Joey was small for his age, as well as poor, and very much ashamed of his drunken father. All these things combined to give him a massive inferiority complex. In old age he even admitted himself that this "might be possible" (after I had pointed it out in a newspaper article) but even then he thought it unlikely. So much for self-analysis.

As a boy he was combative, cocky, an insufferable little know-it-all. He learned later that there were vast areas of human knowledge permanently closed to him, and he acquired just a trace of humility, but to the end of his life he was the battling underdog determined to be the male alpha, the poverty-stricken slum child set on being a world-beater. Even at the age of twelve he was managing this quite well. His former schoolmates remember him as an undersized "crackie" (a small, loud-mouthed dog) but a leader.

In later years Joey looked back on his time at Bishop Feild with the fond glow of nostalgia. But in fact, those years were unhappy and unproductive. In his first year he was only one place from the bottom of the class. Later, because he was able to read and write fluently, he did a little better than that, though he never achieved even moderate distinction. His teachers had little influence on him. He would have learned to read and write as well without any help from the school, from his magazines and penny dreadfuls and the better materials to which he graduated later. He learned no mathematics—at least none that he could remember later—no foreign languages, just a smattering of geography and history, and no science or music or art. He was self-taught, as much as it is possible for anyone to be, and he suffered from the common weaknesses of self-teaching. He understood neither classical logic nor the scientific method, nor the principles of objective criticism. He learned only his chosen subjects in his own haphazard way: some literature, a lot of current politics and economics and social theory, and little else. When he went as an adult to hear public lectures by intellectuals like Bertrand Russell, he found them incomprehensible.

Joey did play the bugle in the Church Lads Brigade, an Anglican cadet corps, and he was perhaps the school's best essayist, but otherwise he made poor grades, and always rebelled against school authority. When he sat for a scholarship and failed to get it, he received only 58% for academic work, 22% for athletics, and 9% for character. The marks reveal more about the school than about Joey himself. To the authorities "character" meant docility, not leadership and daring and imagination; and "athletics" meant team sports, including cricket, which Bishop Feild had imported from the playing fields of Eton. Such "failures" dampened Joey's self-confidence not in the least. In one of his school books he inscribed what he intended to be his future name and title:

> The Right Honourable Joseph Roberts Smallwood, K.C.M.G., P.C., M.H.A. Prime Minister of Newfoundland.

He already knew about prime ministers and privy councillors and Knights Commander of St. Michael and St. George. During his free time at school his favourite place was the visitors' gallery of the Newfoundland House of Assembly, fortunately only about three blocks from the schoolyard.

He did learn some useful things at Bishop Feild, none of them on the curriculum. He learned that most boys from wealthy families were dolts. And he learned to take his knocks, from both boys and teachers—corporal punishment was meted out freely. The headmaster used a wooden paddle; the manual training teacher used a lath, with which he belaboured the boys' rear ends; the older boys sometimes spanked the younger ones—all in the English public school tradition.

He made some lasting and even lifelong friendships among his school fellows. He led a strike in protest against the food in the dining room, demanding "more lassy and less pudding", and believed it was partly successful: there did indeed seem to be more molasses, at least for a time. When he and others were caught skipping their compulsory church attendance and were "gated" for two weeks as punishment, he organized a boycott of the dining room, and the headmaster, obviously a reasonable man, reduced the period of punishment to a few days.

At school Joey also learned something about how the other half lives—the *upper* half. At school he wore decent clothes, never the threads and patches that he wore at home. He sometimes paraded in uniform with the Church Lads Brigade. He had to keep his shoes shined and his hair cut and combed. Because he was a boarder, he had to follow a regular routine of personal hygiene: to wash every day and brush his teeth and take baths. All this was in sharp contrast to life at home, where there was no running water, let alone a bathtub, and where he used an outdoor privy instead of a flush toilet.

Perhaps the most important thing he learned—at least the most important skill—was typing. Before the First World War typing was still regarded as a specialized secretarial skill, and was not taught even in the school's "commercial" streams. So Joey couldn't take typing, but there was a typewriter in one of the offices, and when it wasn't being used he slipped in through the unlocked door and practised on it till he could bang out thirty or forty words a minute by the hunt-punch-miss-and-cuss method. Later practice gave him a respectable degree of speed and accuracy.

There were six grades at Bishop Feild, ending with what we would now call grade eleven. Joey, after fomenting another battle with the establishment, and refusing to accept what he regarded as an unjust "gating," dropped out of school before he had finished grade nine. With his usual vagueness about dates and periods, he thought he remembered "four or five years" at Bishop Feild, but his actual time there was little more than three years. According to his own reckoning, he was fourteen when he quit without finishing grade nine and began hunting for a job.

While the boy was in his early teens, his mother suddenly got religion. A lapsed Catholic until then, she fell in with a group of hot gospellers from the United States, began attending prayer meetings at the Bethesda Mission in downtown St. John's, and was soon "converted." The Bethesda Mission housed one of those emotional sects where people "testified" with tears and cries, rocked and sang and "spoke in tongues." Sometimes they fell to the floor, shaken by hysterical laughter, when possessed by the Holy Ghost.

Joey went with his mother on various occasions to the Bethesda Mission. Even late in life he could recall the names of many of the prominent members of the congregation. He probably enjoyed the emotional atmosphere and the loud singing and praying, and perhaps learned from these meetings something about how crowds can be swayed by mass emotion. He never allowed his own head to be turned the slightest bit, but must have seen the preachers work the crowds into a state of frenzy. Later, he would use many of the same tech niques himself: the endless repetition of simple slogans, the loudness and earnestness of voice, the straightforward appeal to simple, basic emotions.

This was not the kind of rhetoric taught in the socialist circles that he frequented a few years later; it was the special rhetoric of the fundamentalist preacher. Later in New York, he listened to other preachers, consciously studying their style, but it was at the Bethesda Mission in downtown St. John's that the young agnostic of twelve or thirteen learned his earliest and most valuable lessons in how to sway mass audiences.

As a speaker, Joey was no great stylist. He developed only a single technique, which he seemed unable to change or adapt to the needs of his audiences. It irritated many intelligent listeners. Even when he was invited to speak at national conventions or university convocations, he sounded rather like a junior highschool teacher trying to hammer a few elementary ideas into a class of slow learners. He had great admiration for imagistic oratory, but never learned to use it.

# CHAPTER 2

# Airplanes and Moonshine

ALL HIS LIFE JOEY HAD THE DUAL AMBITION TO BE A GREAT POLITICAL leader and a great writer. As a writer, he wanted to be a polemicist, a propagandist, a teacher, a journalist with a message, but always a journalist, even when he published in hard covers. So it is scarcely surprising that he went to a St. John's newspaper when, at the age of fourteen, he needed his first full-time job. The First World War had begun in August 1914. By the following spring Europe and America were operating under a war economy, and it wasn't hard to find work in St. John's. Indeed, in 1915 anyone with a skill or even an aptitude could find suitable work in any North American city. Unemployment would be mostly unheard of for the next five or six years.

At that time it was quite usual for journalists to start their careers as printers. Editors, and even some owners, of North American dailies often started that way. And a career in journalism was one of the normal routes into politics. Most Newfoundland prime ministers were former newspaper editors or owners or both. Joey got his first job with the St. John's *Plaindealer* at $1.50 a week as a "printer's devil." Apprentices were called devils not because of their character, but because their hands, face, and clothes were so often black with printer's ink. Joey did all the menial jobs in the print shop: he washed off the hand-set type with water and lye, swept the floor, ran messages, inked the forms on the platens, and did a little typesetting under the watchful eyes of the printers, who, in the case of the *Plaindealer*, were also editors and owners.

Later that year Joey moved to another weekly, *The Spectator*, a one-man-and-a-boy operation on Theatre Hill (named for the Majestic Theatre, which stood, domed and magnificent, at its foot) but he was there only a few weeks before the paper folded. He immediately got a better job at higher pay with *The Daily News*. It was the beginning of a career of job-hopping that was to continue until he settled down, more than thirty years later, into the one job that really suited him.

Now aged fifteen, he still wasn't a reporter, but an apprentice printer. Even that didn't last long: the paper moved him from its printing room into its mail room; from there he moved again to the bookkeeping department, where he became a bill collector. Meanwhile, he was getting the occasional bit of writing into print—if not in his employers' newspaper, then in *The Fishermen's Advocate*, published by one of Joey's all-time heroes, the leader of the Fishermen's Protective Union, William Coaker.

Coaker had a powerful formative influence on the young Smallwood. Born in St. John's, educated at Bishop Feild, he had become, by the outbreak of the First World War, one of the most powerful politicians in Newfoundland, and a social reformer of great force. Coaker had organized his first union back in 1903, and by 1908 had made himself leader and spokesman for the Newfoundland fishermen. Within a year he organized some fifty local councils of the Fishermen's Protective Union, and eventually was head of an organization with about twenty thousand members. In 1913 Coaker and seven followers were elected to the House of Assembly as members of the Fishermen's Union Party. Until then the sacred halls of the Colonial Building had been inhabited only by merchants, lawyers, and newspaper editors—an exclusive club of the power elite, conservatives to the backbone, regardless of their labels. Coaker's crew had walked into the House to take the oath of office dressed in fishermen's guernseys, to the consternation of the men on the government benches dressed in morning suits. It seemed for a little while that the revolution had arrived, and the Royal Navy was alerted by the governor to keep a cruiser in readiness, in case the king's peace should be threatened at St. John's.

To Joey this was all heady stuff. Coaker was at the height of his power and influence, he was the great working man's hero, and though the war was already undermining his authority, this did not become apparent until later. Joey might be working for the Tory press, but his heart and head were with Coaker and the Fishermen's Protective Union. He was in full sympathy with their expressed intention to "make the grass grow on Water Street," where the fish merchants had always ruled the land from their stores and offices. There is no doubt that the fifteen-year-old Joey already saw himself as another, even greater Coaker, and the time would come when the fishermen would see him that way too, after Coaker had failed, and left them for the booby prize of a knighthood, a merchant empire, and a home in the West Indies.

A year or so earlier the boy (already calling himself a socialist among his schoolmates though he had but the vaguest idea what socialism was all about) had met Coaker's *éminence gris*, the intellectual George Grimes, in a dentist's waiting room, and had received from Grimes two books that purported to explain socialism for blue-collar workers. Written at a grade three reading level in a series of punchy slogans, they made a deep impression on Joey, who continued to think in slogans for the rest of his life. Having digested—indeed *memorized*—them, he considered himself an instant expert on the coming revolution.

During this part of his career the youngster, now earning six dollars a week, lived with Grandfather David on Springdale Street, a stone's throw from his old home on Coronation Street, but ate lunch daily with his father at the Salvation Army soup kitchen, where coarse but substantial meals could be bought for ten cents each. Though Joey may not have been the socialist revolutionary that he believed himself to be, he was quite clearly a proletarian.

It was at some time during this period that he joined the MCLI—one of the crucial steps in his career. The Methodist College Literary Institute was a debating society founded by teachers and former students of the Methodist College (later Prince of Wales College) in St. John's. Because even Methodist ministers might be excluded from membership, they stretched the constitution to include members of the church who had not attended the college either as students or teachers. It took some imagination, but Joey could be regarded as either a Methodist or an Anglican, so he got in. No amount of redefining the membership requirements, however, could admit all the skilled speakers in Newfoundland, so the MCLI relied heavily on guest debaters. One way or another, nearly every orator in the island, every major politician, and many a skilled defence lawyer, learned his trade there. The gallery of MCLI presidents looks remarkably like the gallery of Newfoundland prime ministers and attorneys-general.

The society not only taught its members how to speak, how to debate successfully, and how to be fast and effective in rebuttal, but also specialized in teaching parliamentary procedure. Half the fun of any MCLI session consisted of the points of order, the arguments over amendments to the amendments, the niceties of laying a resolution on the table, and the tricky business of getting it off. "Moving the previous question," a form of closure, was one of the delights of the more experienced members. No parliament in the Empire was conducted with more rigour than the sessions of the MCLI. But above all, this wonderful parliamentary training was *fun*. Joey became not only an attendant at every debate, but one of the institute's perpetual debaters. He and Cyril Parkins and Bert Butt, and the marvellous, silver-tongued orator Nimshi Crewe, carried the torch for the Left against such shell-backed Tories as Captain Abram Kean, Herb Russell, Cal Pratt, and William White.

Joey was too young to have debated there with Sir Robert Bond, but was in time for the debates led by Sir Richard Squires (both of them great debaters and prime ministers). Smallwood had a close association with the MCLI for thirty years: he and Squires debated there as a team in 1920, and he and I did the same in 1948. As a journalist, he started the practice, which continued for some forty years, of reporting the debates in full in the daily press, giving a summary of the arguments advanced by each speaker, as well as the resolutions and the vote. This became particularly important after 1934, when for fifteen years Newfoundland had no parliamentary government. During that period the MCLI's weekly debates covered every public issue as it came up, and the debates were reported at increasing length. In this way the tradition of public debate was kept alive, and important issues were kept before the public eye in a country ruled by seven men sitting in a closed room, answerable only to the Dominions Office on the other side of the ocean.

Joey's big break into journalism came after he had spent nearly two years as office flunkey and bill collector at *The Daily News*. In 1918 *The Evening Telegram* advertised for a reporter. Then, as now, it was the most important paper in the island, though it was only one of six dailies being published at St. John's. The paper was officially and rabidly Liberal, in a Gladstonian sort of way. That is to say, *The*

*Telegram* was an enthusiastic supporter of British imperialism; the Union Jack was (and still is) its emblem; it was violently opposed to every revolutionary reform movement in the world; but above all it was violently opposed to the Newfoundland Tories, whom the editors regarded as a bunch of self-serving scoundrels.

"At least you can work with the Liberals," Joey used to tell his fellow socialists. "You can't work with the Tories. They're blind and deaf. They're incapable of seeing that change is inevitable." Not all of his fellow socialists agreed with this, but a surprising number of them ended up, like Joey himself, in the Liberal Party.

The founding owner and managing editor (though not the editor) of *The Evening Telegram* was a charming old conservative named William J. Herder. Like Joey, he had started life as a printer's devil, but had gone on to found a publishing dynasty. His son Ralph was now working with him. His younger sons and grandsons later entered the business and made an enormous success of it until they finally sold out to the Thomson newspaper chain in 1969. Liberal or not, Herder was an idealist. He had gone to jail for contempt of court (and his editor had gone to jail with him) rather than compromise the ethics of journalism by revealing the name of a correspondent. Herder had spent his time in jail dressed in his red flannel longjohns because he refused to wear the prison uniform.

Such was Joey's new boss, and they got along famously, even though Herder was well aware that he was nourishing a socialist viper in his conservative bosom. William Herder and his successors never made an issue of their writers' politics. If they could produce lively copy, and didn't slip in too many radical ideas, the Herders would back them all the way. Joey started at $12 a week, but *The Telegram* was soon paying him $18, and finally $25—a substantial wage at the end of the First World War, when master mariners were often glad to get a ship at $50 a month.

*The Telegram's* editorial department then consisted of the editor, who selected copy for the editorial page and wrote the leaders, and two reporters, assigned respectively to the east end and the west end of the city. Joey was fortunate to get the west end, which happened to include the departure points for the pioneer Atlantic flights. He worked at first opposite Ned Smith, and then opposite Pat O'Reilly, who continued to cover the eastern beat as a *Telegram* reporter for more than forty years—until long after Joey became premier. O'Reilly, who shared a newsroom with me for six years, always remained friendly with Joey, but like many people who knew him as a youth, regarded him with mixed respect and amusement: "He's fine. Just remember to take him with a grain of salt."

No cub reporter ever had greater luck. Joey landed his first job as a journalist with an ambitious paper anxious to improve its news coverage just as some of the most dramatic stories in Newfoundland's history were breaking. First there was the massive victory parade at the end of 1918 (Joey covered it on horseback.) Next came the invasion of Flat Islands by the Royal Navy. Then there were the first daring attempts to fly across the Atlantic Ocean in the kite-like planes of the war. For reasons of geography and prevailing wind, all such flights originated in Newfoundland, which had rarely before been a centre of world attention.

The Flat Islanders were independent Bonavista Bay fishermen who liked their drop of 'shine. When the local police arrived to seize their stills, the Flat Islanders got out their swiling guns and drove the invaders from their shores. Alfred B. Morine, a Mainlander who had become Newfoundland's attorney-general (and the parachute member for Bonavista Bay), was appalled by this daring act of lawlessness. Through the governor he sent off a secret appeal to Britain to send a cruiser at once to put down the insurrection.

When HMS *Cornwall* arrived at St. John's from the West Indian station in June 1919, no one thought anything about it. Cruisers were in and out of the harbours frequently, and only the ladies of the waterfront paid them any great attention. But Joey scented a story. Off he went to Morine's office. "She's going to Flat Islands, isn't she?" he demanded.

"You want to go with her?"

"Well, of course."

Morine smiled, picked up his phone, and asked for the inspector general of police. "There's a reporter from *The Telegram* named Smallwood," he said, "wants to go to Flat Islands on the *Cornwall*. Take him along as your secretary—no need to have any fuss about a reporter being on board." So the head of Newfoundland's police force smuggled Joey on board the king's ship, disguised as his private secretary.

Next day they cruised around Bonavista Bay firing practice shots at icebergs until they judged that the rebels were well cowed. Then they sent a landing party creeping through the fog to Flat Islands with orders to grab every able-bodied man in the place and clap him into irons.

It was true comic opera, with a proper anticlimax. By the time the *Cornwall* arrived, all the able-bodied men of Flat Islands had left for their summer's fishing down on the Labrador. A company of marines, half a dozen policemen, the inspector general, and secretary Joey all swarmed ashore to be welcomed on the wharf by the entire population of women and children. They searched the settlement for hidden fishermen, and found six senior citizens, all that remained of the male population. These they carted off to St. John's for trial, where they were quickly acquitted and given passage back home. But for Joey it was wonderful copy. He wrote it up as a farce (and a sly attack on the whole clumsy apparatus of British imperialism) and *The Telegram* sold more than a thousand extra copies on the street that afternoon. His reputation as an enterprising reporter was made.

Meanwhile Britain's *Daily Mail* had initiated a great trans-Atlantic air race by offering a prize of ten thousand pounds to the first airplane to reach the British Isles from North America. In effect, this meant from Newfoundland, for the island was about four hundred miles closer to Britain than any other part of the New World. Teams of volunteer workers at Harbour Grace scrambled to build the first gravelled airstrip in Newfoundland. Lester's Field in St. John's, part of a large pasture near Mundy Pond on the city's northwestern edge, was put at the disposal of international flyers. Planes began to arrive, shipped in crates from Europe, and teams of mechanics began assembling and testing them.

Vast crowds turned out, almost around the clock, to watch the preparations. The planes were among the first most Newfoundlanders had ever seen, and were part of the greatest, most dangerous sporting event of the era. Newfoundland in 1919 was like Cape Canaveral in the 1960s, but the excitement was more intense, because flying the Atlantic was no mere technological feat, like landing on the moon. It was the ultimate high adventure, with enormous risk to the flyers. Not one of the planes that made the attempt in 1919 had actually been built to cross the Atlantic. At best, they had only been modified to cover long distances. Predicting the weather was a matter of guesswork, and bad weather could bring any flight to an end after its point of no return. So the odds were against any plane making it to Europe in safety, and indeed most of them crashed, ditched, or vanished without a trace.

Seeing them take off was literally seeing men fly in the face of death. The press and the public, both local and foreign, just lapped it up.

Joey scrambled back and forth between St. John's and Harbour Grace, with occasional visits to Trepassey, trying to cover the preparations at all these departure points, filling *The Telegram's* columns with accounts of test flights, with the crashes-on-takeoff that were all too common because every plane was loaded beyond its normal capacity with fuel, and with interviews in which the heroic "birdmen" told of their deeds, their dreams, and their death-defying escapes from repeated disasters. But as the two likeliest candidates neared their zero hours, he was forced to choose between St. John's and Harbour Grace, almost a day's travel apart. He decided to bet on the favourite, a huge Handley Page bomber brought from England by Admiral Mark Kerr, flying out of Harbour Grace. The opposition, at St. John's, was a smaller Vimy bomber, built by Vickers, and converted for long-range cruising. Commanded by Captain John Alcock, with Lieutenant Arthur Brown as navigator, and stuffed with gasoline instead of bombs, it was quite capable, if luck was on its side, of spanning the ocean with flying time to spare.

Hawker and Grieve had already ditched in mid-Atlantic and had been rescued by a ship. Raynham and Morgan had crashed so badly on takeoff that their plane was out of the race. An entire flotilla of American amphibians, among the largest planes in the world, were sitting at Trepassey near Cape Race, each with a five-man crew and thousands of men in support, and an American warship stationed every hundred miles all the way to the Azores. But the Americans were hampered by the very size of their operation: machine shops, wireless stations, weather stations, and fuel dumps all had to be set up. A chain of communications stretching from the United States to Newfoundland to the Azores and on to Portugal had to be set up and functioning. The planes themselves had to be checked and rechecked for "malfunctions."

While all this was going on, with excitement at fever pitch, Alcock and Brown slipped quietly into the air at St. John's, disappeared over the Atlantic, and landed sixteen and a half hours later in an Irish bog, mistaking it for a field. The race was over, the prize won, and Joey had bet on the wrong horse. But he continued to cover Admiral Kerr until Kerr took for Long Island, New York, in a bid to be the first to fly non-stop from the United States to Britain. His huge plane crashed at Parsboro, Nova Scotia, and that was the end of his venture.

One of the four Navy-Curtis amphibians from Trepassey also made it across the Atlantic, but not entirely by air. It came down in the sea hundreds of miles short of the Azores, then managed to taxi on the surface (shepherded by American warships) to the mid-Atlantic islands, where its malfunctioning engines were restored to service. Then it flew on to Lisbon.

Although Atlantic and round-the-world flights continued from St. John's and Harbour Grace that year and for many years thereafter—some of them truly suicidal attempts in light, single-engined planes—the excitement was dying down, and Joey began wondering about the next stage in his career. Meanwhile, there was the first Newfoundland general election in which he was able to take an active part. He worked for the Labour Party, the first of several labour parties to contest seats in St. John's, sometimes successfully. That year Joey discovered the thrill of working in smoke-filled committee rooms, canvassing for votes, inventing slogans, and convincing yourself that your candidates were going to win. They didn't. In the election of 1919 the three candidates were defeated, though they made a good showing in St. John's West. Among those elected in the capital were Richard Squires, soon to become Joey's hero and exemplar, and Sir Michael Cashin, nominally a Liberal, though in fact an independent without political philosophy or allegiance to anything but himself. He led a patched-up faction called the People's Party but changed its name to Liberal-Progressive before the election. Squires was leading a faction called the Liberal Reform Party (as Joey would do half a lifetime later). But party lines were tangled and meaningless except as tags. It was a dog's game, with every dog for himself, leading straight to chaos and disaster.

By 1919 Coaker had degenerated from a radical with a mission, determined to revolutionize the economy and reform society, into a bourgeois politician leading a union faction in coalition with Squires. He captured ten seats in the north, and Squires fourteen in the south. Twelve seats went to Cashin and his followers. So Squires became prime minister, and Coaker minister of fisheries. How Joey reacted at the time to all this political footwork he has never said, but within a few years he had transferred his political allegiance totally to Squires, and though he continued to call himself a socialist, at least among socialists, his loyalty to Squires never wavered.

The foxy St. John's lawyer who led the Liberal Reform Party was no socialist, no populist, no reformer—no liberal, in fact. He was a pragmatist through and through, a successful player in the power game, with no visible political convictions, right, left, or centre. It was one of Smallwood's deep inconsistencies that he professed to be a lifelong socialist while choosing a man like Squires as his political model.

During the election of 1919 *The Telegram's* editor, Charles James, took leave of absence to run for Cashin's Liberal-Progressives in Burgeo-LaPoile (where he collected a pitiable 231 votes out of the 1,659 votes cast). This gave young Joey his chance to sit at the great man's desk and pontificate to his heart's content, writing leaders for the paper. He wrote all the editorials during James's absence, and got all but one of them past the eagle eye of old man Herder, who wisely insisted on seeing every one before they went to the typesetter. In later life Joey used to claim that he had been editor of *The Telegram* at the age of eighteen—a claim the paper itself never endorsed. However, it cannot be disputed that he was, for a time, the editorial *writer*.

Besides writing for *The Telegram* (then supporting Cashin, but later switching its support to Squires, when it became obvious that Cashin's group was neither liberal nor progressive) Joey was also helping to produce the weekly labour paper *Industrial Worker*, which, of course, supported neither Squires nor Cashin, but the three Labour candidates, Linegar, Cadwell, and Foley. He never did explain satisfactorily how he sorted out those conflicting allegiances, or why William Herder didn't at least ask him to take leave of absence for the duration of the election. Perhaps leader writers were hard to find in 1919.

Once the election was over, there was really nothing to keep Joey in Newfoundland. Where would he go? Obviously to New York, the capital of the world. Besides, the United States was one of the three countries next in line for the socialist revolution that had already happened, to everyone's astonishment, in Russia. The other countries on the list, according to Karl Marx, were Germany and Great Britain. These assumptions did not appear as wild then as they do now. Britain was on the verge of returning the first Labour government in any western country, and the difference between British Fabian socialism and the Kerensky regime in Russia was not yet clear. Germany was also tottering on the verge of a revolution that might go either to the far left or to the far right. Gangs of thugs from both sides were fighting and murdering each other, but eventually the German Left went down in a blood-bath before the march of Hitler's National Socialists.

In the United States such mass movements as the One Big Union and the Industrial Workers of the World were urging the urban proletariat—the vast majority of the people not living on farms—to use their votes to take control of the government.

Joey was determined to be part of all this, and to fight in the revolution as a journalist. But there were obstacles. He had neither the cash nor the credentials to get to New York and land a job as a reporter. He decided that he would have to work his way south by the natural steps—first Halifax, then Boston. William Herder gave him a letter of recommendation. More important, he got a letter from Sir Patrick McGrath, a Newfoundland journalist with an international reputation. Then he went by train (using a rail pass issued to reporters by the Reids, owners of the Newfoundland railway) and by boat to Halifax, where he promptly got a job with the *Herald*. He stayed with that paper only two months, long enough to accumulate the funds for a ticket to Boston, but it was valuable experience just the same. While working in Halifax he discovered a talent for interviewing the rich and the famous—such interviews being the most popular kind of non-news in the papers of the time. The $25-a-week reporter found that he was perfectly at ease with movie stars and industrialists and multimillionaires. They were just people like himself, after all—and he remembered this later when he hobnobbed with the Rothschilds and the Nixons and the Churchills. They might find him naive. They might laugh behind his back. But he always met them on what Stephen Leacock slyly described as "a footing of open-handed equality."

At the end of his two months in Halifax, Joey took a train to Yarmouth and then a ship to Boston. In that old capital of the New England states, he worked for another two months on the *Herald-Traveller*. There he listened to and interviewed his first soap-box orators—single-taxers, flat-earthers, and the like—who made their pitches on the Boston Common. This was his introduction to street-corner oratory, an art he was to practise successfully for the next half century. Finally, at the end of October 1920, four months out of St. John's, he landed in Manhattan, and immediately got work as a casual reporter with New York's socialist daily, the *Call*.

# CHAPTER 3

# How the
# Other Half Lives

DURING THE FIRST WORLD WAR THE NEW YORK CALL HAD BECOME AN important and influential newspaper. Then revolution swept through Russia in 1917, and there was international excitement over seeing one of the world's largest countries undertake the experiment of organizing a Marxist government—the first of its kind. The circulation of the socialist *Call* zoomed to over a million. But during the succeeding three years came disillusion and disappointment, and the tide of radicalism in the west receded. As America "got back to normalcy" the paper's circulation collapsed to about a hundred thousand. That's where it was when Joey arrived.

Even then it was the liveliest and most provocative general circulation paper published in New York City. The standard of reporting was high. A number of famous journalists had worked for the socialist daily at one time or another—among them Dorothy Day, who later won readers by the tens of millions with her syndicated columns, and John Reed, the brilliant young chronicler of the coup organized by Lenin and the Bolsheviki, who wrote the bestseller, *Ten Days That Shook the World*.

Joey had a lot to live up to and a lot to learn, so he flung himself into the job with the enthusiasm and the limitless energy for which he was to become famous.

"It seemed like heaven," he told me some twenty years later. "I was at the nerve centre of North American socialism, working with the people who were making socialist policy, and meeting the most famous names on the Left: Eugene V. Debbs—you must have heard of him—perhaps the greatest orator of his time, a real saint, a working-class hero. He spoke to twenty thousand people in Madison Square Garden when he came out of Leavenworth Prison. He said: 'Comrades...I come to speak to you on behalf of our comrades who are still inside the prisons—and it's a subject I know something about—you might say that I have inside information.' In that vast auditorium you could hear a pin drop. It was like being present at the Resurrection. He'd run for president of the United States, you know, on the Socialist ticket. I knew his successor, Norman Thomas, very well. He was presidential candidate in later elections. I knew Marcus Garvey—now there was a man!—a Jamaican Negro who started the whole movement for black power in the United States. They jailed him on a trumped-up charge of using the mails to defraud, selling tickets for a charter voyage to Africa—a perfectly legitimate thing to do. Eleanor Roosevelt—she wasn't a socialist, of course, but like her husband she was working for the people, for reform, and she and I once spoke at the same meeting, in the open air to a crowd of at least twelve thousand people. Then there was a night in Buffalo when I shared a hotel room with Frank Crosswaithe, the man they called the Negro Debbs."

The hotel room was in the black ghetto to which Joey had been spirited away by a bodyguard of black men in a car after he had made an inflammatory anti–Ku Klux Klan speech at an open-air rally in the hotbed of Klansmen that Buffalo was in those days. Such foolhardy courage was one of Joey's ingrained qualities, perhaps acquired in childhood. The greater the danger, the more outspoken he became. He was always convinced that the tongue was smitier than the sword.

In New York he discovered the hidden meaning of "democracy" as it was practised in a land where the political machine had supplanted the voter as boss. He got a close look at Tammany Hall's control of the state, at hirelings bribing officials and fixing the results of elections, so that the results came out the way the political machine dictated, regardless of how the people voted. He saw corrupt officials counting ballots that had never been cast, and came close to being beaten up by hired political thugs. He could still get angry about all this thirty and forty years later, when he was in the business of manipulating elections himself. It was a question of methods. Manipulating voters with slogans and promises and the razzle-dazzle of million-dollar campaigns financed by people paying for special privilege he seemed to regard as fair play. Beating them, intimidating them, destroying their ballots, refusing to allow them to register for the vote, he regarded as another matter entirely. "All's fair in love and politics," he used to say "so long as you don't violate people's rights and freedoms under the law."

Throughout his life, early as well as late, he had a great respect for law and order, and for the institution of justice founded on the courts. Unlike the radicals who came along a generation later, he never regarded the courts as part of the apparatus of repression.

Joey spent a whole year in New York before deciding, like a true Newfie, to go home for Christmas. Always improvident, always broke, even when he was earning good money (as he sometimes was), he managed to make it back as far as Halifax on his last dollar, where he sold an article to the *Herald* about his experiences in New York. Then he wired his father for $50, and the money arrived the next day— perhaps supplied by Grandfather David or Uncle Fred. Then he and another expatriate St. Johnsman used the money to get as far as Port aux Basques. From there they travelled on to St. John's using the rail pass that the Reid Newfoundland Company had issued two years earlier to "Joseph R. Smallwood and one friend." They arrived, according to Joey, "Without two cents to rub together," but his talents were always in demand in his native town, and he was able to get casual work as a writer and editor to carry him through the winter. He continued to visit St. John's, and to work there for an average of two or three months a year, mostly in winter, the whole time he was in New York. He was never separated from Newfoundland for long.

When he returned to the cultural capital of the Western world in the spring of 1921, he made a serious bid to get a job on the *New York Times*, and says he was promised one later that year. Presumably he had to wait for an opening. Meanwhile, he tried to make his few dollars stretch to cover the waiting period, because work at the *Call* had now practically dried up. He slept in flophouses and ate in soup kitchens, husbanding every cent. This time he really got close to the bottom of the heap, eating ten-cent breakfasts and thirty-cent dinners, and sleeping in a fifty-cent bed. When even that proved too expensive, he moved to a twenty-five-cent flophouse on the edge of the Bowery, where he slept among lines of alcoholics in beds separated by chicken-wire partitions. Wary of the unwashed sheets, he spread newspapers over the blankets, and slept there in his street clothes. When the weather warmed up, he moved out to a park, and slept on a bench, saving his quarters for food. There he suffered the ultimate indignity of the down-and-out deadbeats of skid row—that of being awakened in the morning by a policeman who walked around the park giving each sleeper a sharp rap with his nightstick across the soles of the feet. Fortunately, there were public washrooms, where even the dregs of the city could clean up and shave after a night of sleeping in the park.

By no means were all of Joey's companions of the streets full-grown men. Far more pitiable even than the broken-down deadbeats was the floating population of "street Arabs" that he met there morning and night: homeless boys aged from their early teens down to as young as six or seven, most of them barefoot, all of them in rags, sleeping in groups for warmth in the corners of alleyways, living on cigarette butts scavenged from the gutters, on scraps from garbage pails, and on coffee at one cent a cup.

All of this entrenched Joey's sense of the evil of capitalism, and of its political wing, the bourgeois parties. It provided him with material for the soap-box oratory that he practised in season and out on behalf of the American Socialist Party. He may never have learned the fine points of socialist theory, but he was a confirmed populist, and was now a regular circuit speaker. This meant speaking not only at political rallies, but also to groups of human rights protesters, to trade union meetings, and to working men's conventions. His job was to supply the oratory, the inspiration, the ringing propaganda of the working class for which the trade union leaders themselves were sometimes ill-equipped. For each such appearance at an organized meeting he received a fee of $10, and that was all the money he earned in the spring and early summer of 1921.

When he was not haranguing the toiling masses, he was in a public library devouring books, or at the Rand School of Social Science listening to the teachers and philosophers of socialism. He regarded the Rand School as his university, and believed that he got a better education there than he could have had at Harvard. It was, at any rate, an education of a less orthodox kind.

There were also lectures at the Labour Temple, for the American trade unions of the 1920s were making a serious effort to help their members acquire the skills and the theory that they would need to run democratic organizations, to meet employers across the bargaining table, and to take part in government if they had the opportunity to run successfully for public office, as quite a few of them did. Joey's blindness to science, logic, and mathematics lasted all his life, but in some other departments he did receive as good an education from the Rand School and the Labour Temple and from his private reading as many run-of-the-mill university graduates got from their classes— perhaps, as he insisted, his education was a good deal better.

He happened to arrive in the United States at the time of the Great Red Scare, when it looked as though the working class might really take control of the country in spite of the best efforts of Tammany Hall and its allies. The workers were electing socialists to Congress. There were socialist mayors in some of the cities. There were even socialist judges (also elected, according to the American system). For the first and only time in the history of the United States it looked as if a socialist government in Washington might some day be possible. This would have been quite in line with the theories of Karl Marx, who expected the proletarian revolution to happen not in countries with peasant economies, but in the places where capitalism was most highly developed, and it was a time when socialists, as well as communists (who differed mainly on questions of method), were convinced Marxists. Joey, like most of the socialists of his time, had never read Marx, but had absorbed Marxist theories at second or third hand from the works of less difficult writers.

During his visits to Newfoundland, Joey was able to continue his socialist contacts through the Newfoundland Industrial Workers Association, the principal working-class movement in the island at that time. The NIWA was patterned on the American industrial unions, especially the powerful Industrial Workers of the World (the IWW, or "Wobblies") led by the able and charismatic Big Bill Haywood. (Joey interviewed Haywood on the eve of his escape to Moscow, after he had been temporarily released from prison and was living under the threat of renewed imprisonment and assassination.)

At NIWA meetings in St. John's, Joey met and got to know people who continued to be associated with him for the rest of his career: men such as Sam Hefferton, later a perennial member of the Smallwood cabinets; Warwick Smith, a leftist intellectual; and Michael Foley, then a working-class leader, but a humble camp follower in the time of Smallwood's triumph.

It was not among the waterfront urchins of St. John's that Joey acquired his sense of compassion, his deep commitment to the welfare of the dispossessed. Those urchins believed, even while licking stolen molasses from their fingers, that they were lucky and privileged. Joey's genuine sympathy for the toiling masses, as he called them in public, or the "ragged-arsed artillery," as he preferred to call them in private, came from his association with the bums and street Arabs of the Bowery, the Jews of the Lower East Side, and the blacks of Harlem. He seemed to have a gift for winning the sympathy and confidence of all kinds of minorities. He became such an habitué of New York's Jewish ghetto that many Jews began to accept him as one of themselves, and the socialists began sending him as a regular speaker to Jewish rallies. His appearance might have helped as much as his attitude, for the dark-haired, lean, sparrow-like Smallwood, with his hooked nose, rimless spectacles, and studious look, might well have been a Jewish intellectual. His appearance might even have helped with the blacks; it was a time when American Jews were close allies with the blacks on almost every front.

Joey's one serious *affaire de coeur* in New York was with a young Jewish woman whom he met on a picnic in New Jersey in 1923. Lillian Zahn was a college student, a socialist, and the daughter of orthodox immigrants. Throughout that summer they were always together while he took her for rides at Coney Island, and she tried to teach him to enjoy classical music, theatre, and contemporary art. Joey paid careful court to her, but her parents were utterly opposed to her marrying a Goy, and with the waning of summer, his passion, too, began to wane. In three months it was all over. She went back to her studies, and he went back to Newfoundland. As far as he could recall, he never saw her again.

He never did get the job on the *New York Times*. Instead, he teamed up with a movie promoter whose speciality was organizing small local companies to make regional movies with regional capital. Ernest Shipman had already made successful regional films in parts of Canada. Joey wanted him to try St. John's, and went back to Newfoundland at Shipman's expense to promote a film company. Shipman later joined him, and they tried as a team to promote film companies not only in Newfoundland, but in the Canadian Maritime provinces as well. None of the companies ever reached the stage of incorporation, and no film was ever made. The only lasting effect of the venture was to give Joey his first tour of the Maritimes and some acquaintance with their financial and political leaders. It also gave him his first look at fur farming, an industry then flourishing in Prince Edward Island, and one he tried to duplicate on a large scale in his own province several decades later.

Joey's failure as a film promoter was the first of a long series of such failures extending over the next sixty-five years, throughout his career as a successful politician, and beyond that into his retirement. He never did learn that he was incapable of dealing successfully with businesspeople; he never did learn that he knew nothing about promotion, nothing about how to organize and run a company, nothing about how to judge the chances of success or failure in a particular enterprise. All his life he went from one financial disaster to the next—in motion pictures, newspapers, farming, and publishing— and when he got his hands on hundreds of millions of dollars in public funds, he perpetrated catastrophes in manufacturing, papermaking, oil refining, even candy making. Everything he touched was a financial fiasco. Yet, through it all, he was personally successful and increasingly popular. If he could have learned to leave financial affairs to his financial advisors, instead of insisting on controlling everything himself, he would have been brilliant in all his undertakings. Instead, he fell into bankruptcy or near-bankruptcy time and again, from the age of twenty-five to the age of eighty-six.

With the collapse of his movie-making venture, Joey returned to New York and the soap box, where he was learning his trade as a rabble rouser and crowd pleaser. He once estimated that in his five years as socialist propagandist he might have earned a total of $1,500 in speaking fees—that would be one official speech nearly every week for the whole time that he was in New York. When he wasn't speaking himself, he went to hear others. He even went to church to hear the patrician oratory of the Unitarians and the sulphurous thunder of the fundamentalists. He was especially impressed by the American evangelists, who practised the same techniques he had seen and heard in the Bethesda Mission in St. John's, with even more striking success. They had learned better than professional actors the art of playing on people's emotions, and what they did in the churches and mission halls, he learned to do in the public squares.

His voice developed and hardened with the continuous exercise, until he could out-bellow the best barrel-chested tub-thumper in the labour movement. It had a somewhat harsh quality, but was effective and persuasive. He developed stamina, too, until he could go on at full volume for hours at a stretch. Learning the art of persuasion, learning the language of the uneducated, and learning to play on mass emotions, to kindle hopes and dreams in his listeners, was for Joey an exalting experience. He began to believe that he really could change the world for the better—at least that part of the world that mattered so deeply to him, his native land.

Joey's four and a half years in the United States included two presidential elections, one at the beginning, and one at the end of his stay. The first was in the autumn of 1920, the second in the autumn of 1924, and he campaigned hard in both. It was the period during which American socialism, so filled with promise at the end of the First World War, virtually collapsed. Toward the end of that period even American workers tightening bolts on production lines or capping bottles in breweries began to believe the American dream, the fiction that they could grow rich by gambling in penny stocks, and that the lowliest of them, if he stuck with the system, might have a Ford in his future.

The Great Red Scare had worked in the way its authors had intended. The radicals were dead, in jail, or driven out of the country. America would remain safe, at least for another generation, for the banks and the trusts, the cartels and the multinational corporations.

Joey witnessed the election of Warren Harding, and the swift humiliation and death of that lame-duck president. He witnessed the election of Calvin Coolidge, a man of modest ability promoted by the same interests that had boosted Harding into the White House. In 1924 he and the socialists—what remained of them—supported the Progressive Party, which seemed to have some hope of gathering populist support. Like all American third parties, it collapsed, as the Socialist Party had collapsed before it. Soon Americans would be talking about the "two-party system" as though it were one of the articles of their constitution, and superior to all other means of electing governments. It was very disillusioning, and it became more and more difficult to keep faith with a ragged-arsed artillery that aimed and fired its guns the way it was told to do by the likes of Harding and Coolidge and their unseen bosses.

Joey remained aloof from all this, keeping a clear head and drawing his own conclusions. Unlike thousands of others, he did not become a tired radical. At the end of his American period he believed even more in the cause of the toiling masses and in his own destiny as their leader than he had at the beginning. But he had begun to sense that his destiny lay not on the world stage in New York, but in his own small homeland, which might yet be transformed by the combined forces of industry and socialism into a little working man's paradise.

Nourishing this naïve dream, he returned to Newfoundland in February 1925 as a temporary organizer for the International Brotherhood of Pulp, Sulphite and Paper Mill Workers.

CHAPTER 4

# Cub in the Political Jungle

JOEY'S STYLE BORE THE INDELIBLE STAMP OF THE POLITICS OF THE 1920S, the time when Newfoundland, like Canada, attained the dignified status of a British Dominion, while her statesmen might have taken lessons in ethics from any pack of wolves. Joey's great exemplar, Sir Richard Squires, won the election of 1919, was chased out of office for graft and corruption in 1923, grabbed power again in 1928, only to escape lynching "by luck and by God" in 1932.

Looking back dispassionately at Squires's career more than twenty years after his death, Michael Harrington, editor of *The Evening Telegram*, described him as undoubtedly the most controversial prime minister in Newfoundland's history. He was brilliant and brainy. Born at Harbour Grace, he came to St. John's as a student, and won the Jubilee Scholarship, awarded to the Newfoundland student with the highest marks in the public examinations. He later graduated from Dalhousie with a law degree, and became junior law partner to Sir Edward Patrick Morris, who was Newfoundland's prime minister from 1909 to 1917. Squires was awarded his K.C. a mere three years after being called to the bar. No Newfoundland politician could have started his career with greater promise of success. He was first elected at the age of twenty-nine. Four years later he was a member of the Cabinet and chairman of the Executive Council. In 1915, at the age of thirty-six, he became a Knight Commander of St. Michael and St. George.

Squires was a consummate debater and organizer, with a gift for patching together unlikely groups into shaky political alliances under his temporary leadership. The party he led to power in 1919 (named the Liberal Reform Party because he had invented it himself, and needed to distinguish it from the old Liberals) never had fewer than three separate gangs of political soldiers of fortune in its ranks, each of the three at cross purposes with the other two. At the same time there were never fewer than two factions in the Opposition—the Roman Catholics and the Water Street Tories—always willing to listen to proposals from government benches on how to form new alliances that might be able to take office once the government had been defeated on a confidence vote.

During one of the endless conversations that he and I had during the 1940s, Joey told me that he believed Squires had never gone to bed any night in his life with the certainty that he would still be prime minister by the end of the next day. Squires's perennial insecurity impressed his disciple with the need for a political organization of which he would be the absolute, unquestioned leader. Although he admired Squires greatly, he was determined never to lead a party himself that was made up of power-hungry factions.

The clever and ruthless Squires had served in the government of Edward P. Morris from 1913 to 1917. Morris, formerly a Liberal Cabinet minister, now led the People's Party (mainly Tory), but ran a "national" government during the First World War, including elements from the Liberals and the Fishermen's Union Party. Before the war ended he retired to England and was elevated to the peerage—a reward, presumably, for Newfoundland's war effort. But it was the war that had wrecked his country's fiscal structure beyond repair. Because of his government's decision not only to raise and equip a regiment of infantry to fight in Europe throughout the war, but also to underwrite the expenses of the Newfoundland war effort, the country began sliding towards bankruptcy. The war left a burden of capitalized expenses totalling $35 million (including war pensions, widows' allowances, etc.) in a country whose annual revenue was barely a tenth of that amount.

To make matters worse, Newfoundland was still paying off the debt on a trans-insular railway it had built at the end of the nineteenth century. Between the railway and the war, the public debt was far greater than the little country, with a population of about a quarter of a million, could possibly afford. And though the railway was a vital piece of social capital, without which the mills at Grand Falls and Corner Brook and the mines at Buchans would never have come into existence, it piled up additional annual deficits that had to be met, sooner or later, out of tax revenues. By the mid-1920s half of Newfoundland's tax collections were being spent on debt service, and by the end of the decade the government was borrowing money every year to meet its annual interest payments. Newfoundland might have been able to afford either the railway or the war, but not both.

It is important to realize that—contrary to the often-expressed opinion—corrupt and inefficient government had little or nothing to do with Newfoundland's slide toward bankruptcy. From 1919, when Squires came to power with his patched-together Liberal Reform party, bankruptcy was inevitable. And it was against the background of approaching financial disaster that his career played itself out. And yet, together with the Reids of the Reid Newfoundland Company, he succeeded in putting together the deal that created the pulp and paper industry in Corner Brook—the island's second, after Grand Falls. The creation of this industry in the midst of fiscal and political ruin remains Squires's principal claim to greatness.

The three elements of the Liberal Reform Party of 1919 consisted of a few old Liberals from the party formerly led by Sir Robert Bond and subsequently by Sir William Lloyd (this might be described as the Squires faction, even though Squires himself had first entered public life as a Tory supporting Morris against Bond); a strong group of the Fishermen's Union Party (the Coaker faction); and a group of businessmen and lawyers (the Warren faction) committed to the eventual promotion of William Robertson Warren to the premiership, once Squires had served their purpose and could be shooed out of office.

On the day Squires first entered the House of Assembly as prime minister, he faced an Opposition motion demanding his removal on the grounds that he was a criminal who had bribed a former member to vacate his seat. The Liberal Reform majority defeated this motion, and there is no record that the commission of enquiry appointed to investigate the charge of "criminal misconduct" ever brought in a report.

The strongest faction in the Squires government was the Fishermen's Union, whose leader, William Coaker, disliked and distrusted Squires intensely. Second strongest was the Warren faction, which, however, could not hope to achieve power except by an alliance with the Opposition, because the Fishermen's Union distrusted the Warren group even more than they distrusted Squires. The prime minister could count on the loyalty of only about four, or at most five, of his followers.

Four years after taking power the Squires government disintegrated. The marvel is that he held it together as long as he did. It went down in the midst of the most sensational charges of graft and corruption ever brought against a Newfoundland administration. Squires's closest colleague, Dr. Alexander Campbell, was revealed to have used government funds to defray election expenses, and to have diverted payments on poor relief into party support. If that was not bad enough, the head of the Board of Liquor Control had been advancing money to the prime minister in exchange for his IOUs. Squires had, moreover, received money from the companies operating the Bell Island iron mines in exchange for favourable legislation.

The amounts involved were large by the standards of the times. At least $20,000 from the Board of Liquor Control had gone into the prime minister's "own pocket" as professional historians have frequently pointed out. What they should have added, however, was that there was no distinction between Squires's "own pocket" and the Liberal Reform Party treasury. Squires was not only his own party treasurer, but ran the treasury literally as a series of cash transactions. All political contributions went into his pocket, and all expenses came out of it.

The corruption of which the Squires regime was quite clearly guilty was the normal, ordinary, accepted corruption by which all the bourgeois political parties of North America financed their elections. There was no way such parties could pay for campaigns except by selling privilege, taking kickbacks on government purchases, or subverting government funds, all of which they did regularly and as a matter of course.

Several years after the scandal broke, it was revealed that members of the House sitting opposite Squires had milked the Board of Liquor Control just as ruthlessly as he. It was such a standard, accepted practice, in which they were so deeply involved themselves, that they howled for Squires's blood only faintly: their own heads were equally in danger. Sir Michael Cashin, the most powerful member of the Opposition, though not the Opposition leader, a former prime minister whose reign had lasted little more than a year, had, for example, imported forty cases of whiskey and three octaves of rum in 1919 without ever paying the government duty of $1,100. Later, when he was in the Opposition, he had sold liquor to the Board at inflated prices, and had been paid by means of cheques made out to a third party totalling $22,198, a transaction on which he probably cleared $10,000 or more.

So Squires was not alone. The difference was that he got caught publicly, with his paw in the public chest. The story broke in the press, which had never heard of such goings-on—heavens, no!—and Squires resigned in disgrace. Warren succeeded him as prime minister, but only by making a deal with the Opposition to take several of its front-benchers into his Cabinet.

William Warren, born at St. John's but educated in England, was a lawyer and a patrician, and had been minister of justice in the Squires administration of 1919. He had led the Cabinet revolt that defeated Squires in the House, and had a party already patched together to take office without the need for an election. Included in the deal Warren had made with the Opposition was the appointment of a royal commission to investigate the Squires scandal. And a further part of the deal was to narrow the wording of the terms of reference of the commission so that the inquiry could not extend to investigating the wrongdoings of past governments, or of members of the Opposition.

The British Colonial Office appointed Thomas Hollis Walker, a prominent English barrister, to conduct the inquiry. Restricted by his terms of reference, he made no general investigation into how the Newfoundland government was run, but confined himself to the specific charges against Squires, Campbell, and certain civil servants. He confirmed that Squires and Campbell had indeed received large sums of money that should have been in the public treasury. Among the recent massive deals *not* investigated by Walker was the purchase of the Newfoundland Railway by the government, and the promotion of the Corner Brook mill. Many years later, when Smallwood was premier, he told me that Squires and Coaker, at one point, had split "a cool million," one-quarter going to Coaker and his Fishermen's Union Party, and three-quarters to Squires and the Liberal Reform Party. Since the two leaders concerned were Smallwood's two principal political heroes, he must surely have believed what he said, though on what evidence (if any) I have no idea. He may even have been quoting Squires himself. In any case, he would not have regarded such party financing as morally wrong. The only way to finance political campaigns, then or for many years thereafter, was by such deals.

Following the report of the Hollis Walker inquiry, Warren had

Squires and Campbell arrested and indicted. He had predicted that "sectarian interests" would safeguard Squires from conviction, and indeed something of the sort proved to be the case. The Grand Jury simply refused to bring a true bill against Squires despite overwhelming evidence, and that was the end of the matter, so far as Squires was concerned. Dr. Campbell was sent for trial by the Grand Jury, but was acquitted in open court, where he was regarded, perhaps correctly, as a sacrificial lamb.

Meanwhile, Warren did not have long to enjoy the fruits of his political double dealing. His government lasted nine months, from July 1923 to April 1924. At that point Squires, who was out on bail, and four of his followers, crossed the floor of the House, leaving Warren with one less vote than he needed to survive a confidence motion. His government fell on April 24.

Warren then deserted the Fishermen's Union Party, and joined the Opposition himself, hoping to pull enough of the conservative elements together to form another government. But his new administration lasted only four days. The governor then invited Sir William Coaker to become prime minister—a reasonable move, since Coaker led the largest single faction in the House—but Coaker was convinced that the gang of political adventurers with which he was surrounded would not permit him to govern for more than a few weeks at most, so he declined the invitation to join the parade of Newfoundland's prime ministerial ephemera.

Finally, an administration was patched together under Albert Hickman, a self-made merchant from Grand Bank who had founded an aggressive business firm in St. John's, and who was a member of an Opposition party, but not a member of the House. Hickman's government lasted a month and a day. He then led elements that were more or less regarded as Liberal into a general election in June 1924, and was defeated by the Tories under Walter Monroe.

Monroe, like Warren and Hickman, proved to be an inept prime minister, but he did manage to hold the party together, and to govern the country continuously from 1924 to 1928. Not a Newfoundland native, Monroe was born in Ireland and educated in England. He arrived in Newfoundland as a young man to enter a business firm owned by an uncle, and later went on to found various mercantile and manufacturing businesses of his own. A Tory by ingrained conviction, he ran what was perhaps the most reactionary government in Newfoundland history, doing such blatant things as removing the income tax, and the import tax on automobiles in the very same budget in which he increased the tax on boots and shoes and fishermen's clothes.

At the end of Monroe's term Squires made the most spectacular comeback in the parliamentary history of the British empire. Smallwood took the credit for having brought Squires and Coaker together once more, with Squires as leader. It took months of careful negotiation during which the two politicians refused to speak to each other, but eventually they agreed to contest as a single party the election that was to be called in the autumn of 1928.

By now Monroe was so unpopular, especially in the outports, that almost anyone could have beaten him. His place as Tory leader was taken by his cousin, Frederick Alderdice. Squires was swept back into power, leaving the Opposition with only eight seats. And that was virtually the end of the Fishermen's Union Party. Henceforth, Coaker and his followers would be indistinguishable from other Squires Liberals, and Coaker himself would not be far removed from other big fish merchants except that he operated his business out of Port Union instead of Water Street. Smallwood, with his penchant for giving more loyalty to an individual than to a cause, seemed to go on believing that neither Squires nor Coaker could do any wrong.

Against this background Joey formed his own political method, as distinct from his political philosophy, which, in his own mind at least, continued to be socialism. In eight years he saw seven Newfoundland prime ministers come and go, at least five of them with no discernible political convictions, unless you count Sir Richard Squires's conviction that Newfoundland must "develop or perish." Squires may have lacked all trace of political philosophy, but at least he was convinced that Newfoundland could not continue to rely on the fishery as the only major factor in its economy. He picked up from the Reids the belief that Newfoundland had massive potential for forest and mineral development, and for at least some manufacturing and farming. He passed this conviction along to his disciple, until it became the driving force behind Joey's aims and ambitions.

As for method, Joey had swallowed such massive doses of Machiavellianism during the 1920s that he was never able to see practical politics in any other light. He believed firmly that this was the way politics had to be. Moreover, he had seen such double dealing among political leaders that he was determined, once he made his own bid for power, that it would be with the backing of a large personal following whose loyalty, not to theory but to *himself*, would be unquestioned.

Throughout the decade he was involved not just in backstairs politics, but in other spheres of Newfoundland public life as well. First of all he became a union organizer. Except for his flirtation with the Newfoundland Industrial Workers Association, Joey had no early experience with unions. Then in 1925 the International Brotherhood of Pulp, Sulphite and Paper Mill Workers sent him from New York to Grand Falls, Newfoundland, where a paper mill had been operating for twenty years. He was paid $46 a week.

There had been two unions at the Grand Falls mill almost from the day it had opened its doors. Canadian paper makers, brought to Newfoundland as experienced tradesmen, had formed a local of the elite International Brotherhood of Paper Makers at Grand Falls. Labourers and minor tradesmen at the mill had organized a local of the International Brotherhood of Pulp, Sulphite and Paper Mill Workers, an industrial union. But Grand Falls had experienced a disastrous strike, and the larger union, which had once claimed 1,700 members, had suffered a steady decline until fewer than a hundred men were now paying their dues. Joey's job was to reorganize Local 63 of Pulp, Sulphite—no easy task. Gamely, he set to work with all his best powers of persuasion, and persisted for three or four months until he had won back about seven hundred of the lost sheep. Then, judging that the Grand Falls union was capable of keeping up the momentum, he headed for Corner Brook, where the new paper mill, soon to be even larger than the one at Grand Falls, was just getting into commercial production.

Unions were no novelty in Newfoundland. Sealers and seal skinners had been forming unions off and on for nearly a century. Craft unions dated back to the St. John's Mechanics' Society founded in 1827. By the 1850s there were unions of coopers, tailors, carpenters, seal skinners, and shipwrights. Printers, typographers, and retail clerks unionized soon afterwards, and by 1891 the first labour federation was formed in St. John's. The powerful Longshoremen's Protective Union dated from 1903.

Internationals were not new to Newfoundland either. One of the strongest was the Mine, Mill and Smelter Workers which had organized a local in 1923 and 1924 at Bell Island, where the largest iron mine in the British Empire was then in operation. The skilled railway trade unions were also organized as locals of American internationals—as were the electricians, machinists, and paper makers at Corner Brook. Even the unskilled labourers had struck successfully for higher wages during the construction of the mill. It was a labour-conscious town where Joey found fertile soil for his organizing. Anyone who was not already a member of a craft union was welcomed into his International Brotherhood of Pulp, Sulphite and Paper Mill Workers.

When I was at Corner Brook in 1975 I met retired mill hands who remembered him from fifty years earlier "buzzing around like a blue-assed fly," organizing his union. It was a great success. He sneaked into the mill during working hours to hold little meetings in out-of-the-way corners. He collected groups as they came off-shift at the mill gate. He went to Humbermouth on Sunday afternoons when the trains arrived and everyone turned out to meet them. There he would climb on a barrel and proclaim the need for unions not only in the mill, but in the community at large. His early evangelism no doubt helped Corner Brook become the most solidly organized pro-union town in Newfoundland. Before the summer was over Local 64 of Pulp, Sulphite was launched and well on its way. Joey had worked himself out of a job, for there were no more paper mills to organize in Newfoundland.

The summer of Joey's one great success as a union organizer was also the summer of his great romance. While working for the international union he boarded with Mrs. Serena Baggs at Curling, in what is now the west end of the city of Corner Brook. Visiting her that year was her cousin Clara Oates from Carbonear. The romance flowered quickly. Clara, a beautiful and talented young woman, could swim, dance, read music, and play the piano. Joey and Clara spent all their free time together and agreed to be married at Carbonear that autumn. Meanwhile, Joey rushed ahead with his other affairs. At no point in his life did love or marriage distract him or slow him down or make him into what could properly be described as a family man. Clara and his children, then and for the next half century, were to occupy a place somewhere at the edge of his life. Nevertheless, he and Clara stayed together to celebrate that rare event, a diamond wedding anniversary.

Late that summer he undertook on his own the difficult job of organizing the Newfoundland Railway's casual workers. It was difficult because the workers were scattered in twos and threes along seven hundred miles of rail line and could never get together in a meeting. And Joey, no longer working for an international union, would have to be supported by the union he was organizing.

Most of the casual workers were maintenance crews—"section-men" as they were called—who were stationed every seven to ten miles along the tracks, living in small houses built by the railway and operating small hand-powered trolleys called "speeders." They had been told they would have to take a pay cut of two and a half cents an hour, so they were ready and eager for organization.

When Joey told me this story in 1948 he said that he walked all the way from Port aux Basques to Bonavista, from Bonavista back to Clarenville, from Clarenville to Whitbourne, and all along the Brigus Junction Line to Bay de Verde and back, a distance of at least 750 miles. Doubtless he did walk a good deal of this distance, perhaps even most of it. According to his own story, he wore out three pairs of shoes tramping from tie to tie for nearly two months.

But in the summer of 1941, as an energetic schoolboy, I was doing some walking myself. I hitched a ride from White Bay to Sandy Lake on a logging truck, and across the lake on a boat to Howley. Then I walked from Howley to the Gaff Topsail, spending a night outdoors in a horrendous electrical storm before arriving at Gaff Topsail Station, where the section foreman was kind enough to give me a night's shelter. As we talked, I mentioned the sectionmen's union of 1925. "Oh yes, I remember it well," the section foreman said. "Joey Smallwood came riding through the country on speeders. I paid my fifty cents and joined his union. I guess we all did. And it worked, too. He stopped the pay cut." Joey later admitted that he rode on hand-powered speeders occasionally, but said he found the work even harder than walking.

Joey was lucky enough to meet the general manager of the railway at Whitbourne, and to present him with a membership list that included all but one section man between Whitbourne and Port aux Basques. The railway couldn't afford a strike by its maintenance crews. The line was in such bad shape that lack of maintenance would stop the trains in less than a week. There and then they made a deal. The pay cut was off, and so were any further demands by the sectionmen's union. What happened to the organization? That was the end of it. What happened to the $300 Joey had collected? Perhaps most of it went to help found his next venture, a weekly paper called the *Labour Outlook*, which he published in St. John's that autumn. His subscription list was made up almost entirely of the six hundred casual employees of the railway.

Having started his paper, Joey dashed off to Carbonear to be married into the old, genteel Oates family. Then he carried Clara back to a rented flat in St. John's, the first of many such temporary homes she would occupy before she moved into the palatial Canada House as First Lady of the Tenth Province. The marriage was happy because she proved to be capable of putting up with almost anything—gypsy-like living, poverty, even neglect. During the next few years Joey often had no permanent home. At those times Clara would return to Carbonear to live with her parents. But they were together whenever Joey had a roof to call his own. Their son Ramsay was born in 1926, William in 1928, and their daughter Clara in 1930. Like his wife, his children became loyal supporters of all Joey's undertakings.

The *Labour Outlook* lasted only a few weeks. Joey then became editor of the daily *Globe*, published in St. John's by Richard Hibbs, and fiercely opposed to the government of Prime Minister Walter Monroe. When Joey took over the paper, its former editor, Dr. H. D. Mosdell, sued the owners successfully for breach of contract, and was awarded damages of $700. Since the *Globe* had nothing in its till, the bailiff stopped the presses while Joey rushed off to try to raise the money to pay off the debt to Mosdell. He tried Opposition Leader A. E. Hickman unsuccessfully; then he went to Sir Michael Cashin, no longer a member of the House, but a bitter foe of Monroe. Cashin put up the money to keep the *Globe* alive, and Joey remained its editor until it went bankrupt six months later. Clara then returned to Carbonear, while Joey went off to sit at the feet of the Fabian socialists who, led by Ramsay MacDonald, had managed to squeeze into power as a minority government in Great Britain.

The money for Joey's steerage ticket to Liverpool on a Furness Withy passenger steamer came from another of his publishing ventures: a Newfoundland *Who's Who*. It was about half finished when he sold it to Richard Hibbs, his former boss, and it subsequently came out in several handsome editions.

While in England Joey worked for the Labour Party in a by-election, wrote a small book, *Coaker of Newfoundland*, which was published by the Labour Publishing Company; and did some occasional writing for the socialist press, but most of the time he sat listening to debates in the House of Commons, or holed himself up in the British Museum reading Fabian literature. He discovered London's used bookstores, and continued to patronize them for the rest of his life. They were mines of used and remaindered books from all over the Empire, some with tens of thousands of titles in stock. Among this miscellany Joey began to locate and put together his own remarkable collection of Newfoundland titles. By the 1960s he had the largest array of Newfoundlandia in existence—more than three thousand books and documents.

Otherwise, his visit to Britain was no great success. Unlike the American socialists, the British Fabians were *in power*, with a million willing hands to work for them. They scarcely needed help from a wild colonial boy. But Joey added to his knowledge of practical politics, and saw for the first time an orderly British parliament in session, running strictly by parliamentary rules, as strict as those of the MCLI in St. John's. The thing he watched in the House of Commons was not a dog fight. And he was impressed. When *he* ruled the roost, he vowed, that was the way things would be managed. Everyone would revere and bow to the Speaker. Everyone from the sergeant-at-arms to the Opposition back benchers would toe the parliamentary mark. Anyone who broke party ranks on even the smallest issue would be sent packing across the floor. Decorum, ceremony, and correct parliamentary behaviour would be rigidly enforced. Politics might be as savage as ever below the surface, but their savagery would be that of gentlemen.

By living in the cheapest Bloomsbury rooming house he could find, and cooking his meagre meals on a gas ring, Joey managed to stretch his English visit to six months, and somehow accumulated the money for a steerage ticket back to St. John's. He arrived in the early summer of 1927, broke as usual. But he borrowed the money for a rail ticket to Corner Brook, and landed a job there with the International Power and Paper Company, an American firm that had recently bought the mill from its British and Newfoundland owners.

I. P. and P. sent Joey with a group of engineers to investigate the possibility of building a third paper mill on the Gander River. They came to the same conclusion that several other companies did later: the available wood supply could not support another mill. The dream of the "Gang on the Gander" continued to haunt Joey for the rest of his career. That this dream continued to elude him while seeming perennially to be within reach was one of the greatest disappointments of his life.

Joey settled down in Corner Brook for a long stay, and since it was the centre of a new political district, slated to send a member to the General Assembly at the next election, he began promoting himself as the district's future representative.

First he started a weekly newspaper, the *Humber Herald*, in competition with the *Western Star*, a weekly paper long established at Curling, and recently acquired by I. P. and P. The *Humber Herald* would be no company organ, but a crusading community voice, demanding all the things that Corner Brook ought to have, from paved streets to children's playgrounds and community planning. Like all the papers Joey edited and published (quite a slew of them from first to last) it was less a newspaper than a propaganda sheet—but it contained very popular propaganda. He hand-set the copy himself, composing the articles as he went along, and printing one page at a time because that was all the type available in the little print shop on Corner Brook's West Side (well beyond company jurisdiction), where the *Humber Herald* was born.

The eight-page tabloid was an instant success, popular and influential, its press runs of two thousand selling out immediately. But then Joey made the same mistake that he would make time and again throughout his career. He plunged from a modest success into an ambitious failure. He organized a company, sold shares, bought a new linotype on long-term credit, and built an annex to the little print shop to house his great new plant.

The paper continued for another two years, sinking deeper and deeper into debt, even while its subscribers increased. Its revenues never quite met its expenditures. When it was facing financial collapse the paper company bought it out, glad to be rid of the one opposition voice in the region. The company then moved the *Western Star* from Curling to the *Herald's* fine new plant, took over the *Herald's* subscription list, and the *Herald* disappeared.

For Joey, 1928 was a momentous year. His second son, William, was born. His second book, *The New Newfoundland*, was published. It painted a picture of a small but booming nation, its towns glowing bright with mines, mills, and factories, its hills white with sheep. The New Newfoundland hadn't actually arrived, of course; it might take Squires another ten or twelve years to complete the transformation, but it was just then coming to birth. Corner Brook, the happy, booming mill town, was the first swallow heralding the summer. In this election year Squires would lead a great, united party to victory, and the new era would begin. Joey had every intention of being part of that victory and of establishing himself as Squires's successor. He went to every hamlet in Humber district, preaching the gospel of the New Newfoundland, promoting himself as its prophet. His election was assured.

And then Squires, the calculating politician, decided to sacrifice Smallwood in his own interests. He needed an easy district, one where he could win a seat with no more than a few token appearances, leaving him free to do his serious campaigning in districts where his electrifying oratory might win doubtful seats for the Liberals. (For the first time in many years the two parties were campaigning under the straightforward names of Liberal and Conservative.) Once Joey had Humber "sewed up," Squires announced that he intended to run there himself.

The Conservatives offered to pay Joey's campaign expenses if he would run as an independent, but he turned the offer down without hesitation. "I'd do this for no one else," he told Squires, swallowing his disappointment. He agreed to become campaign manager in Humber district and if possible he worked harder for Squires than he had worked on his own behalf. By election day, October 29, 1928, he had spoken to virtually every voter from Deer Lake to the capes at the entrance to Bay of Islands, and could predict the results within fifty votes. Squires, who had spent a mere two days campaigning in Humber, polled 3,011 votes to his opponent's 632. In that election he beat Prime Minister Frederick Charles Alderdice by a landslide: twenty-eight seats to Alderdice's twelve.

While Squires went off to run the country, Joey remained in Corner Brook publishing the *Humber Herald*. When it went under, a year and a half later, he returned to St. John's to the editorship of yet another political propaganda sheet.

This came about in a curious way. The Tories had a paper called *The Watchman*, which they mailed to a list of supporters throughout the country hand-picked by their ward heelers. Every issue blasted Squires, blaming him for the economic depression, which was worldwide by then and beginning to affect Newfoundland's markets, and blasting him for the unemployment rate, which by the beginning of 1930 had climbed to 30 percent. But by now even the Tories were feeling the pinch of the worldwide economic crisis. They failed to pay their editor. He sued. The court issued a writ, and the bailiff put the *Watchman*—offices, printing plant and all—up for sale at auction.

At this point, Squires called Joey into his office. "I want you to buy it, Smallwood," he said. "Here. This ought to be enough to enable you to outbid anyone from the Opposition. They'll hardly have the money in cash."

He reached into his pocket, hauled out the Liberal Party treasury, and peeled off $3,000 in large bills. The astonished Joey went off to the auction, and not only got the keys to the plant and the offices, but found in a drawer the complete Tory mailing list, which he pocketed and took home.

"Mustn't leave those benighted voters without their reading matter," Squires told him. "Now that you're editor you can tell them the truth, instead of a pack of Tory lies."

So *The Watchman* became *The Watchdog*, with its print and masthead looking exactly the way they had looked before, except that now there was a large, flattering photograph of Squires on the editorial page, and article after article telling what wonderful work he was doing for the country. It went out to everyone on the Tory mailing list, and also had a large popular sale on the streets of St. John's. To make matters worse, the Tories could not find another printer prepared to issue a competing paper.

They immediately applied to the Supreme Court for an injunction to stop publication of *The Watchdog*, alleging that it was fraudulent, and issued under false pretexts. Judge Kent, a famous jurist, heard the case and, according to Joey, "threw it out." However, according to Leslie R. Curtis, Squires's law partner and Joey's lawyer at the trial, what the judge actually did was reserve judgment and never render a decision. The case was still on the books marked C.A.V. (the Court wishes to advise itself) fifty years later.

CHAPTER 5

# *Young Man with a Microphone*

DURING SQUIRES'S FIRST TERM, HE HAD "PUT THE HUM IN THE HUMBER," as he'd promised. During his great comeback campaign he promised to "put the gang on the Gander"—that is, to build a third paper mill on the Gander River. It is unlikely that he could have accomplished this, even if the world economy had remained stable. But when the American stock market crashed in the autumn of 1929, the idea became an impossibility. By 1931 the price of Newfoundland fish going to the West Indies had dropped to less than two cents a pound. Few fishermen could live on the proceeds of their catch, and were forced, at least during the long off season, to take the government dole of six cents a day. Privation in the outports was widespread, and unemployment was general in St. John's. The government seemed unable to help in any way beyond issuing poor relief.

During Squires's last two years in office (1930–32), Joey was constantly at his side. The prime minister had at last begun to appreciate Smallwood's political talent, and was relying on him more and more to help run Liberal Party affairs. It was rather like helping to run a morgue. By 1932 the party was in a shambles.

In April of that year many fishermen discovered that they would not be able to get an "outfit" from a merchant for the summer's fishery. Some of the branch stores in the outports had closed. Others were refusing credit to fishermen, and without credit few of them could buy the gear, the gasoline, or the salt needed to catch and cure their fish. Many working-class families in St. John's were also hungry, ragged, and desperate.

Against this background a group of merchants and politicians called a public meeting, chaired by the king of the merchants, Eric Bowring. Among the Opposition politicians who attended was Peter Cashin, Sir Michael Cashin's son, who had been elected as a Squires Liberal in 1928 and appointed Squires's finance minister, but in 1932 had crossed the floor, charging Squires with falsifying minutes of council.

At the meeting, held in the big Majestic Theatre in downtown St. John's, and said to have been attended by more than a thousand people, Cashin made an inflammatory speech (one of many such in his long and fiery career) again charging Squires with dishonesty, and blaming his government for the economic disaster. After a number of such speeches, none quite as violent as Cashin's, the merchants announced that Water Street would close down the next day to allow for a massive march to the House of Assembly, where they would present the people's grievances and demands.

It was not a time when responsible public men would have risked mob action, even against a leader they disliked as much as Squires. The paper mills were running on short time. The logger's earnings had dropped from $2.50 a cord to $1.50, and in some cases as low as $1. Teachers had taken a cut of 25 percent in their already miserably low salaries. Railway workers were being laid off. At Bell Island the mining company had retrenched until fully half the miners were idle. Casual workers in St. John's could no longer find jobs of any kind. Even tradesmen were sometimes being paid by company vouchers redeemable in kind at grocery stores, instead of in cash. Approximately one thousand of those formerly employed in the small factories around the city were now on the street, and in most cases on the dole.

An election was due that autumn. What the merchants and Opposition politicians hoped to accomplish by forcing Squires out of office six months before his term expired is now difficult to imagine; it is equally hard to believe that they really expected a change of government to make any great difference to the economic disaster. In any case, they did encourage the mob to march on the Colonial Building, and once the mob was there—an estimated ten thousand— the demonstration turned into a riot.

Joey had attended the meeting at the Majestic Theatre on the night of April 5, 1932, but when he had tried to defend the government, he had been thrown bodily out of the hall. The next day he was in the House at Squires's side when the mob arrived, sent a delegation into the building, waited a long time for an answer, and then began smashing the windows with stones. They also hauled down the Union Jack from the flagstaff, and hoisted something else in its place. It was reported to be green. But perhaps it was just a scarf or a large handkerchief, not the republican flag of Ireland, as many people supposed. Anyway, in a country that had seen a number of bloody riots between the English and the Irish, it was regarded as the emblem of armed insurrection.

After smashing every window, the mob broke into the Colonial Building, defying a charge by police armed with clubs, and dragged the furniture—chairs, desks, tables, and a piano—into the grounds, where they piled it all into a heap, and started a huge bonfire.

Five people, including Squires, his wife (also an elected member of the House of Assembly), and Joey, had barricaded themselves into the Speaker's Room adjoining the Assembly Room, and crouched there in the gathering darkness while the mob rampaged through the beautiful chambers of the House of Assembly and the Legislative Council, wrecking everything.

A group of Opposition MHAs managed to get to the Speaker's Room and escorted Helena Squires to safety. Then they returned for Sir Richard, took him out by way of a side door in the basement, and made for the street through the thinnest part of the crowd. With his glasses off, and a cap pulled down over his eyes, they hoped he might not be recognized. But a shout went up: "There he goes! Get the goddamned bastard!" The mob immediately dragged Squires from the arms of his would-be rescuers and swept him along in a crush of bodies across Military Road and into Colonial Street, which leads downhill toward Bishop Feild College and the waterfront. "Drown him!" the mob shouted. "Down to the harbour with him!"

The street was narrow, with doors opening directly onto the sidewalk. About a block past Military Road someone opened a front door, grabbed Squires, and pulled him inside. Then a Roman Catholic priest, who had been trying to quiet the mob in the Colonial Building grounds, jumped up on the steps in his vestments and stood in the doorway, arms outstretched, trying to keep the lynchers at bay. Fortunately, most of the mob was unaware of what had happened. The thousands behind, jamming the narrow street, kept pushing the few hundreds in front, so that the mob, carried by its own momentum, swept past the priest and on down Colonial Street toward the harbour.

Meanwhile, someone hustled Squires out the back door of the house, across the backyard, through a hole in a fence, and into the back door of another house on Bannerman Street, which runs parallel to Colonial Street. From there he was able to phone a cab and escape, while the mob surged downhill to Water Street and began looting the liquor stores.

Soon the crowd was roaring drunk on limitless quantities of free booze, and began breaking into the department stores owned by the very merchants who had started it all. They continued to rampage around town all night, but dispersed before dawn.

The Newfoundland Constabulary, wearing the Bobbie hats patterned on those of the first colonial police force in Dublin, Ireland, and armed only with night sticks, were incapable of dealing with large mobs, even if, as happened on rare occasions, they had guns issued to them. So the government recruited squads of special police from the Great War Veterans Association, and the special police began patrolling the streets dressed in civilian clothes, identified by white arm bands with stencilled lettering.

The next morning Squires drove unescorted to his law office, and later stalked out to his car through a mob of several hundred men. No one ever accused him of lacking courage. This time not a hand was raised against him. The governor wired for a British cruiser, and ordered the Riot Act to be read to renewed gangs of looters. (This would permit police to fire their rifles over the heads of the crowd or even *into* the crowd, if it refused to disperse.) But the ginger had already gone out of the mob. Some of the men had drunk so much rum that they were still vomiting in the gutters the next morning.

Squires refused to resign, but asked the governor for dissolution of the Assembly, and led his party into a general election that he was certain to lose. In the June 11 vote the Liberals were wiped out, returning only two members out of twenty-seven: Gordon Bradley in Humber, and Roland Starkes in Green Bay. One of those defeated was Squires himself. Another was Smallwood, who had run for election for his first time in the district of Bonavista South. He was beaten by Herman Quinton (later to become a Smallwood Cabinet minister) by 3,528 votes to 812. It was the only time in his life that he would suffer personal defeat at the public polls.

Frederick Charles Alderdice, the new prime minister, was much less a politician than a businessman of the old school. Like his cousin Walter Monroe, he belonged in the Victorian era, and like him had been born in Ireland, coming to Newfoundland as a young man to work in a family business. He became successively manager of the Colonial Cordage Company (operators of the Ropewalk at Mundy Pond), prime minister, leader of the Opposition under Squires, and finally prime minister by right of election as leader of the majority party in a bankrupt dominion.

Alderdice had campaigned on a promise to investigate the question of appointing a commission to replace the elected government of Newfoundland for a number of years. In a sense, therefore, it might be said that Newfoundlanders *voted* for Commission of Government, even though Alderdice never held the referendum that he had promised on this question. Indeed, despite what he had said during the campaign, it is unlikely that he would have allowed the demise of his own government had he not been forced into it: the public debt had now reached $100 million, 60 percent of all revenues being spent on debt service. There was no way the government could either meet the next round of interest payments or raise another loan. Alderdice tried to lease Labrador to British developers for an annual rent, but failed. The banks refused to give the government even short-term credit.

At the time it was considered "unthinkable" that a British dominion should default on its bonded debt. So when it became obvious that Newfoundland simply didn't have the cash or the credit to meet the interest payment due on January 1, 1933, Great Britain offered to meet two-thirds of the amount due, on condition that Newfoundland accept a royal commission to consider the country's future. The commission, under Lord Amulree, made the expected recommendation: it blamed Newfoundland's problems on corrupt and inefficient administration. In effect, it said that Newfoundlanders were unfit for self-government, and recommended that the country be put under British trusteeship until it became self-supporting. Alderdice accepted all this, tendered his government's resignation, and became one of the six commissioners appointed to rule the country under the chairmanship of the British governor, and under the ultimate control of the Dominions Office in London. On February 16, 1934 the Commission of Government was sworn in. It would be fifteen years before Newfoundland elected a government again.

Without politics or political newspapers to occupy his time, Joey headed off to the outports to take up the job at which Coaker had failed so badly—the organization of the fishermen. He believed that what they needed was a true producer-consumer co-operative, not a fisherman-owned limited liability company, like that organized by Coaker. But he wanted to keep the name "union" to identify it as a successor to the FPU, so he called it the Fishermen's Co-operative Union.

To launch this new enterprise he went to live in Bonavista, the largest all-fishing outport, close to the centre of the old FPU empire, which was now defunct, though remnants of it, such as the Fishermen's Union Trading Company, remained quite strong. At first, he lived with friends. Then, as the union began paying him a pittance for his full-time organizing, he was able to rent a house for $8 a month and to bring his wife and children north to live with him. For a while he also had a thirty-six-foot boat with a one-cylinder gasoline engine and sails. Wisely, he never tried to run it himself. He left the navigation to a retired skipper and the operation of the engine to a young fisherman.

Some six or seven thousand men joined Joey's union at one time or another, and undertook to pay dues of fifty cents a year—more than most of them could manage. Indeed, some of them hadn't had fifty cents in cash since 1930. So they brought him bags of potatoes and turnips, cabbage, carrots, and parsnips grown in their gardens, and loads of firewood hauled from the forest. The Smallwoods spent the better part of three years in Bonavista, living on such fare, on much the same level as the better-off fishermen, but never quite as poor as the hundred thousand Newfoundlanders living on the dole.

Some writers have said that Newfoundlanders were "destitute beyond parallel in North America" during the Great Depression, but this is not true. A number of families were indeed destitute. A few people in remote places actually starved, and there was much malnutrition in the outports as well as in the cities. But on the whole, Newfoundlanders were far better off than people living in such places as the Dust Bowl of the West. They could get most of the food they needed from their gardens and the sea, as they had always done. There were limitless crops of wild berries. The forest provided wild meat, and all the fuel they could use. Outport Newfoundlanders had always lived off the land, and they continued to do so, right through the 1930s. Most of them were very poor; their houses went unpainted; their clothing wore out and could not be replaced; thousands of children had no boots or shoes, and some of them stayed out of school because of lack of clothes, but few of them were ever on the edge of starvation.

Their diet was grossly inadequate, but this was as much from igno-
rance as from poverty: many of the poorest people insisted on eating
white bread, for instance, instead of bread made from the nutritious
whole-grain flour distributed by the government. They despised
"brown bread" as the food of the destitute. So diseases of diet
deficiency were rampant. Tuberculosis was epidemic. Pneumonia was
common. There were a few cases of beri-beri, and many early deaths
from contagious diseases, as there were all across Canada and the
United States in the Depression years.

Joey, who had never spent time in the outports before this, was
shocked, his outlook permanently altered by the conditions he found
in a few fishermen's homes. Many times he told the story of being
invited to the house of the first man he met when he entered the little
settlement of Tickle Cove in Bonavista Bay after walking across the
neck from Keeles. The man thought he looked hungry (he was) and
invited him to share his dinner. The dinner turned out to be a slice of
bread fried in pork fat because there was no butter or margarine, and
black tea without sugar steeped in a tin can because there was no
teapot or kettle, in a little house furnished with biscuit boxes. It was the
sort of incident that Joey came to associate with the fishery, and that he
kept conjuring up years later when he was trying to rescue the
fishermen from the industry of their ancestors, and give them jobs on
production lines in factories—jobs for "good cash wages."

The Fishermen's Co-operative Union could hardly be called a
success. You just can't create a great co-operative movement out of a
population with nothing to buy or sell and with incomes averaging less
than $100 a year. But it wasn't a complete failure either. In one place at
least, the village of Pouch Cove, near St. John's, where the fishing is
reliable, and the people determined to make a go of it, the producer-
consumer co-operative that Joey organized flourished and grew, right
through the Great Depression. It was still healthy, after some rounds
of reorganization, when Newfoundland entered Confederation.

But from 1933 to 1936 the economics of the Newfoundland fishery
continued to grow worse and worse. It reached the stage where Joey
could no longer pay his $8-a-month rent in Bonavista and he was
forced to concede that his effort to organize the fishermen was a
failure. In 1935 he threw in the sponge and moved back to St. John's,
where he might be able to eke out a living as a freelance journalist and
publisher.

He had an idea for an ambitious publishing project: a large, glorified scrapbook about Newfoundland, a mix of history, geography, folklore, pictures, *everything*, a book that every literate family of Newfoundlanders at home or abroad would want to own. He estimated that it would cost at least $5,000 to launch such a project, and he knew only one place where he was likely to get that kind of money. He went to Ches Crosbie.

Chesley A. Crosbie, son of Sir John Crosbie, who had been Monroe's finance minister, was an adventurous businessman who in the course of a short lifetime made and lost fortunes in everything from whale blubber to Coca-Cola, but by the end of his life was the wealthy owner of an airline, a shipping company, and a dozen other corporations. He put money not only into sound, imaginative ventures, but also into unlikely ones, big and small. He had helped finance the fishermen's co-operative at Pouch Cove, an action that any other fish merchant would have regarded as madness.

Ches Crosbie didn't back Joey's enterprises—this one or later ones—out of any personal regard for Joey. First of all, he was the kind of free-enterprise gambler who would back *anything* that looked as if it might have a chance of success. Secondly, like Smallwood, Crosbie had passionate feelings about Newfoundland. If someone proposed a scheme that looked good for his little sea-girt isle, he'd back the scheme to the best of his ability. Now and later Joey was often doing the kind of thing that Crosbie would have liked to be doing himself, given the time and talent. So he was often willing to risk money on Smallwood enterprises, even though he may have regarded Joey himself as anything but a sound risk, and certainly not as a personal friend (the way Joey regarded Crosbie).

Crosbie was a limited man, with little education and no gift for public appearances, but with daring and courage and a heart that was "in the right place," as the saying went. It was for all these reasons that he agreed to grub-stake Joey's *Book of Newfoundland*, and he did so very handsomely indeed. Crosbie not only underwrote the publishing costs of the two volumes, but also provided an office and a secretary who doubled as assistant editor, a man named Leo Moakler, formerly a printer with the George Andrews firm on Water Street. Crosbie also supplied as many as ten typists when they were needed. The offices of *The Book of Newfoundland* were on the top floor of the Crosbie building, and Joey was able to call on the resources of the Crosbie firm as required.

He rounded up all the experts he could find on every subject from

Newfoundland stamps and coins to the Newfoundland dog and Newfoundland's part in the First World War. He added folktales and anecdotes, ballads and poetry. Most of the writers gladly worked for nothing, although a few of them may have been paid a little. Some of the longest pieces in the book Joey wrote himself. Moakler was paid $8 a week, a salary he says he was glad to receive, and the typists too were paid, but Joey was not. At the time he was boarding in a cheap rooming house on Water Street, the Falcon House, and may have managed to squeeze the room rent out of his expenses, but that was all. He lived from hand to mouth, and hoped to make a profit from the book to pay off some of his accumulated debts. But profit or not, he was doing what he wanted to do, singing the glories of his native land, and that was what mattered most to him. He was never really interested in money, viewing it mostly as a necessary nuisance.

Some of the costs of *The Book of Newfoundland* were underwritten by including a large section of company advertising at the back of each volume. Oliver L. Vardy, an enterprising young Newfoundlander recently returned from serving a jail term for armed robbery in the United States, volunteered to sell the advertising on commission. Joey reported that Vardy made several thousand dollars out of the deal—more money in a few weeks than he himself had ever made in an entire year in his life. It was the beginning of a long association between Vardy and Smallwood.

Despite the advertising, Crosbie had to put up most of the $25,000 it cost to bring the various elements of *The Book of Newfoundland* together, and to have it printed and bound. It was produced as a handsome two-volume set, in red imitation crocodile leather and gold leaf, with well over a thousand pages and about a thousand pictures, mostly black and white photographs. The print run was 10,000.

But even at five dollars a set the book failed to sell. Few Newfoundlanders in 1936 were able or willing to dig up five dollars for *any* set of books, even books as handsome and informative as those. Most of them sat in the warehouse in St. John's for six years. Then, in the 1940s, Canadian and American servicemen stationed in St. John's discovered them, and bought them all up to send home as souvenirs. The edition sold out, and Crosbie finally got his money back. Joey just got his expenses. Years later, however, when he was premier, and when the cost of the original set had risen among rare book dealers to $150, he brought out volumes three and four in the same print and binding, and a reprint of volumes one and two. Eventually he published volumes five and six. In the end the project returned him a reasonable profit—about $100,000—but he waited a long time for it.

The six volumes were truly a mine of information on just about every possible subject connected with Newfoundland. The information was not always reliable, for it depended on the care and research of scores of individual writers. Much of it was mere hearsay, some of it strongly prejudiced by political and other opinions, but with these reservations *The Book of Newfoundland* remained the most thorough and remarkable set of books ever published about any Canadian province.

When the expected income from his great publishing venture failed to appear on schedule, Joey found it necessary, at the depths of the Great Depression, to scrabble around for a living. He still thought of himself as a writer, so he went to *The Daily News* with a proposal for a column. It was a grab-bag of short items that he had dug up during his years in the outports and his months in the Gosling Memorial Library at St. John's, doing research for the book. *The Daily News* took his column, and paid him $20 a week—not much, it seems now, but adequate to meet basic living expenses for a small family in St. John's in 1937. It was the beginning of a great change in his personal fortunes.

The column was called "From the Masthead." His by-line was "The Barrelman," for he saw himself as a ship's lookout, spying out information for the people on deck. After a few weeks, he went on the air with it, a quarter of an hour nightly, and he became instantly famous. "The Barrelman" was one of the three great radio hits in Newfoundland in the years just before the Second World War. The others were the "Gerald S. Doyle News Bulletin" (like "The Barrelman," broadcast by the government station, VONF) and a kind of marine soap opera set on board a sailing ship, the *Irene B. Melon*, produced by local actors and musicians and broadcast by the privately owned station VOCM.

The "Gerald S. Doyle News Bulletin" at 7:45 P.M. was sponsored by a firm selling patent medicines and cod liver oil, and Doyle, a Water Street merchant, became widely known in the outports as "Dr. Doyle." His bulletin broadcast a mix of local news, notices of all kinds, including private messages, and reports of how outport patients were faring in St. John's hospitals. If they were recovering they were "recovering rapidly and hoped to be home soon." If they were dying, they were "doing as well as could be expected." Everyone understood the euphemisms, and prepared for the best or the worst, as the case might be. And everyone listened. People without radios in outports that had no electricity crowded into the homes of those lucky enough to have wind chargers, or battery-powered sets. Soon they were crowding into the same houses in equal numbers to hear *The Barrelman*.

After running his program unsponsored for a couple of weeks, Joey went to Frank O'Leary, a commission merchant more or less in competition with Doyle, and persuaded him to sponsor the show. It became "F. M. O'Leary Limited, presenting *The Barrelman*, in a program of making Newfoundland better known to Newfoundlanders." A ship's bell rang out, and Joey came on, invariably with the greeting: "Ladies and gentlemen, good evening." Then followed his grab-bag of anecdotes, letters, historical items, ballads—anything he thought would interest his listeners and make them proud of their country—each item separated by a clang from the ship's bell, and all of it interspersed with commercials for O'Leary products. It was purely a one-man show, never anything except Joey and the bell. Mail began to arrive by the bagful. Soon he was adding tall tales from his listeners to his repertoire.

He tracked down Newfoundland's oldest resident, Mrs. Helen Carroll of North River in Conception Bay, and made an annual radio extravaganza of her birthday. When she turned 114 on October 11, 1942, he reported showers of presents and messages from the king, the Pope, and the governor general of Canada, all of which Joey had arranged by writing to the people concerned. It made superb radio copy and proved, once again, what an exceptional race of people Newfoundlanders were.

The program extolled their bravery, resourcefulness, and talent for survival in adversity until Newfoundlanders began to believe it all themselves. When they entered Confederation they refused to give up the self-image that Joey had built for them over the previous twelve years, and continued for generations afterwards to be the only English-speaking province of Canada with a true national ethos and a sense of national identity.

No program in the history of radio ever achieved greater popularity. He had absolutely 100 percent listenership. The competing St. John's station at first tried to run a news program in the parallel time slot, then quit, and merely broadcast recorded music to show that it was still on the air. But while the recorded music was playing, the people in the competing studio tuned their radios to *The Barrelman*.

Joey also edited F. M. O'Leary's monthly newspaper, which was sent free to tens of thousands of outport homes, advertising O'Leary products. The mailing list, compiled by O'Leary's outport dealers, was of great use to the Newfoundland Confederate Association some ten years later when it helped to form the basic mailing list for *The Confederate*. Joey had always been prudent about keeping copies of things that might be useful to him later.

The program helped turn Frank O'Leary, a small-time commission merchant, into a millionaire, and it made Smallwood a household name. Everyone in the island old enough to listen and young enough to hear recognized his voice the moment it came over the airwaves. He and the radio, it turned out, were made for each other. It became his very own medium.

By any previous standards Joey was now well-to-do, earning $75 a week—a good, solid middle-class income in the 1930s—and he began to act a little less like a penurious drifter. He bought his first bottle of Christmas port. He bought his first house, a substantial two-storey structure on LeMarchant Road, by now a respectable neighbourhood that even included a few small merchants. Then he bought his first farm—four acres of cleared land and thirty-six acres of woods and berry barrens on Kenmount Road northwest of the city, with an old farmhouse and a new barn. There the children ran barefoot in the fields, Clara picked berries on the hill and started a garden, and Joey plunged into farming on a grand scale.

Even before he bought the place on Kenmount Road, Joey had been dabbling in experimental farming. My first memory of him in the flesh (though not in the voice) was when he came to the door of my grandfather's house on Campbell Avenue, near Mundy Pond on the northwest edge of St. John's, looking for a place to board a couple of purebred goats that he had imported. But the goats, like all Joey's farming experiments, were abandoned somewhere along the way. By the time he moved to Kenmount Road (much further out of town than Mundy Pond), he had decided on laying hens.

He built up a flock of 1,500 that should have grossed between $30,000 and $40,000 a year, for he was retailing his eggs at a dollar a dozen, and people were glad to buy them at that price. But he could never get his hens to lay properly, and finally he sold them off at a loss.

Then he tried pigs, and was nearly wiped out by an epidemic of hog disease. By instinct, he was a husbandman, not a gardener. All his farming consisted of trying to make some species of bird or mammal pay for its keep.

Fortunately, *The Barrelman* went merrily on its way, paying for some (but not all) of the losses on the farm. He ran the program for six years, at the same time doing some work for Water Street firms as an advertising writer, and some research into family histories. He wrote one such history for R. B. Job, a fish merchant, and another for Cyril B. Carter, whose family included five generations of lawyers, judges, and politicians.

In such matters Joey had the enthusiastic assistance of his lifelong friend Nimshi Crewe, an accountant working for the government, whose passionate hobbies were history, antiques, and genealogies. Crewe was a socialist, Newfoundland's most fluent orator and debater, a man who might have been a brilliant political or religious leader in another time and place, but who found no scope for his remarkable talents in the Newfoundland of the thirties and forties.

During his years as the Barrelman, Joey was able for the first time in his life to afford a car. In it he and Crewe took to touring the outports together during the one month each summer when *The Barrelman* was off the air. Crewe spent the month collecting antiques, and became an expert at restoring old furniture. Joey collected folklore and anecdotes for his program. In this way he visited many of the places that could be reached by Newfoundland's still scanty road system. He saw those outports during the time of their recovery at the end of the thirties and the beginning of the forties when the Great Depression was over, when prosperity was beginning to return to the fishery and especially to the logging industry. The Bowater Corporation, through its subsidiaries, the Bowater Paper Company, and Bowater Newfoundland Limited, had begun logging in 1938 for the mill at Corner Brook, which they had purchased from International Power and Paper, and also for their mills in Europe.

So the Great Depression ended in Newfoundland in 1938; by 1939 it was difficult to find enough hands to man the bucksaws, and Joey came back from his journeys with renewed confidence in the country and its natural resources. All you had to do to create the New Newfoundland of which he had been dreaming for so long was to concentrate your efforts on forestry, mining, farming, and manufacturing, instead of on the fishery, with its twin problems of periodic fish failures and cyclical market collapse.

By all the rules of common sense Joey should have stayed with *The Barrelman* until he was ready to step straight out into politics, but common sense was never his strong point. He abandoned the program (it was taken over by his young friend Michael Harrington, later to become editor of *The Evening Telegram*) and went off to Gander to raise pigs for the combined air force messes of Great Britain, Canada, and the United States.

Gander Airport was one of the providential creations of the Commission government. Built with remarkable foresight in 1936, before there was any trans-Atlantic air traffic, it was completed a year and a half before the outbreak of the Second World War, and became the western base of the Atlantic Ferry Command. For several years it was the largest and busiest airport in the world, with Canadian and American planes taking off for Britain at the rate of one a minute. The waste from the mess halls could easily nourish a thousand pigs, and Group Captain David Anderson of the Royal Air Force persuaded Joey to undertake the venture.

Once again he went to Ches Crosbie, and once again he got the money he needed. With some help from the RAF Welfare Fund (obviously not restricted to gilt-edged investments) and with much surplus material from military construction, they built the largest piggery Newfoundland had ever known, and flew in Canso-loads of weanling piglets from Prince Edward Island. Eventually they ran about a thousand pigs at a time, and processed about two thousand carcasses a year. From dressed carcasses they went on to hams and sausages and pickled pork. Perhaps because he was not in sole charge, the Gander piggery was the one farming venture in Joey's lifetime that proved an unqualified success. It operated from 1943 until well past the end of the war.

It was still booming along in December 1945, when Joey hitched a ride on an air force transport to Montreal and went on to Toronto to investigate the possibility of starting a feed mill in Newfoundland. The restless Smallwood was now contemplating raising herds of beef cattle.

On his way home on December 12, 1945, he stopped over in Montreal, and bought a copy of the *Gazette*. On the front page was a Reuters dispatch from London announcing the impending election of a national convention in Newfoundland to examine the country's financial condition, and to debate the merits of future forms of government to be placed before the people in a national referendum.

"SELF RULE IS PLAN FOR NEWFOUNDLAND" the headline announced. "Colony Soon to Have Own Government after 12 Years of Commission." The *Gazette* was misinterpreting Newfoundland affairs. The country was not a colony but a dominion with suspended constitution, and self-rule was not promised—what was promised was a referendum in which Newfoundlanders could decide what future form of government they wanted, self-rule or otherwise.

But no matter. Joey ignored the errors and concentrated on the substance of the announcement. Of course he would have to get himself elected to the national convention. That would be his first step toward becoming prime minister. The next step he could imagine only vaguely. He was too excited to stay in his hotel. Out he went, pacing the street for most of the day. That afternoon he wound up at an apartment owned by Ewart Young, a Newfoundland journalist working in Montreal as freelance reporter and magazine publisher.

Young told him at once that the only sane course for Newfoundland was to seek confederation with Canada. They argued about it over dinner and through the night until 3:00 A. M., and Joey gradually came around to Young's point of view. Young maintained ever afterwards that he had made Joey a confederate. Smallwood didn't exactly deny this, though he preferred to believe that he had received the inspiration straight from heaven, with, at most, a little help from his friends. Young clinched the argument by pointing out that the man who led Newfoundland into confederation would not only become the premier of the province, but would be a national hero forever afterwards.

Joey had never thought of confederation with Canada as a possibility. Now he discovered that a strong minority, including a number of thoughtful Newfoundlanders, supported the idea. Gordon Bradley, the last Liberal House leader in Newfoundland, was already a confederate. So was Phil Forsey, a teacher and well-known MCLI debater in St. John's. So was Greg Power, a poet and brilliant satirist, who owned a small farm at Dunville, near Placentia. So were thousands of fishermen along Newfoundland's south coast, many of whom had worked in Canada and on Canadian ships plying the Great Lakes.

Although Joey didn't know it at the time, and was probably unaware of it throughout the subsequent campaign, federal union of *all* British North America had been British imperial policy since the 1850s. This policy had been made plain time and again. Britain had never tried to force the various colonies into union, but had offered encouragement through the Colonial Office and through her governors, and had refused to have anything to do with weakening the union, once it began to emerge.*

Joey was nobody's pawn. He invented the confederate movement out of his own thinly thatched skull. Nobody chose him to lead the crusade. He chose himself. Indeed, to people outside the island he looked like the most unlikely of leaders: a drifter, a tired radical who had become a pig farmer. It took him a long time to get politicians in Ottawa and London to take him seriously, to convince them that he had even an outside chance of success. Even inside Newfoundland very few people, including very few confederates, believed at first that Joey could bring Newfoundland into the Canadian union and become the first premier of the tenth province. At the end of 1945 that idea was about as bizarre as the idea of a manned expedition to the moon.

I was one of the first people—perhaps the very first—who believed that he was going to do it. He once said to me: "You have to believe in yourself first. Then, later, other people may come to believe in you. You have to believe in your destiny, your star. I have never doubted myself. Never. Not even once."

The day after his long argument with Ewart Young, Joey made up his mind to take destiny by the forelock. He hitched a ride on an air force plane back to Gander, already planning to sell his interest in the piggery as soon as he could, aiming to plunge straight into Newfoundland politics as leader of the confederate faction.

Everything combined to make this Joey's main chance. He was forty-five—old enough to be a leader, but young enough to have a long political career ahead of him. He'd had all the training he could possibly need. By good luck his name and voice were well known and well liked throughout Newfoundland. A few intellectual snobs in St. John's laughed at him, but what did they matter? Also by good luck, he was not one of the "old politicians" who would forever be tainted by the disaster of 1932. He was a new leader with a new cause,

---

*The policy led to something called the "conspiracy theory" among Newfoundland historians and popular writers, a theory so ill-supported by facts or documentary evidence that it is unworthy of serious examination. The conspiracy is supposed to have been hatched between the governments of Canada and Great Britain.

asking Newfoundland to go forward into a new adventure, not back into the past, to the politics of the twenties and thirties.

There were men just as able as he on the other side, some of them with pleasanter voices, many of them better educated, some of them equally well known, well respected, and capable of rousing the enthusiasm of their listeners. But none of them had a cause like his, a cause that invited Newfoundlanders to venture into a challenging future, instead of retracing a course that had been tried before. Silver-tongued persuasion, clever use of media, all the money on Water Street, the power and influence of the Roman Catholic archbishop—all of this was ranged against him to no effect.

Back in Gander, the first thing he did was to write letters to the prime minister of Canada and the premiers of all nine Canadian provinces (he had to phone a friend to find out their names!). He outlined his intention to run for the national convention and explained his interest in confederation. He asked for their most recent budgets and budget speeches, and for information on public services. An avalanche of official documents descended on his desk in Gander, and he began sitting up every night until near dawn digesting the stuff. He used the information in his campaign for election, and to write a series of long letters to *The Daily News* in St. John's, outlining exactly how confederation worked, and pointing out how it would benefit Newfoundland. The letters ran daily for more than two weeks, and were read by thousands of thoughtful subscribers interested in the future of their country. They probably didn't create any army of converts. But they did start the debate going. People everywhere began discussing the pros and cons of confederation, at least in an academic way.

The MCLI took up the subject, and packed the Pitts Memorial Hall for the biggest debate that had taken place in St. John's since the suspension of responsible government. To widespread public astonishment, Joey and his team won the debate for confederation on the basis of votes cast by those present.

He sold the pig farm and, as he put it, "took the train to St. John's with $5,000 in cash in my pocket—the most money I'd ever seen in one place in my life." Whatever share of this belonged to Joey himself went to pay off back debts—there would be nothing to help him run his election campaign. When it came to financing his tour of Bonavista Centre, which included the section of Gander where he had been living, he had to look to others for funds. He got $1,500 from Tony

Mullowney, a friend and fellow confederate who worked at the airport. That was Mullowney's share of the profits from a small *coup* they had pulled off together, buying and selling war surplus blankets. Joey's wealthy backer, Ches Crosbie, had financed that deal, as well.

A little later Smallwood also sold the farm on Kenmount Road. Even he—deeply committed as he was to pigs and steers and poultry—realized that for the next couple of years at least he would have no time for farming. Later he might join some of the other Canadian premiers as a gentleman farmer. For now he was working sixteen hours or more a day learning about every aspect of the Canadian system, especially about relations between the federal government and the provinces. Before he was through, he probably knew more about federal-provincial relations than any person in Canada.

Because Kenmount Road was on the verge of development as a major commercial area of the city, he sold the farm at an immense profit. His total outlay for the farm, including the improvements he had made to it, was approximately $6,000. He sold it for $125,000. That was more money than he had ever imagined he could possess, but virtually all of it went to pay off his back debts and even that amount didn't succeed in clearing them entirely. He was a lifelong debt-accumulator, a terrible credit risk, with the glib ability to persuade people to lend him funds. Once during the confederation campaign, I saw him go through his personal mail, sorting out all the bills and throwing them unopened into the fireplace. Long after he was premier there were still uncollected back debts to St. John's merchants that had been outstanding for several years.

He got through the campaign in Bonavista Centre on Tony Mullowney's $1,500 and whatever else he could scrape together. Travelling up and down the district by chartered boat, he held meetings in packed halls. Although Bonavista Bay had voted solidly against confederation in 1869, he gambled on his ability to sell the idea to the voters this time. Everywhere he went he enthralled his listeners with three- and four-hour speeches about the benefits Newfoundland would enjoy as a Canadian province. And in this first round of political salesmanship he had nearly total success. He was elected to the national convention on June 21, 1946, by a vote of 2,129 to 277. His opponents in St. John's should have taken notice, but they didn't. They felt the election was a popularity contest and confederation a still-impossible dream that would vanish during the deliberations of the national convention.

The Commission of Government had retained the economists Chadwick and Jones to prepare a report on the issue. The study appeared that summer, and all elected members of the convention received copies. Then the Commission appointed an economic advisor and a secretary to the convention, and Justice Cyril Fox of the Newfoundland Supreme Court to the chair. As those preparations took nearly three months, the convention did not begin sitting until September 11.

Most members of the national convention were inexperienced and naïve. The Commission, with the best of intentions, had stipulated that all representatives be residents of their electoral districts. The result was that only a few able men came in from the outport districts, and most of them were not natives, but people who had been employed there. Such were Joey himself, the Reverend Lester Burry from Labrador, Isaac Newell from White Bay, William Keough from St. George's, Malcolm Hollett from Bonavista North, and Gordon Bradley from Bonavista East. These were the outport delegates who had some impact on the convention, not one of them a native of the district he represented, unless you count Joey's birth at Mint Brook.

It was more or less accidental that this handful of capable men represented the districts that they did. No fewer than eight seats were *uncontested*. Many of them fell by default to people of little ability and no experience in public affairs. Even where the seats were contested, the results were much the same. Of the men elected from districts where they were native or long-term resident, it is difficult to find more than two or three, outside the St. John's districts, who contributed anything to the convention debates, or to the subsequent public life of Newfoundland.

# CHAPTER 6

# *Resurrecting*
# *a Lost Cause*

I MET JOEY IN 1946, JUST AFTER HIS ELECTION TO THE NATIONAL convention, and before the convention began sitting. We had a common friend, Nimshi Crewe, and we met at Crewe's home on Lower Battery Road overlooking the Chain Rock and The Narrows at the entrance to St. John's harbour. That house was a delight to the visitor, a fine old Victorian structure filled with restored furniture: Sheridan chairs, Queen Anne sideboards, chests of antique silverware, even a massive kitchen table that had once been cabin furniture in a great sailing ship. Even more delightful, however, was Crewe's conversation. He'd invited me to his house that night to discuss the philosophy of William James and his *Varieties of Religious Experience*, and Joey happened to drop in. He was hardly equipped to discuss philosophical systems, nor was he interested in them, but he listened to us with flattering attention. It was the first and last time Crewe had ever known him to listen more than he talked.

At the end of the evening he invited me to visit his home on Devon Row where he had rented a flat in what had once been a classy apartment house, a short walk from Lower Battery Road. I went eagerly the next evening for a long chat. Talk on almost any subject seemed to me in those days to be almost an end in itself. For Joey's part, he must have considered me a good prospect for conversion to the confederate cause. I was a budding freelance writer, helping to write, edit, and print the first *avant garde* magazine in Newfoundland.

I was also far more deeply involved in the labour movement than Joey had ever been himself. Formerly a member of the powerful Longshoremen's Protective Union, I had gone on to organize unions of labourers, fish plant workers, and minor tradesman in Burin, Argentia, and St. John's. I was president of one of the biggest unions in Newfoundland, chairman of the Building Crafts Council, and influential in both the St. John's Trades and Labour Council and the Newfoundland Federation of Labour. Indeed, at twenty-two I was the boy wonder of the Newfoundland labour movement. Joey just then was eager for converts, but few of them came rushing in from the outside, convinced by his newspaper letters. Most he had to cultivate slowly and carefully, one by one, gathering the forces that two years later would turn into a powerful political machine.

I was a left-wing socialist, and some of my friends were card-carrying communists. From them I had learned a good deal about successful labour tactics, and made no secret of the fact. Joey didn't mind any of this. He talked as one socialist to another. He, too, had formed friendships with communists, though he found them hard people to work with, purists, separatists, the Jehovah's Witnesses of the socialist movement, so to speak. He was determined, he said, to have a socialist government in Newfoundland once we had won the battle for confederation. It would probably have to be organized under the name of the Liberal Party, but that wouldn't make the slightest difference. Socialist it would be, in all but name. He even talked about reviving the Legislative Council, the old appointed upper house, as a sort of provincial senate. "We'd fill it," he said, grinning wickedly, "with retired trade unionists and cooperative organizers."

In those days Joey was an outspoken agnostic. In private he made no secret of his utter scorn for all religious institutions. In public he preserved a discreet silence. But even at that early stage there was an underlying strain of bigotry in his character. Although he cultivated Roman Catholics, he had a deep distrust of their Church. More than once in the 1940s I heard him say that the Vatican was the real enemy of world peace, not the Kremlin.

He had a personal magnetism, a charm, an enthusiasm, that came across even more powerfully person to person than it did on the radio or from the platform. His sincerity, his conviction, his energy, were all hard to resist, and even stubborn individualists like myself were drawn into the vortex of his influence like chips into a whirlpool. There was no real question of his being anything but the leader of any group with which he was associated. He sought advice, and often listened to it, but it was always in the spirit of a king listening to the advice of his council.

I was converted to Smallwood before I was converted to confederation. One or two nights after being immersed in his confederate propaganda, I visited the home of my friend and fellow trade unionist Irving Fogwill, a man twenty-two years my senior, who had introduced me both to the union movement and to contemporary literature.

"He's going to win," I said. "He's going to make it. He's going to get confederation, and he's going to become the first premier of the province of Newfoundland."

"Impossible!" said Irving. He was, in any case, a confirmed pessimist. "He'll never take this country with him!" Nevertheless, within a few months both Irving Fogwill and his wife Janet became committed workers for the confederate cause, very close to the inner core of the Newfoundland Confederate Association. Like my brother, my father, the rest of my family, and thousands of other Newfoundlanders, they became confederates by imperceptible degrees. At some point they began to realize that they were convinced, converted to the cause, and then they often worked for it with zealous enthusiasm, accepting the slogan coined by Phil Forsey, "Confederation is the only salvation."

I always thought of myself as Joey's first convert, certainly the first in St. John's. The other members of the Inner Four were not converts. Forsey and Greg Power (and many other members of our organization) had been confederates long before Joey himself.

Forsey, born at Grand Bank in 1912, educated at Memorial University College and Mount Allison University, was then a teacher at Prince of Wales College, a leading debater at the MCLI, and an outspoken socialist. He had run for the national convention in St. John's West, and had been narrowly defeated.

Power had inherited from his father a small farm at Dunville, where he raised chickens and grew cabbages. He had been the chairman and moving force behind the General Workers' Union of Argentia. A year younger than Forsey, he too had a college education, and had once been a world-class athlete, setting a record for the hop-step-and-jump at the British Empire Games, which remained unbroken for more than a generation. Power's family had deep roots in Placentia district, where his grandfather had been one of the Placentia Giants. (They were six brothers, all well over six feet tall, who had carried their own rowing shell from Placentia to St. John's to win the championship race at the annual regatta.)

The Inner Four—Smallwood, Forsey, Power, and myself—were the real heart of the Newfoundland Confederate Association.* There were others with higher official positions, but they were window dressing. Gordon Bradley, for instance, became the association's chairman, and there were other officers who, we hoped, would look more or less respectable in the public eye. You could hardly run a national organization in the Western world of the 1940s with three of its four leaders out of the trade union movement, and all four professed socialists.

But we were the ones who made the decisions, often after long discussions, shaped every piece of strategy under Smallwood's leadership, and worked as a unit. He *listened* to us and acted on our advice. He discussed all his own ideas with us before taking them to the public. No one who saw the way he functioned in that small circle could ever accuse him of being a dictator, as so many outsiders did once he had achieved power. He was unquestionably the leader, but arrived at decisions by consensus.

Smallwood spent nearly every waking hour in the company of one or more of us. Greg Power, who had fought a long battle with pulmonary tuberculosis after his days as an athlete, and whose health was still a little shaky, often retired from our sessions shortly after midnight. Joey insisted that Power needed his sleep, and must never be allowed to catch cold or get the flu. But Forsey and I would sit up with Joey night after night until 3:00 or 4:00 A.M., discussing first the strategy that he used in the national convention, and later the strategy of the two campaigns for the national referenda.

Devon Row, where Joey lived, was a line of three-storey brick houses built in the previous century, a sort of high-class "town house" development of its time, right in the shadow of the Newfoundland Hotel, on the top floor of which the government radio network (headed by station VONF) had its studios. It was not more than a seven-minute walk away from the Colonial Building, where the national convention was to meet in the same chamber from which Squires had barely escaped with his life. The Commission government had restored the edifice, refurnished it, and touched up the remarkable

---

*Officially, it didn't exist for another two years, but *de facto* it was alive and active before the convention began to sit.

Baroque decorations in vermilion and gold leaf with which a Polish prisoner had adorned its ceilings in an earlier era.

So the modest apartment on Devon Row was the ideal meeting place for an embryonic political party not one of whose members owned a car. It was there that the battle for confederation was planned, and its strategy decided. There was a small sitting room with a tiny fireplace (more for decoration than heat, but useful for burning bills and other junk mail), around which four or five people could sit and talk. There was a dining room table around which a dozen people could crowd for food or work. There was a small kitchen—Clara's domain—with an everlasting supply of boiling water and numberless pots of tea.

Clara Smallwood was, in a sense, the perfect wife for her little dynamo of a husband. She was not much help in a political campaign—in fact, she seemed incapable of making any kind of public appearance other than to stand up and smile—but that was quite enough. Joey always had plenty of campaigners. Clara never even hinted that she had any ideas about her husband's career. She accepted his impatient domineering with absolute docility. And domineering he was. He treated her not as a consort so much as a domestic servant. When he sat up all night discussing political strategy, she sat up all night too—in the kitchen, reading, ready to make pots of tea as required. Joey would never have gotten away with treating any of his three grown children the way he treated his wife. They tended to have their father's spirit and their mother's good looks, together with some of her talents: Ramsay, like his mother, was a good amateur musician. The children took Joey with a grain of salt, but they pitched in and helped willingly when extra hands were needed to stuff envelopes or count names on petitions; his family backed him up at every turn.

Emotionally, Smallwood seemed to be closer to Greg Power than to anyone else. They were so close and seen so often in each other's company, that their political enemies sometimes made snide remarks about them, hinting that one or both might be something less than a true-blue, red-blooded American Male. Such attempted smears were frequent in Newfoundland politics. They had been used against Coaker and Bond; Smallwood would use them later against his own political enemies.

I was closest to Smallwood in the professional sense: Power was his friend; I became his alter ego. I got to know Joey so well that I could answer his letters in exactly the same style that he would use if answering them himself, learned to imitate his signature so that even he couldn't tell which of us had signed a membership card. I also learned to imitate his style of journalism, which was much different from my own.

Forsey continued teaching at Prince of Wales College throughout the sittings of the national convention and the political campaigns that followed. He was brilliant and full of ideas, and pretended to a hard-boiled cynicism. He also had contacts among the merchants, friends among the wealthy, and even a pally relationship with some of our political opponents. He was able to exploit all those contacts later. Forsey was the only one of the four who had a weakness for alcohol. Joey was almost a teetotaller. Power and I enjoyed our rum and coke but there was never any danger that our drinking would get out of hand. Forsey, even then, tended to drink compulsively, but seemed to have the compulsion under control; the disciplined life of a school teacher kept his drinking within bounds. I should have foreseen (but didn't) that the undisciplined life of a politician would destroy him, because I knew him better than any of his other friends. With Forsey and his wife Doris and six children I had as close a friendship as with anyone in my life.

The national convention opened quietly, almost sedately, like a gentlemen's debating club rather than an explosive mixture of Irishmen, Orangemen, fish merchants, and populist orators. It didn't remain gentlemanly for long. There were soon verbal brawls on the floor of the convention, and even physical ones in committee.

Newfoundland had been a long time without political debate, with only the MCLI to continue the discussion of public affairs. Perhaps it was for this reason that the Commission government decided to broadcast the proceedings of the convention in full, informing the Newfoundland public, and reintroducing them to parliamentary government, which everyone expected to be restored, in one form or another. The debates were not broadcast live, but were recorded in the afternoon for broadcast that same evening through the network of government stations. Every word spoken at the afternoon debates was broadcast at night, and the national convention soon replaced *The Barrelman* as the most popular radio entertainment in Newfoundland. In the outports, at least, everyone sat up as long as the show was on the air. This was usually three hours, from 9:00 P.M. to midnight, but sometimes extended to four hours, starting at 8:00 P.M. And Joey was the undisputed star. There were other media personalities in the convention, but none as clever as he, none who was such a natural behind a microphone.

His most effective opponent on the air was Peter Cashin, who was ten years older than Smallwood. A native of Cape Broyle in Ferryland, Cashin had risen from the ranks during the First World War to become a major in command of the Newfoundland machine gun corps. He returned to Newfoundland in time to enjoy his father's brief term as prime minister, and then to replace him as member for Ferryland in 1923. He was a major player in Squires's downfall, then disappeared from public life until after the Second World War when he began a series of radio broadcasts savagely attacking the Commission government and demanding the immediate return of responsible government to Newfoundland.

Gordon Higgins, born in St. John's in 1905, was not as spellbinding a speaker as Cashin, but he was far more intellectual and came from a family that contributed five prominent members to Newfoundland politics. His father had been Speaker of the House of Assembly, minister of justice, and a judge of the Supreme Court.

Malcolm Hollett was the only effective Smallwood opponent who came from the outports. Born at Burin in 1892 into a merchant family, he was a Rhodes scholar, educated at Oxford, and had been a magistrate at Grand Falls before his election. A tireless and effective speaker, he was Smallwood's most persistent political enemy, not only in the national convention, but for many years afterwards.

Ches Crosbie was also a convention member, backing the cause of responsible government, and fighting against confederation, but his effectiveness in debate was almost nil. His reputation as a businessman was useful to the responsible government supporters, but his voice was clearly a liability.

Joey's strategy was, first, to talk directly to the people of Newfoundland, to spend as much time as possible on his feet explaining why Newfoundland should seek union with Canada; second, to win support among the delegates; third, to get the convention to send a delegation to Ottawa to explore with the Canadian government the possibility and implications of a union between Canada and Newfoundland.

Joey never once forgot that he was on the air, and he timed his important propaganda announcements to coincide with prime-time listening. Every day, on his way from Devon Row to the Colonial Building, he would drop into the Newfoundland Hotel and take the elevator to the top floor, the VONF studio. There he'd ask about broadcast times that night, and translate afternoon debate times into evening broadcast times.

"The convention will be on directly after the Doyle News? Let's see. That means that eight o'clock at night will be the same as three o'clock in the afternoon, and eight-thirty will be the same as three-thirty. That's when I'm going to speak to the people of Green Bay and Humber District about the future of logging and the importance of the pulp and paper industry in Canada."

His friend Dick O'Brien, then a young broadcaster, recalls such visits vividly: "Joey was living on the $15 a day he got as the allowance for an outport delegate, and he rarely had a dime to spare. So his second reason for the visit was to 'borrow' enough cigarettes to get him through the afternoon. Sometimes he got them from Al Vardy, who broadcast the foreign news in those days, but Vardy treated him with scorn. He'd take a half pack of cigarettes, and throw them on the floor, like tossing something to a dog, and Joey would stoop and pick them up."

He *needed* those cigarettes more than his pride. A chain smoker, he didn't begin worrying about what a hundred cigarettes a day might be doing to his health until some time in 1947, when he began using a cigarette holder with a filter. Then he'd take out a used filter, dripping with tar, and gaze at it dubiously. Eventually he dropped the habit altogether, but that was years after the convention had closed, and his financial worries were over.

Making himself the convention's media star was the easy part. Manipulating its internal politics in order to get his delegation to Ottawa took a lot more planning—and cunning. Most of the delegates had no intention whatsoever of seeking any information from Canada. Their minds had been made up long before the convention began to sit. The only thing they wanted was the return of responsible government, and a chance to run for office.

But Joey soon found support among the outport delegates, especially those from the north and west coasts. There was, of course, Gordon Bradley, from Bonavista East, a respected lawyer, and a great debater. Already sixty years old when the convention opened, Bradley had been a lawyer since 1915, and had begun his political life as a Tory backbencher with Monroe in 1924. Before the next election he switched sides, and he came back with Squires to be appointed solicitor general. From 1932 until 1934 he was Liberal House Leader. He was active in numerous local and national organizations, in church affairs, and in volunteer community groups. Above all, he had a marvellous speaking voice, and a commanding platform presence.

Joey found a supporter of great intelligence in Isaac Newell, from St. Anthony. Newell was an intellectual, a minor poet, and later a university professor. His speeches were filled with well-reasoned argument, but he was neither charismatic nor a gifted speaker. Bill Keough, a former co-operative field worker from St. George's, was both.

A handsome, powerfully built man, gentle, slow moving, and soft-spoken, Keough took fire the moment he rose to his feet, and produced thunderous orations that kept his listeners enthralled even when they disagreed with his conclusions. He came from an area with strong ties to Canada, and had been working among fishermen and small farmers. He was eloquent beyond anyone in the confederate ranks, and was equalled only by Cashin as he pleaded the cause of the little people in the outports against the selfishness and cupidity of the St. John's merchants. The delegates sat in dead silence as they listened to him, even though most of them intended to vote the other way. His first speech to the convention was a complete surprise. No one there had suspected that the delegate from St. George's was as great an orator as Cashin, with a deeper and richer voice, and an even greater gift for imagery. When the speech was finished, and the echoes died among the rafters, there was a spontaneous burst of applause from all sides of convention, including even the fish merchants. Smallwood stood up and walked to Keough's seat to shake his hand. It was a moving moment, but it won no converts to the confederate cause.

Few of the delegates from St. John's or the Avalon Peninsula even considered the *possibility* of confederation. There seemed to be about thirty who would never budge and only sixteen who were prepared to entertain the idea. That's how it was when the convention opened, and that's how it was when it closed, a year and a half later.

So Smallwood was forced to work from a minority position. He tried without success to win new converts among the delegates. He dangled senatorships and government portfolios before hopeful eyes. He may even have *promised* such things, though of course any promises he made would be contingent on his first getting elected and being in a position to give advice on such matters. It is true that the Newfoundland Confederate Association sold some senatorships later, on the instalment plan, but none were sold to members of the convention.*

So what Joey couldn't get by bribery he set out to win by guile. But first, by moving a resolution on October 28, 1946 he launched a major debate on confederation:

"WHEREAS it is desirable that the National Convention and the people of Newfoundland should be fully informed as far as possible of all facts having any bearing upon forms of government that might be submitted to the people in a national referendum; therefore be it

"RESOLVED that the appropriate authorities be advised that the Convention desires to inform the Government of Canada of the Convention's wish to learn that government's attitude on the question of Federal Union of Newfoundland with Canada; and further wishes to ascertain the terms and conditions on the basis of which the Government of Canada consider that such Federal Union might be effected; and be it finally

"RESOLVED that the Delegation should have no authority whatsoever to negotiate or conclude any agreement or in any manner to bind the Convention or the people of Newfoundland."

This mere fact-finding resolution might have been expected to pass without much trouble. Instead, it unleashed the most violent and emotional oratory, a debate that lasted for five days, and caused such emotional turmoil that one delegate, Ken Brown from Bonavista South, collapsed with a stroke, while on his feet denouncing Canada. He crashed full-length to the floor, his face suffused with blood, upsetting his desk as he fell. He was rushed off to hospital, and pronounced dead. A few days later the chairman, Justice Cyril Fox, also died, of a heart attack, and the delegates elected Bradley to take the chair. The debate ended on November 5 with the defeat of the resolution by a vote of 25 to 18. (One delegate was dead, one was in the chair, and one was absent from the chamber.)

"It did two things," Joey told us the next day. "It drew the lines. We know now where everybody stands. The whole country knows it. And it got the message out by radio for the first time. Now we have to work on getting that delegation to Ottawa. Next time it won't be me. Someone else will move the resolution."

---

*Readers may ask, "In what way were they sold?" The answer is, in the same way that peerages were sold in Great Britain. More of this, later.

"If it's going to pass it had better be someone from the other side," I suggested. "Ches Crosbie would be ideal."

He grinned. "Yes, indeed he would. But I don't think there's any way to get him to do it. I'll have to work on someone else."

That someone else turned out to be the Honourable R. B. Job, a former member of the Legislative Council, chairman of Job Brothers (a fish and mercantile firm), and director of the Royal Stores, Browning-Harvey, and Colonial Cordage. He was also the oldest member of the convention, and, by general consent, its senior statesman. Job had his own hobby horse to ride: he hoped that Newfoundland could get special tariff privileges from the United States, a form of reciprocity for the American right to import goods duty-free to their military bases in Newfoundland. The idea was not entirely crazy, for the Americans only had property rights on their leased bases, with extraterritorial privileges, while sovereignty remained with Newfoundland. The Americans had always ignored this distinction, but when it came to dealings between governments, the distinction might prove important.

The dream of getting duty-free fish into the United States had been cherished by Newfoundlanders for generations, and was one of the great disputes between Newfoundland and Canada, for Canada had intervened to prevent the implementation of the Bond-Blaine treaty back in 1890, by which Newfoundland had indeed secured such a right. Newfoundlanders had never forgiven Canada for destroying the fruits of their greatest diplomatic *coup*. Smallwood went to Job and offered to support a fact-finding delegation on the American question if Job would support a fact-finding delegation to Ottawa. It seemed reasonable, and they made a deal.

"While we're at it," one of them suggested, "we should find out what the British are prepared to do if we return to responsible government, or how far they're prepared to continue assistance under the Commission."

"One motion should cover all three fact-finding missions," Smallwood proposed. "I think you should move it, and I'll find a seconder, and get whatever support I can."

So Smallwood got his resolution to send a delegation to Ottawa (as well as London) and had it moved and seconded not by confederate supporters, but by two strong advocates of responsible government, one of whom was the convention's senior statesman, while the other was the leading lawyer of the responsible government faction, Gordon Higgins.

The resolution proposed that the convention approach the Commission government to ascertain:

"1. What steps if any can be taken for establishing improved economic or fiscal relationships between the United States of America and Newfoundland, particularly bearing in mind the present occupation of certain Newfoundland territory and the fact that free entry is given to the United States for its importations to Newfoundland.

"2. What financial or fiscal relationships could be expected between the Government of the United Kingdom and Newfoundland

1—Under continuation of Commission Government in its present form;

2—Under a revised form with elected representatives thereon;

3—Under Responsible Government in approximately its previous form;

4—Under any other suitable form of government.

"3. What could be a fair and equitable basis for Federal Union of the Dominion of Canada and Newfoundland, or what other fiscal, political or economic arrangements may be possible."

Only eight delegates recognized this portmanteau motion as a trap and voted against it; the others allowed it to pass virtually without debate; many of them were not even present for the vote. Among those voting against were Peter Cashin and Malcolm Hollett.

When a committee of the convention approached the Commission government they were told that the government would facilitate fact-finding missions to London and Ottawa, but that an approach to the United States would have to be made, if at all, at the diplomatic level. This ruled out an approach by the convention. Resolutions to send missions to London and Ottawa then passed without opposition.

The delegation to London, chaired by Bradley, received a cool reception. Britain was still in an economic bind, paying for the Second World War, and had difficulty converting pounds into "hard currency" like Canadian and American dollars. The new socialist government there was in no mood to promise long-term aid to distant parts of the Empire, which, in any case, they were in process of dismantling. When a colony became self-governing, it should also be self-supporting, and dominions in particular should not expect Britain to underwrite their economies. All this was made abundantly clear very quickly. Newfoundland might decide to return to the status of a

Crown colony. Or Commission government might be extended for a period, without elected representation. But if Newfoundland wanted responsible government, either as a separate dominion or as a province of Canada, British responsibility would end with the passage of the necessary legislation in the British parliament.

This was what Joey had expected and hoped for—bare justice, and a cold shoulder—but some of the members of the London delegation were very angry indeed. They had expected gratitude for Newfoundland's part in the two world wars, for the interest-free loans that Newfoundland had extended to Britain in wartime, and for the private financial support of the war effort made by the people of Newfoundland through savings bonds, and through the outright gift of Spitfire aircraft. Instead, the British felt that *they* were the ones who deserved the gratitude for saving the world from Hitler. Peter Cashin, the strongest personality in the London delegation, had expected nothing better than this. He suspected the British of trying to prolong Commission government in order to get their hands on Newfoundland's accumulated surplus, which amounted to between $45 and $50 million and which would be readily convertible into Canadian or American currency. Let them restore responsible government as they had promised, Cashin insisted, and Newfoundland would go it on her own. The talks in London lasted barely a week. On April 9, 1947, the delegation left London for Newfoundland empty-handed.

After a brief debate on the London report and another unsuccessful attempt to get a delegation to Washington, the convention elected the delegation to Ottawa, and talks began there on June 25, 1947.

Bradley also chaired this delegation. Its other members were Joey Smallwood, the Honourable R. B. Job, Gordon Higgins, the Reverend Lester Burry, Charles Ballam, and T. G. W. Ashbourne. Ashbourne and Ballam were lightweights who would contribute little if anything to the negotiations. Burry was a confederate (like Ballam and Ashbourne) and something of an expert on Labrador, having spent most of his professional life there as a United Church missionary. Job was by now in failing health, but had a thorough knowledge of the fishing industry. Higgins would be useful as devil's advocate: a determined opponent of confederation, he would be well able to raise the needed objections, point by point, as the negotiations proceeded. Bradley was confederate and experienced in politics, a man of intelligence, presence, and ability, but he had some severe deficiencies. He not only lacked ambition, but had a fatal lack of physical energy. He spent his life in a state of near-exhaustion that energetic people just couldn't understand. Privately, Smallwood would call him "as lazy as a Newfoundland dog." He never really appreciated the fact that Bradley suffered such chronic fatigue that he literally had to make a determined effort just to get up out of a chair.

So Joey carried the ball about 90 percent of the time, which was just what he wanted. He was the only delegate who was completely familiar with the Canadian federal system, knowledgeable about federal-provincial relations, and determined to secure from Canada a realistic offer that would give Newfoundlanders something worth voting for. He negotiated hard and long, arguing cogently with minister and mandarin, so that the meetings, instead of being concluded in two or three weeks as expected, stretched on for months through the whole of that long, hot summer, from June 25 to September 30.

If Joey had only minor support from the other members of the delegation, he had massive support from interested Canadians: at first it was Frank Bridges, the federal minister of fisheries, a New Brunswicker, but Bridges died suddenly that summer. Then support came from R. A. MacKay, an economist and diplomat who happened to have made a thorough study of Newfoundland and who had recently edited and published a scholarly book on the subject. But above all, Joey had the support of J. W. Pickersgill, a brilliant backstairs politician, who was the special assistant and advisor to Prime Minister Mackenzie King. Joey also had the continuous advice of Scott Macdonald, the Canadian High Commissioner to Newfoundland. Pickersgill and Macdonald were both determined confederates, willing to make almost any effort to bring Newfoundland into the Canadian union, though most of their political bosses in the federal Cabinet were lukewarm to the idea.

As the talks progressed, the federal civil servants compiled two large volumes outlining relations between Canada and the provinces, and in particular detailing the public services that the federal government would provide for Newfoundland. Bound in black and later distributed to all members of the convention, they became known as "the black books," the bible of the confederate movement. By summer's end the negotiations had also produced a set of tentative special terms of union—in effect, an *offer* from the government of Canada to Newfoundland that might provide a basis for confederation. As it turned out, this offer was far from generous, or even adequate, because Mackenzie King was afraid to offer Newfoundland anything that the Maritime provinces didn't already have. But inadequate as they were, the tentative terms showed that Canada was at least interested, and prepared to negotiate. To Newfoundland, used to extreme austerity, the tentative terms of union might even have looked attractive. The terms were not sent back with the delegation, but were sent later, to the governor, as an offer from one government to another.

While all this was going on, many of the national convention delegates remaining in St. John's were most unhappy. They had expected the talks to last a few weeks. When they had stretched to a month with no end in sight, five of the delegates telegraphed Gordon Bradley demanding that he break off the talks and call the convention back into session. Bradley replied that the delegation had not finished the work that the convention had appointed them to do, and that they would return as soon as possible after it was completed.

The five delegates then called on the governor, asking him to reconvene the convention and make plans to hold a referendum in the autumn of 1947. The governor wired Bradley saying that the matter would be left in his hands. Later, an even larger group of delegates, supported by prominent members of the Responsible Government League, took out a full-page advertisement in the St. John's *Evening Telegram* repudiating the Ottawa delegation and the negotiations that were going on there.

On September 8, twenty-one convention delegates signed a telegram to Bradley and to Prime Minister Mackenzie King, dissociating themselves from the negotiations, and demanding the immediate return of the delegation to St. John's. By now Smallwood was worried. It sounded too much like a popular revolt. He phoned Greg Power daily to ask for news from the outports, and he wired me, asking my opinion on how the public in St. John's was taking it. I replied that he could rest easy; it was a tempest in a teapot; the public cared little whether the convention resumed its sittings in September, October, or November. He calmed down, but was still on edge.

Joey was upset not only by the rumblings from St. John's, but even more by an ill-considered statement issued to the press by Lester Pearson—not yet a member of the government, but an influential civil servant as undersecretary of state for external affairs, treading exactly the same road to power that Louis St. Laurent had trodden before him. Pearson, who knew nothing of the history of Newfoundland politics, explained to the press that the Newfoundland delegation had no power to negotiate, adding that Canada would prefer to deal with an elected government "to forestall any possibility of future complaints by Newfoundlanders that they had no voice in the actual negotiation of terms." This was precisely what the Responsible Government League had been saying all along: "Get responsible government first. Then if we want to discuss confederation, we can deal with Canada as an equal." It sounded reasonable. But Pearson was unaware of the hidden agenda: once responsible government was a fact, every kind of fillibuster, every trick in the book, would be used to prevent negotiations from ever starting.

When Bradley read in the St. John's *Daily News* a story based on Pearson's statement, together with editorial comment, he nearly threw in the sponge and left Ottawa. The Canadians, he believed, were playing games, jack-easy about making any deal with Newfoundland. By instinct he felt he should rush home in anger and denounce them. Smallwood had to use all his powers of persuasion to keep Bradley in Ottawa until the Canadian government gave them at least *something* to take back with them. Fortunately, Bradley's waffling did not become public knowledge until several years later.

The Canadian government itself was divided on the question of whether an offer of any kind should be made. Mackenzie King was uncertain. From Ottawa's point of view Pearson's statement looked perfectly reasonable. The prime minister—a somewhat paranoid politician at the best of times—always feared that the Maritime provinces were ready to desert him at the slightest provocation, perhaps even ready to elect governments of separatists, as had happened once in Nova Scotia during the early days of Confederation. But his secretary of state for external affairs, Louis St. Laurent, was determined not to send the delegation home without an offer. He impressed upon King what a triumph it would be for him, personally, to complete Confederation by bringing Newfoundland into the union. This appeal to King's vanity probably tipped the scales, and he mentioned in his diary "the value it would be to my name and to the future to have Newfoundland come into Confederation while I am still Prime Minister." He called a special Cabinet meeting to discuss offering terms, with Scott Macdonald as consultant, and he and Macdonald talked the Cabinet into agreement.

Crucial negotiations then began, with Smallwood stressing that the special terms of confederation must protect Newfoundland's special interests. He was particularly fearful of alienating Roman Catholic voters, who made up a solid third of Newfoundland's population. Denominational education must therefore be regarded as sacrosanct. The matter of divorce was almost equally dangerous. There must be no easy divorces in Newfoundland. He wangled from the federal government the strange provision that Newfoundland's denominational schools should be protected by a special section of the terms of union. In effect this meant that denominational schools in Newfoundland would become a part of the Canadian constitution, in complete contradiction of the constitutional principle that primary education was a provincial responsibility. Absurd as that sounds, Joey had his way, his powers of persuasion reinforced by St. Laurent, who knew something of the influence that the Church could wield in secular affairs. The delegation also insisted that the terms should specify no divorce courts in Newfoundland. As in Quebec, divorces would be granted only by Act of Parliament. There was a third matter, which was perhaps even more crucial, not to the religious hierarchy, but to all Newfoundlanders—and that was the ownership of Labrador. The delegation insisted that Labrador's ownership be spelled out in the terms of union, even at risk of Canada's humiliation, for Canada (not Quebec) had tried to take Labrador from Newfoundland back in the 1920s: "The Province of Newfoundland shall include the territory of Labrador *defined by the award of the Judicial Committee of the Privy Council in 1927 as Newfoundland territory.*" This term was written in, and once the Act of Union became law in Newfoundland, Canada, and Great Britain, neither Quebec nor Canada could ever secure a change in the Labrador boundary without Newfoundland's consent, for the Newfoundland terms of union were to be a contractual relationship, unchangeable except with the consent of both contracting parties.

There were also special financial matters: Canada would have to take over such costly services as the Newfoundland Railway and the coastal shipping around Newfoundland and northward into Labrador, and it would have to provide a car ferry service across Cabot Strait as soon as Newfoundland had built a road between Port aux Basques and Corner Brook. The delegation also insisted on a transitional grant to cushion the loss of Newfoundland's revenues from customs and excise taxes. Later, there would have to be a permanent grant to enable Newfoundland to maintain its public services without imposing taxation "more burdensome, having regard to the capacity to pay, than that obtaining in the Maritime Provinces." Thus was born the principle of *equalization grants*, later to become an established practice in Canada. They would not, in fact, make all the provinces equal or correct the exploitive market relationship between central Canada and provinces on the fringes of the country, but at least they would *tend* in that direction.

The negotiations were hard going, and the delegation's proposals met a lot of opposition not only from members of the government who did not want to make the deal look too attractive, but also from influential civil servants, who were deeply concerned about making changes in the structure of the Canadian federal system.

After many weeks of negotiations, Smallwood, assisted by R. A. MacKay and Pickersgill, came up with proposals that both sides could accept, at least provisionally. This was one of Joey's finest hours. He showed that he was no mere propagandist, no simple populist politician, but that he was also a statesman, capable of compromise, of considered negotiations, of putting the case for his country appropriately, and of manipulating the art of the possible. The former pig farmer gained the respect, and to some degree the admiration, of such diverse federal politicians as Louis St. Laurent, C. D. Howe, and J. W. Pickersgill. During those months in Ottawa, it became perfectly obvious that Smallwood was Newfoundland's future leader.

The delegation finally returned, and the national convention resumed its sittings at 3:00 P.M. on October 10. We knew that the responsible government delegates intended to propose a motion of no-confidence in Chairman Bradley as soon as the sittings began. The plan was to vote him out of the chair and elect a new chairman, thus delivering a strong symbolic blow to the confederate cause, but Bradley, warned in advance, had a brief speech of resignation typed out, ready to deliver at the first hint of rebellion.

The session started quietly. Smallwood, as secretary of the Ottawa delegation, laid the black books on the table, and read the five-page introduction to the delegation's report. He sat down, and A. B. Butt (St. John's West Extern, a debater of note, and a former friend of Joey) asked for the floor. He rose and began to read the preamble to his motion, which was to have been a powerful indictment of Bradley and the behaviour of the Ottawa delegation, but the chairman interrupted:

"Just a moment, Mr. Butt."

Butt sat down. Bradley stood in his place on the speaker's dais and read the few lines of his resignation, his voice ringing with indignation as he described the contemptible actions of the delegates during his absence in Ottawa. Then he announced: "This convention is without a chairman." And he strode from the platform, a tall, commanding figure, his black gown flowing around him, down the aisle and out of the chamber.

Pandemonium broke loose, led by Joey, who tossed papers into the air and kept shouting across the floor that the convention was no longer in session. To emphasize the point, he lit a cigarette, and started to blow smoke around the hallowed chamber.

But even though the session was indeed at an end, Convention Secretary Gordon Warren took the chair and called for order. He suggested, and the delegates agreed, that they should ask the governor to appoint a new chairman.

Governor Gordon Macdonald, as it happened, was prepared for this, and John B. McEvoy, a prominent lawyer who had been a special advisor to the Commission government, had already agreed to accept the chair, should Bradley resign. McEvoy had never been involved in politics, was neutral on the question of confederation so far as anyone knew, and had built a great reputation both with the corporations and in the courtroom. The convention resumed under his chairmanship on October 13, with the delegates in a somewhat chastened mood. They had heard the broadcast of the short session three days before, and must have realized that Bradley had made them look like a bunch of naughty little boys being read a stern lecture from their teacher.

The history of the national convention falls neatly into two parts. The first part, before the Ottawa delegation, was dominated by Peter Cashin and the other advocates of responsible government, with Smallwood and his supporters a minority voice, advocating an apparently hopeless cause. The second part, after the Ottawa delegation, was an all-Smallwood show. It was then the convention became his platform for preaching "the gospel of confederation" to the people of Newfoundland by radio. He dominated the proceedings. The twenty-nine delegates opposed to him were permanently on the defensive, fighting a losing battle, trying vainly to stop him. Phil Forsey, watching the debates from the visitors gallery, used to chuckle with glee: "They've been outflanked, out maneouvred, and outgeneralled. They might as well quit."

There was a minor debate in October over accepting the report of the Ottawa delegation. On October 29 the governor received the proposed terms of union from Canada. Printed in a slim volume with a gray cover, the terms were tabled in the convention for later debate, and became known as the Gray Book. On November 20 the convention moved into committee of the whole to consider the Canadian proposals point by point.

Smallwood's job was to "pilot the terms through the committee" in the same way that ministers "pilot" their budget proposals through committee when the estimates are being debated in parliament. This gave him unlimited opportunity to explain the terms in detail and to answer every single criticism from his twenty-nine opponents. He had the backing of some excellent speakers, including Bradley, who, no longer in the chair, was free to enter the debate at any point he chose.

It would be wrong to portray Smallwood as standing in his place for three weeks fending off the slings and arrows of the Responsible Government League. He was on his feet only about 80 percent of the time. Whenever someone raised a point against one of the proposed terms of union, he took off with another speech, explaining in laboured detail what great benefits it would bring to the Newfoundland people, and contrasting those benefits with the miseries endured under responsible government.

"I know it sounds laboured and repetitious to you," he told me, "but it's not you I have to convince—it's the voters out in Scratch-Ass Tickle, where it will only sink in if I say it ten times over in slightly different words. I'm talking to the Huskies and the Jakitars and the swile hunters, even though I have to address my remarks to Johnnie McEvoy."

During the committee debate Joey worked like a galley slave, and enjoyed every minute of it. He spent the nights preparing his arguments for the next day, working in his flat on Devon Row until dawn, then sleeping until noon and turning up at the Colonial Building when the daily session started at 3:00 P.M. The debate would normally end at six, but twice a week (later it became five times a week) there would be night sessions from nine until midnight. Then he would spend almost the whole afternoon and evening on his feet in the chamber. Now and then one of his supporters would make a speech, giving Joey the opportunity to bow to the chairman, and go stand in the doorway (technically outside) feeding his nicotine habit with a borrowed cigarette. During the long debate his opponents watched and waited and kept giving him more and more rope, believing that sooner or later he would have to collapse, or his voice would give out. He even instructed us to spread rumours about how close he was to

Joey at the beginning of his political career, aged forty-six, when he launched the campaign to bring Newfoundland into the Canadian union. On his little portable typewriter he churned out millions of words of political propaganda. (Photograph copyright Marshall Studios)

Counting names on the confederate petition in the little flat on Devon Row, St. John's, 1948. Standing, left to right: Joey, Irving Fogwill, William Smallwood; seated: Janet Fogwill, the author, Joey's daughter Clara Smallwood , Roy Pike, Bill Case, Max Howell and Herb Wells. Fifty thousand people petitioned Britain to include confederation as a choice in the national referendum.

Joey denounces John Crosbie in the House of Assembly. Heir apparent Crosbie had resigned from the cabinet after a dispute over financing the new industries. Heir apparent Ed Roberts works at his desk immediately behind Joey's, unimpressed by the legislative drama. Joey's longest-serving cabinet colleague, L.R. Curtis, is seated at his right.

The author, aged twenty-five, addresses the first session of the Newfoundland legislature after confederation. On his right are Liberal members George Mackinson, Edward Russell, Edward Spencer, Baxter Morgan, Samuel Hefferton.

Joey explains to Premier Jean-Jacques Bertrand of Quebec just where the Quebec-Labrador boundary lies. Though Quebec premiers were forced to recognize Labrador as Newfoundland territory in order to secure mining and hydro developments, they refused to issue maps showing the boundary. In negotiations they referred to it as "Point A." (Canadian Press Photo)

Fishermen demonstrate against Smallwood's policies after the phosphorus plant he promoted at Long Harbour spread pollution across the fishing grounds. He had already lost the support of the loggers and of the middle classes in the cities. The fishermen were his last remaining constituency.

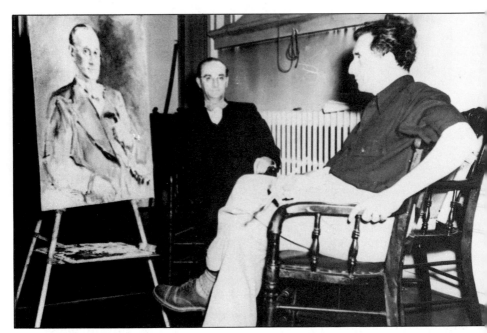

Sitting for an oil portrait by Steiger, who did oils of all Newfoundland prime ministers. Steiger made him look older and more statesman-like than he was at that time, and he did not grow into the portrait image, as might have been expected.

exhaustion. But he was actually as strong at the end of the three weeks as he had been at the beginning.

During the dinner recess, or after the night session ended, he would sometimes take half an hour off and play solitaire to relax. Solitaire was the only game I ever saw him play. He could absorb himself completely in this pastime, and come back to his work refreshed, as though he had been practising transcendental meditation.

Throughout the sittings of the convention he remained almost as poor as ever, supporting his family on the tiny sessional allowance, unable to afford a car or even a new suit of clothes. He wore his suits until they were threadbare, and often the parts didn't quite match. He was still wearing such odd pieces of old suits the year after confederation, when the Canadian Tailors' Association voted him "best-dressed man of the year." He grinned delightedly at the honour: "That's the first time anybody got it for wearing a black vest with a navy blue jacket!"

As he culled the sheaves of bills from the mail and threw them into the fire, he'd remark, "I'll see my creditors after I become premier." By that time, of course, many of them would be anxious to forget old debts in the hope of future favours. But while he was still plain Joey, some of them became a real bother. Bowring Brothers of St. John's issued a writ for the collection of $985 outstanding for a number of years. According to Joey, this was the remainder of a debt for feed supplied to his disastrous poultry operation on Kenmount Road five or six years earlier. He agreed to pay it off in small monthly instalments.

Joey always managed to shrug off such minor personal annoyances and devote his attention single-mindedly to his major task. Only several years later would he begin to think about "personal security" as a necessary base from which to operate effectively. Throughout the confederation campaign he seemed to be hampered not one whit by the fact that he was forever on the brink of personal bankruptcy.

His opponents in the national convention knew just as well as his friends that Joey's personal finances had always been in a state of chaos. They knew he was unable to deal with money, or with figures of any kind. Often he was unable even to remember the date of the month, though he could recall thousands of names of people he had met once or twice years before. His opponents therefore kept harping on his weakest point: finances, figures, taxation. Peter Cashin challenged him to show that Newfoundland would be solvent under confederation, and declared, from his own knowledge as a former finance minister, that this would be possible only if the province imposed crippling taxation. Cashin was even able to demonstrate such impending insolvency with strings of figures that he could pull out of the air like magic during an extemporaneous speech—he hadn't been Opposition finance critic for nothing. This, Joey's opponents felt, would be the clinching argument against confederation. There was still a lingering fear of bankruptcy in Newfoundland, and it appeared that the province would be able to survive only by taxing everyone's house, every fisherman's boat, every slice of bread on his table.

On December 5 the debate had been going on for twelve days and nights, and everyone was convinced that Joey would have to wind it up on the following Monday, December 8, with the arguments about taxation left unanswered. But when the convention recessed that night for the weekend, he called Phil Forsey and me into conference. He had secured a copy of the latest Newfoundland budget and estimates from the Commission government. He also had the now-famous black books, which set forth every item of proposed federal government spending inside the province-to-be.

We sat up until dawn in Joey's little sitting room, subtracting from the Commission government's departmental estimates every item of expenditure that would be taken over by the federal government, adding what we hoped would look like generous amounts for such vital services as welfare and education, subtracting from revenues such wicked impositions as customs duties, adding subsidies and returns from taxation agreements, federal rentals, and other receipts.

We projected a very modest increase in provincial revenues annually over the next eight years, not forgetting the transitional grants from the federal government, which were such an important item in the proposed terms of union. We added *no new provincial taxes whatsoever*.

This time Joey knew enough not to trust himself with figures. He had a sound knowledge of how the services would be distributed, but the financial implications, the adding and subtracting, he left to Forsey and me. My own knowledge of budgets and government finances (on which I was considered an expert during my eight years with *The Evening Telegram*) stemmed mainly from that weekend.

In the hours before dawn on Saturday we produced a tentative budget for the provincial government during the first year of confeder-ation, and a generalized eight-year projection of revenues and expenditures, showing a budgetry surplus for every one of the eight years. After that, the terms of union called for a financial review to determine what additional assistance, if any, Newfoundland would need to maintain its services at the level then achieved.

By 3:00 A.M. Sunday our job was complete. Joey did the rest himself, on Sunday afternoon and evening and into the small hours of Monday. He dressed the figures in the robes of official rhetoric, and had them all ready to lay on the table of the convention later that day.

He went into the session on Monday afternoon and "brought down" the budget, together with the eight-year projection. His opponents were stunned. If he had literally pulled a swarm of rabbits out of the soft felt hat that he wore in those days, they could not have been more astonished. What is more, the budget stood up to Opposition criticism, and to searching examination by Cashin. He attacked it, of course, and advanced all sorts of arguments against it, but they sounded unconvincing. Needless to say, it bore hardly any relationship to what actually happened after confederation, when the new government began spending money the way Joey had always spent it whenever it happened to be lying around. What it did do was to demonstrate beyond reasonable argument that Newfoundland *could* survive as a province without imposing new taxation of any kind, and without curtailing services, but actually improving and extending them.

It took all day just to present the document. On Tuesday the debate on the budget began, continuing through Wednesday, Thursday, and Friday. It was such an overwhelming success from the confederate point of view that the responsible government delegates adopted a new way of shutting Smallwood up: they walked out of the chamber, leaving one member behind to direct the chairman's attention to the fact that there was now no quorum. The session adjourned in disorder, and J. B. McEvoy seriously considered resigning the chair at that point. Smallwood, Bradley, and others persuaded him to remain. He agreed, and the convention went into its Christmas recess.

The debate resumed on January 5 amidst widespread disorder on the floor, and widespread applause for Smallwood's performance from the visitor's galleries—a sharp contrast to the early days of the convention when every mention of confederation had brought hisses from the spectators. As usual, I was sitting in the front row. At one point Peter Cashin rose in response to the applause, glared in my direction, and barked, "Mr. Chairman, those galleries have been ... fixed up!"

At recess time Ike Newell walked up to me and asked, grinning,

"Are you the lad who rigged the galleries?" It mattered not in the least. The applause had gone out loud and clear to every corner of Newfoundland: the sound of the toiling masses applauding the confederate leader while the wicked merchants hampered him and heckled him and tried to stop the debate. He stood up, a lone little figure surrounded by his enemies, from January 5 to January 15, hammering home the point that confederation would mean increased services, increased opportunities, and increased revenues for the government, all without increased taxation. It convinced not one single member of the convention, or at any rate changed not a single vote—the sixteen confederates were still confederates; the twenty-nine antis were still antis—but it convinced a lot of people in the country at large.

Apart from his own ability, Smallwood enjoyed many advantages that his opponents did not have. He was aided by a corps of intelligent, well-informed people inside and outside the convention, by those who would later form the Newfoundland Confederate Association, and by high-calibre Canadians like MacKay, Macdonald, and Pickersgill—and there was no question about the leadership: we were united behind him.

Apart from A. B. Perlin, columnist and editorial writer for *The Daily News*, there was no such help for Smallwood's opponents, and they were a house divided: Ches Crosbie, Peter Cashin, Gordon Higgins, and possibly Malcolm Hollett all cherished leadership ambitions. They were often at cross-purposes and hard put to conceal their differences. Smallwood, personally, was more effective than any of them, not only because of his natural endowments and training, but also because of his lifestyle. He was an ascetic. None of his time or energy was wasted on cocktail parties, social pursuits, or bouts of solitary drinking. At least three of his major opponents were tipplers, and two of them alcoholics—Hollett, an intellectual who, in many respects, had the capacity to be a leader, was the worst of the lot when it came to handling booze. His bouts of drinking could incapacitate him, even land him in hospital. Cashin was not much better as a leadership candidate. Though fluent and fast on his feet he was a rabble rouser for whom slogans and unfounded accusations took the place of reasoned debate. He failed, consequently, to convert the uncommitted voter; his appeal was to those already convinced. Crosbie, though brilliant in business, was not a very smart politician, or even a passable speaker; when coached and trained and groomed for a speech which he had rehearsed again and again at home, he still delivered it in a half-intelligible rumble. Higgins was a man of respectable intellect, a good speaker, a first-class lawyer, but he had never learned to use the language of the semi-literate radio listener, as Cashin and Smallwood had done. He always sounded like a professor speaking to a law school class. Cashin was the only one who coined memorable phrases. His description of Joey—"That self-appointed Moses, trying to lead us to the promised land across the Gulf of St. Lawrence"—amused if it didn't convince.

Higgins delivered the final appeal for responsible government in the convention, moving, on January 19, 1948, that the convention recommend to the government of Great Britain that two forms of government be included in the coming referendum: Commission government as then constituted and responsible government as it existed in 1934 before the Commission was established.

After a four-day debate this motion passed unanimously. All the confederates voted for it because they felt that the people should have the opportunity to choose the form of government that they preferred and there were three clear choices, two of which were in Higgins's motion. Each of those choices would undoubtedly be favoured by large numbers of voters. Their support for Higgins's motion cast their opponents in a bad light.

On the following day Smallwood moved "that the national convention desires to recommend...that the following form of government be placed before the people of Newfoundland in the forthcoming referendum, namely, confederation with Canada upon the basis submitted to the national convention on November 6 by the Prime Minister of Canada."

This motion launched yet another heated debate that went on day and night for nearly five days, ending in an all-night session on January 26–27 when the chairman "refused to see midnight" on the clock. Smallwood, under the parliamentary rules, had the right to close the debate with a final speech, and he did so with one of his most eloquent efforts. That speech was the last one broadcast from the convention, and it was moving and persuasive. At 5:00 A.M. the vote was taken, and the motion was defeated 29 to 16. The vote notwithstanding, tens of thousands of listeners were convinced that the confederates had won the debate hands down.

There can be no doubt that the governor and the Commission of government unanimously regarded confederation as at least a desirable option for Newfoundland, and did whatever they could do, in fairness and impartiality, to have this option placed before the people, along with the others. Undoubtedly, the governor discussed the matter with the Dominions Office in Great Britain, and was told that His Majesty's government viewed confederation in a favourable light, as British governments had done since the 1850s.

There is, however, not a shred of evidence that Canada or Great Britain were parties to any kind of underhanded or secret dealing in the matter. On the contrary, the more closely the documentary evidence is examined, the clearer it becomes that the issue was truly in doubt up to the last moment, and that few people in the Canadian government had any more than a mild interest in the matter.

I should add, perhaps, that it would have been very difficult to have a conspiracy to chivvy Newfoundland into confederation without Joey Smallwood himself being party to it. And he very clearly was not. Indeed, he was on tenterhooks, waiting for the British Government's decision as to whether confederation would even be on the ballot.

Before the formal dissolution of the convention on January 30, 1948, the telegrams of protest began to pour in from the outports. A typical message, signed by a Protestant minister and all the members of his small congregation, read: "If ye will not trust the people, the people will not trust ye."

# CHAPTER 7

# Cash, Crosbie and Comic Union

JOEY WAS OUT OF BED, AS USUAL, BY MID-DAY, BOUNCING AROUND LIKE A ball coach whose team had just dropped the opener in the World Series.

"Now the real job begins!" he announced. "We'll show those twenty-nine dictators who's going to rule this country!"

"What do you want us to do?" I asked.

"We'll begin organizing. But just hang on till I finish writing this speech. It's for Bradley."

He was pounding rapidly at his ancient little portable, the only typewriter he ever used. For a two-finger typist he was remarkably fast.

"The twenty-nine dictators! We'll keep harping on that!" The phrase had been used in one of the telegrams of protest sent to the national convention. Joey recognized it instantly as a winner, grabbed it, and made it his own.

Some of the twenty-nine dictators were his personal friends, but Joey kept friendship and politics in separate compartments. A personal friend might be a dangerous political foe. If so, he would reach back into the store of Biblical vituperation he had picked up twenty years before while sitting at the feet of the fundamentalist preachers to choose a suitably nasty epithet for the erring brother. He had always been friendly with the Honourable John S. Currie, publisher of *The Daily News*. Currie was almost painfully respectable, a former member of the Upper House, and a pillar of the United Church.

When he published a particularly violent attack on confederation, Smallwood sat brooding at his desk, a far-off look in his eyes.

"I've been searching for the right word," he said. "I think I'll call him a *whited sepulchre.*"

When the convention closed, Joey talked Bradley into remaining in St. John's long enough to deliver a radio address denouncing the twenty-nine dictators and appealing to his listeners to send in telegrams demanding that confederation with Canada be placed on the referendum ballot as a third choice.

"Does that mean I've got to stay here to receive the telegrams?" Bradley demanded. He was itching to get back to Bonavista, the only place where he was moderately content.

"No," said Joey, "just deliver the speech. We'll do the rest."

Bradley, a greater actor even than Joey, was superb that night. His voice trembled with indignation, rose fervently, and sank to a modulated croon as he talked of the people's right to make their own choices. He was in the time slot formerly occupied by convention broadcasts, and nearly every radio in the outports must have been tuned to his words. His indignation was catching.

The result, as Smallwood wrote later, was electrifying. The next day the telegrams came pouring in. Boys on bicycles delivered them by armloads to the little flat on Devon Row, where Joey had to set up a long table to receive and sort them. Ten of us worked day and night for the next four days recording the names and addresses of those who responded.

Among the people who worked on the petition were Janet and Irving Fogwill, Irene Ebsary, Phil Forsey, Roy Pike, and the entire Smallwood family. We took the petition from door to door in St. John's. I covered the Mundy Pond region, then virtually a small rural town, mostly Irish Catholic, on the outskirts of St. John's. It was the centre of St. Theresa's Parish, where many of the people were factory workers employed at the neighbouring Ropewalk, manufacturing ships' cables and lines, or at the Newfoundland Butter Company, a margarine factory owned by the Crosbies. Though most of those Irish factory workers would later vote against confederation, persuaded to do so by their priests and bishops, I had a wonderfully friendly reception; they invited me into their homes, and nearly all of them signed the petition.

By the end of the week we had 48,960 signatures. The official count, when Joey delivered the petition to Government House for transmission to the British government was 49,769. But the responses were still coming in; names from local petitions were arriving by letter. There was no final count, but the number exceeded 50,000. As Joey pointed out, this represented more people than had voted to elect the members of the national convention two years before. Had a referendum been conducted the week we launched the petition, there can be no reasonable doubt that confederation would have won by an outright majority on the first ballot. But many things took place in the intervening months, and we would be hard put indeed to defend the gains that Joey and his supporters had made by the time the national convention closed.

Looking over the names and addresses that we had copied from the telegrams, Joey was ecstatic:

"There's our organization!" he crowed.

We combed the lists for leadership potential. There were magistrates, ministers, priests, small outport merchants, many school teachers. One was an aging Inuk named Abel Abel, Chief of the Council of Elders at Nain, Labrador. He claimed, probably with justification, to speak for the entire Inuit population. He was a pre-Smallwood confederate, who later showed me correspondence on the subject between himself and Mackenzie King dating back to the Second World War.

"We'll launch the Confederate Association with 101 vice-presidents," Joey exulted. Each principal petitioner—usually the first name on a list from a large settlement—became vice-president for that area. Not one declined the honour. We took out a full page in *The Evening Telegram* under a Confederate Association banner and published the list.

Meanwhile, Joey was like a cat on hot bricks waiting for the British government's answer to the convention's recommendations and the confederate petition. A week or two after delivering the petition to Government House he learned that it had not been forwarded to London.

"That son-of-a-bitch!" he raged, pacing up and down. Joey had been sure that the governor would send the petition, perhaps by courier, to the Dominions Office, if not to Buckingham Palace itself.

"But he sent the *results* to London, of course," I said.

"Oh yes, a cable, so Ken Macdonald* tells me. But that's not the same thing! They should have got the original, with all the names. Just imagine! That pile of telegrams! And the bastard didn't send them! It's criminal!"

To relieve the tension of the long wait, to have something to do, Joey decided on a formal, official launching of the Newfoundland Confederate Association. We rented the ballroom of the Newfoundland Hotel for the evening of February 21. Bradley came to town for the occasion, and was unanimously elected the association's president. He made a fine, extemporaneous speech, too. Joey, who, at his own request, was elected secretary and campaign manager, was the star of the evening, and received an ovation when he spoke. Various committees were assigned to the rest of us. But the committees never met, the president never presided, and the secretary was far too busy ever to attend to his secretarial work.

Historians have sometimes wondered what could have happened to the records of the Newfoundland Confederate Association. The answer is simple: there never were any records. There was correspondence, of course—great stacks of it—and a lot of it survives in Smallwood's truckloads of papers. But the only meeting the Newfoundland Confederate Association ever had was its founding convention. There were never any minutes or books of accounts. Its officers and committee members ran into each other from time to time during the campaign, but there was never such a thing as a committee meeting or a meeting of the executive from the night it was founded to the day it faded quietly away, its mission accomplished. The "association" was really just an exercise in public relations.

That, too, was Bradley's function. He wasn't expected to *do* anything except sign membership cards. His job was to be the outward and visible sign of our tenuous respectability—the proof that confederation was not just a communist plot hatched by the little cell of wild-eyed revolutionaries who were, in fact, running the show.

Joey, in those days, was still regarded as a wild-eyed revolutionary, and the people he had chosen for associates did nothing to dispel that notion. There was Power, the most conservative of the three, and the nearest to being respectable, but nonetheless a union leader who had

---

*Kenneth Macdonald was Sir Gordon's son, one of the governor's aides. As well as being the governor's press secretary, he was, at this time, the principal pipeline for "leaked" information at Government House. If you wanted something to reach the governor's ear unofficially, he was the man to see. Needless to say, Joey was in touch with him frequently.

been chased off the American base at Argentia with riot guns. Although he was a Roman Catholic, he had attended a Protestant school and hadn't heard mass since his university days. Then there was Forsey, known for the extreme leftist position he took as an MCLI debater and Horwood, leader of the most radical wing of the St. John's labour movement. That was the reality behind the Confederate Association, those were the people who ran it from the dingy little office on Water Street, and who were known far and wide as "The Four Bolsheviks."

158 Water Street was a logical choice for confederate headquarters. It was near the government radio station (the only one with power enough to reach most of the outports), close to the cable offices, close to the main post office, and almost next door to the plant where our newspaper would be printed.

"Right in the lion's den," Joey chortled, "the lair of the twenty-one millionaires!"

Those millionaires were another of his inventions. He had decided on twenty-one as a nice, convincing figure. No one really knew how many of the Water Street merchants were millionaires, but no one ever challenged Joey's statement. The twenty-one pre-confederate millionaires became a fixed part of Newfoundland mythology. (By the time Joey got around to writing his political memoirs in the 1970s, he had forgotten the figure himself, and reduced the millionaires to twenty. He also forgot the number of vice-presidents of the Confederate Association, and reduced them to one hundred.)

On the morning of March 2, 1948, a rumour spread through the town that the governor had received Great Britain's answer to the resolutions and petitions that had come out of the national convention. Someone at Government House had leaked the information to a number of interested people. The dispatch had been sent to the studios of the Newfoundland Broadcasting Corporation, and would be opened and read at twelve noon, precisely.

Joey hurried from his apartment up the short hill to the Newfoundland Hotel, hoping to get an advance hint of what the dispatch might contain. When he arrived on the top floor he found Peter Cashin pacing the corridor outside the VONF studios. Malcolm Hollett was leaning against a wall. Several others from the Responsible Government League had also heard the rumour, and were standing around anxiously awaiting the results.

At that point the only person outside Government House who

knew the contents of the British dispatch was the young broadcaster Dick O'Brien, who had been left in charge of the station during the temporary absence of William Galgay, the manager. O'Brien had received the sealed papers that morning.

"It came by courier in a plain brown envelope from Kenneth Macdonald," he recalled, "with orders that it was to be shown to no one until it was read on the air at noon. I took it to the men's bathroom, locked myself in, and opened it. Only then did I realize that what I was holding in my hands was the British government's decision on the Newfoundland referendum. I read it over, and later took it to the studio. Just before it was to go on the air, I walked from the control room into the glass-walled room reserved for the announcers. There on the outside were Cashin and company, and Joey, with his nose pressed against the glass like a kid at a candy-store window. I looked at the clock. The hand was just reaching twelve. The microphone was switched on. Then I turned toward Joey—the others couldn't see—and gave him a broad, slow wink. He leaped about two feet into the air, and began to caper about the corridor, while I sat down and started to read "an important message which we have just received from Government House."

The statement from Philip Noel-Baker, Secretary of State for Dominion Affairs, was long and formal, acceding to the national convention's request that responsible government, as it existed in 1933, and Commission government, be included on the referendum ballot, but adding that Commission government, should the people choose it, would be limited to an additional period of five years, after which the question of future forms of government would be re-examined. Then came the crucial decision:

"... having regard to the members of the convention who supported the inclusion of confederation with Canada on the ballot paper, His Majesty's Government have come to the conclusion that it would not be right that the people of Newfoundland should be deprived of the opportunity of considering the issue at the referendum and they have, therefore, decided that confederation with Canada should be included as a third choice on the referendum paper . . . ."

Noel-Baker took note of the fact that most of the members of the convention felt that confederation should not be considered except as an issue between elected governments, but argued: "The terms offered by the Canadian government represent, however, the result of long discussion with a body of Newfoundlanders who were elected to the convention, and the issues involved appear to have been sufficiently clarified to enable the people of Newfoundland to express an opinion . . . ."

The terms offered, in fact, would not be final, and the people would not be voting on the terms, but on "the issues involved." It was a hard slap to the Responsible Government League and to the twenty-nine dictators who had hoped the referendum could be run off without the trouble and expense of a political campaign. The date for the referendum was June 3, leaving a full three months for campaigning, and if no form of government received an overall majority, a second referendum would be held with the form receiving the fewest votes dropped from the ballot paper.

We had a great bash and got down to work. But the Responsible Government League was off the mark well ahead of us. Four days after the announcement they were on the air with their first broadcasts, denouncing Britain's decision as a betrayal of the pledge made in 1934 to restore responsible government at the request of the people when the country was self-supporting.

We didn't regard the announcement as any kind of betrayal. The country was self-supporting, and the people were now being asked their opinion. If they requested responsible government as it existed in 1933, then it would be restored in that form. If they preferred to have responsible government as a province of Canada, then it would be restored in *that* form. If they did not request responsible government at all, then Commission government would remain. The talk about betrayal was absurd, and everyone knew it.

The Responsible Government League was also first off the mark with its propaganda sheet, *The Independent*, which began appearing in March. It was a cheap-looking, amateurish job, the work of a penny-pinching organization. But responsible government had other, much abler spokesmen. *The Daily News*, though it remained a legitimate newspaper, took as strong an editorial stand against confederation as it was possible to take; any news that tended to damage Canada's image was given front-page headlines; anything favourable to Canada was relegated to the back pages, or dropped altogether. The editorial page became an outright propaganda organ for responsible government. Indeed, most of the anti-confederate propaganda *originated* there, with the editor, Albert Perlin, who wrote the leaders in addition to the newspaper's only column of comment and analysis.

*The Western Star* at Corner Brook was forced by its owners, the

Bowater Paper Company, to take a pro-responsible government stand. Bowater manager in Corner Brook, Monty Lewin, a cocky little fighter remarkably like Smallwood, was well respected, a friend to everybody, and the most paternalistic of town and company managers, but feared that confederation would bring an end to the special tax status enjoyed by Bowaters in Newfoundland. (He was right; it did.)

The Grand Falls *Advertiser* was, if possible, more rabid in its support of responsible government than *The Western Star*. But despite the paper companies and their captive newspapers, the voters in both towns remained strongly pro-confederate, especially in Corner Brook.

The weekly tabloids—even *The Fishermen's Advocate*—were equally fixed in their support of responsible government. By far the strongest of the weeklies was the St. John's *Sunday Herald*, a Saturday tabloid published by Geoff Stirling, then just at the beginning of a career in radio, television, and financing. *The Sunday Herald* claimed to have a circulation larger than even the biggest daily in the island. During the campaign Stirling turned it into a propaganda sheet for responsible government and for his own special dream of economic union with the United States.

The only newspaper in Newfoundland that attempted to take a reasoned look at the choices in the referendum was the St. John's *Evening Telegram*, which had the largest daily circulation, and was soon to have the largest weekend circulation as well. *The Telegram* took no specific stand for or against any form of government, but attempted to give full coverage to the views of all sides. In fact, *The Telegram's* editor, C. E. A. Jeffrey, was a convinced confederate, but could not swallow the idea of Joey Smallwood as leader. He distrusted the man then and distrusted him later when he became premier. Joey always said this was because Jeffrey had been one of his school teachers "who took a dislike to me for some unknown reason." In fact, there was nothing emotional about Jeffrey's distrust of Smallwood. A few years later I became Jeffrey's editorial protégé and eventually his successor. As I got to know him it became obvious that he simply believed Joey lacked the necessary intellect and education to be a suitable premier. Above all, he believed that Smallwood's judgment was faulty, perhaps to a fatal degree. Had Bradley, rather than Smallwood, been the real head of the confederate party, Jeffrey would have been a lot happier, and a lot more outspoken in his support for the movement, and the Herder family, owners of *The Telegram*, would have concurred.

In these circumstances it was imperative that the Confederate Association publish its own propaganda organ. And it must be a paper of the highest professional quality. *The Confederate* was slow off the mark, its first issue not ready until April 7, 1948, but when it did appear it was the liveliest, most entertaining, most professional-looking political paper ever published in Newfoundland. *The Independent* was dull by comparison.

Joey wrote a dozen or more short, punchy articles for each issue of *The Confederate*, describing the success of the campaign, talking about tax cuts in Canada (a general election was due the next year), showing how prices would fall with the removal of customs duties, and so on. Greg Power wrote a clever political satire for each issue, always devastatingly funny. He also produced some outrageous political verse and slogans. I didn't write a great deal for the early issues. I selected the pithiest bits from our stable of speakers for reprint, and, as Joey became busier and busier with the campaign, I wrote more of the short pieces in the style he had adopted for the early issues. Forsey did some writing, too. We had the cleverest, most effective political cartoons ever published in Newfoundland. They were drawn by a mainland artist, Jack Booth, who worked for Toronto's *Globe and Mail*. Some of them were based on his own ideas, but most were suggested by Joey. No one in the opposing camp seems to have guessed that the cartoons were being drawn in Toronto—perhaps because they showed such an intimate knowledge of the local scene.

*The Confederate* appeared weekly, and we tried to get it into every home in Newfoundland. Its total cost must have been in excess of $50,000, but we got excellent value for the money. Above all, it gave our supporters confidence. *Their* party had the liveliest, best-looking, funniest, and most entertaining paper they had ever read.

The confederate headquarters at 158 Water Street consisted of two dingy back rooms behind a barber shop just across Water Street from the harbour front. Access was by way of a small door and a narrow hall. For the first few days of the campaign it was a very lonely place, and *The Independent* had great fun describing the Four Bolsheviks huddled in their little office borrowing bus fare from each other. The picture wasn't so wildly off the mark. Except for Forsey, who had his teacher's salary (and a large family to support) our combined personal incomes would hardly have exceeded $50 a week. We didn't look much like a band of world beaters about to change their country's history.

But volunteers began showing up, looking for ways to spread the gospel. Some of them were moderately respectable: Bill Frampton, past president of the Newfoundland Federation of Labour; Billy Bond Taylor, a live wire, the moving spirit behind the St. John's local of the International Retail Clerks. Both had run as Labour Party candidates for local and national offices, and had been narrowly defeated. Irving Fogwill was a widely respected intellectual. His wife Janet was a living dynamo with a gift for organization; she not only worked as a volunteer herself, but brought many other willing hands into the movement.

Joey had a blind spot when it came to women. He never understood that they were fully adult, fully endowed humans, with as much intellect and ability as men. When he met a brilliant woman he set her to stuffing envelopes; no woman ever ran on one of his tickets. Janet Fogwill was the first with whom he missed the boat. Brilliant, educated, personally magnetic, she would have made a perfect candidate in St. John's West, and a Cabinet minister of true distinction. Instead, he had her leading a women's auxiliary called the "Lady Liberals Association," and finally she drifted off to become one of his sworn opponents.

Some of our volunteers, like Frampton and Taylor, became almost full-time workers. Among them appeared my younger brother Charles, a black-bearded union leader, tall and lanky, who could have played a nineteenth-century stage villain. Joey thought he looked like Rasputin.

"Don't *you* start coming in here," I greeted him. "They'll think we're making bombs."

Ted Russell, who, like Keough and Newell, was a gifted co-operative field worker, arrived with a furtive air, shepherded in by Phil Forsey.

"Where do you stop and look around to see that no one's watching before you go in?" he asked.

Russell, a Lincolnesque figure of forty-three, was from Coley's Point, Conception Bay. He had begun teaching at the age of sixteen, went on to become a magistrate, and was director of co-operatives for the Commission government in the 1940s. He was a skilled debater with a subtle sense of humour.

As he entered our office his eye fell on a map of Newfoundland that I had put up on the wall opposite the door. I had decorated it with pins in four colours to suggest that the Confederate Association had tentacles reaching into every corner of the land. The pins meant absolutely nothing, but the map was a great morale booster for visitors. I was adding a red pin to a northern outport when Russell arrived.

"Hullo," he said, "What's this? Another vice-president being born?"

Such levity lightened the work of the organization but did nothing for our greatest problem, which was, to put it simply, money. Joey brooded for a long time about how we were going to raise the funds (or the credit) to run a three-month campaign. He had only a vague idea of what it would cost, but a hundred thousand dollars seemed like the absolute minimum.

Besides printing and mailing *The Confederate* to everyone whose address we could find, we'd need trucks, boats, vans, loudspeakers, and a chartered plane to fly Joey to a hundred isolated outports that could not otherwise be reached in time. Indeed, a hundred thousand dollars would probably not begin to cover the essentials. And we had hardly a hundred thousand pennies among the lot of us. There was plenty of money in St. John's, of course, but it seemed to be all on the other side, fattening the coffers of the Responsible Government League. We wished earnestly for a conspiracy, with funds slyly passed on from London and Ottawa but—alas!—no conspiracy appeared. We were on our own.

When we had assembled the first issue of the *The Confederate*, Joey went to *The Evening Telegram*, which had a large job-printing department, and bargained on a price per issue for a four-sheet paper with an initial press run of thirty thousand copies. *The Telegram* agreed to set up and print the paper for a starting price of $2,000 an issue. It went up to $3,000 later, as we needed larger and larger press runs. *The Telegram* didn't ask for money in advance, but insisted on being paid before the papers actually left the plant. It might have been possible for Joey to talk the Herders into extending credit to the Confederate Association, but *The Telegram's* treasurer wasn't a Herder: he was a hard-headed if somewhat soft-hearted business manager named Ron Martin, who had a small financial interest in the paper, and firm ideas about the bottom line.

So Joey got the type set up, took the galley proofs back to the office, and there, with scissors and paste, made it up into full-sized page dummies. These he took back to the compositors, to get the pages ready for the press. He still had no idea where the money for that first issue was coming from. The Lord would provide. And sure enough, the Lord appeared in the person of Phil Forsey. Forsey and his wife and six children had no money of their own. His house was mortgaged. He still didn't own a car. He had only a teacher's salary. But he knew a bank manager who would advance a loan on his ninety-day note. He knew Joey as well as any of us, and what Joey's promises were worth when it came to repaying money, but he took the risk anyway, borrowed the money on his own credit, and paid for the first issue of *The Confederate*.

What's more, Forsey had friends who weren't living absolutely from hand to mouth. Some outport merchants and even one or two St. John's merchants were among his confidants. In some instances he had tutored their sons and heirs over rough spots in high school, saving them from failure and disgrace. In others ... well, he just seemed to have a gift for winning people's confidence.

One of Forsey's friends was Sandy Baird, a maverick businessman who had broken ranks with the twenty-one millionaires. He had told Forsey privately that he'd be willing to support confederation, at least quietly. That meant *money*. What about a senatorship? Forsey asked. Well ... yes ... there'd been a lot of talk about the Confederate Association having senatorships for sale. If confederation should become a fact, and if the Canadian government should decide that his career of public service made him worthy of a senatorship, Baird wouldn't refuse it.

Clyde Lake, a wealthy fish merchant from Forsey's region of the south coast with his headquarters in St. John's, also dreamed of a senatorship. Lake came from a part of the country that was solidly pro-confederate, and Forsey cultivated him avidly. Between them, Baird and Lake should be good for a few grand, perhaps enough to put us over the next two or three weeks.

I was in the confederate office when Sandy Baird sent a messenger with his first instalment, a cheque made out to the Newfoundland Confederate Association. (I forget the amount, but it was enough to pay our postage bill, at least.) The boy asked for a receipt, and I made one out and signed it. It may have been the only receipt ever issued by the Newfoundland Confederate Association for a political contribution of more than one dollar. When Smallwood learned what I'd done, he read me a mild lecture. A political party's financial affairs should be entirely *sub rosa*, he declared. Everything should be done on the basis of gentlemen's agreements, nothing on paper.

"You shake hands," he said. "You don't sign receipts." Ideally, you'd even insist on taking the money in cash, so there'd be no cancelled cheques as a possible source of future embarrassment. Look what had happened to Squires! I took this lecture to heart and later negotiated thousands of dollars in political deals, without, so far as I know, leaving the faintest trace behind me.

It soon became obvious that the sale of senatorships was not going to keep us solvent. Jocy (with Forsey's help) explored every other possible avenue. He appealed to the fishermen by radio, and to the 101 vice-presidents by letter. Membership in the Newfoundland Confederate Association cost only one dollar, but perhaps some members could afford to give two dollars, or even five. The money for memberships came trickling in—some three thousand dollars all told, and Bradley cursed and grumbled because he had to put his signature on so many membership cards. But on the whole, the membership drive was a disappointment.

Newfoundlanders had never been asked to join and support political parties before. Parties were organized from the top down, never from the bottom up, though the Fishermen's Union Party may have been a partial exception to this rule. But in any case, their funds came from somewhere up there, never from the people they were supposed to represent. So fifty thousand people might be prepared to vote for us, but there certainly weren't fifty thousand prepared to pay a dollar each for the privilege.

Jocy's first try for the financial big time was a scheme we later referred to as Charley Penney's Mission. Penney, an insurance salesman who lived in St. John's West Extern, had been defeated as a Labour Party candidate in the 1946 election for the national convention, and had subsequently attached himself to the Confederate Association. If he could sell insurance, Joey argued, he should be a good door-to-door canvasser. So Joey sent him abroad, carrying the names and addresses of hundreds of Newfoundland families who had moved to Canada. He also carried a letter from the Association appealing for funds and establishing his credentials as its trusted representative. He was to ask expatriate Newfoundlanders to lend their names to the cause, and to contribute as much money as they could to the campaign. He might get a five dollar or a ten-dollar bill from some people, but here and there he might meet an expatriate with such deep feelings for the Old Rock that he'd collect a hundred dollars—or a thousand!

Joey, who had read about encoded correspondence in *The Life of Lenin*, invented a cipher for exchanging information with Charley Penney. It was based on a set of definitions in *The Little Pocket Oxford Dictionary*. The cloak-and-dagger business of encoding and decoding telegrams to and from his travelling salesman tickled Joey's fancy no end. I was never sure just how serious he was about this business (or where he got the names and addresses, for that matter: perhaps his Canadian allies knew someone with access to the census files and ransacked them for "Country of origin: Newfoundland"). Anyway, Joey had a lot of fun with Charley Penney's Mission, and having fun was still important to him in those days. In practically everything he did there was an element of play. He didn't just *look* like Puck. He acted that way. What's more, Charley collected numerous endorsements for confederation, and we were able to publish the names of many mainland Newfoundlanders who thought Canada was the cat's pyjamas (any who thought it was the sinkhole of the universe were simply ignored). Charley also got quite a substantial amount of money—almost enough to pay his entire expenses across the country and back.

Long before his return, Joey had sought out the only likely source of really heavy funding. He made a frantic, desperate appeal to the Liberal Party of Canada for help. The appeal went by way of the Liberal bagman in the Maritimes, whom Joey happened to know, but was passed along to the top brass in Ottawa. The Liberals in Ottawa at first seemed doubtful about the propriety of meddling in Newfoundland politics. Newfoundland was still a foreign country, even though part of the British Family, and the Liberal Party wasn't the CIA. They could not, they explained, dip into the Liberal treasury to finance political campaigns in foreign lands, *even supposing the Liberal treasury had any money in it*, which it usually did not.

But C. D. Howe, the major force in the party from the end of the war until his defeat in 1957, thought of a way out of the difficulty. He couldn't see anything wrong with private Canadian citizens donating funds to a worthy cause in Newfoundland if the spirit should so move them, and he thought he knew how the spirit could be induced to do just that. Pick out a trusty, discreet businessman, Howe suggested, and "send him to me."

The man Joey chose for this delicate mission later became a well-known senator. The trip (actually a harrowing *series* of trips) was known as Petten's Pilgrimage. Smallwood has written, repeatedly, that he asked his "old friend Ray Petten" to become "treasurer of our movement." But in fact Petten was never treasurer. The treasurer was Charley Garland, a small Water Street businessman who always insisted that he had been a confederate long before Smallwood himself (and the only *private* citizen for whom the flags flew at half mast on Confederation Building after his early death). Petten was something far more important, the party's principal bag man.

C. D. Howe supplied Ray Petten with a letter of introduction to be used among his friends in the Canadian business community, and sent him off to Senator Gordon Fogo, who was head bag man for the Liberal Party of Canada. Joey, fearing a wire tap, would never mention those names in phone conversations. Talking by phone to Bradley, for instance, Howe became "the man who knows *how* it's done." The senator was simply, "the man from Fogo."

Gordon Fogo gave Petten a copy of the Liberal party's hit list: corporations that could be reliably tapped for funds at election time. Many of those corporations turned out to be in one branch or another of the liquor business. They were merchandisers, brewers, vintners, and distillers, and with a little prodding by way of Howe's letter, they coughed up surprising amounts of cash. No one knows just how much, since no records were kept. Perhaps the records of a bank account exist somewhere, and this might give a rough approximation, but only an approximation, for considerable sums of money passed through our hands without ever seeing the inside of a bank. For example, I myself received a single donation of $3,000 in cash, and spent it in cash: half the amount on printing bills, and half on travelling expenses.

In addition to the sources mentioned above, it was widely rumoured that some of the giant chain stores had put up money for the campaign. I cannot confirm or deny the rumour. Altogether, the confederate campaign must have cost about a quarter of a million dollars and the election campaign that followed probably cost another hundred thousand—but these are only informed guesses.

So we got the money, and Mr. Petten got his senatorship and a profitable string of liquor agencies as a sort of bonus. He also got an ulcer and a heart condition. These may not have been due entirely to the rigours and worries of the campaign, but you could see him turning grayer week by week as our demands for money became more and more pressing.

At one point Petten had to pledge his own credit to keep us afloat—as Forsey had done on a more modest scale when the campaign started. Knowing Joey as well as he did, Petten must have realized that he was risking financial ruin. Poor Ray! If anyone ever deserved his senatorship, Petten did. And since he didn't live long to enjoy it, his son Bill succeeded him in the Senate—"the first hereditary senatorship in Canada," as someone caustically remarked.

With seemingly limitless funds now at his disposal, Joey put on the most dazzling campaign in Newfoundland history: flags, music, guns, bands marching, blizzards of campaign literature—it seemed less like an election campaign than a national triumph.

At first we chartered just one small aircraft—a single-engined Cessna on floats flown by Captain Eric Blackwood with Joey as its sole passenger, and so much baggage that it could barely stagger into the air. But later we had two and three planes at a time, including a Norseman that cost $50 an hour. We didn't just rent public address systems. We *bought* them, the most powerful amplifiers and speakers we could find. We installed one of them in the belly of an airplane so Joey could circle through the clouds and speak to the outport people "from heaven."

We sent out an army of door-to-door canvassers. We paid expenses for any of the 101 vice-presidents who wanted to do some campaigning. We sent experienced speakers like Russell and Forsey and Keough to the outports, hiring halls and holding pro-confederate rallies, often to the thunder of swiling guns and the blare of Salvation Army bands. We hired radio time, and rounded up everyone who had some influence or reputation and would agree to speak for us.

Joey, furious worker that he was, wrote most of the speeches. He could still work circles around the rest of us. But Greg Power wrote some of the talks, even one or two of those delivered by Gordon Bradley. Phil Forsey and I wrote our own, and Forsey also wrote speeches for those campaigning on his native south coast, an area that he knew better than Joey or anyone else in the organization. Sam Hefferton, Joey's old friend from the days of the Newfoundland Industrial Workers Association and now supposedly a man of some influence among Anglicans, also wrote his own speeches. Hefferton had eventually lived down his radical reputation as editor of *The Industrial Worker* and had gone on to become a teacher at Bishop

Feild College, and president of the Newfoundland Teachers Association, a post he continued to hold throughout the campaign for confederation. Ted Russell wrote his own, too. He was better than Joey at the kind of speech he could deliver so well, combining intellectualism with common sense and down-to-earth folksiness. He had a voice that sounded absolutely like the best "sea lawyer" on an outport stage head.

But regardless of who wrote them, Joey glanced at every speech before it was delivered over the radio. There was to be no danger in our outfit of people speaking at cross-purposes, as happened so often in the camp of the responsible government supporters—the "stable of the sacred cow" (responsible government) as Power described it in his continuing series of satires.

It was perfectly obvious to everyone that we were outspending the Responsible Government League by a factor of at least two or three to one, and there were loud demands from our opponents to know where the money was coming from. Cashin was sure the wily Brits were behind it. Others suspected the Canadian government. Obviously, they said, Joey must be the patsy of powerful foreign interests that had designs on Newfoundland, probably just a puppet playing out the script of a plot hatched in London and Ottawa.

We who had been the butt of jokes about bus fare a few weeks earlier couldn't say just *nothing*, and it would be hardly good public relations to admit that we were spending Canadian money milked from the liquor trade. We were forced to invent fictitious sources of funds, and that's how the story got around that scores of thousands of fishermen were sending in their one-dollar bills and two-dollar bills (and even a few four-dollar bills saved from the nineteenth century when there really were such things in Newfoundland) each with a little note pinned on, saying something like, "God bless you, Mr. Smallwood, for what you're doing for we poor people. We'm praying for you."

There actually were a great many letters (but few of them with money). At the beginning, Joey answered them himself on his overworked little portable. Then I took over, and he merely signed the letters. As soon as we were able to afford hired help he got the services of an absolutely superb secretary-typist, Mrs. Anna Templeman, who could take dictation at almost any speed and turn out faultless copy at seventy or eighty words a minute. By that time I knew exactly what Joey would say in reply to almost any letter, so it was often I, not he, who dictated the replies to his mail. But all the letters went out over his name. When he became premier, Mrs. Templeman continued as his confidential secretary, and did a superb job in a very demanding position. She even learned to tolerate Joey's long-haired tortoise-shell cat, who had a habit of sleeping in the out-basket on her desk.

We were all supremely confident of success. The only bad scare we got during the campaign leading up to the first referendum was when Ches Crosbie, seconded—perhaps one should say *managed*—by the able and popular young radio salesman Don Jamieson, started the Economic Union with the United States Party. Despite its clumsy name, this was a real threat, for then, as now, the idea of free trade with the United States looked to many Newfoundlanders like the pot of gold at the end of the rainbow—and had about as much substance. But the idea had been good for many an election campaign in the past (as it would be in the future, too) and it proved to be the bait that almost persuaded Newfoundlanders to swallow the responsible government hook.

Economic Union was a smokescreen, of course. It is difficult to believe, in retrospect, that its most eloquent advocates could have been anything other than hypocrites. But in fact most of them were slick young men in their twenties, totally ignorant of political history and they thought they had a brilliant new idea that had never been tried before. They probably didn't know that Macdonald and Bond and others had virtually flogged it to death in the nineteenth and early twentieth centuries.

What the United States was supposed to get out of such an unlikely alliance as one with Newfoundland in the late 1940s it is hard to imagine. Some American newspapers (mainly those owned by Colonel Bertie McCormick) speculated on the chances of Newfoundland's becoming "the forty-ninth state." That, indeed, might have looked tempting to American politicians, some of whom had never given up the old American dream of the encirclement and absorption of Canada—but no such thing was ever really in prospect. The idea of extending to Newfoundland trading privileges denied to Canada—America's principal export market, and its main source of raw materials—was never for a moment entertained in Washington.

"For a brighter tomorrow—vote for economic union with the United States today!" A double-barrelled slogan that almost worked. The Economic Union Party picked up tens of thousands of supporters, not all of them previously committed to responsible government.

Two of our 101 vice-presidents bolted and joined what looked like the bandwagon. The Responsible Government League at first hesitated, worried by the deception, and perhaps concerned also about the fact that if they won under the economic union banner they would be forced to accept Ches Crosbie as prime minister. But they discovered that they had no choice. Jamieson's musical parade just swallowed them up. Cashin, Higgins, all the other former heavyweights, sank into virtual insignificance. Soon there was just the dance music, and Ches Crosbie, booming away in his semi-intelligible rumble, and his brilliant stage manager, Don Jamieson, telling everyone what it was that Mr. Crosbie had said.

As a last-minute gambit, cleverly timed to tilt the scales in a close election, economic union might have succeeded. But it was introduced so early in the campaign that we had ample time to expose it as a fraud. Still, it brought responsible government, the sacred cow that had begun to smell like she was dying, violently back to life.

It looked so bad at first that Joey lost his nerve—the only time in those early years that his political judgment faltered. He went to see Ches Crosbie—a thing easily arranged, since they were old acquaintances who had shared many small business ventures in the past—and offered to make him premier of Newfoundland if he would discover that the United States wasn't interested in economic union with Newfoundland after all, and if, following this discovery, he'd swear allegiance to confederation instead.

There were a number of reasons for this lapse on Joey's part. He not only overestimated the strength of Crosbie's party; he had always overestimated Crosbie himself, his ability and his popularity. He thought Crosbie was universally respected, even by the fishermen and the rest of the "toiling masses." In this instance, Power and Forsey and I were right, and Joey was wrong. The three of us never took Crosbie seriously. Power invented the term "Comic Union" for the economic union movement, and it gained instant currency. In Power's satirical columns, Crosbie became "Sitting Bull" and Jamieson became "Donald Duck." Both names were wickedly apt. Crosbie was a stolid, dour-looking man with little to say, while Jamieson was a rotund, baby-faced bouncer whose voice never seemed to stop, quack, quack, quack. Power was convinced that they could be laughed out of court. Forsey and I believed that economic union could be exposed as mere bait to make people swallow the old hook that Cashin and company had failed to get them to take. Hefferton called it "a little fresh snow sprinkled over the thin ice of responsible government as it was in 1933."

We were informed, on the day following Joe's chat with Ches, that the whole sorry conversation had been secretly recorded on tape. Since they had sat together in Crosbie's living room, this seemed entirely possible. Jamieson could easily have been lurking in the next room, with microphones hidden a few feet from where they were sitting. The tape, we were told, would be broadcast, suitably introduced by Mr. Jamieson, on his program *For a Brighter Tomorrow*.

Ches Crosbie later told me that no such tape was ever made. But he did succeed in giving Joey a violent case of the jitters for a day or so while we waited for the fatal broadcast and he dangled the imaginary tape over our heads.

Crosbie didn't believe that Joey would ever make him premier of Newfoundland. First, he didn't trust Joey that far. Second, he didn't believe that Joey could do it, even if he intended to. I am personally convinced that Smallwood was sincere in his offer (though of course he intended to succeed Crosbie after one term). He really would have promoted Crosbie as the first provincial leader of the Liberal Party. But in the end it wouldn't have worked. Crosbie would have been rejected, and Joey would have been "drafted." In fact, Joey tried to make Crosbie the finance minister in his first elected government after confederation, and Crosbie then endorsed him and agreed to run in the district of Grand Falls. But Greg Power, almost single-handedly, engineered Crosbie's defeat at the Liberal convention, and so saved Joey from the consequences of his own folly.

On May 8, three and a half weeks before the first referendum, J. B. McEvoy delivered the death blow to the Economic Union with the United States Party. He returned from a visit to the United States with documents that demonstrated the virtual impossibility of a customs union (much less a full economic union) between Newfoundland as an independent colony or nation, and the United States. He published the documents in *The Evening Telegram*. Then *The Confederate* came out with a screaming page-one headline: COMIC UNION BLOWS UP! As usual, the headline was Joey's own work.

The principal document in McEvoy's file was a memorandum on union by Judge Manly O. Hudson of the World Court, who was also professor of international law at Harvard. The memorandum made absolute nonsense of the Economic Union Party's claims. McEvoy also published a letter from Arthur Monroe, head of the largest fresh fish business in Newfoundland, opposing economic union on the ground that it would reduce the Newfoundland fishery to a mere appendage of the New England fishery. But Monroe's missive was just icing on the cake.

The Economic Unionists rallied as best they could. Geoff Stirling collected and published the names of a long list of American senators who said they'd be willing to talk to a delegation from Newfoundland. Eventually (but not until the first campaign was over), he and Jamieson secured what was supposed to be a statement read by Senator Brooks, Bertie McCormick's man, and Stirling's principal backer in the U. S. Senate. They launched a campaign of advance publicity for a broadcast on which "the words of Senator Brooks" would go out over the Newfoundland airwaves, assuring everyone that economic union between Newfoundland and the United States was a very active possibility indeed.

The effort was another fiasco. "The words of Senator Brooks" may well have been written by the senator himself, or at least approved by him, but they appeared to have been recorded by someone else, an actor or a radio announcer in the United States, and the effort to pass off the recording as a statement by the senator was stopped by the Newfoundland Broadcasting Corporation.

"It was completely contrary to corporation policy to broadcast a recording by an actor impersonating a public figure," Dick O'Brien recalled. "You had to have *documentation* before you could broadcast a recording purporting to be by a public man, and they certainly didn't have that. We didn't want to ruin their broadcast, but we couldn't allow the deception, either. In the end, they were allowed to broadcast excerpts, as *reports* of what Senator Brooks had said. But the effect was lost."

In fact, it was generally believed that the economic unionists had tried to work a deception, and had failed. It did them much more harm than if they'd never tried it at all. Years later, Stirling still insisted that what he had brought back from Washington was a recording of the senator's own voice, but Jamieson, O'Brien, and others connected with the incident, were certain that he was wrong—a striking case of the total unreliability of human memory.

With economic union effectively out of the way, Joey had high hopes that confederation would head the poll in the first referendum. And it certainly would have headed the poll, perhaps even with an outright majority, except for the intervention of the Roman Catholic

Archbishop of St. John's, the Very Reverend Edward Patrick Roche, a man of enormously greater influence than Ches Crosbie.

Roche was Archbishop of St. John's (and Metropolitan in Newfoundland) for an incredibly long time. When he entered the lists against confederation he had already worn the ring and mitre for thirty years in a compact little kingdom of his own, answering to no one closer than the Vatican. Besides his private (and perhaps unconscious) motives for opposing confederation, Roche also feared, with some justification, that confederation would expose Newfoundland Catholics to secular and materialistic influences from the mainland—to consumerism, divorce, birth control, public education, to all those mainland trends that would weaken the power of the Church and put Catholic faith and morals in jeopardy.

In fact, that is exactly what happened. So from the archbishop's point of view he was quite right to oppose confederation. Whether he was justified in the methods he used is another question. He took a small parish newspaper, *The Monitor*, turned it into a major propaganda sheet for responsible government, and had it mailed to every Catholic home in Newfoundland. He also brought his influence to bear on the parish priests in his own archdiocese, and, so far as he could, in the dioceses of other bishops throughout the island. Some parish priests who had been supporters of confederation bowed to his wishes, and either fell silent or instructed their people to vote for responsible government in accordance with "His Grace's intentions."

Roche carried the Bishop of Harbour Grace with him willingly. Indeed, Bishop J. M. O'Neill went even further than the archbishop, an austere and restrained cleric, would have thought proper. It was O'Neill who said, "I do not mean to insinuate that the confederate leaders are communists. Perhaps they are not. But I do say that they used communistic tactics." Communism was, of course, the bugbear of the Roman Catholic world of that time, the antichrist in the flesh. Power, going to church for reasons of respectability for the first time since his marriage, saw the priest stand at the altar and declare, "It isn't only in Russia, my children, that the communists are abroad. We have them right here, in our midst, in the Parish of Placentia, spreading their black poison." It was the sort of scare campaign that could be quite effective with ignorant and superstitious voters, many of whom came to believe that by voting for confederation they would be putting their immortal souls in jeopardy.

Even within the archdiocese, one or two brave priests remained unregenerate confederates (and were banished to the parishes of "Little Siberia" in Placentia Bay). On the west coast, where at least half the Catholics were staunch confederates, the Bishop of St. George's told everyone to vote according to their own consciences, regardless of what they might read in *The Monitor*.

So there was anything but a solid Catholic vote for responsible government, and the further you moved away from St. John's, the less solid it became. But in the capital city feelings reached a murderous pitch. The few prominent Roman Catholic families who were known confederates feared for the safety of their children in the Roman Catholic schools, and in some cases took them out of school altogether. To consolidate the support of those St. John's voters who rejected the advice of the archbishop, Joey decided that we had to have a monster rally in the final days of the campaign.

His first rally in St. John's was almost his last. It was held in the CLB Armoury, the largest assembly hall in Newfoundland, and we packed it with confederates. They cheered themselves hoarse (and there was a solid minority of Catholics among them). Meanwhile, the street outside was packed with Peter Cashin's supporters, many of them from the Southside Hill, or "The Brow," as St. John's people called it. They filled the road from curb to curb, and refused to leave when the rally was over. Many of them were drunk, and some of them were there for blood. For the second time in his career, Cashin had come close to inspiring a lynching.

Irving Fogwill, veteran of the bitter labour strikes of the 1930s, had organized a trained bodyguard of tough young men to protect Joey in case of attack by thugs, and Joey was accompanied by several members of the bodyguard when he walked down the front steps of the Armoury that night toward a waiting car. But the lynch mob closed in and caught the bodyguard in a vice. People were knocked down and trampled. Joey's glasses were smashed. Without them he was virtually blind. But the guards were even tougher than the mob. They hoisted Joey on their shoulders, and kicked and butted their way to the side of the car. It was impossible to get a door open, so they sat him on the roof, and the driver began crawling forward in low gear. The mob parted, knowing full well that the car would run over them if they didn't. It picked up speed. By the time some of the crowd had gathered rocks to throw, it was too late. Half a mile down the road Joey got off the roof and inside the car, and went to a hotel. He didn't dare go home.

We boasted of "the biggest political rally in Newfoundland history" and spread the word that the responsible government gang had tried to lynch the people's champion. There were people in the outports who seriously talked about organizing a massive march on St. John's to take over the city if necessary. The next time I saw Joey he pulled out a small six-gun given him by a supporter. I think it must have been designed to fire .22 calibre shells.

"It's not loaded," he said, "but I bet it would make those toughs back off if they came for me."

"You know," I joked, "we really need a martyr to crown our cause."

"You can be the martyr if you want," he retorted. "It's not going to be me if I can help it."

He had, among his other qualities, what seemed to be limitless physical courage. Threats, instead of intimidating him, charged him with the will to fight. He spent the last three days of the campaign in a whirlwind tour of Conception and Trinity Bays, trying to sway votes in the one area where it seemed there might still be some hundreds or thousands of people who hadn't yet taken a definite stand.

On the night of June 3 the count came in, and we sat up until nearly all the polls had reported, and we knew within a few hundred votes how it had gone. The final tally was:

Responsible Government: 69,400

Confederation: 64,066

Commission Government: 23,311

There was foolish rejoicing at Responsible Government League headquarters (though, Jamieson reported, not among the leaders, who knew they had to win first time out or not at all). And there were a few foolish tears shed in the committee rooms of the Newfoundland Confederate Association. We'd lost! And by a mere 5,000 votes! The impossible had happened!

I was with Joey and Greg Power in a private room that night, listening to the counts. When nearly all the votes were in, we knew that victory was now within our grasp. We shook hands. We patted each other on the back. Then we went down to the committee rooms to congratulate our friends.

Behold the long faces! Women shedding tears! Irving Fogwill was there, pointing out (in vain) that the second referendum was coming, that responsible government had failed to win by a margin of ten thousand votes, and that the twenty-three thousand people who had voted for another five years of commission, were never going to vote for a return to responsible government.

Nobody seemed to be impressed by Fogwill's reasonable arguments, but it took Joey only a few minutes to put renewed heart into his followers. He said much the same things that Fogwill had been saying, but he said them with such conviction, such confidence, he was so obviously delighted with the results, that he soon had the crowd convinced.

"All we have to do is buckle down to another six weeks of really hard work," he said, "and we'll be more than on top in the second referendum."

His voice was almost gone, but he could still manage a convincing croak. Beaming happily, he left the committee room, went and had a bath, and fell into bed, telling us to meet him the next afternoon.

CHAPTER 8

# *His Grace's Intentions*

THE WEEKEND FOLLOWING THE FIRST REFERENDUM GEOFF STIRLING'S *Sunday Herald* made the most serious mistake of the campaign. On page one near the bottom, under a single-column headline, it ran a small news item stating that in the referendum, for the first time in history, the Roman Catholic nuns had left their convents and gone out to vote. The archbishop had released them from their vows for the occasion. No one who read the story had the slightest doubt about how the nuns had voted.

"Have you seen this?" I asked Joey as I entered the Confederate Association's office with a copy of the paper. He was busy with yet another map of Newfoundland on which he was colouring in black the electoral districts that had voted against confederation. Without exception, they were heavily populated with Irish Catholics.

"What I propose to do," I said, "is buy up a couple of hundred copies of this paper, and mail them out to all the Orange lodges in Newfoundland."

"All right," he agreed instantly. He was in an angry mood. "If it's going to be a wedding, let it be a wedding. I'll get you the names and addresses you want."

Unlike his hero Squires, Joey had never been a member of the Loyal Orange Society, but Gordon Bradley was a Past Grand Master, and some of our strongest supporters in Conception Bay were the masters of local lodges. I went off with a wallet full of petty cash to buy up all the copies of the *Sunday Herald* in all the stores along Water Street.

I took the papers back to the office, tore off the front pages, circled the item in heavy blue pencil, and mailed the tearsheets to the officers of every Orange lodge in Newfoundland. There was nothing in the envelopes but the single sheet of marked newsprint. That was all I needed to send.

Joey, meanwhile, had one of his frequent brainwaves. Our new campaign would be for *British* union, and the Union Jack would become the flag of the Confederate Association. He rushed off in a great tear to get window posters and bumper stickers printed in red, white, and blue, with the word "Confederation" sandwiched between pictures of the Grand Old Flag for which so many Newfoundlanders had fought and died in two world wars. *The Evening Telegram*, already carrying the Union Jack on its own masthead, was more than happy to add it to the top corners on the front page of *The Confederate*.

The issue printed the week after the referendum carried the banner headline, "Tail Tries to Wag Dog." At the bottom of the page was Joey's map with the anti-confederate districts coloured in black. If you wished to do so you could interpret the "tail" as the Avalon Peninsula, most (not all) of which had voted for responsible government. You could equally well interpret it as the Irish Catholics, who constituted only a minority of the Newfoundland population. Either way, it was designed to consolidate confederate support among the outport Protestant majority.

A lot of our supporters were very unhappy about this turn of events—myself among them. Even though I had helped to fuel the fires of bigotry, I really had no stomach for the job, and in the middle of the second referendum campaign, when we were, in effect, urging people to go out and vote against the Pope, I was so fed up with the whole thing that I went off and spent ten days in a cabin in the woods (making it possible for Joey to describe me later, when we were no longer allies, as a supporter who "blew hot and cold"). Our Catholic campaign workers in St. John's all remained loyal to the cause, but they were tight-lipped, and white around the gills. Joey himself disliked it. His only feeling about religion was that it was a waste of time. But he did have a strong prejudice against Vatican politics, which had always opposed socialism and most other kinds of reform.

Less than a week after I'd mailed out the *Sunday Herald* tearsheets, two Orange lodges met and called for a special Grand

Lodge meeting because "the Roman Catholic Church is attempting to dominate Newfoundland." Within the month, the Grand Lodge met to pass a resolution condemning political interference by the Catholic clergy, and urging Orangemen "to use every effort to bring such attempts to naught." Orangemen had always been a strong political force in Newfoundland, quite out of proportion to their numbers.

Meanwhile, one of the supporters of the Responsible Government League played straight into our hands in a manner even more surprising than the originator of the *Sunday Herald's* gaffe. Forsey had friends in both camps. He was such a good listener that it was easy for people to fool themselves into believing that he agreed with them when in fact he was just sitting there, attentive, saying nothing. One of his drinking companions, an Irish nightclub owner, was infuriated by the slogan "British Union," which we were distributing in an edition of ten thousand to anyone who would display it. Couldn't everyone see that Canada wasn't Britain? One Saturday night after closing time, well along in his cups, he began making posters: "Confederation means British Union with French Canada."

"Where should I put 'em up?" he wondered.

"Well ... there'll be a lot of people going to church tomorrow morning," Forsey suggested slyly.

"That's it!" the zealot enthused. "No sense putting them near the Catholic churches. It's the Protestants who need the message."

He started off in his car with several helpers, while Forsey prowled behind in a taxi to see the job well done.

The posters went up beside all the Protestant churches, on poles if poles were handy, but otherwise *right on the churches themselves*. The first posters were hand lettered, some of them rather crude, but a couple of days later, printed versions appeared, and were mailed out to some of the outports. The reaction was violent: Desecration! Sacrilege! Outrage! The Anglicans, who regarded their Cathedral of St. John the Baptist with almost superstitious reverence, were especially shocked. Nailing notices to church doors might have been all right for Martin Luther, but it wasn't done in Protestant St. John's. Every Newfoundlander heard what had happened. Joey was horrified. Even the archbishop's decision to release the nuns from their vows and send them out to vote wasn't half as bad as this!

The reaction was so strong that Don Jamieson felt compelled to broadcast a formal statement to the effect that the Economic Union with the United States Party had not been associated with the posters in any way whatever. He was just as shocked as the Confederate Association by the desecration of the Protestant churches. A day or two later the Responsible Government League added its voice to the condemnation. Eventually an obscure St. Johnsman of Irish extraction claimed credit for putting up the posters. In fact, he had just been one of the tavern owner's assistants.

Newfoundlanders were not a pious people. In general, they tended to take their religion as a kind of entertainment, along with their drinking and swearing and fornicating. But if they were not pious, they *were* ingrained sectarians, a stance that was strongly reinforced by the system of church-owned schools and interschool athletics. Even adult sports were run by clubs whose members had gone to one or the other of the sectarian schools. This and other factors fed the pervading racist conflict between British and Irish. Irish Catholics and English Protestants had battled in the streets time and again. At one point Irish elements in the Newfoundland regiment had staged a mutiny. An Orange parade that had marched provocatively through the Irish section of Harbour Grace in 1883 was met by gunfire, and two of the marchers were killed. A riot between Catholics and Protestants at St. John's in 1861 had ended with three people dead and twenty wounded.

So, piety aside, it was still possible in 1948 to sway sections of the electorate on the basis of religious prejudice alone. How much effect the campaign of sectarianism had it is impossible to say. But it had *some* effect. I knew a few Protestants in St. John's who voted for responsible government in the first referendum, but switched to confederation in the second referendum, apparently because of the stands taken by the Catholic clergy and the Orange society. And there were certainly some supporters of Commission government who would not have voted at all in the second referendum had it not been for the sectarian hysteria. In the end these people went out and voted for confederation not because they believed in it particularly, but because they weren't going to allow the archbishop to decide the fate of the country.

During the campaign leading up to the second referendum the Confederate Association finally breached the walls of the establishment. Late in the campaign Joey was able to publish in the daily press and in *The Confederate* a list of names of people who had decided to lend their influence to his cause. Every one of those on the list would have been invited to the annual Government House garden party in the days when such an invitation drew the line between the classes and the masses.

To those of us who had fought and won the real battle it was all rather laughable: the Outerbridges, the Monroes, the Bowrings, the Winterses all climbing on the confederate bandwagon. And how many votes *that* swayed is equally hard to say. Some. Members of their own families, and perhaps the small class of social climbers at St. John's who'd follow any fad espoused by Sir Leonard and Lady Outerbridge.

Two of the three Newfoundland members of the Commission government not only supported confederation, but did so publicly, in speeches on the radio. The third, Sir Albert Walsh, a Roman Catholic, was also pro-confederate, but elected not to make a public statement.

Even with such heavy guns, Joey was still campaign manager, and still completely in charge. The commissioners wrote their own speeches, but submitted them to Smallwood before they went on the air. The more prominent of the two was Herman Quinton, an Anglican, a former magistrate, and a former Tory, who had defeated Joey in his first bid for election in 1932. The other was a leading United Church layman, Herbert Pottle, a scholar with a doctorate, who was fluent in foreign languages, and held strong opinions in favour of social reform. Perhaps the most useful action taken by the two commissioners was to line up at least some of the former supporters of Commission government (the senior civil service, for instance) in the confederate camp.

This sudden flood of support from on high created a great change in Joey. Here he was, unexpectedly hobnobbing with the people he had always pretended to despise, but had actually envied from afar. They treated him with something like respect, at least to his face, no matter what they might be saying behind his back. He may or may not have made a deal with the two commissioners. Neither he nor they ever said a word on the subject, but they were, in any case, conspicuous members of his first Cabinet, sworn into office the day the Commission took its final bow, while the third Newfoundlander on the Commission became lieutenant-governor. All three simply stepped from one government into another.

Outerbridge was Joey's nominee for lieutenant-governor (an office which Smallwood always viewed as a purely decorative one, overlooking its constitutional responsibilities). But there were rumours that Joey might not be the Outerbridge family's first choice for premier. Sir Leonard's wife was widely quoted as saying, in front of a roomful of socialites, "Reahlly, Leonaad, you surely aren't going to invite that *dreadful* little man to be Premyah!"

In fact, there was no constitutional precedent for what was about to happen. A lieutenant-governor would be sworn into office, chosen by the king on the advice of his ministers, and he would then call upon someone—a person who had not yet been elected, and was not even the leader of a parliamentary party—to form an interim or caretaker government. In theory, the lieutenant-governor could pick anyone his fancy might dictate. In reality, the Canadian government's choice would probably be standing at his elbow when he was sworn into office, and he would either make that choice his own or be fired from his job the next minute. But the rumours about the Outerbridges reached Ottawa, and raised enough doubt to cause concern there, as well as in St. John's.

Joey's head was turned a bit by the attentions of the members of the establishment—the Newfoundland Family Compact—who had previously refused to acknowledge his existence. He talked no more about an Upper House filled with retired union leaders. He worried, instead, about whether he could persuade a Winter, a Bowring, a Crosbie to sit under him in the government. And he began talking about "reconciliation." Above all, where was he going to get the necessary two or three *respectable* Roman Catholics to form a government that would not look too sectarian or class-conscious?

A letter from the Grand Orange Lodge was issued about a week before the vote in the second referendum—time enough to drive a few confederate Catholics to cover (some of them just didn't vote at all) and time enough to stiffen the resolve of the men in charge of the lodges. Bradley was present at the Grand Lodge meeting that issued the letter. It went out over the signature of Grand Master Chesley Fillier of Clarke's Beach, Conception Bay, an outport merchant and one of our strong supporters. Sent as a private communication to the members of the Loyal Orange Society, it of course became public at once. And it served to make the last week of the campaign one of extreme tension, with grave danger of violence in some of the outports, as well as in St. John's.

"We're going to have one more giant rally in the CLB," Joey announced, "three days before the end of the campaign."

The air was electric with tension. Once again the great auditorium was packed to the doors with a standing audience. Once again the street was jammed to the curbs with a mob of Peter Cashin's followers. A public address system mounted on the outside of the building carried the speeches out over downtown St. John's for a good half-mile. Joey, as usual, was superb. The crowd shouted itself hoarse. Greg Power, Phil Roche and a few less well-known Catholics were visibly present to demonstrate that not everyone of Irish extraction was supporting Peter Cashin and the archbishop.

Smallwood's personal bodyguard was reinforced, each armed with his own choice of weapons—a piece of chain, a set of brass knuckles, a bottle with the end broken out. Two guards from His Majesty's Penitentiary, both of them of Irish extraction, showed up as volunteers. They weighed about two hundredweight each, stood around six-foot-two, and were armed with blackjacks—sand-filled weapons guaranteed to knock a troublemaker unconscious without fracturing his skull.

One or two hecklers dared to raise their voices that night—they must have been either very drunk or very brave. They were manhandled out the front door and tossed into the arms of their friends at the foot of the steps. Irving Fogwill had instructed our heavies never to shed blood or break bones. "When two or three of you have got him pinioned," Fogwill said, "as you're rushing him out the door, *squeeze his testicles*."

The mob seethed and bawled in the street, waiting for Smallwood to appear on the steps, as he had done on the previous occasion. Few people even knew that there was a back way out of the Armoury, a fire escape by way of a flight of steps leading down directly from a small room off the back of the stage. Behind the Armoury was a patch of vacant ground with a broken fence next to a supermarket parking lot. We had backed a car through the fence, and kept it waiting beside the steps with its lights off, the driver at the wheel. While the crowd was still cheering and the chairman was still making announcements, Joey and Greg Power, accompanied by a couple of guards, quietly left the stage, got into the car, and drove off across the empty parking lot. An hour later they were comfortably settled in a small outport hotel. Joey's wife and family had been moved out of town for safety the day before.

The last announcement from the stage of the Armoury that night was, "Mr. Smallwood has already left for a tour of Trinity and Conception Bays. He'll be appearing in all the towns there within the next few days."

The mob howled uselessly. A few of us remained in the Armoury, with members of the bodyguard, while the mob surged off eastwards along Harvey Road, some shouting and some singing. We learned the next morning that they had gone down to Devon Row, collecting stones and bricks and empty bottles as they went. There they attacked the house that they thought was Smallwood's. It turned out to be the house next door. They smashed all the windows, and littered the inside with bricks and rocks. A few of the missiles had obscene messages tied on them with string.

That morning, Joey and Power were joined by one of the Confederate Association's travelling vans, equipped with music, microphones, and a powerful public address system. In two days, Joey made fifty-six speeches in fifty-six outports. He'd park the van on a hill overlooking a village, play a little music, and begin addressing the voters. As a rule, most people would come to their doors to listen. The speeches were short—about twenty minutes each—but he took a little more time in a few of the larger places. Altogether, he spoke for nearly twenty hours. Then, near the end of the second day, his cast-iron vocal chords quit. When he cast his ballot on the morning of July 22, he was virtually reduced to a whisper.

The second referendum was almost an anticlimax. We'd had no doubts at all about winning. The only surprise was that responsible government made as strong a showing as it did. We won by a margin of 4.67 percent, which would be regarded as decisive in any election, but was considerably closer than we had expected.

If you looked at the vote district by district instead of all in a block, if you looked at the results the way they would have appeared in a general election instead of in a referendum, the result amounted to a confederate landslide: twenty-nine districts for confederation, nine for responsible government (using the distribution followed in the national convention). Or, counting by seats, with eight seats in the four St. John's districts, you still had only thirteen seats for responsible government, and thirty-two for confederation. (One of the St. John's "seats" had gone confederate, in St. John's West Extern, where Bert Butt had backed the wrong horse.)

For the sake of a proper historical perspective it is important to keep the actual number of votes and the distribution of votes in mind, because misinformation about the second referendum has been published and repeated so often that it has become accepted folklore. The final count of votes was as follows:

Confederation with Canada: 78,323

Responsible Government: 71,334

This has been described by Don Jamieson, for example, writing many years after the event, as "a majority of five thousand." Richard Gwyn, in *Smallwood, the Unlikely Revolutionary*, called it "wafer thin." Bren Walsh, in *More Than A Poor Majority*, also called it "the five thousand majority" but Walsh made fewer such slips than the others. Jamieson, in another place, called it "the narrowest of margins," "splinter thin," and even "about one percent." According to Gwyn, "it could not have been closer."

Such writing is not only nonsense. It is *inaccurate* nonsense. The difference between the two votes was exactly eleven votes short of seven thousand, not "a majority of five thousand." It was not "wafer thin" or "splinter thin" or "about one percent." It was 4.67 percent. Seven thousand is not five thousand, and 4.67 percent is not "about one percent"; it is "about five percent."

The confederate victory was a close one, but it could have been a lot closer, and still would have been decisive. The margin of seven thousand votes was a lot wider than the margin by which responsible government had beaten confederation in the first referendum. Confederation had picked up more than fourteen thousand votes between the two referenda. Responsible government had picked up less than two thousand.

Some historians and journalists, sitting at their desks looking at the results long afterwards, have made much of the fact that the total vote in the second referendum was lower than in the first. There is a difference of slightly more than seven thousand. It has been suggested that seven thousand of those who supported Commission government simply stayed home. One or two writers have even published the wild suggestion that the second referendum was fraudulent, and that seven thousand votes for responsible government were destroyed, all as part of the official conspiracy—this fraud being carried out, somehow or other, under the noses of scrutineers from the various responsible government parties, who sat in all the polling booths.

Such speculations could only have been made by people who knew nothing about the social realities of Newfoundland in 1948. On June 3, when the first referendum was held, nearly everyone was at home. On July 22, when the second referendum was held, almost ten thousand fisherman were at sea, and only a minority of them managed to reach a polling booth. Few of the Labrador floaters (as distinct from the stationers) and few of the banking crews, got the chance to vote at all. Had they been able to reach polling booths, the confederate majority would have been increased accordingly.

On the day following the vote, Ches Fillier and his friends organized a massive outdoor celebration on the beach between Bay Roberts and Spaniard's Bay. People came in cars from St. John's (a motor parade with bunting and blowing horns) and Brigus and Carbonear, and perhaps from places even more distant. In a surviving photograph I am able to identify some of the faces in addition to those of Joey and myself. Clara Smallwood and her daughter are both there, and her son Bill. Sam Hefferton, Bill Frampton, and Billy Bond Taylor have come from St. John's. But not a single Irish face is visible in this Orange stronghold—not even that of Greg Power.

Too late to affect the results, the Responsible Government League began a series of desperate manoeuvres to try to anul the confederate victory. They sent telegrams on July 25 to Prime Minister Mackenzie King and to Opposition leaders in Britain, describing the referendum as illegal, and asking its results to be set aside. Four days later, they asked King to receive a delegation, but he refused.

Meanwhile, King himself had been waffling. He had expected a larger majority, one way or the other, and wanted to take time to think it over. Actually, as Smallwood has pointed out, he could hardly have refused to accept *any* majority, since to do so would have been an act of bad faith on Canada's part, once they had made their offer and allowed it to go to a vote. But in any case, the seven thousand majority was a clear and unmistakeable decision by the people of Newfoundland. Pickersgill, knowing well how King's mind worked, looked up the results of the voting in all of King's own elections, and discovered that only once had he received a larger share of the popular vote than confederation had received in Newfoundland. When King asked his opinion, he put on a great show: "Why, it's wonderful, Mr. King!" he enthused. "Do you realize. . ." etc. etc.

"Is that so?" King replied. "Well. . .that puts the matter in a new light, Pickersgill." He went off to Cabinet and relayed the same information to his colleagues and then, on July 30, announced that Canada would accept Newfoundland into Confederation. The same day the Commission government at St. John's announced a new delegation to negotiate the final terms of union.

The next day Ches Crosbie issued a statement advising the members of his Economic Union with the United States Party to accept the decision of the majority as expressed in the referendum. The Crosbie faction, in fact, would soon be lined up with the winners, worming their way to positions of power. Three days later Crosbie himself was named by the governor as one of the members of the new delegation to Ottawa. The others were Albert Walsh (chairman), Gordon Bradley, J. R. Smallwood, J. B. McEvoy, Gordon Winter (one of Joey's late converts, scion of an old family, and head of a manufacturing firm), and Philip Gruchy, the paper company manager from Grand Falls.

Walsh had first been elected as a Squires Liberal in 1928, and had been Speaker of the House and later a member of the Cabinet. Defeated in 1932, he became, in turn, chief magistrate, labour relations officer, and commissioner for home affairs and education. At the time of confederation he was commissioner for justice, and deputy chairman of the Commission.

The negotiations at Ottawa would not begin until October 6. Meanwhile, the Responsible Government League sent a delegation to London to enlist British members of parliament in the fight to keep confederation from being enacted. They received what Cashin called a brushoff from Philip Noel-Baker, whom he described as a "lizard," but got the glad hand from an opposition independent, Sir A. P. Herbert, and also from Lord Sempill, an eccentric peer of the realm who agreed to introduce a bill, "An Act for the Liberation of Newfoundland," into the House of Lords. The bill would have restored responsible government forthwith.

Meanwhile, in St. John's, six members of the last Newfoundland legislature issued writs out of the Supreme Court against Commission of Government, claiming that the procedure in the election of the national convention and the holding of the two referenda had been unconstitutional. Judge Brian Dunfield heard the arguments for the writs on December 6, and rendered judgment on December 13, ruling them invalid. On January 14 the plaintiffs filed notice of appeal against Justice Dunfield's judgment, and on February 8 the Supreme Court granted leave for an appeal to the Privy Council on the constitutional issue.

Herbert's private member's bill never did get a hearing in the House of Commons in London, and Sempill's bill suffered a similar fate in the House of Lords. But both announced that they would vote against the Newfoundland bill or introduce amendments when it came before parliament. Herbert, in fact, managed to round up a few

Opposition members to support the Responsible Government League. He introduced an amendment to the Newfoundland bill which was defeated by a vote of 217 to 15. The bill then passed into law with no further opposition. The appeal to the Privy Council was dropped without a hearing.

While all this was happening, the governments at St. John's and Ottawa were taking orderly steps toward confederation. The delegation from St. John's met a committee of Cabinet in Ottawa advised by senior civil servants. The Canadian team included such stubborn negotiators as the axe-faced economist Mitchell Sharp (later a tough finance minister) and the formidable C. D. Howe, whose specialty was driving hard bargains with American multinational corporations in the course of transferring large blocks of the Canadian economy to their management.

Such men were unlikely to be generous. But the Newfoundlanders did win some minor concessions. They demonstrated beyond any doubt that the proposed transitional grants were inadequate to replace the revenues that would be lost to Newfoundland as a result of union, and got an increase of some $20 million a year.

Various small details overlooked in the earlier negotiations now received attention. Newfoundland war veterans were to receive Canadian pensions. Where their pensions were paid by Great Britain at a lower standard than Canada's, Canada agreed to pay the difference. Railway pensions were specifically guaranteed. The ferry and coastal freight services to be taken over by Canada were to be maintained at a level not lower than that then prevailing.

NAFEL—Newfoundland Associated Fish Exporters Limited— had the sole right to export dry cod from Newfoundland, and this, under Canadian law, would be considered an illegal cartel. Its continuing operation was sanctioned for five years. After that, presumably, the Canadian government would set up a marketing board to replace it.

There was even a special term to protect the Newfoundland Butter Company, the Crosbie family's margarine factory. Banned in the rest of Canada because of the influence of the dairy lobby, margarine was almost universally used on Newfoundland tables. According to the terms negotiated it would continue to be legal in Newfoundland. (And, because provinces were specifically forbidden by the British North America Act to erect trade barriers against each others' products, it soon would become legal in the rest of Canada, too.)

Despite the margarine concession, Ches Crosbie refused to sign the revised terms of union, because he regarded the revised transitional grant as still far too low. He walked out of the meetings, and returned to St. John's before the signing. Sir Albert Walsh was also unhappy, and agreed to sign the deal only because he believed that nothing better could be wrung from the tight-fisted Canadians, not because he believed it was just or adequate. They signed the terms in the Senate Chamber on December 11, 1948, using the cut-glass inkpot that had been used to sign the first pact between the colonies back in 1867. But this time they did it under a barrage of popping flashbulbs.

The deal was unique; it was the first time a sovereign country had entered the Canadian union. The terms of union, therefore, had the force of a treaty, a contractual relationship between Canada and a foreign country. Once passed into law, the deal could conceivably be annulled, but never altered unilaterally.

As 1949 dawned, a few Newfoundlanders would become the last Canadians ever to receive formal honours bestowed on them by the king in the traditional "honours lists." Two or three would be knighted. Others would receive the Order of the British Empire. Since Canadians were not allowed to receive knighthoods or any of the lesser orders of chivalry, this was a last-chance deal. If you weren't Sir Chesley Crosbie by March 31, 1949, you never would be, unless you moved to Great Britain. (Crosbie didn't make it.)

Joey was an obvious choice for such an honour, and the final decision about the matter rested with the governor, Sir Gordon Macdonald. Macdonald was all for it, but Joey succumbed only slowly to the blandishments of power. When the governor's son Ken told him that he would be recommended for a knighthood should he care to accept, Joey decided to think the matter over. He asked my opinion: "You know, Harold, there's something to be said for it: Sir Joseph Roberts Smallwood, K.C.M.G. Talk about respectable!"

"No!" I said without hesitation. "Everyone knows you as Joey, and that's how they want you to stay. If you start accepting knighthoods, they'll think you're going over to the merchants, like Coaker."

"Coaker didn't go over to the merchants."

"Perhaps not. But it *looked* that way."

He accepted this argument and refused the honour. I'm sure that all he really wanted from me was confirmation of what he'd been thinking himself. But he must surely have regretted it in later years when symbolic honours began to look important to him, and he collected honorary degrees like scout badges. Sometimes I've regretted it, too. A provincial government, the only one in Canada, headed by a Knight Commander of St. Michael and St. George would have been a delightful anachronism, and a reminder of our special status as the only truly latecomer to the Canadian union.

While such grave questions were being discussed at St. John's, Pickersgill was moving things along in Ottawa. Civil servants drafted the Newfoundland bill, mapped out federal ridings in Newfoundland, and sent out notices that Newfoundland mothers should register for family allowances.

Pickersgill had foresight enough to realize that in January or February navigation to the far northern outports of Newfoundland and Labrador might cease, and that no mail might be delivered to some of them until May or June, whenever the drift ice decided to move. So he arranged to have family allowance cheques made out months in advance, and sent in bundles to the post offices before navigation closed that winter. The cheques were to be delivered to their owners in April and May. This ensured that most people would receive at least one month's benefit, and probably two, before it would be possible to hold a provincial election.

An army of civil servants and justices of the peace worked frantically to register as many people as possible for the federal freebees. Not only family allowances, but also old age pensions and veterans' pensions had to be applied for and documented. In the absence of a birth certificate, acceptable documentation included a record of a baptism, a marriage certificate stating the ages of the parties, or even a page cut from a family Bible. At the risk of angering the Holy Trinity, hundreds of such pages were actually clipped out and mailed to Ottawa. But no one was struck dead, and the pages, returned to their owners, were reverently pasted back into place.

Additional justices of the peace had to be sworn in to take statements on oath and do all the paperwork for people who had never done any paperwork in their lives. I was a justice of the peace myself for a couple of months, and I discovered some strange situations: a man in his seventies who had put aside enough money for "a decent funeral," and feared he would be required to spend it before he could apply for his pension, just as he would have been required to do if applying for relief under the Commission government; a man who had deserted from a French ship nearly sixty years before, and had no documentation whatever as to his age; a woman who hesitated to apply for family allowances because her child had been fathered by her brother, and she was afraid to enter his name in the blank space marked "father."

In some instances where there was absolutely no documentation in support of age, we took affadavits from older people, if we could find them, stating that the person in question had been an adult, apparently twenty years old or more, half a century ago. The Ottawa mandarins rolled their eyes up to heaven and took such things as legal proof of age. They had been instructed by their political bosses, who had been requested by Pickersgill, to give every case the benefit of the doubt. In the end, though there were some delays, no one was denied a pension because of lack of strictly legal proof of age.

The mandarins wanted Newfoundland to enter Confederation on April 1, 1949, because that was the first day of their financial year. But Joey balked at having it happen on April Fool's Day. So after pondering the question the government agreed to move back the actual act of union to a minute before midnight on March 31. The extra minute would save Joey's feelings without embarrassing the federal treasury.

By the beginning of March Joey was choosing his interim Cabinet, which would govern the country for six or seven weeks while the first provincial election was arranged and run off. There was an embarrassment of Protestants and an embarrassing lack of Catholics. There was Bill Keough, of course, from the solidly Catholic and confederate district of St. George's, and he even had the blessing of a bishop. But Keough stood alone. Joey needed someone from the Irish Catholic districts of the east coast, preferably some leading Catholic layman, and Greg Power, who'd just recently been seen inside a church after a lapse of some twenty years (and whose father had actually taken his pew out of the church at Placentia and carried it home after an argument with the priest) just didn't fill the bill. Joey needed a real Catholic, one who went to mass a decent number of times each year, and was on speaking terms with the hierarchy. Or at least he *thought* he needed this. He approached a number of Catholic businessmen and professionals at St. John's without results.

By scraping the bottom of the barrel, Power came up with Michael Sinnott, from Placentia, certainly not a leading Catholic layman, or friend of the archbishop, but at least a former magistrate. So Joey managed to squeeze two Catholics into a ten-man government. Sinnott, in his eighties, was so old as to be almost feeble, and so inconspicuous in government affairs that Joey actually forgot his existence. When he came to write his memoirs, he referred to his first Cabinet as having "but one Roman Catholic in it, my dear friend Bill Keough." Sinnott appears only in a list of his ministers obviously prepared by one of his stenographers.

Forsey presented a problem. He told Joey that he had no wish to enter politics—at least not yet. He wanted to finish his year as teacher at Prince of Wales College in St. John's, then take the summer to think the matter over. Ike Newell had not just waffled, like Forsey. He had flatly refused to have anything to do with entering the government or running for election. I, too, told Smallwood I didn't want to run in the election.

"What's this?" he demanded of me. "Am I simply going to be deserted by the whole lot of you?"

I should have said "yes" and walked away. But I didn't. I kept silent.

"Harold," he resumed, "you know Forsey better than any man alive knows him. Go and talk to him and make him resign from that school. I want him in my government."

So I went and sat with Forsey over a bottle of booze and talked him into doing the thing that cost him his reputation, his self-respect, and finally his life. Deep down, Forsey must have known himself even better than I knew him. His instinct warned him to steer clear of the dangers and temptations of power. He was a man of tender sensibilities and inner contradictions, with a deep commitment to children and a harsh cynicism about adults. He should have been left to deal with his problems in private life.

Joey was quite incapable of understanding that there were other careers just as important as politics, other routes to self-fulfillment. He dragged Forsey into political life (with my help) and the results were tragic. The cynicism took over. Forsey became a sensualist and an alcoholic. Joey fired him from the Cabinet. For a while he got a menial job in the Department of Highways. For a while I managed to get work for him as an editorial writer. Two years after being fired from the government he escaped to Ottawa and got a job teaching school once more. He died in Ottawa at the age of fifty-two. During the few years that he was minister of supply, he was known as "Ten Percent Forsey." The ten percent, however, did not go into Forsey's pocket. Any monies he collected went to the party.

Had Ike Newell been living in St. John's instead of in St. Anthony, Joey might have managed to drag him into public life, too. He dragged me in, over my protests, but I was tough enough to escape almost at once. Bill Keough apparently went willingly. His fate was not as obvious, as public, as Forsey's, but for Keough, too, it was a process of gradual, but fairly rapid, destruction. It took only five years for Forsey to reach rock bottom. Keough remained in the House of Assembly and in the government, sinking into a progressive silence, until he died prematurely in office in 1970, a man whose tremendous promise had never been fulfilled, the last, and not the least tragic, of Joey's angry young men.

There was one further hitch in the smooth progress toward provincehood: the matter of the lieutenant-governor. Louis St. Laurent, who by now had succeeded Mackenzie King as leader of the Liberal Party and prime minister, sent his parliamentary assistant Walter Harris to St. John's to interview Sir Leonard Outerbridge, who was universally believed to be in line for the appointment. Harris came away from the interview quite uncertain that Outerbridge intended to send for Smallwood, as planned, on April 1. Smallwood himself was touring the south coast by ship, lapping up the adulation of that solidly confederate region, and could not be reached. So St. Laurent made a quick decision. He asked Sir Albert Walsh, about whose intentions there could not be the slightest doubt, and Walsh agreed to accept the appointment.

St. Laurent, a Catholic layman who had spent his life dealing successfully with the Catholic hierarchy in Quebec, thought this would be a clever choice not only because Walsh was a distinguished public man and a known supporter of confederation, but because he was one of the two or three leading Catholic laymen in Newfoundland, whose appointment would "make distinguished Catholics such as the archbishop and Bishop O'Neill less apprehensive." But St. Laurent didn't know his bishops as well as he thought he did. Later that year, when he visited St. John's as prime minister, Archbishop Roche refused him an audience.

April 1, 1949, dawned mild and foggy. A few fading patches of blackened snow melted into the St. John's gutters, and as the morning progressed, shafts of wet sunshine gilded the forest of ceramic chimney pots along the skyline of Newfoundland's ancient capital. Here and there a Union Jack flew mast high and defiant, but at least half the city was in a kind of unofficial mourning. The pink-white-and-green flags of Britain's oldest colony* hung everywhere at half-mast. Black crêpe draped one or two doorways. Men walked the streets wearing black ties, as was customary at funerals.

There was little rejoicing even among confederates. Joey was far too busy to celebrate. He stood beside Sir Albert Walsh as the lieutenant-governor was sworn into office by Chief Justice Sir Edward Emerson. Colin Gibson, the Canadian secretary of state, also attended the ceremony, but only as a spectator. Then, a few minutes later, Smallwood himself was sworn into office by Lieutenant-Governor Walsh, and one by one his nine Cabinet ministers also took the oath: Leslie R. Curtis, Q.C., not a confederate, but Sir Richard Squires's former law partner, became attorney-general; Gordon Winter, past chairman of the Newfoundland Board of Trade, became minister of finance; Herman Quinton, who the day before had been a commissioner, became minister of health; Dr. Herbert Pottle, also from the Commission, became minister of welfare; Michael J. Sinnott became minister of public works.

Finally, there were four who had actually been members of the Newfoundland Confederate Association: Charles Ballam, one of the two former union leaders elected to the national convention from Corner Brook, became minister of labour; Bill Keough became minister of natural resources; Sam Hefferton became minister of education; Phil Forsey became minister of home affairs.

Smallwood has often been accused of surrounding himself with second-rate men, but not all the members of his first Cabinet were second rate. Four of them: Curtis, Pottle, Keough, and Forsey, were very able men indeed. Only one of them, it is true, ever achieved any political distinction. That was Curtis, who remained for many years the only man in Cabinet who could restrain Smallwood's impulsiveness, and inject a bit of caution into public policies. The others never achieved much distinction not because they lacked ability, but because they were quite unsuited to the role of politician in the kind of government in which they had to serve.

There was another factor, too. Able men tended to wither in the glare of Smallwood's presence. He was overpowering, so overpowering that even the best-equipped intellect could often do no more than

*Actually, this was the *Irish* flag of Newfoundland, if you can believe there was such a thing; the *English* flag of Newfoundland was a red ensign with the dominion's badge (not the same thing as the coat of arms) in the fly.

echo his ideas. He exuded an aura that killed debate and nearly paralyzed the mind. A great pity it was, too, because he was badly in need of intellectual guidance. No intellectual himself, and badly educated, he could have benefitted enormously by powerful minds like those of Pottle and Forsey had he been able to sit still and listen to them the way he had listened to Nimshi Crewe and me one night three years before—a night that now seemed half a lifetime ago.

While the subdued installation ceremonies were taking place in St. John's, a much flashier celebration was going on in Ottawa under the self-satisfied eye of John Whitney Pickersgill, who had arranged it all and done the backstairs work. There was a salute with cannon on Parliament Hill. The Newfoundland flag (the English one) was run up beside the flags of the other provinces. Prime Minister St. Laurent and Gordon Bradley climbed together up ladders to a platform that had been erected over the door of Parliament's centre block, and there made the first strokes with a stone-cutting chisel to carve the Newfoundland coat of arms into a blank shield that had been conveniently left by the builders in 1920 for the use of a possible future province. A shield with the cross of St. George, lions and unicorns in the quarters, the whole flanked by Indians and surmounted by a caribou, with the motto *Quaerite Prime Regnum Dei* (Seek Ye First the Kingdom of God), it had been granted to Newfoundland by King Charles II of England while mainland Canada was still populated only by Indians and fur-traders. The ceremony concluded with a carillon of bells ringing out from the Peace Tower across the Canadian capital.

There had been some difficulty about fitting Bradley into the federal Cabinet on Confederation Day, but Joey had insisted, in private talks with the prime minister, that he had to be sworn in on the day Newfoundland entered the union, with a nice high-sounding title like secretary of state. There was already a secretary of state, of course, Colin Gibson, who was at St. John's watching the administrator swear in the lieutenant-governor. But Mr. Fixit Pickersgill had taken care of that, too. He had gone to St. Laurent and suggested that Gibson should move to another post to make room for Bradley.

"What post?" St. Laurent had asked. "There's no vacancy."

"I'm sure you can arrange one," Pickersgill said. "Mr. MacKinnon is a very patriotic man, and I happen to know that he doesn't plan to run in the next election. I know this because he discussed the matter with Mr. King in my presence. I'm quite sure if he were asked to resign he'd do it, and accept an appointment to the Senate."

James A. MacKinnon had held a series of Cabinet posts under King and St. Laurent, and was then minister of mines and resources, a portfolio he had held for less than a year. He readily agreed to resign from the Cabinet and to accept a seat in the Senate a month later. Colin Gibson was glad to move to the vacant portfolio, a more senior one than secretary of state, but did not make the move until April 1. This allowed him to go to St. John's to see the swearing-in of the lieutenant-governor as Canada's official representative, leaving behind him a letter of resignation, so Bradley could be sworn into his vacant ministry later that day.

So Bradley became secretary of state for Canada on April 1, 1949. In the federal election of June 27 he won the riding of Bonavista-Twillingate by a resounding majority of 9,724 votes to his Progressive-Conservative opponent's 1,415. A superb politician out on the hustings, he had little effect in government. Before his first term in Ottawa was at an end he accepted an appointment to the Senate, and took virtually no part in public life thereafter. He died in 1966 at the age of 80.

# CHAPTER 9

# At War with the Press

AND SO WE WON THE WAR AND SET ABOUT LOSING THE PEACE. BETWEEN Joey and his friends in Ottawa there had always been an understanding that he was going to lead the Liberal Party in Newfoundland, and support it federally. The Liberals had been in power in Ottawa since the end of R. B. Bennett's single term in the 1930s, and it looked as though they were going to remain in power forever.

His sympathies, he told us privately, were with the CCF (the socialist party of that time and the predecessor of the NDP) but there was no way he could see the CCF financing an election campaign in Newfoundland. All the money, federal and provincial, would simply come down against it. Besides, in Newfoundland you could easily have socialism under the name of the Liberals. The CCF, after all, were only "Liberals in a hurry, Liberals gone to wing."

"You can *work* with the Liberals," he told us, as he had told the Fishermen's Union Party and the NIWA a generation earlier. "You can't work with the Tories. But you can work with the Liberals and achieve the same results as if you were working under the name of socialism."

At this point Joey could have led anything—even the Rhinoceros Party—to victory in Newfoundland. Money might have made the difference in only one or two close seats. He was well aware that many of his closest followers—Phil Forsey, Bill Keough, Ted Russell, myself, and possibly Greg Power—would have been far more comfortable in the CCF than in the Liberal Party, and that was also true of many in the next-to-closest circle: Irving and Janet Fogwill, Ike Newell, Billy Bond Taylor, and others.

However, there was never any question of having a genuinely socialist, or even mildly leftist, government in Newfoundland. Except perhaps for a few years in New York, the Liberal Party was as far to the left as Joey had ever gone, except in his own fancy. His concept of socialism was "being on the side of the toiling masses," and his concept of what the toiling masses needed was jobs in factories owned by free enterprise helped out with large government loans if necessary.

"Our first job," he told us the week after he came to power, "is reconciliation."

Some of us assumed that this meant reconciliation with the Roman Catholic people, and even the hierarchy, if possible. But for Joey it meant, above all, reconciliation with the Water Street merchants, and especially with the Family Compact that had ruled Newfoundland both before and after responsible government was achieved in 1855, and had continued to do so, with limitations, even under the Commission of Government.

In fact, no effort at reconciliation was needed in that quarter. The merchants came flocking to his court in droves. The Roman Catholic voters on the east coast were more difficult to woo (it takes a while to get used to voting for antichrist) but they soon learned that Joey had been telling the truth about confederation, while his opponents had spread a lot of false propaganda, and they fell into line. The Archbishop of St. John's and the Bishop of Harbour Grace proved to be much more stiff-necked, but Joey set out to win their tolerance if not their support, with statements about the untouchability of the school system, and how unthinkable it would be to have divorce courts in Newfoundland. (For years and years only Newfoundlanders with money could get divorces by paying for bills with such titles as "A Bill for the Relief of Hezekiah Hammerford," the relief in question being relief from his marriage.)

One of the effects of Joey's wooing of the Roman Catholic Church, and his consequent support of denominational schools, was that he had to support the claims of all the other denominations, too. These included the radical fundamentalist sects, who soon had their own schools supported at government expense, where they could teach students that the universe had been created in six days by divine fiat six thousand years ago, and that Joshua had stopped the rotation of the earth so the Israelites would have plenty of time to complete the massacre of the Amorites.

Even when it came to framing a charter for Memorial University later that year, promoting it from college to degree-granting institution, Joey felt it necessary to include a clause proposed by Catholic and Protestant fundamentalists forbidding the university to teach "any materialistic philosophy" or anything else likely to contradict the religious traditions.

So much for socialism. In his interim Cabinet Joey had one corporation lawyer, one establishment merchant, two small businessmen (one of whom had been a union leader in his youth and now held the labour portfolio), two career civil servants, two teachers, and one co-operative organizer.

Almost from the day he was called to office, Joey began referring to "His Majesty's outport government," implying that for the first time the outports, not the St. John's merchants, were ruling Newfoundland. But it is worth noting that only three members of the government were from outside St. John's. Some of them would later be elected in outport constituencies, but they had never lived in the outports, at least not since childhood, and never would. And two of the three outporters in the interim Cabinet hastened to buy or build houses in St. John's, and to move there permanently.

Smallwood and Bradley had both attended the national Liberal Convention as guests in the summer of 1948. They had been invited to speak, and Joey had made a great hit there, receiving a standing ovation. After that, he rarely missed the opportunity to address mainland audiences.

Because Canadians were not much accustomed to colourful speakers, because they were used to politicians who stood at lecterns in heavy horn-rimmed glasses and *read* what had been written for them by their speech writers, he got a great reception everywhere he went. Joey was not an orator like Keough, but he was a born actor, and a fluent, extemporaneous debater of a breed that seemed to have died out in Canada shortly after the time of Sir John A. Macdonald. He was entertaining as well as informative, passionate as well as persuasive, and Canadian audiences from coast to coast discovered him with glee.

He preened and strutted a bit, basking in all this mainland adulation.

"I am becoming a national figure," he told us, as he paced the floor of his Devon Row flat, "a *nat*ional fig*ure*." Forsey, behind Joey's back, stuck his thumbs into the sides of his vest, and strutted about, repeating the phrase to anyone who'd listen: "A *nat*ional fi*gure*."

The province that Joey inherited on April 1, 1949, had substantial assets as well as great liabilities. The liabilities were economic. Newfoundland had essentially a two-industry economy: forestry and fishing. The paper mills at Grand Falls and Corner Brook had flourished until the daily output of the Corner Brook mill was the largest in the world, and their combined exports were worth more in dollars than the combined exports of the fishery. And the fishery itself was an industry of huge proportions, with greater volume than any other Canadian province, and greater value than any except British Columbia's. Under the Commission government, the fishery had undergone a lot of reorganization. The government had opened bait depots and founded fresh-fish plants for the export of frozen fillets, so that production of both salt and fresh fish was now soundly based. Marketing they had overhauled completely under the able administration of Ray Gushue, Chairman of the Newfoundland Fisheries Board. But the fishery was still liable to catch failures and to the uncertainties of markets in third world countries.

Newfoundland's only important mines were at Bell Island and Buchans, the one mining iron ore for the Sydney smelters, the other, silver-lead-zinc for the American market, and supporting between them a population of some 16,000. There was no manufacturing for export, just light industry around St. John's to supply the local market. Agriculture consisted of subsistence gardening by fishing families, and the production of dairy products, poultry, and root crops for St. John's and Corner Brook.

Social capital was also in short supply. Newfoundland had few roads, most of them badly built and badly maintained. The railway was a narrow-gauge line in a bad state of repair. Electric power reached only certain parts of the Avalon Peninsula, the Corner Brook area, Grand Falls, and Gander. A few villages had little hydro plants of their own and some had diesel generators. There was not even the foundation of a provincial grid. Public services such as hospitals, schools, and libraries were scarce and poorly endowed.

Newfoundland's greatest assets were natural resources: the largest fish stocks in Canada; forests with much potential for development, especially in Labrador; considerable undeveloped mineral wealth; and untapped hydro power sites capable of generating some ten million horsepower.

A second class of asset was the cash surplus accumulated by the Commission government—some $45 million—combined with the fact that Newfoundland was the only province with no public debt.

The third class of asset, difficult to measure, but important to both social and economic development, was the high level of organization in the Newfoundland workforce. At confederation more than 45,000 Newfoundlanders were members of trade unions—most of them locals of American "internationals"—which represented one of the highest levels of organization in North America. The only large block of unorganized workers was in the fishery, where the fishermen's union had flourished and foundered a generation earlier. At confederation Canadian labour organizations sent representatives to Newfoundland to begin the process of gathering the new province's workers into the fold, and found to their amazement that there was virtually no gathering left to be done. For the most part they had to content themselves with splitting up such large existing unions as the General Workers of St. John's into locals of the Teamsters, Hod-carriers, public service unions, and so on. There was virtually no *new* organizing until much later, after the new hospitals were built, and the Labrador mines came into production.

Smallwood's interim provincial government contented itself with facilitating the changeover to confederation and preparing for the first general election. There was, of course, no new legislation, because there was no legislature. For the months of April and May, 1949, everything was directed to a single end: putting together the Liberal Party of Newfoundland, and winning the first provincial election by as large a majority as possible.

The founding of the Liberal Party of Newfoundland was a spectacular media event, but also a massive exercise in "democracy." Leading confederate supporters from every district in the island joined the Liberals. Some delegates to the first convention were former supporters of responsible government who had since seen the light. A few delegates literally invited themselves (a process easier than most people realized, or the convention might have been much larger than it was). There was a caucus from every district, and every district voted to elect a Liberal candidate to stand in the coming election.

To bring delegates to St. John's we chartered a train which started at Port aux Basques, with Greg Power and myself on board as shepherds, while Joey organized matters in St. John's. Delegates joined the train at every principal stop along the route. At Deer Lake we picked up, along with the local people, delegates from St. Barbe and White Bay. At Gander we were joined by delegates from Twillingate, Fogo, and even Labrador. The last big influx came at Brigus Junction, where some of the delegates from Trinity and Conception Bays had arrived by a branch line. Hundreds of other delegates came by car from Placentia and Conception Bays, and the Southern Shore. The exact number attending the convention was never recorded, but it was reported by the newspapers to be approximately 1,500.

The trip across Newfoundland was one big party, and it gave Power and me an opportunity to work on the delegates to get them to agree to the choices of candidates Joey had already made. We weren't blatant about it at that stage, and we operated in a relaxed atmosphere of good fellowship. Indeed, we spent much of the trip playing poker and sipping rum. Power was a keen hand at the poker table, and so was Police Sergeant Joe Seward, a delegate who had formerly been a member of the Newfoundland Ranger Force. As the train crawled its way up the slope of the Gaff Topsail in central Newfoundland, Seward was having an astonishing rush, with a full house on several occasions. He capped it by filling the first straight flush I had ever seen at a poker table.

We arrived in an exuberant high, and the high carried us through the next three sleepless nights, as we spent twenty-four hours a day rigging the convention the way Joey wanted it rigged. This task was not as simple as it might seem. First, Joey had to place his key people, those he relied on to form the political core of his following, in districts where they could be elected. Next he had to find seats for the neo-confederates who would increase our respectability. Last, but not least important, we had to see to it that each district voted for a candidate of the right religious complexion. Catholic districts must have Catholic candidates. Anglican districts must have Anglicans. Only in the "Non-Conformist" districts would there be a degree of latitude. There you might get away with running a United Church candidate, a Presbyterian, a Fundamentalist, or even someone with as little religion, formal or informal, as Joey himself. As a result of all this (and following the distribution of districts handed down from responsible government days), the three main religious groups would be assured of equal representation in the House of Assembly, and the Liberal caucus would have some balance, with at least a few Catholics.

In the CLB Armoury, crowded with well over a thousand delegates at any one time, the plenary sessions featured speeches by Joey, Bradley, and each candidate as he was declared elected by the delegates from his district. They cheered themselves hoarse, presented silver cups of gross proportions to Joey and Bradley, drank numerous cases of rum, and retired to separate quarters to vote as they were told.

This was the point where the blatancy came in. Forsey and Power and I were among the round-the-clock "persuaders" chivying the delegates into line—a task not inordinately difficult, considering the instruments of persuasion that we had at our disposal. In the coming year or two there would be hundreds of new jobs to hand out, tavern licences to be granted, and restaurant licences where no tavern could be opened. There would be appointments to government boards, most of them brand new. There would be purchases from merchants large and small. Everyone already knew that Power was going to be in charge of handing out the liquor licences, and that Forsey was going to have a lot to say about government purchasing.

In only one district did the vote go against Smallwood's wishes. That was in Grand Falls, where Greg Power decided to do his best to save Joey from himself by promising tavern licences and other goodies to anyone who'd work to elect a local boy instead of the former head of the Economic Union with the United States Party, Ches Crosbie. As it turned out, the delegates really needed little persuading, but Power's work tipped the balance, and Grand Falls elected Ned Spencer, contrary to Joey's explicit wishes.

The next day, Joey met Power in the corridor of the Newfoundland Hotel. "You did that!" he snapped, stabbing his finger at his Machiavellian friend.

Power demurred. "It was a democratic election," he said, grinning. "You can't blame them for turning down a Water Street merchant, now can you?"

Joey walked away, muttering. Later he took Spencer into the Cabinet because he felt that Grand Falls was too important a district to leave out, but he disliked Spencer intensely—indeed, I believe he was the only member of his many governments, first or last, whom Smallwood personally hated. But Spencer continued to serve in the House and in the government for seventeen years, until his voluntary retirement in 1966.

I suggested to Joey that we should put out one more issue of our paper as part of the election campaign, changing the name from *The*

*Confederate* to *The Liberal*. He agreed, and left the job entirely in my hands. I had learned in the late weeks of the Confederate campaign to imitate his journalistic style to the point where neither of us could tell which had written one of the short articles. (Joey always wrote the lead articles himself, and believed, in later years, that he had written most or all of the short ones, too.) As he became busier and busier with campaigning, I had written more and more of the paper, and when it came to *The Liberal*, I wrote every word that went into it, took the proofs from *The Telegram's* job printers, wrote the headlines, and pasted the whole thing up into pages for the press. Everyone assumed that the thing had been written by Joey himself. Actually, the first time he saw any part of it was after it was in print. I managed the financing of the paper by selling patronage to a Water Street merchant who, a few months previously, had been telling everyone that Horwood ought to be "shipped back to Russia, where he belongs."

The result of the election was more of a foregone conclusion than Joey had supposed. He elected twenty-two Liberals, including three Roman Catholics. The Opposition elected six, including one Protestant in St. John's East. St. John's West returned two Liberals. But that was not the whole story. Even in St. John's East the vote was close. One of the two Liberals was defeated by less than 200 votes, and the other by less than 400.

The Liberal in the solidly Catholic district of Placentia–St. Mary's lost by less than 150, two Liberals in Harbour Main–Bell Island by approximately a thousand. Peter Cashin, who ran as an independent in Ferryland, where he enjoyed immense personal popularity, was the only Opposition candidate elected with more than a slim majority. The Progressive Conservatives came within inches of being wiped out altogether. There could be no more convincing demonstration of the fact that by May 27, 1949, the overwhelming majority of Newfoundlanders had accepted confederation and Smallwood's leadership. The Liberals received more than 65 percent of the vote, the PCs less than 33 percent, and the independents 2 percent.

Joey now faced a completely new challenge—that of running the government and managing government affairs in the legislature. He had never sat in a government or in any elected assembly. Indeed, no one on the Liberal side of the House had ever been in a legislature before, so Joey not only knew little about the job, but had no one in his caucus to give him advice.

He did what he could, drawing on his reading and his own

experience. Consequently, he ran the government the way he had run the Newfoundland Confederate Association. The idea of a true democratic government, a government by committee, was wholly foreign to his experience. He was good at parliamentary rules and procedures, because he had learned them thoroughly many years before at the MCLI and had watched them at work in St. John's, London, and Ottawa. However, he had never been an active member of any democratic body such as a town council or a trade union. He had approached them from the outside, as propagandist and organizer; he had never been a grass-roots member of anything. Consequently, he really knew little about how democratic institutions functioned: parliamentary procedure, yes; democratic procedure, no.

So his government became a one-man show, as the Confederate Association had been. He sought advice from those whose opinions he respected, but he acted on it or rejected it in the spirit of a monarch, not in the spirit of a democratic leader. He was never arrogant, but the effect of arrogance was there just the same—the result of his combined forcefulness and loquaciousness. In the end it was he, not the government, who ruled.

His behaviour in Cabinet and his behaviour in the caucus consisted of selling his colleagues his ideas, his programs, his policies, which had been coined not inside those democratic bodies, but outside them.

Never once did he sit quiet, as chairman of the Cabinet, to listen to his ministers developing policy. Never once did he sit still in caucus to listen to the Liberal members of the legislature discussing the party platform. Not that none of them ever spoke—the problem was that they had to speak within such strict limits. Ministers might raise matters from their own departments, indeed they did so quite regularly, as requests were passed on to them from their deputies. Any member might raise questions concerning his own district, if it was a matter that required the attention of the whole government, but the only part he took in the formation of policy was to vote "yea" to government measures in the House. It was Joey who had all the answers.

Rarely, if ever, was there a formal vote on any issue in either body. In Cabinet meetings Joey always tried to get consensus, which in effect meant trying to get everyone to agree with him. After all criticism had been silenced, overridden, or beaten down by the sheer weight of Joey's personality, he would then turn to the clerk of the executive council and say: "Enter a minute to the effect that that was passed." It would then be so written. On the very rare occasion when there was a serious disagreement, he would postpone the decision, knowing that sooner or later he could count on unanimous support. To Joey this whole regime seemed to be the very essence of democracy. It bothered him greatly that outsiders considered him a dictator, and that insiders were obviously unhappy much of the time. If he had known how to make the process more democratic he certainly would have tried to do it.

Some of the ablest minds in the province withered under Joey's brand of democratic government. After a year and a half Herman Quinton gladly accepted an appointment to the Senate. Ted Russell lasted only a year before he crossed the floor of the House and joined the CCF. Dr. Herbert Pottle stood it for six years before making his escape, and, soon afterwards, leaving Newfoundland altogether. When the time came, Pottle could not talk to Smallwood about his resignation. Whispering "I'm sorry, I have to do this," he stood in his place and read a prepared statement to the House of Assembly. Forsey stuck it out for five years and Keough for twenty, but it was terrible to watch Keough shrivelling from a great orator who could move even his enemies to cheers, to the stature of a flunky whom Smallwood treated like an office boy. The only *able* minister who could cope with Smallwood's approach was Curtis, the toughest, most pragmatic member of the government, and the only one who ever learned to deal with Smallwood as an equal.

To Al Vardy, the ex-con from Albany prison who had tossed cigarettes contemptuously on the floor and made Joey stoop to pick them up, the premier was amazingly loyal. He invited Vardy to run, in company with former deputy-mayor Jimmie Spratt, in the first election in St. John's West, and when both were returned to the legislature, Smallwood invited them both into the Cabinet.

Spratt, like Vardy, had a dark shadow in his past, but one for which he could in no way be blamed. His son had been hanged for murder, a crime of passion, in which he killed his fiancée with a "blunt instrument." The Commission government, with complete insensitivity, had decided to proceed with the hanging, despite a massive public outcry in St. John's, and demands from all sides for a commuted sentence. It was the last time capital punishment was applied in Newfoundland. The public was so horrified by the execution that Newfoundland effectively abolished the death penalty then and there, a full generation before it was abolished in Canada. Some fifteen subsequent murderers brought before the courts, including some who had committed brutal killings in the course of robberies, either had their convictions reduced to manslaughter, or their sentences reduced to imprisonment.

Early in the life of the first elected Smallwood government an unusual petition was introduced to Cabinet by Attorney-General Les Curtis. The hangman who had been brought to Newfoundland from Quebec to spring the trap under young Spratt claimed that the Commission government had never paid his fee in full. He was now petitioning for the balance. Curtis laid this letter on the Cabinet table while Jimmie Spratt was sitting there as one of the ministers. Joey nudged Curtis with an elbow to try to shut him up, but Curtis turned and inquired, "What's the matter with you?" then went on to explain what the letter was all about—it was as though he didn't realize that the man whose son had been hanged was sitting across the table. Spratt rose from his place, his face white, shuffled from the room, and never attended another Cabinet meeting. He remained in the legislature for two and a half years, then retired from politics.

Vardy ran for re-election in 1951 and remained in the Cabinet, but he quickly resigned under threats from Peter Cashin to expose his criminal past. Vardy's record was an open secret in St. John's, but apparently he did not realize this. He never made any mention of having been in jail, or any public reference to his prison experiences. Consequently, it was quite easy for Cashin to drive him from office. Joey remained loyal. When he could no longer have Vardy in his Cabinet he made him director of tourist development.

Many years later Vardy died, a fugitive from Canadian justice, in the United States, but he had meanwhile enjoyed twenty-three fat years of Joey's favour. He was a mere tourist director for only a short time, eventually becoming deputy-minister of economic development. He teamed up with some of Joey's wealthiest supporters in financial deals that made him a millionaire, and finally led to his downfall.

Vardy continued to make snide remarks about Joey behind his back, but Joey never uttered a word against Vardy. If questioned about Vardy's past, he would refer to it as "a youthful indiscretion."

When the Tories finally came to power after a full generation in the wilderness, they appointed a royal commission to investigate some of the financial shenanigans of their predecessors. One of the fish they caught was Vardy, who had been part-owner of a company renting seven properties to the government at what the commission regarded as almost twice their rental value.

Worse was to come. The RCMP raided Vardy's penthouse apartment in St. John's, and later charged him with fraud, bribery, and breach of trust. Vardy himself could not be found in Canada, but the RCMP traced him to Panama. The Panamanian secret police arrested him there at the request of the Newfoundland government on January 22, 1974. He was then flown to Miami with a police escort on his way to Canada.

There he escaped, and applied for bail to an American court. The court granted bail of $5,000 with sureties of $45,000, but ordered him to remain in southern Florida while the Canadian government pursued extradition proceedings. The fraud charges against him totalled $218,000. Vardy spent the next six years in Clearwater, Florida, fighting attempts by the government and the RCMP to take him to Canada for trial. He died in Clearwater, at the age of seventy-three, on April 13, 1980.

It would be a mistake to picture Joey as governing Newfoundland entirely alone. He sought advice all the time, but mostly from outside the Cabinet and outside the party caucus. The only minister he consulted extensively was Curtis, because Curtis had a long experience with the law, and, indirectly, with government. Besides this, he continued to consult those who had been his principal advisors in the Confederate Association, and, to a lesser extent, the two ministers who had been members of the Commission government. On matters of procedure he often consulted Will Carew, the clerk of the executive council, and secretary to the Cabinet. Carew had lengthy experience as secretary to eight Newfoundland prime ministers and had been secretary to the governor-in-commission for fifteen years. Such people helped Joey make policy, and, since the consultations were carried on outside the structure of government, Joey's friend Nimshi Crewe began referring to the panel of advisors as "Smallwood's kitchen cabinet."

But we were no longer meeting in a kitchen, or even in the old downtown living room where we had started the confederate movement. Instead, we had the run of an impressive three-storey mansion on Millionaire's Row—exclusive Circular Road—at what was once the back of St. John's, where the nineteenth-century plutocrats had built their great town houses overlooking the picturesque valley of Rennie's

River and the hills to the north of the city. The great house had the advantage that it was separated from the Colonial Building, where both the Cabinet and the legislature met, by a distance of only a few hundred yards across a small park and along a quiet street a block long.

Canada House, as it was called, had been built in 1902 by a *nouveau riche* Irish immigrant. It had later been the home of Sir Michael Cashin, and in 1941 had been bought by Canada as home and offices for the Canadian High Commissioner in Newfoundland. At confederation, the house and offices fell vacant, and the Canadian government leased them to the Government of Newfoundland at an extremely modest rental. Joey and his family moved into the spacious living quarters at the east end of the building. The west end became the premier's offices.

Here Michael Foley, Joey's old friend from the NIWA, now grown fat and diabetic, became "doorkeeper in the House of the Lord," admitting visitors to the waiting room and arranging them on chairs and benches in the order in which they would later be received into The Presence. It was Joey's policy to see everyone who called, first-come first-served, and to give each visitor his undivided attention, at least for a minute or two. You didn't need to make an appointment. You didn't need to phone in advance and say you wanted to see the premier. You just walked up to the door, and gave your name to Mike Foley, who showed you to a seat and sent your name into the next room. If you waited long enough, you got to see the premier.

The only people who didn't have to wait in line were those Joey had *asked* to call. Otherwise, bishops, bookies, and bums got the same treatment. Sometimes he'd be off to a Cabinet meeting while his visitors still sat in the waiting room. But if they wished, they could remain there until he returned. His day never ended until the last visitor had either left in despair or had been ushered into his inner office to solicit help in organizing a town council or repairing a cod trap or applying for an old age pension. One of Joey's enduring qualities was his endless patience with "the ragged-arsed artillery."

Inside the waiting room a double-thick green baize door separated it from the office inhabited by Mrs. Anna Templeman and Joey's tortoise-shell cat. It was Mrs. Templeman who took all his phone calls at first, though later on she had an assistant secretary. She managed his confidential correspondence, and ushered visitors in and out of the Inner Sanctum. There was also a door connecting this office to the living quarters, which of course also had their own entrances, making it possible for confidential visitors to enter by a confidential route. Members of the Smallwood family might come and go to this office (though not to the Inner Sanctum, except by invitation) and the tortoise-shell cat was occasionally joined there by a handsome white husky dog named Wolf.

The Inner Sanctum itself was cluttered with trophies and memorabilia collected during Joey's travels, and though you had to get past both Mike Foley and Mrs. Templeman in order to enter it, Joey was completely exposed to the public on the other side, through a massive undraped picture window that looked out on to Circular Road and the park. He perhaps never realized how easy it would have been for an assassin to shoot him through this ground-floor window, as he paced about his office. Once he became premier he lived entirely without benefit of security guards.

In the spacious drawing room at the other end of the house, Mrs. Smallwood installed new floor-to-cciling drapes, new thick carpeting, a new upright piano, and a sound system that was then regarded as "high fidelity." Her record collection included Beethoven symphonies and concertos and sonatas, the piano parts often played by Arthur Rubinstein. In the evenings after the last visitor had left his office, Joey would often relax there, and listen to the piano, or to Clara's classical records. He appeared to have no musical talent, but in the course of his haphazard education he had acquired a taste for the popular classics.

Among occasional evening visitors to that drawing room were a new breed of personal friends: small businessmen, young, on the make, determined to tie their fortunes to Smallwood's political star. Among them were such small fish as plumbing and electrical contractors who had been mere journeymen two or three years before—men like Ed Learning, who played the guitar on the hustings and sang comic songs (his son Walter, later famous in Canadian theatre, might then have been a boy of seven or eight); men like Joe Ashley, whose electrical business burgeoned along with the Liberal Party until he was able to buy Canada House in 1960, when the Tories were in power in Ottawa and they had, on Prime Minister Diefenbaker's personal orders, told the premier to go packing.

Joey's running feud with the press began almost as soon as he was elected, and continued as long as he remained in office. He always felt that modern reporters were a degenerate breed, far inferior to the reporters of his own era (1919–25) and that he could show them how to report the news properly if only they'd listen. He got his own way with

the press most of the time. They reported uncritically even his most
fanciful schemes for economic development: the orange juice factories, the gazelle-skin gloves. They gave him banner headlines every
time he painted a picture of a new city rising on the shores of
Conception Bay or Octagon Pond. But he wasn't satisfied with this.
They didn't treat the Tories as roughly as he thought they should. And
even though their news pages treated his dreams as reality, their
columns and editorials were sometimes critical. Nothing short of total
subservience would have satisfied him.

His first major blast at a reporter came on March 28, 1951, after
Resources Minister Ted Russell had left the government, charging it
with financial irresponsibility. The story of Russell's resignation was
carried in *The Daily News* even before Russell announced it to the
House, and the premier charged *News* reporter Burnham Gill with
having partly inspired the resignation, hinting also that he had written
parts of Mr. Russell's resignation speech. He called Gill a "contemptible cur, beneath the respect of decent men, a man who is an insult to
the great profession of journalism, a journalistic knave." This contemptible cur had started his career as a member of the Newfoundland
Ranger Force, and later became editor of *The Western Star*. Eventually he was administrator and chief archivist of the Newfoundland
Archives.

Joey kept lecturing the press gallery on what a sorry lot they were,
but did not really hit his stride until I began writing a daily column for
*The Evening Telegram* in 1952. "Political Notebook" started as a
miscellany of political chit-chat (at Joey's own suggestion) but soon
developed into the principal organ of government criticism. From
1953 to 1958 I published a long series of revelations about backstairs
politics, uncovered a number of minor scandals, and shaped the course
of many public attacks on the government.

Joey responded with weekly, and sometimes daily, blasts, in which
he described me as"a snake, a crocodile, a loathsome scavenger, and a
literary assassin," among other things. His favourite name for any
*Telegram* story that he disliked was "a Horwood lie." He suggested
repeatedly that I ought to be barred from the press gallery, and *The
Telegram* itself silenced.

Finally, after a speech in which he declared that my proper place
was "behind bars," he referred my reports to a special Committee of
the House on privilege, predicting darkly that I would be thrown into
prison and *The Telegram* padlocked. Under an ancient rule dating

back to the English parliament, the House, acting on the report of such a committee, had the power of arrest and imprisonment without trial. At least once this rule was invoked in Newfoundland when a certain Dr. Kielly was sent to prison without trial for insulting a member of the House, and the chief justice was arrested and imprisoned for issuing a writ of *habeas corpus* on his behalf.

Committees of the House, however, always include at least one member from the Opposition. In this case it was Jim Higgins, a skilful lawyer and later judge of the Supreme Court. Perhaps through his influence, the committee appointed to deal with the supposed breach of privilege never tabled a report.

After a campaign of investigative reporting by *The Telegram*, in which it was revealed that a number of Liberal members of the House were engaged in the liquor business, at both the wholesale and the retail levels, Joey denounced the paper as disrespectful and inaccu- rate—"a once-great paper that has fallen into the hands of illiterates." Unable to deny the facts revealed in the stories, he attacked the paper on other grounds, and wound up by suggesting that it was cooking its circulation figures.

*The Telegram* replied to this by publishing figures from the Audit Bureau of Circulations, showing that its circulation had soared to unprecedented heights during the battle with Joey, and Joey actually stood in his place in the House and apologized for having misrepre- sented the paper's circulation—the only time he ever apologized for any statement he or his associates made about the press.

*The Telegram* was later the subject of a number of libel actions by members of the government, and by companies doing business with the government, culminating in a suit by all eleven ministers collec- tively, alleging libel in stories about liquor and organized prostitution. This case, the only one that was not dropped by the plaintiffs before it came to trial, was thrown out of court by the chief justice, who awarded costs to *The Telegram*. The costs were not paid. *The Tele- gram* then initiated, and won, a civil suit for the collection of the costs, which were still not paid. In none of the actions did *The Telegram* make any apology or any out-of-court settlement.

In September 1954 the premier issued a directive to the civil service forbidding the release of news or the making of any statements to the press by deputy-ministers or others without a specific clearance each time from the government. Since this amounted to a blackout on how government programs were being implemented, the Newfoundland Press Club responded by publicly expelling the premier, who had been its honorary president until that time.

Shortly after the opening of the 1956 session, *The Telegram* carried a story to the effect that three Liberal members of the House who had recently announced their resignations would have been the subject of an Opposition motion to unseat them under the Legislative Disabilities Act, had they remained in the Legislature. Opposition Leader Malcolm Hollett issued a statement confirming the story, but Joey attacked the paper as having inspired the whole thing out of pure malice.

This time, besides calling me a snake and a crocodile, Joey also suggested that I might be a communist, a card cheat, an embezzler, and a "degenerate." I invited him to repeat any of those things outside the House so we could settle the matter in court, but he declined the invitation.

The personal vendetta ended in 1958 when I left *The Telegram* to work as a freelance writer and novelist, but Joey's war with the press continued. Later that year he called an unnamed reporter "a drunk and a fool," then three days later threatened action for the way this story was reported, and warned the press gallery that they must not accuse him of shouting and bellowing in the House.

That year, in one of those *coups* that reporters dream about, Malcolm McLaren, who worked for *The Telegram* and later for the CBC, brought down the budget a week before it was due to be released in the House. There was pandemonium in the legislature, and Joey delivered a withering blast, ending by pointing at McLaren in the press gallery, and stammering, for once at a loss for words, "That ... that ... that ... that THING."

But nothing that ever happened in Newfoundland matched the drubbing that Joey received from the mainland press after he tangled with the unions and brought down the worst antilabour legislation of his era in 1959. And that was not the only event that led to bad press for the premier. After the early honeymoon years between Canada and Newfoundland, the mainland press was frequently hostile. Although Joey was always "good copy," he was often portrayed not as the consummate politician of his time (which he was) but as a mountebank.

By the 1960s, journalists like Tom Alderman (for the *Star Weekly*) and Boyce Richardson (for the *Last Post*) were doing long feature profiles that presented Joey as an incredible combination of tinpot dictator and clown, the sort of figure that might have inspired a Charlie Chaplin film.

None of this really bothered Joey. His image in the mainland press was of little interest to him. Shrugging off the criticism, he made the typical Newfoundland comment: "They just don't understand. They don't understand Newfoundland and they don't understand me."

The attitude of the local press, on the other hand, bothered him a great deal, but the greatest efforts of the press to undermine his authority and popularity seemed to do him not the slightest harm at the polls. Between 1949 and 1966 he ran in six elections, without ever losing more than eight seats, mostly in the metropolitan centres where people read the newspapers.

# Fishing in Troubled Waters

THE TASK OF THE OPPOSITION IN NEWFOUNDLAND RIGHT AFTER confederation was not an enviable one. The immediate effect of union was to put a flood of cash from Ottawa into circulation in outports where cash had previously been very scarce indeed. People had been skeptical of Joey's promise that every mother would receive monthly cheques on behalf of her children, every old person a substantial pension, every disabled war veteran enough to make him wealthy by outport standards. But then it happened—in April and again in May— and ten days later the election was held.

The Progressive Conservative Party had inherited personnel from the decimated ranks of the Responsible Government League, for whatever good that might do them. The Economic Unionists had already bolted to the winning side. The PCs had the greatest difficulty even finding a credible leader to contest the election.

They tried Ray Gushue, chairman of the Newfoundland Fisheries Board and later president of the university, a man of high reputation and international standing who would have nothing to do with such a lost cause.

They tried J. B. McEvoy, who would indeed have been a great catch, since it would have removed a little of the anti-confederate colour with which the PCs were so deeply stained.

They tried Captain Len Stick, an outporter and regimental number one from the Royal Newfoundland Regiment, who had been promoted to captain in the field. Stick told them he was a Liberal, and later won a seat in the House of Commons.

They tried Cal Pratt, who looked like a sound choice, a business-man connected with a string of companies and the Board of Trade, with a reputation for soundness, integrity, and intelligence. (Pratt later became a Liberal senator.)

They finally settled on H. G. R. Mews, an insurance manager and city councillor who later became mayor of St. John's. Mews had a lot of charm and political ability. Moreover, he had not been conspicu-ously anti-confederate. But he failed to win a seat in the legislature, defeated in St. John's West by Spratt and Vardy.

Cashin had been elected as an independent, leaving the PCs with five seats, headed by John G. Higgins of St. John's East. All five Conservatives were elected in Catholic districts, by narrow margins. In many of the outports respected candidates running for the PCs collected pitiably few votes. Cyril Parkins, a brilliant speaker and debater, captured a mere 293 in Twillingate; the universally admired Captain George Whiteley received only 190 in St. Barbe; Sam Grant, a well-liked merchant who ran against me in Labrador and knew the district far better than I, received only 133 votes.

Cashin helped matters not at all. He did nothing to conceal his contempt for the pathetic PC Opposition, and set resolutely about becoming an effective one-man Opposition himself.

Smallwood's task, by contrast, was easy. He had boundless popu-larity, the backing of the federal government, and what seemed to be limitless money in the treasury. His first job would be to use some of this money to improve the lot of the less fortunate members of the toiling masses. His second job would be to use the rest of it to finance economic development.

Joey was sincere in his populist politics. The months between the coming of confederation and the coming of the sinister Director-General of Economic Development, Dr. Alfred Valdmanis, were filled with social legislation that put Newfoundland, in this respect, ahead of all the other Canadian provinces. Joey seemed to be deter-mined to make the province a welfare state if not a social democracy.

Federal pensions and transfer payments were well enough, as far as they went. But it was up to the province to supplement them by providing the social services that the feds overlooked. So Newfound-land instituted mothers' allowances, a special kind of welfare for women who had been left to provide for a family by death, desertion, or a disabled husband. Some tut-tutting was heard from the puritans because Joey insisted on including unwed mothers. The Opposition took up the cause. "Subsidizing immorality!" they cried. But Joey was adamant. Children must not be penalized because some man had decamped in the face of a shot-gun wedding. It all sounds rather Victorian today, but the Tories were voicing the majority middle-class opinions of their time.

While dismissing their arguments, Joey coined one of his memorable slogans. "Never again in Newfoundland will there be a hungry child!" he thundered. And Ed Learning, the prankster, taught this slogan to his dog. "What did Joey say?" Ed would ask, and in reply the dog would produce a series of yelps and whines that sounded tolerably like, "Never again in Newfoundland will there be a hungry child."

To the benefit of labour, he produced a new Trade Union Act, providing for registration after supervised votes, comprehensive mediation, union shops, and checkoffs. Workmen's compensation was also needed, so he appointed Irving Fogwill head of a committee to study this complex matter and draw up legislation. Later Fogwill became chairman of the Workmen's Compensation Board.

Joey felt that all medical services ought to be provided without cost to the consumer, but after a committee presented the projected costs of such a service if the provincial government shouldered the burden alone, he backed off, temporized, and introduced medicare for everyone up to the age of sixteen. Even this step had been taken by no other province, and it happened years before medicare was introduced with much fanfare and struggle in Saskatchewan. Newfoundland doctors never uttered a peep against it. After Joey's plan was introduced, a national survey showed that Newfoundland doctors had the highest incomes in Canada, although they served the province with the lowest *per capita* income.

Meanwhile, the Tories made their final effort: they sued Joey for "sitting on the public chest."

The mistake was made during the federal election of June 1949, in which Joey had campaigned vigorously in the two ridings where he still had some opposition: St. John's East and St. John's West. He came close to electing Liberals in all seven seats (a trick he pulled off four years later). But in Ferryland, Peter Cashin's territory, where the pious Catholic lawyer William J. Browne was running for the Tories, Joey overstepped the mark: "I'm sitting on the public chest," he told the voters. "I don't need you. I've been elected. But you need me. I'm sitting on the public chest, and not one red cent will come out of it for Ferryland unless Greg Power is elected."

Browne, interpreting this as intimidation of voters under the Canada Elections Act, collected eighteen affadavits from people who had heard Smallwood speak, and hauled him into court. Under the Act Joey's "crime" could have carried a sentence of two years at hard labour, and Browne, who yearned to see the antichrist hauled into court in handcuffs, asked to have him arrested. The magistrate refused, and issued a summons instead. But that was bad enough. The Tory *Globe and Mail* called it "the most brazen bribe ever offered to Canadian voters." St. Laurent, while washing his hands of the issue, quietly dropped Joey from his list of speakers in the national campaign. The lawsuit was also quietly dropped, after Browne had won the election by the slender margin of 516 votes.

St. John's East was won for the PCs by Gordon Higgins, one of the two best representatives Newfoundland ever sent to Ottawa. The other five seats went to Liberals, whose performance in parliament was disappointing without exception. Joey, it seemed, could deliver the seats, but not the talent. The lopsided popular vote revealed that his star was still rising in Newfoundland: Liberals 72 percent; PCs 28 percent.

Joey now turned his attention to the House of Assembly, which was about to have its first post-confederate session. Well aware of the importance of ceremony in public affairs, and of the crowd-pleasing effect of ritual, he surrounded the legislature with colourful traditions, old and new. He installed pages, impeccably dressed. The sergeant-at-arms wore a sword, and carried a new, gold-plated mace that looked as though it might have come straight from the mother of parliaments itself. Much of the furniture (including the mace) was supplied by Newfoundland's sister provinces, who had asked Joey what Newfoundland would like as a coming-out gift.

Sir Leonard Outerbridge had now replaced Walsh as lieutenant-governor, while Walsh had moved on to the Supreme Court. Outerbridge was almost too perfect in the role. He also wore a sword, and a plumed hat that would have done justice to Napoleon III. His black uniform, covered with silver scrolls, weighed eighty pounds. When he opened the House and read the Speech from the Throne, Outerbridge looked not so much like a lieutenant-governor as King Edward VII. All he needed was a crown.

There were parades, inspections of the guard (the Newfoundland

Constabulary actually carrying rifles), and salutes with field guns. Not content with reviving old ceremonies, Joey invented new ones. The presentation of the Address in Reply to the Speech from the Throne was another opportunity for a parade, he decided. So the members lined up in their morning suits and top hats behind the sergeant-at-arms and walked to Government House, where Outerbridge, in all his finery, received the illuminated address inscribed on parchment from Mr. Speaker in his black and white robes, while the flashbulbs popped. Press and radio referred to it as "the traditional parade to Government House," apparently never suspecting that this was a tradition which Joey had dreamed up himself while listening to Clara's recording of a Beethoven military march in his sitting room.

We had fun during that first session. Occasionally Joey would sit in his place wearing his gray fedora, to the astonishment of the press gallery, who didn't know it was a privilege going back to the British parliament. He'd doff it ostentatiously when rising to address the Chair. He lounged with his feet on his desk, and was unsuccessfully called to order by the Opposition. Though I usually wore a black suit and bow tie, I came to one sitting dressed in clothes made by the Nascaupi Indians of Davis Inlet, but when I asked for permission to present a petition from northern Labrador in the original language, Inuktitut, Mr. Speaker unfortunately ruled that it had to be translated into one of Canada's official languages.

Once a day Joey sent a page to fetch a large chocolate malted milkshake from the soda fountain in a small nearby store, and sat in his place consuming it with great relish while the Opposition turned green at the sight. On one occasion he had a lobster brought to him in its shell, and busied himself with it while speakers on the other side tried to keep their attention focused on the debate. When the leader of the Opposition complained, Joey called a page, and sent the honourable gentleman a claw.

Most members of the legislature were quite unused to being waited upon by pages, but Joey kept them hopping up and down the stairs to the legislative library, and back and forth across the floor with notes. We also circulated bits of doggerel (mostly written by Ted Russell) and caricatures of honourable members. It all helped to relieve the tedium of the debates and the business of slogging through the proofreading of bills in committee of the whole.

Joey rarely left his place on Mr. Speaker's left hand, where the government traditionally sat in Newfoundland, because in the days before central heating that was the warm side of the chamber, near the fireplace. It also happened to be the side where the evening sun shone directly into ministerial eyes. Joey put up with this for only a few weeks before ordering venetian blinds for the tall western windows, and teaching the pages to draw them at a signal. He would leave his place for a cigarette several times during a sitting, but went only as far as the doorway, where he stood blowing smoke into the chamber, and listening to the debates.

That year Joey continued to gather information eagerly, and to make his peace with those who had opposed him. To do both, he and I went to Corner Brook and visited Monty Lewin, the anti-confederate Bowater manager. We travelled in a private rail car and lodged in luxury at Sir Eric Bowater's house, the Viper's Nest (named for his coat of arms). His house servants, trained in pre-war traditions, waited on us as though we were dim-witted British lords.

The trip was about forest policy, for one thing, and we had the luck to meet at the Viper's Nest one of the oddest people I had ever encountered—Sir Shane Leslie, a British forester dressed amid the slush of Corner Brook in kilts and sporan and silver-buckled shoes, complete with a little dirk at his leg.

Forestry, Leslie explained, was not enough. Countries with limited resources of timber and pulpwood must practise *sylviculture*. Joey was impressed not only by Sir Shane's opinions, but perhaps even more by the fact that he was a cousin of Sir Winston Churchill. In any case, he was soon lecturing his followers about the right way to harvest trees, and the need to make forests thrive by seeding and spraying fertilizer from the air. Before long, he had a sylviculturist of his own, imported from Scandinavia. The sylviculturist took a look at the square miles of match-stick fir growing up through the layers of slash left by Newfoundland logging contractors, and recommended controlled burning to get rid of the weedy growth and give spruce a chance to regenerate. Joey recoiled in horror. Start forest fires? Even for the best of reasons? The sylviculturist quietly disappeared.

Joey and Power and I also went to Ottawa in the early summer of 1950 to discuss, among other things, federal services for the Indians and Inuit of Labrador. The federal Indian Act applied to treaty Indians only. We insisted that this was unfair, and such federal services as education were extended to Newfoundland's native peoples, but it took five or six years to accomplish this small bit of elementary justice.

On that trip we flew to Moncton, where Ches Crosbie kept a car for his convenience. In the borrowed car we then drove along the Gulf coast of New Brunswick and Quebec, visiting every town that had a fish plant. Except for the design of the Caraquet longliners, we saw nothing new. In 1950 Canada's Atlantic fishery was less developed than Newfoundland's, and even the longliners were not seaworthy enough for most parts of the open coast.

In the capital we stayed at the Château Laurier, ate in the basement cafeteria, and sometimes roamed the streets of Ottawa after midnight, stopping for fish and chips at a twenty-four-hour restaurant. At that time Joey could still roam around unrecognized, without an official escort. He and I went to see *All the King's Men*, then in its first run at the movie houses. It seemed to be a faithful account of the career of Huey Long, the great American populist-turned-dictator, and Joey was deeply moved by it. We went walking after the show while he discussed Huey Long: "He was misunderstood, you see— deeply misunderstood. A great man, a man with great ideas, a man determined to help the people. And look what happened to him!"

He could dimly foresee that his own career might take such a course. He did not explore the possibility that the fault may have been in Huey Long himself, his character and his political philosophy. Long's ideas on helping the "toiling masses" were uncomfortably close to Joey's own. Those ideas seem to be something Joey never questioned, perhaps never examined, from the early years when he had formed them under the tutelage of Sir Richard Squires, and in the depressed areas of New York.

Joey believed himself to be profoundly committed to unionism, and during his first administration he made an effort to extend unionism to the only major sector of the workforce that was still unorganized (apart from public servants). The fishermen's union organized by Coaker had failed mainly because the Roman Catholic hierarchy at St. John's had forbidden Catholics to join. So when Joey decided to revive it under a new name, he brought in as keynote speaker one of the most famous Catholic priests in Canada, Monseigneur Moses Coady, founder of the famed Antigonish Movement of producer and consumer co-operatives. It would be difficult even for the Archbishop of St. John's to proscribe an organization endorsed by Coady.

On April 2, 1951, 240 fishermen's delegates arrived in St. John's, expenses paid by the government. They divided the map of the province into regions, each of which would have a fishermen's local (like Coaker's) and then spent six days listening to speeches and debating clause by clause a constitution which I wrote for them. They then went home to organize the locals in their regions.

The Newfoundland Federation of Fishermen had an annual operating grant from the government and a general secretary hand-picked by Joey himself—former magistrate Max Lane (who, in 1956, became a member of the House of Assembly and of the Cabinet). Lane ran a full-time office in St. John's and tried to represent the fishermen's interests, but the organization never had any grass-roots drive, never got around to collective bargaining for fish prices, and did its only worthwhile work organizing fish-selling pools so fishermen didn't have to bargain individually with the merchants' buyers. But even that activity was restricted. There was no provision in the Newfoundland labour code for collective bargaining of fish prices—a situation that continued until 1971. This didn't mean that the federation couldn't bargain, merely that the merchants didn't have to. NAFEL continued to set prices, as it had in the past.

The Canadian Labour Congress offered to accept the Newfoundland Federation of Fishermen as an affiliate, but Joey balked at this. Affiliation, he made it clear, would mean the end to government subsidies. Lane and his assistants looked at the possible results of that, and decided the matter should go no further. It was never put to a vote of the membership.

Some of the fresh fish plants were organized, with local unions and collective agreements. The oldest was the Fishermen's and Workmen's Protective Union of Burin, which I had organized in 1946 as an affiliated local of the Newfoundland Federation of Labour. Six other plants were subsequently organized by the Canadian Labour Congress. But all this work was unrelated to the Newfoundland Federation of Fishermen, and the union membership only included people working for wages in the plants—most of them members of fishermen's families, but not fishermen themselves.

Joey was no doubt sincere in his desire to give the fishermen an organization that would effectively represent their interests, but he simply didn't know how to go about it. Despite his claim to have organized unions right, left, and centre in his youth, he really had a very sketchy connection with the labour movement, and no more than vague ideas on how unions were organized, or how they functioned.

His overriding interest, in any case, was not social reform, but industrial development. Industry—*heavy* industry—was his dream, the object of his devotion, his golden key to the kingdom.

In the early 1950s C. D. Howe, Minister of Trade and Commerce, controlled such a wide range of activities in Ottawa that he was nicknamed Minister of Everything. So it was to Howe that Joey went with his need for heavy industry in Newfoundland. He had created the Department of Economic Development with himself as minister, and had hired Gordon Pushie, a former journalist, as his deputy, but up to that point nothing much had happened. He and Pushie just didn't know how to go about getting Algoma Steel or General Dynamics or Alcan to set up shop in Newfoundland. And these were the kinds of industries that Joey had in mind—not fish plants or sail lofts.

"I know just the man for you," Howe told him, and sent Joey off to see one of his departmental flunkies, who, in turn, introduced him to an obscure Latvian with a part-time job teaching economics at Carleton University.* Alfred Valdmanis was also occasional advisor to Howe, and had appeared before the Department of Immigration (smoothing the way for former Nazi collaborators to settle in Canada, it later appeared).

Joey accepted Valdmanis's story uncritically: the Latvian government had educated him, the most brilliant student of his generation, until he had three doctorates; then made him minister of finance, economics and trade, and president of a corporation named Latvian Steel, all before he was thirty. In 1939 the Russians arrived and threw him into jail, but he escaped and hid in the woods. Then in 1941 the Germans arrived, and jailed him again. He was waiting to go before a firing squad when Hermann Goering intervened to save him because they were both Grand Commanders of the Order of Stellar Polaris, conferred by the King of Sweden. He was then forced to work in Germany, but served later at the headquarter of General Eisenhower, Supreme Commander of the Occupation forces, and at the International Relief Organization in Geneva.

Joey made him an offer on the spot, but there were difficulties. Pushie was deputy-minister of economic development. How would he place Valdmanis?

"My Premier," the little Latvian said, "I cannot serve under a deputy. But if you wish I can have a special position. I can be your

---

*Richard Gwyn thought Joey had invented Howe's part in this long after it happened. However, Joey recounted the events to me in this way the day he returned from Ottawa.

director-general of economic development, responsible directly to you."

So Valdmanis, who insisted on always being addressed as "Doctor," received this Germanic title, the first of its kind in North America. There was one more hitch: salary. Deputies, in those days, got about $6,000 a year. Valdmanis couldn't be placed on that level. Joey offered him $10,000, and he accepted. It wasn't the money; it was the prestige, the status. When he discovered that Joey had hired another expert, Clive Planta, to crate the "chart and compass" by which the Newfoundland fisheries were to steer themselves into the twenty-first century, at the unheard-of salary of $15,000 a year, he could not endure the slight. So his salary was reconsidered. Would $25,000 be appropriate? Yes, Valdmanis thought perhaps it would. So that's what he got.

"My Premier," he promised in the summer of 1950, "I will give you one new industry within one year." It turned out to be a cement mill, followed almost at once by a gypsum mill making plaster of Paris and plaster wallboard. Valdmanis knew cement and plaster well because that was part of the work he had done for Hitler—he had been in charge of cement and gypsum production at Biebrich—but he didn't reveal that detail.

The plan was to build the factories using Newfoundland's surplus, sell them, and then build others with the money from the proceeds of the previous sales, and so on ad infinitum. To find builders Valdmanis went to Germany and returned with quotations from Miag for the cement mill and Benno-Schilde for the gypsum mill. They were lower than bids that had come in from the United States, and the plants were built (not at all on schedule, and not within the estimates) at Humbermouth, in the east end of Corner Brook.

Some of the Germans who had come to Newfoundland to build the plants remained to operate them, and they went into production with no more than the usual problems. The only part of the plan that misfired was the matter of selling them to private corporations at anything even close to the cost of construction. It turned out that nobody wanted them. The government would be stuck with the two plants, and the portion of the surplus that had gone into building them (some seven million dollars) would be tied up indefinitely. Moreover, during the first few years the government would have to provide operating capital and cover the annual deficits.

Soon a third plant was on the way. Located at Donovans, just west of St. John's, it was to manufacture plywood and other veneer products from local birch and imported hardwoods. This time there was no trouble finding an operator. The Dawe family, sawmill owners for generations with plants at Bay Roberts and St. John's, had been trying for many years to promote an industry based on Newfoundland birchwood. Chester Dawe Limited gladly took on the management of the veneer mill. The only problem was that Chester Dawe did not have the capital needed to actually buy the plant.

These ventures took care of most of Newfoundland's accumulated surplus. Some of it had gone to build roads and public buildings and some of it had covered a shortfall in revenue, but the rest had gone into the three plants. In future, capital account, whether for public works or economic development, would depend on borrowed money.

But in 1951 Joey told the legislature: "It is unthinkable that we should ever borrow." He thought he had discovered an ingenious alternative. Crown corporations were exempt from federal taxation, and a province could organize a crown corporation which included minority private interests, as long as the private interest did not exceed 10 percent. Joey's brainchild was the Newfoundland and Labrador Corporation—NALCO—with paid-up capital of a million dollars: nine hundred thousand from Newfoundland and one hundred thousand from an array of financiers, including Wood, Gundy and Company; Harriman, Ripley and Company; and Cement and General Development. These truly were names to conjure with, and you may be sure that Joey did just that to great effect at press conferences and in the legislature until Newfoundlanders began to believe that the financial and corporate giants of North America were practically knocking down the doors to get in on the ground floor of vast developments in forestry, minerals, and hydro power.

Joey's spellbinding was as effective as ever, and the press were still reporting him uncritically. If he said that a couple of small mills in Corner Brook would "create more than a thousand new jobs," that's how it was reported. No one bothered to compare the mills with North American plants of similar capacity. Had they done so, they would have discovered that the two mills could not possibly employ more than three hundred people between them. The other seven hundred "new jobs," if they ever existed at all, would be in service industries presumably made necessary by the direct employment of the three hundred mill hands.

NALCO was intended to do more than merely develop natural

resources. It was also supposed to take on the burden of borrowing capital. It would have to raise the money for new mines, mills, hydro installations, and gangs of loggers to cut down the forests of Labrador. That was the reason for shareholders like Wood, Gundy and Company, who were past masters at floating bond issues. If NALCO had functioned as it was supposed to do, it would have become a huge multinational corporation, as vastly in debt as Brazil or Poland, holding almost all the resources of Newfoundland and Labrador as collateral and leaving the government itself free of all direct debt.

But despite the enthusiasm and admiration of Dr. Valdmanis, who told Joey, "My Premier, you have invented a new thing; you have created a new idea in the realm of economic thought," it didn't work at all. Eventually NALCO was sold for the nominal sum of $2 million.

Many of Joey's friends and some of his closest colleagues disliked and distrusted Dr. Valdmanis from the moment they first met him. He looked, dressed, and acted like an undersized storm trooper. He was arrogant, and he was an obvious phoney, a *poseur*. Just as obviously, he held the democratic process in utter contempt.

But to Joey, he appeared to be Newfoundland's saviour. Always a sucker for a smooth con-man, he was never more thoroughly hoodwinked than by the little Latvian "doctor." Within a matter of months, Valdmanis had become, along with Joey himself, the real ruler of Newfoundland, so that Peter Cashin could justly refer, in the House, to "the Smallwood-Valdmanis government."

The first reaction came from Ted Russell, who had succeeded Keough as Minister of Natural Resources in 1950, and who resigned from the government and crossed the floor of the House in March 1951, a year and ten months after his appointment. It was no sudden decision. Russell and I and other "dissidents" had been discussing the government's economic policies for months past, and had agreed that at least some of the new industries were going to go down the drain, taking most of the accumulated surplus with them. We felt that Valdmanis had been an unmitigated disaster. I argued that we should make no move until the first new industry collapsed, but Russell felt that he could not continue to support "the economics of disaster" a minute longer. Joey had predicted in the House that the three new industries would earn "a clean net operating profit of $1.25 million a year." We knew that they would show a net operating loss instead, and indeed that is what they did.

Joey was taken by surprise when Russell left the government and the party, but he quickly recovered and issued dark threats as to what would happen to his former colleague.

"By the time I'm through with Ned Russell," he predicted, "there won't be enough of him left to stuff a thimble."

Russell didn't join the Tories, who might have been able to look after him one way or another. Instead, he became a member of the CCF, and had a very thin time indeed. He ran unsuccessfully in the next provincial election, struggled to find some kind of work by which he could make a living, and even tried selling insurance. Eventually, he invented "Uncle Mose," an outport character who became a great hit, assisted by Russell's excellent voice and good acting, on CBC radio. Later *The Evening Telegram* ran Uncle Mose as a comic strip. Eventually, Russell went back to the profession he had practised as a young man just out of school, becoming a Latin teacher at Prince of Wales College. But it was all hard sledding, for anyone who dealt with him risked Smallwood's displeasure. From Joey's point of view, Ted Russell was a Judas Iscariot. While he was premier, Joey found it easy to forgive his political enemies, to take them into his Cabinets, to exercise what Nimshi Crewe called "the Christian grace of forgiveness." But he was quite unable to forgive a friend who was forced by conscience to disagree with him.

Meanwhile, Joey had taken off with Valdmanis on the first of his many European tours, and was amazed to find that Valdmanis had instant access to virtually every industrialist in Germany. They met the Farbens, the Erhards, the Krupps, all of whom received Valdmanis as if he were an old friend. Alfred Krupp, head of the steel clan that had engineered the rearmament of Germany, was still in jail for war crimes, but Valdmanis had contrived to visit him, carrying messages back and forth to Joey, who hoped, among other things, that Krupp could be lured to Newfoundland to start up a steel industry.

They returned with cases and cases of German wine, which they could bring into Canada because of diplomatic immunity. Using the haul, Alfred Valdmanis started a private wine cellar in St. John's, and tried to refine Joey's tastes, which had never extended beyond the sophistication of the occasional glass of port. The campaign to educate Joey's palate was not a success. Thirty years later his favourite wine was still sweet sherry.

Valdmanis, disliked intensely by members on both sides of the legislature, appeared to have Joey in thrall: "The time will come when Newfoundland will build monuments to Dr. Valdmanis," he declared,

"... I wouldn't want to be head of the government without him ... I'd rather resign ... he's closer to me than any of my brothers or sisters have ever been ...."

Valdmanis had now come up with a new plan for economic development. It was described as a fifty-fifty deal. The government would put up half the cost of each new industry, usually in the form of guaranteed loans. That would relieve everyone except the banks of the need to find the actual cash. The German industrialists, unable to provide money in dollars, would ship machinery to Newfoundland, and find the manpower and "know-how" to a value equal to that of the government-backed loans. The loans would eventually be paid off out of profits—at least, that was the theory.

Joey assured the House that he was "fishing in troubled waters." The Germans, he said, were expecting the Russian armies to sweep over western Europe at almost any time. They were willing to make any sacrifice to escape to Canada in advance of the communist hordes. His announcements of new industries, always made in person, usually at a press conference called for that specific purpose, now came thick and fast.

In June 1951 he announced a great logging operation for Labrador. It was to be headed by Dr. Arthur Seigheim, a Swiss magnate in forest products. The operation, centred on Lake Melville, was to employ 1,500 loggers, settled with their families in two new townsites complete with schools, churches, and shopping centres.

In July he announced a leather tannery, to be built in Conception Bay. Two days later it was an associated plant for fur dressing, dyeing, and the manufacture of leather goods. A glove factory would make fine specialty goods not only from local skins, but also from gazelle skins imported from Africa. A large textile plant, manufacturing cotton goods from imported fibre, would be built on the outskirts of St. John's.

"Fifteen thousand new jobs before the end of the next two years," he announced confidently. "Soon we are going to have two jobs for every man in Newfoundland." He spoke with such conviction that people almost believed the jobs were already there. It was difficult to credit that it was all hype.

That was the period when, according to folklore, Joey advised the fishermen to burn their boats. Actually, he never did anything of the kind, never made any statement or recommendation that could be construed in that way, but he did say many times that most of them would be better off working in the new "plants" at "good cash wages." The nearest anyone came to advising fishermen to burn their boats was in a speech to the legislature by Gordon Janes, the Liberal member for Fogo. Salt fish ran into severe market conditions that year, and many fishermen were discouraged. Janes, from an all-fishing district, echoed their frustration, and the hope for jobs ashore by pounding his desk and repeating, "Their boats are on the bank—and that's where they're going to stay!"

On its first venture into fisheries development, Joey's government had been badly ripped off by the Iceland boat fiasco. It began when a group of smooth-talking foreigners arrived at his door explaining that they were from Iceland, the skippers of herring seiners, and that they were anxious to move to Newfoundland where everything was on the rise, and opportunities for expansion seemed limitless.

Joey was all ears. What did they need? Money. Working capital. With that they could get their boats out of hock and organize a great new herring industry in Newfoundland. No sooner said than done. The Iceland boats arrived, looking like candidates for the scrap heap, and after some delay, they were put to sea with their crews. Nine months later, with six barrels of herring to show for their efforts, and $412,000 in government funds gone down the drain, the Iceland skippers disappeared, leaving the fleet of decrepit seiners behind them. The ships lay around for three years. Then the government "loaned" a local operator $55,000 to "buy" them.

The budget speeches, and the speeches from the throne of this period, reveal the government's reckless haste and naïve optimism. Needless to say, Joey wrote all such speeches himself. The lieutenant-governor, or finance minister, as the case might be, was merely his mouthpiece. The speech from the throne of October 24, 1951, is typical. Here is a brief excerpt:

> The new cement mill at Humbermouth has been completed, and cement is now being manufactured in it. The outlook for this great industrial enterprise is exceedingly bright, and it is anticipated that there will be no difficulty in selling the entire production of cement at profitable prices. It is reliably estimated that for each of the next three years there will be used in Newfoundland more than eight times as much cement as the new mill can produce, and should the deepening of the St. Lawrence Seaway be commenced in the near future, a great additional market for Newfoundland cement will undoubtedly be open. The Humbermouth mill will produce Portland cement of the highest quality, and it will not be

surprising if the mill's productive capacity has to be doubled or trebled within the next year or two . . . .

Very much the same situation is true of the new gypsum plaster, plasterboard, and plaster lath mill. This mill, which is now rapidly nearing completion, will commence production a few weeks hence. It is one of the most modern and efficient factories of its kind in the world, and for its output there is a very brisk demand at profitable prices, both within and without Newfoundland.

The third of the new industries to be launched is the birch veneer and plywood mill. This mill will produce also hardwood flooring, and hardwood doors . . . . The market demands for the products of this mill are quite incapable of being satisfied, and my Ministers have now under consideration a proposition from a very substantial European owner of several such mills for the establishment of a second veneer and plywood mill in Newfoundland. Investigations have revealed that this province contains very large stands of healthy birch, both white and yellow, to provide the raw material for two modern plants. . . .

Construction of the new tannery is proceeding rapidly at Carbonear, and a start has been made on the construction of the large new machinery factory at Donovans. This latter seems likely to become perhaps the largest single labour-giving enterprise in Newfoundland, apart from the fisheries. It is expected, within the next two years or so, to employ five thousand men in full-time work, or more than the number now fully employed in the Corner Brook and Grand Falls paper mills, and the mines of Bell Island, Buchans, and St. Lawrence, all counted together.

The first of the machinery for the new cotton textile mill is scheduled to leave Europe for Newfoundland on the fifth of November next. Construction of the buildings is expected to commence even before that date.

The new leather goods factory is expected to commence early in November, and indeed, before the close of the present calendar year a number of other new industries are due to commence actual construction. My Ministers expect that by the spring of 1962 more than twenty new industries will have commenced production or else be in course of construction.

There were early signs of trouble with some of the "new industries." One of them was a "rubber plant" brought from Germany by a small manufacturer, and installed in a futuristic-looking building at Holyrood, some thirty miles west of St. John's on the shore of Conception Bay. It was to manufacture "all kinds of rubber goods," Joey announced, but persistent reports insisted that the principal product of the factory was intended to be rubber condoms, for sale in what was believed to be a rapidly burgeoning market in Latin America.

Holyrood was an all-Catholic village, and the parish priest was somewhat more than horrified by those rumours. He laid down the law. French safes were against Roman Catholic faith and morals, he declared. If the rubber factory began producing them, he'd order everyone in his parish to refuse to work in it. There was even a suggestion that it might be picketed—permanently.

The rubber factory began producing rubber boots. They leaked. They were dumped on the Montreal market where they retailed for $1 a pair. The rubber factory staggered along, losing money every day it functioned. Finally, it turned out that the machinery in the plant had come from Germany, right enough, but that it had virtually no commercial value. It was obsolete stuff that had been discarded from American factories, and shipped to Europe under the Marshall Plan at the end of the Second World War. Some of the machines still had little metal plaques attached, with the words "Gift of the people of the United States of America for the rehabilitation of Europe."

By the time the rubber factory closed its doors for the last time, it had cost the government many times more than the Iceland boats. The day it closed there was an enormous bonfire in the yard. The pillar of smoke that rose into the sky above the village of Holyrood was seen by passing ships more than a hundred miles off the coast. The futuristic factory then lay vacant for several years, until someone agreed to lease it as a storage shed.

The rubber factory was an extreme example, but it was nonetheless typical of the new industries introduced to Newfoundland by Dr. Alfred Valdmanis. The only ones that could be considered even moderately successful were the first three. They lost money, but they continued to operate, and though the government never got back its investment, it did manage to give them away, or lease them at a purely nominal rate, to parties that continued to operate them without further infusions of government capital. Employment in the cement and gypsum mills at Corner Brook never came anywhere near the figures announced in advance; it fluctuated a great deal, but settled at about 250 jobs for both plants.

The plywood plant at St. John's was eventually joined by another small plant producing chipboard, or pressboard, from scrap and otherwise commercially useless wood. Like cement and gypsum, this was a rational industry, with a local market. The same could not be said for most of the other industries introduced by Valdmanis.

The cotton mill got into production, but soon went bottom up. A battery plant at Topsail operated briefly and unsuccessfully. It was supposed to specialize in sub-zero storage batteries for the Arctic. A small boot and shoe factory operated at a low level. So did a knitting mill. A chocolate factory produced perfectly good chocolate bars, but failed completely when it came to marketing. The gazelle-skin gloves turned out to be in lower demand in the carriage trade than had been supposed.

All this was going on under the "Develop or Perish" slogan, taken from a Smallwood speech in which he had declared, "Newfoundland cannot stand still. We must go ahead, or we will go astern. We must go forward, or we will go back. We must develop or perish!" It was little more than a rewrite of speeches that Sir Richard Squires had made back in the 1920's but Joey thought so well of the harangue that he had it printed for free distribution with the salient passages in boldface type. Then he called a snap election.

The excuse for the election in the autumn of 1951, two and a half years after his landslide victory of 1949, was that the government needed "a specific mandate for the policy of economic development." The real reasons were fiscal, as Smallwood told me privately. The government had spent the cash surplus accumulated by the Commission government. The plan to use NALCO as an agency for floating bonds had failed, since the development corporation just didn't look all that attractive to the financial houses. The government was going to have to go to the bond market itself, and Joey didn't want to start running up a provincial debt a year or two before an election. Newfoundlanders, having been burned before, had a great fear of public debts. Starting to pile up a provincial debt shortly before a general election would just provide the Tories with too much ammunition. Then there was the sales tax. Joey hated the idea of imposing a sales tax, but he could see no other way of balancing even the current account. "It's a direct way of increasing the cost of living," he lamented, "but it seems to be the only thing we can do." Eventually he would extend the sales tax even to basic items of food, but not until well into his second term, and then the Tories would shame him into making food exempt once again by referring to "the food tax" at any and every opportunity.

He waited until the last legal moment before announcing the election, in order to catch the Tories completely off guard. He certainly succeeded. In the election of November 26, 1951, the Progressive Conservative Party failed to nominate candidates in White

Bay, Green Bay, Twillingate, or Labrador. In those four districts Liberals were returned by acclamation.

Joey was upset because two members of his caucus, George Makinson (Port de Grave) and I, refused to seek re-election. The middle-aged Makinson was already drawing a federal pension and developing a cattle farm, so his decision was understandable, but Joey was shocked when he learned I was refusing to run. He had already publicly named me as his heir apparent (the first of many), and he assured me that I'd fill the first Cabinet vacancy. I assured him that nothing would change my mind, that politics simply wasn't my game. So we parted good friends—for a while.

The PCs elected five members and the Liberals twenty-three, but the Liberal Al Vardy, elected in St. John's West, resigned almost immediately, and in the by-election of February 7, 1952, he was replaced by Malcolm Hollett for the PCs. This reduced the Liberal strength to twenty-two and increased the Tory strength to six. But in Ferryland, where the Tory Gus Duffy had defeated Myles Murray by only two votes, a recount discovered irregularities in the election, and a by-election, held September 25, 1952, returned Murray by a margin of 336 votes. The Liberals were thus back to twenty-three and the Tories to five, but in Hollett the Opposition at last had a leader who would serve continuously for the rest of the 1950s.

A year later, with a federal election looming, Joey pulled off one of his minor political *coups*. He got rid of Peter Cashin, by far his most vocal critic in the House of Assembly, and at the same time managed to elect a Liberal MP in St. John's East, which until then had been the most solidly Tory riding in Newfoundland. Cashin resigned his seat in the legislature to run as an independent against Gordon Higgins. As Joey foresaw, this split the Tory vote, and for the first time the riding of St. John's East returned a Liberal, A. M. Fraser, to the House of Commons.

In the same election, Janet Fogwill and I and several others set out with determination to defeat W. J. Browne in St. John's West. Jim Power won the riding for the Liberals by a margin of 940 votes. Thus, for the first time, the Liberals made a clean sweep of the Newfoundland ridings. It was a feat Joey would repeat ten years later in the general election of 1963.

Browne, the defeated Tory MP, then had himself nominated for Cashin's vacant seat in the Newfoundland legislature, and took it by acclamation on March 9, 1954. The Tory strength, which had fallen to four seats was now back up to five, under Hollett's leadership.

Joey rewarded Peter Cashin for helping him pull off this stunt by making him director of civil defence (later "emergency services") for Newfoundland, a position that he held, virtually free of all duties, until his retirement ten years later.

While those political machinations were afoot, the economic development program went ahead full speed. The greatest project of all was the machinery plant built at Octagon Pond, west of St. John's. At first, Joey explained, it would have just one or two large buildings, but once into production it would expand rapidly until it covered scores of acres and employed tens of thousands of workers. The plan included an adjoining housing development that amounted to a satellite city.

Joey brought C. D. Howe to St. John's to open the machinery plant in September 1952, and assured us privately that the Canadian Department of Defence would place a massive order for machine gun barrels that would keep the first stage of the plant busy for years. Also at the opening was the then-mysterious figure of Sir William Stephenson ("the man called Intrepid") who had managed important areas of the British intelligence network during the Second World War, including the tricky business of liaison with the Americans. Stephenson was now chairman of NALCO, the Cement and General Development Corporation, and various other companies.

One of Stephenson's plans as chairman of NALCO was to raise a ten-million-dollar bond issue with which to buy the first three new industries from the government of Newfoundland. The offer of the bond issue had fallen flat. Not a bond had been sold. A little over a month after the opening of the machinery plant, Stephenson resigned his chairmanship.

The order for the machine gun barrels never materialized either. Instead, the machinery plant made truck bumpers and school desks for the Newfoundland government. It never expanded beyond its original size—one fairly large building—and never employed more than a few score people. Indeed, it was just a fairly large machine shop. But like the first three industries, it never quite closed down either. It eventually passed into the hands of the MacNamara Construction Company at a great loss to the government.

Perhaps the most astonishing incident of the economic development program involved "Dr." Luther Sennewald, the eyeglass specialist. Also involved was a man the Tories called "the sinister Max Braun-Wogan," whom Joey always referred to as "Max Brown," to make him sound like a nice guy from down the street.

Sennewald had apparently met Smallwood in Germany in 1950, and they had discussed what Joey called "an optical factory" for Newfoundland. Eyeglasses, frames, microscopes, and lenses were all to be manufactured by a special process that Sennewald had invented himself. His products were touted as world-beaters. At a meeting in the Colonial Building's Cabinet Room a microscope, reputed to be built by Sennewald, was demonstrated for the benefit of Liberal caucus members. It was small but powerful, and showed beautiful purple images of microbes on a glass slide.

"What are those?" Joey enquired.

"Oh, that happens to be gonococcus."

"Is that what causes the clap?"

"Yes."

Les Curtis, known far and wide as "The Horney Attorney" because of his sexual appetites, was standing by.

"Hey, Les!" Joey called. "Come meet some of your old friends."

Curtis grinned good-naturedly, but tried to marshall the Cabinet against the Sennewald deal. It was postponed and all but forgotten until the last two weeks of the 1951 election campaign when Sennewald wired the Tories from his office in Germany promising to produce "all documents revealing surprising manipulations in both St. John's and Germany behind all new industries. Ready to come immediately if you pay expenses."

The Tories rushed off the expense money and published the telegram. But Sennewald, on landing in Gander on his way to St. John's, mysteriously vanished, documents and all. He had been met at the airport by Max Braun-Wogan, the German mystery man, founder of something called "Neue Technique Corporation", and now a member of Valdmanis's staff. Braun-Wagon whisked Sennewald on board an RCAF Canso bomber borrowed from the Canadian government, and flew him to St. John's. There he was interviewed by Valdmanis and Smallwood, following which he issued a statement saying there had been a serious misunderstanding. Then he flew back to Germany. The Tories said he had been kidnapped, and hinted darkly at methods that might have been borrowed from Hitler's Gestapo.

When the House reconvened for the thirtieth General Assembly, Joey introduced legislation for the optical factory. But after a few weeks Greg Power, who was minister of finance in the new government, received a call from the Bank of Montreal in St. John's, reporting that Sennewald was transferring the money paid by the government for the optical plant to an account in Montreal as fast as he was receiving it. Sennewald himself was in Montreal, and had not been seen in St. John's for some time. Power ordered a search of the warehouse used by Sennewald. His cases of optical equipment, supposed to be equal in value to the government advances, turned out to be filled with stones, scrap metal, packing, and a few small items, such as the microscope, that could be used for show.

Gordon Pushie, the former deputy-minister for economic development and now Joey's executive assistant, rushed off to Montreal with a warrant for Sennewald's arrest. He arrived in the nick of time. Sennewald had already bought airline tickets to three foreign countries. Instead of calling in the police, Pushie persuaded Sennewald to return the money in exchange for immunity from prosecution. He went back to St. John's with $110,000 in a suitcase.

Malcolm Hollett and Bill Browne, from their seats on the Opposition side, did their best to keep alive the names of Dr. Sennewald and Dr. Seigheim, but Joey refused to mention them. By the time he got around to writing his memoirs twenty years later he seemed to have forgotten that they ever existed. "Max Brown" suffered the same fate. He failed to win an entry even in *The Encyclopedia of Newfoundland and Labrador*.

Altogether, the government sank about $50 million into the Valdmanis phase of economic development. Not all the money was wasted: four of the plants survived after a fashion, returning nothing to the government, but giving work to a few hundred people. Even the NALCO deal was not a total fiasco. Its hydro power, forest, and mineral surveys prepared the way for important developments that came later.

The crown corporation had a curious history. First, it was given vast blocks of resources in Newfoundland and Labrador; then, when it proved unable to promote development or float bond issues, Joey decided to "un-crown" it by offering its shares for sale on the open market. The sale began in April 1953, and continued until September. Meanwhile, Dr. Valdmanis resigned as director-general of economic development, to become chairman of NALCO at a salary of $30,000 a year. But NALCO was actually in process of withering away, its assets transferred to two other companies. The British Newfoundland Corporation (BRINCO), a brain child of Joey's, got the lion's share, including thousands of square miles of mineral rights, and the hydro power of Churchill Falls in Labrador. A little company that manufactured iron frying pans in Quebec got the rest.

When Valdmanis moved to NALCO, it was already obvious that his schemes for economic development in Newfoundland had failed. He was by no means the economic wizard that his *curriculum vitae* suggested. But he was bright enough to see within a year of their opening ceremonies that every one of his new industries was in deep trouble. Six months after the election that had been called ostensibly to provide a mandate for economic development, he was already proposing a moratorium on the mad career of factory construction. Joey, still friendly with the Latvian, rejected the advice.

Valdmanis's fall from favour was not the sudden thing it must have seemed to the public. Greg Power, now holding the senior portfolio of finance, had always disliked and distrusted him. By 1953 even Joey would have had to be deaf and blind not to know that there was much more in his director-general's past than the director-general had ever admitted. He had asked the RCMP to look into Valdmanis's record, and the RCMP had given him a clean bill of health. But during the 1950s any European fascist or former Nazi who had not actually been a part of Hitler's inner circle would be likely to get a clean bill of health from the RCMP, as Joey knew perfectly well.

A few of the German nationals who had come to Newfoundland were members of the Social Democratic or Christian Democratic Parties, which had been underground throughout the Hitler era. They declared that Valdmanis himself and the people with whom he was most closely associated were all former supporters of Hitler. Even graver were the charges contained in a document made public by W. J. Browne. It was a statement dating back to 1943 by the Latvian refugee Gregory Miskins, which described Valdmanis as the Latvian Quisling—Hitler's man in the little Balkan state, a Nazi collaborator from the very beginning. The most serious charge of all was that he had been involved in the effort to raise the "Balkan Waffen SS," a proposed army of a hundred thousand men recruited from the Balkan states to fight for Hitler on the eastern front. If the charges were true, Valdmanis was a traitor and a war criminal.

Instead of merely asking the RCMP to check his dossier, Joey might have had the Latvian investigated properly. He didn't. He decided instead to ignore the matter while it rankled at the back of his mind and increased the coldness of relations between himself and the other half of "the Smallwood-Valdmanis government."

When Valdmanis moved to NALCO his star was already setting. It was June 1953. He had been running Newfoundland's economic development program for only three years, but already it seemed like an entire era. His efforts to attract new investments to NALCO were coming to nothing. Six months after his appointment he moved NALCO's head office to Montreal "to be nearer the great investment houses." Actually, his family had always lived in Montreal. In St. John's Valdmanis had enjoyed only the company of his confidential secretary, a gorgeous Latvian blonde named Olga Leikus. She followed him to the mainland.

He had been chairman of NALCO for only eight months when Joey called him into his office and coldly announced, "I want your resignation, right away." Accustomed as he was to dealing with dictators, Valdmanis didn't argue or ask questions. "Yes, my Premier," he said, snapping to attention. "Good," said Joey, and dismissed him with a wave of the hand. Valdmanis clicked his heels and walked out of the office, his back rigid.

He assumed that his dismissal was caused by his failure to create an economic revolution in Newfoundland. In his letter of resignation he thanked the Premier for the "difficult but proud years of co-operation while pursuing your policy of economic development...pray forgive me where I have failed."

What had actually happened had nothing to do with failure. Greg Power had caught him padding his expense accounts and pulling down a double salary as chairman of NALCO while still drawing the last three months of his pay as director-general of economic development. By this means he had pilfered upwards of $10,000. It was the kind of petty greed that Joey despised in some of his ministers.

He now recalled, so his own story goes, that one or two of the German-Latvian community in Newfoundland had tried to question him about Valdmanis's role as a fund raiser for the Liberal Party. Fund raiser? Did that mean graft over and above the small-time stuff unearthed by Power?

Joey had no qualms about party funds. He spent millions of dollars on his election campaigns, and the money didn't all come from impulses of pure generosity among Liberal-minded business houses.

He didn't object to people using their positions to gain special privilege, either. They were all doing it. Newfoundland had no conflict-of-interest legislation. But he tended to draw the line at actual cash payments that went into private pockets instead of into the party treasury.

Late one night, Joey's story continues, he received a visit from "a man for whom I had great respect." Apparently he went so far as to identify the man as "a Latvian engineer." In any case, they cruised around the outskirts of St. John's in Joey's limousine while the visitor told him how Valdmanis had collected commissions from Miag and Benno-Schilde on the building of the cement and gypsum mills. The commissions were supposed to be funds for the Liberal Party of Newfoundland, and amounted to about half a million dollars. The pair drove back to Joey's office, and there the informer repeated his story to Finance Minister Greg Power. The man then left, and Joey called the Newfoundland superintendent of the RCMP, D. A. MacKinnon.

Power is unable to recall the name of the Latvian who helped put the finger on Valdmanis, but he says he was alerted to Valdmanis's impending downfall by his own housekeeper, who happened to be a German-speaking woman in touch with the European immigrant community. Such are the backstairs routes by which the mighty are brought low.

Joey's interview with MacKinnon was brief and to the point. Valdmanis was a rogue, and it was the RCMP's duty to get the goods on him. His last words to MacKinnon were: "Find the money, Superintendent. If you don't find the money, even the Atlantic Ocean won't wash me clean—everyone will believe that the money was truly for me or the Liberal Party."

It might have been just as well for Joey had he never recorded this demand, because neither MacKinnon nor anyone else ever found the money. And it wasn't just half a million dollars; it was much more.

Later that day, Joey says, MacKinnon flew to Ottawa. The RCMP put a tail on Valdmanis and enlisted the help of the FBI. Together, RCMP and FBI operatives went to the offices of the American Express Company in New York, where the German firms were reported to have deposited the "commissions," and secretly photographed the files. Once they thought they had enough evidence, they followed Valdmanis to New Brunswick, where his brother Osvald was manager of a small fish plant manufacturing cat food. At the village of Chamcook, just north of St. Andrews on the Bay of Fundy, they waited until just before three o'clock in the morning of April 24, 1954.

Then they pounded on the door of Osvald's darkened house, swarmed up the stairs, and arrested Valdmanis out of his bed. They took him to the nearest airport in handcuffs, and flew him to St. John's the next day.

The Opposition in the House of Assembly had been carrying on an investigation of their own. They already knew that Valdmanis was part owner of the St. Andrews fish plant, of which his brother was manager. They knew that he owned a Latvian newspaper in Toronto. They knew that he was connected with a company named "Douay Export" in New York. They knew that his Montreal home was beautifully furnished. It seemed to add up to more than could be accounted for by three years of the generous salaries Newfoundland had been paying him. Soon they were spreading a story that Joey had not really initiated the action against Valdmanis, but that it had started with an income tax investigation in Ottawa. The RCMP, they said, had warned him that the tax probe was underway, and he had hastened to take credit for the arrest of the Latvian before the story broke in the press. They demanded Smallwood's resignation.

The trial, when it came, was an anticlimax, because the case was never argued and defended in open court. Valdmanis was at first charged with fraud involving $200,000 extorted from the firm of Benno-Schilde, builders of the gypsum mill. Then he was charged with receiving $270,000 from Miag, who had built the cement mill. The last instalment from Miag had been deposited in New York in 1951, but the last from Benno-Schilde had not been deposited until February 24, 1954. Joey felt this cleared him from the charge that the money had been collected on behalf of the Liberal Party. It was deposited a few days *after* Valdmanis had resigned as chairman of NALCO, though Valdmanis was still a director. Others insisted that this made no difference. The Opposition felt they had Joey on the run, and they hammered away at him relentlessly.

The Grand Jury (*in camera*, of course) found a true bill, and Valdmanis was ordered for trial. As his lawyer he chose Gordon Higgins, the principal Tory spokesman for the province. It took Higgins two weeks to raise the $50,000 bail to get Valdmanis out of jail and into a modest hotel room. From the hotel Valdmanis phoned Canada House and got Joey on the line. He asked permission to come and see him. Joey refused. He pleaded for mercy. Joey told him coldly that the matter would be left entirely in the hands of the courts. He wept. The premier was unmoved. He could not forgive what he regarded as a personal betrayal, and he felt that he had been personally betrayed. Within two days he had Valdmanis back behind bars, this time with bail set at $270,000, the amount his former director-general had allegedly defrauded from the cement mill. He launched a civil suit for the collection of that amount.

"This," Higgins declared hotly, "is persecution, not prosecution." Higgins was unable to raise the additional bail, and his client stayed in a prison cell until brought to court by the police to stand trial four months later.

While in jail awaiting trial it became known that Valdmanis was a barbital addict. He was unable to sleep—virtually unable to live—without regular doses of the drug known in the underground as "goof balls." Interviewed by a Toronto *Telegram* reporter, he broke down and wept. A doctor who visited him in prison reported that had he not known Valdmanis's history he would have judged him to be suffering from acute mental illness, probably unfit to stand trial.

In the end, Attorney-General Les Curtis allowed Valdmanis to cop a plea. The Latvian agreed to plead guilty to one charge—the $200,000 fraud involving the gypsum plant—if the other charges were dropped. This prevented any evidence from getting into open court. Chief Justice Sir Albert Walsh sentenced him to four years at hard labour in Her Majesty's penitentiary, and he was taken back to prison. It was all over, at least as far as the court was concerned.

The matter was now out of Joey's hands, and in the hands of the prison officials, and they proceeded to treat Valdmanis as leniently as possible. He was soon moved from the St. John's prison to the prison farm for first offenders at the Deer Park on the Salmonier Line. He worked there as a school teacher, and reportedly was very popular with the prisoners. He was sometimes allowed to go fishing in the nearby Salmonier River, and once or twice, he had leave to visit St. John's. He was also allowed on medical prescription to have the goof balls to which he was addicted. Within a year and a half he was released on parole.

Joey had nothing whatever to do with this lenient treatment. On the contrary, he would have treated Valdmanis as vindictively as he was treating Ted Russell. He wanted Valdmanis kept in jail for the maximum term, and refused to support his application for parole. But Valdmanis had been cleared by the parole board, and Les Curtis—as he would have done for any other prisoner—proceeded to sign the documents for his release. He was freed, and immediately left the province.

After it was all over, the mystery remained. What had happened to

Some of Joey's John Wesley icons. Writings, books, pictures, sermons, biographies all added up to one of the world's largest collections of Wesleyana. The eighteenth-century religious reformer held a lifelong fascination for the populist politician.

Only stay in hospital during his premiership was at Toronto in 1976, when he had an operation for a detached retina. Until his sudden collapse with a stroke in 1984 he enjoyed phenomenal good health. During all his years in the House of Assembly, he never lost a day because of illness.

He collected cartoons — those that showed him in a favourable light. The far larger number that portrayed him as a tyrant or a clown he ignored.

oey introduces John Diefenbaker to Eleanor Roosevelt. Bringing the former First Lady of America to St. John's for the official opening of the new university campus was one of his triumphs. He had shared a political platform with her in the American presidential election of 1928.

The third and fourth generations. Joey with his grandson, Joey Smallwood II, and his great-grandson, Joey Smallwood III.

"Arrest that man!" At a student demonstration against the oil refinery deal, Joey demands the arrest of a demonstrator who, he said, had spit at him. The heavy-set man at centre is an RCMP plainclothesman. Two students were arrested and released without trial.

the money? How much was it? According to people connected with the new industries, it was a great deal more than the $470,000 mentioned in the two charges. And indeed, why would such a skilled international criminal have ceased his activities with the first two of the fifteen new industries built before his fall from power? Most of those industries were German or German-Swiss, and most of them were brought to Newfoundland through Valdmanis's efforts. Some of them had cost more than the cement and gypsum mills combined.

But one thing became perfectly clear. Valdmanis didn't have the money, and his family didn't have it—at least not in any significant amount. He continued to insist that he had collected it for the Liberal Party, though he never explained by what route he had delivered it, if at all. One of his relatives had power of attorney to operate the account in New York, and payments out of that account had gone to purchase the New Brunswick fish plant—allegedly for far more than the plant was worth. Still, that outlay could accounted for only a small fraction of the total. Valdmanis was said to have muttered "blackmail" on at least one occasion when asked about the money, but there is no real evidence for this either. The possibility cannot be ruled out however. Valdmanis was quite clearly a collaborator who had worked for Hitler, who should never have been allowed into Canada, and who might easily be sent back to Germany to stand trial for war crimes. Thus he was a suitable subject for blackmail, provided someone with the right connections had the goods on him.

When Attorney-General Curtis went after Valdmanis's assets, the Latvian declared bankruptcy. The amount recovered from his bankrupt estate was $13,452.39—just about the value of the furniture then remaining in his house in Montreal.

A few years after his release he was killed in an automobile accident. Fifteen years after his death his heirs were still living in very modest circumstances. Obviously, they had not benefited from the proceeds of massive extortion, or any major part of it. Most of the money had gone somewhere else.

As late as 1988 professional historians were still working on "the Valdmanis problem," trying without success to unravel the mystery of the disappearing money, which—they were now convinced—had actually exceeded a million dollars.

# CHAPTER 11

# A Grand Imperial Concept

ON A FINE SUMMER DAY IN 1950 JOEY WAS FLYING IN AN AIRPLANE OWNED by mining magnate Jules Timmins from Goose Bay to Knob Lake, where Timmins was developing an iron mine that straddled the Quebec-Labrador border. They flew westward along the Hamilton River, Labrador's largest waterway, to the edge of the great Labrador Plateau, where the river surges and tumbles over falls and cataracts for a total drop of a thousand feet, finally plunging over an escarpment twice as high as Niagara's into Bowdoin Canyon. There the plane banked in a tight circle to give the passengers a close look at one of the world's greatest waterfalls. What most of them saw was a river heaped into ridges by its own pressure, then churned into spray that rose like clouds of smoke hundreds of feet into the sky. What Joey saw was millions of horsepower of energy galloping uselessly downriver toward the sea.

At that time Joey had developed a most unlikely friendship with the premier of Quebec, the diminutive leader of the Union Nationale party, Maurice Duplessis, a parochial politician who travelled around his province with motorcade escorts, padlocked the offices of heretics, and was widely regarded as Canada's homegrown Mussolini. They visited Knob Lake together at least twice, the second time for the official opening of Timmins's mine. And according to Joey, they "pissed across the border" to show their contempt for each other's territory. He thought the incident very funny.

With Duplessis he even talked in a friendly, half-serious way about the possibility that Quebec might buy Labrador from Newfoundland. Duplessis thought a hundred million ought to be enough for it. Joey thought two hundred and fifty million nearer the mark.

"It wouldn't have to be in cash, of course," he said. "The annual interest would be fine—say, twelve to fifteen million a year. Know what we'd do with the money? We'd build a road *right around the coast of Newfoundland*, from settlement to settlement." He loved to toy with such dreams.

They visited Sept Îles together for the opening of the Quebec North Shore and Labrador Railway, which connected Knob Lake to the Gulf of St. Lawrence through Newfoundland and Quebec territory, and Joey had fun assuring Maurice that now his claim to Labrador was officially recognized, even by the government of Quebec, he had "no further territorial ambitions." Just the same, the border was to prove a problem in the future, not because Quebec's claim had any substance, but because in that province the border continued to be a political hot potato.

Duplessis was well aware of the power potential of the Hamilton watershed, and also of the five rivers flowing out of Labrador through Quebec to the Gulf of St. Lawrence. Their headwaters were unfortunately controlled by Newfoundland, and some kind of accommodation would eventually have to be made if their enormous waterpower was ever to be developed. But the time was not ripe for it, and before he and Joey could strike any kind of deal (assuming one was possible) Duplessis's political career came to an end.

Two years after Joey's first flight over the falls, he got in touch with Lord Beaverbrook, a Canadian by birth who had risen to the highest councils in Great Britain during the Second World War. Beaverbrook was a personal adviser and close friend of Prime Minister Winston Churchill. Joey asked him to arrange a meeting.

He met Churchill privately at Number Ten Downing Street on August 14, 1952, and carried into the Council Room, where Churchill received him, a large map of Labrador which he laid on the table while he explained to the prime minister his dream of a huge British consortium like the East India Company or the Hudson's Bay Company, organized not for trade, but for development. "The last chance," he called it, "for Britain to undertake a great colonial venture—waterpower, minerals, forests. If Britain doesn't do it, the Americans will: they're already in Labrador developing the iron mines. But this would be an empire in itself. Look at the great Hamilton Falls alone: five million* horsepower—five *million*. We'll make tens of thousands of square miles available. It'll be the biggest real estate deal of this century...."

Churchill latched onto the idea at once.

"It's a grand imperial concept," he growled, then remembered to add a qualifier: "I use 'imperial' in the *good* sense."

"May I quote that, sir?" Joey asked.

"By all means," Churchill assured him. He introduced the visitor to his financial expert, Lord Leathers, whom he asked to expedite the scheme in every possible way.

Joey rushed off to Fleet Street, and next day the English papers were full of the story. They quoted Churchill's "grand imperial concept" over and over. They quoted Joey's opinion that no British company, even the biggest, would be able to carry out the venture alone. There would have to be a huge combination of bankers, mining companies, developers, promoters, experts in every field. A new empire of the north was to be founded.

The British public lapped it up. Seven years after the war, Britain was still deeply in debt, her economy stagnant, her people accustomed to austerity, and looking toward ever-shrinking horizons. The days when "Land of Hope and Glory" had been sung in every school—and believed—seemed to be gone for good. But here they were being offered a scheme that even Cecil Rhodes might have approved. Letters poured into the Savoy Hotel, where the Newfoundland premier was staying. His phone kept ringing. Hundreds of professionals wanted to volunteer their services. Some sent cheques and money orders to help along the promotion (he had to return these). Joey reported it all to the press, and they kept asking for the names of the companies who would undertake the great development, but he had no names as yet.

Then Sir Eric Bowater, whose North American empire had been founded in Newfoundland, and whose family had lived there during the war, mentioned the matter to the Rothschilds, who had helped to finance some of his own far-flung enterprises. After a decent interval, the Rothschilds invited Joey to lunch at their family business headquarters, a pre-Victorian building in which their ancestors had arranged for the purchase of the Suez Canal, and had raised the two

---

*Surveys later boosted this to seven million.

million pounds that the Duke of Wellington needed to finance the Battle of Waterloo.

Anthony de Rothschild, the aging head of the English house, presided with his nephew Edmund de Rothschild, who later inherited the leadership of the bank, and paid several visits to Newfoundland and Labrador. Lord Bessborough, a former governor-general of Canada, who was related to the Rothschilds by marriage, sat with them as well, along with other partners and senior officials.

The Rothschilds' approach puzzled Joey. The meeting seemed to be more like a social visit, in which everyone lingered over sherry, and chatted about world events. They gave him the place of honour at the head of the table while lunch was served, and they listened politely while he talked about Labrador. Still there were no negotiations. Only later did he understand British upper-class customs well enough to realize that bargaining over meals was considered to be barbaric.

The business meeting came afterwards, and lasted an hour. Joey was quite unsure of his success until, as everyone was leaving, Anthony de Rothschild asked, "Do you wish us to put this thing together for you?" He replied eagerly, "Yes, yes indeed!"

Joey rushed off to Winston Churchill to thank him and tell him the news. Churchill nodded and puffed cigar smoke at him and gave him an autographed copy of his latest book, *The Closing of the Ring* (a volume in his continuing history of the war). There was another round of publicity in Britain, and Joey flew home to announce it to the press and the legislature.

The St. John's papers greeted the plan with their usual enthusiasm. No matter what you thought of Joey and his schemes, they were always great copy. But the Opposition, used to seeing those schemes fall flat on their faces, greeted it all with total skepticism. The British Newfoundland Corporation was now known under the acronym BRINCO, and Opposition Leader Malcolm Hollett made one of the great bloopers of his career by standing in his place and calling it BUNCO. Nevertheless, when it came to a vote, he and his colleagues supported the BRINCO bill and the leasing of ten thousand square miles of Labrador resources to the new company.

The Rothschild consortium included many of the great corporate names in Britain—six banks besides their own, such mining giants as Rio Tinto, Frobisher, and the Anglo-American Corporation of South Africa, forestry and development companies such as Bowater's, Imperial Chemical, and English Electric. Finally a pair of Canadian banks, the Royal Bank of Canada and the Bank of Montreal, bought into the company. Churchill arranged a waiver, in BRINCO's favour, of the British regulations against the export of Stirling.

Over the succeeding decade, BRINCO spent tens of millions of dollars on mineral surveys in Newfoundland and Labrador without finding any major field that could be developed into a mine. The vast iron fields of the Labrador Trough were already taken, and what remained was not very promising. True, they made some interesting discoveries: an enormous deposit of uranium ore at Monkey Hill near Makkovik on the Labrador coast, causing Joey to look positively smug as he announced quietly to the House "the discovery of a great new uranium *province*"; substantial copper and copper ore at Seal Lake in central Labrador, including a few chunks of pure copper as large as bricks; and a smaller copper-lead deposit in Newfoundland that could be mined economically. The uranium came too late. Five years earlier it might have started a stampede to Makkovik. But by the time it was discovered, it was already a drug on the market, though it was not yet a dirty word. They had no better luck with the forests. They owned millions of cords of prime black spruce around Lake Melville, but there was no way to market it.

BRINCO was soon concentrating its efforts on one thing: the development and sale of power from Hamilton Falls—shortly to be renamed in honour of Winston Churchill.

The river and falls that drain most of western Labrador have gone through a series of name changes which make the various names under which the development took place very confusing to anyone not familiar with their history. First the Indians called the river the Asuanipi (Ass-you-*wan*-a-pee); parts of the upper reaches still bear that name. The white trappers who travelled the river from coastal Labrador late in the eighteenth century called it the Grand River, and named the falls Grand Falls. Then Sir Charles Hamilton, governor of Newfoundland from 1818 to 1825 renamed the river, and the huge bay into which it flows, in honour of himself. The falls remained Grand Falls, and were rarely visited because the route travelled by the trappers and Indians followed a chain of lakes, circumventing Grand Falls to the north and west. When I began writing about Labrador for the Newfoundland press in 1950 I decided this simply wouldn't do. There was already a Grand Falls in Newfoundland, and another in New Brunswick. I changed the name to Hamilton Falls, and everyone thankfully took it up. That name lasted until February 4, 1965, when, following Winston Churchill's death, Joey renamed the river and falls in his honour.

BRINCO spent $17 million proving the power potential of the Churchill, then faced years of frustration trying to find a way to market it. In the beginning it seemed that the only likely markets were in New England and New York. This gave Joey one of his great slogans. "Labrador power will light Broadway!" he told a New York audience, then repeated it all across the country.

Quebec, however, stood in the way. And Joey's dear friend Maurice Duplessis had been replaced by that far tougher customer, the smooth-talking, gentle-mannered, but iron-hard Jean Lesage, once a Liberal Cabinet minister in Ottawa, now architect of Quebec's Quiet Revolution. Lesage looked at the map, decided that the only way Joey could reach New England with a power line was through Quebec, and proceeded to try to divert the Newfoundland government's share of the profits into his own treasury.

At first he demanded that Quebec must be a full partner in the development. When Joey wouldn't agree to this, Lesage dropped the matter, but proceeded to nationalize Quebec power, and with it Shawinigan Engineering, a company that owned a great power station at Shawinigan Falls, north of the St. Lawrence. Shawinigan also happened to own 20 percent of the Churchill project. Joey was enraged, believing that Lesage was attempting a takeover of his grand imperial project. Lesage denied having such a motive, but suggested that the British ought to be kicked out, and the whole thing nationalized, Quebec and Newfoundland acting in partnership. Joey refused. If that couldn't be done, then Lesage insisted that Quebec must buy the power at "point A" as he called the border, refusing to name it. He would thus control the sale of power and the collection of taxes. All this was eventually conceded, but even then BRINCO and Quebec couldn't agree on a price. A gap of twenty-five hundredths of a cent per kilowatt-hour remained between BRINCO's lowest selling price and Quebec's highest offer. A quarter of a tenth of a cent may not seem to be much, but on a sale of five million horsepower it translated into about $20 million a year.

The whole manoeuvre was disheartening. Lesage suggested that changes might be made to the Quebec-Labrador boundary to "settle the matter once and for all." It had, in fact, been settled nearly thirty years before, when Canada, at Quebec's request, had referred the matter to the Privy Council, the court of last resort, and the Privy

Council had confirmed Newfoundland's contention that the border lay at the height of land. This settlement had later been written into the constitution of Canada, becoming one of the terms of union between Canada and Newfoundland in 1949, but it took a royal commission and eighteen volumes of academic studies to establish this simple fact in Quebec. The "settlement" Lesage wanted was the watersheds of the five rivers that flowed out of Labrador into the St. Lawrence, which would give him masses of undeveloped hydro power in an area easy to reach. That would involve moving the border northward to the watershed of the Churchill. In exchange, he suggested that in the far north the border might be moved westward to the George River, giving Newfoundland about the same amount of territory that she would be giving up in the south. With such a deal, perhaps he'd be willing to compromise on the transmission line, and since few voters ever looked at maps it could be "sold" to Quebec voters as a "settlement" in Quebec's favour.

Joey wavered. He dropped a few hints as to what was afoot, flew a cautious political kite, and got a furious reaction from the uninformed Newfoundland public. Give away Labrador? Newfoundland's fabulous heritage? Heaven forbid! His attitude promptly stiffened, and he made his first public statement on the matter. Yes, there had been feelers from Mr. Lesage about a deal that would involve moving the boundary, but he had rejected them at once. Not *one inch* of Newfoundland territory, he declared loudly, would ever be alienated while his government was in power. And that was the end of the matter. He turned, instead, to the question of building a power line around Quebec to the east.

This proposal—"the Anglo-Saxon Route"—painted Quebec politicians as a greedy, unreasonable gang with whom you couldn't do business. Better to deal with Nova Scotia, filled as it was with true-blue Anglo-Saxons, the province of New Brunswick, and the friendly state of Maine. Joey talked with the two premiers and the governor of Maine and found them reasonable. Meanwhile, negotiations for passage through Quebec were simply dropped.

The Anglo-Saxon Route received a flood of publicity. The proposal was to build a transmission line eastward (*not* southward, as Joey kept saying) a distance of four hundred miles to the Strait of Belle Isle, then under the strait by cable to Newfoundland, southward three hundred miles to Cabot Strait, thence sixty miles by undersea cable to Nova Scotia, and then another five hundred miles by transmission line to the American border. The total distance would be more than twelve hundred miles, by far the longest transmission line ever built, and the undersea cables would be a problem. Only in the Soviet Union had anything even remotely like it been attempted.

Nevertheless, engineering firms retained to survey the route declared it feasible: the cables could be buried in trenches to protect them from icebergs and fishing trawlers. Cost was another matter. The Anglo-Saxon Route would cost more than twice as much as the route through Quebec, and would increase the cost of the entire project by about a third—$350 million. Lesage kept his cool and waited for BRINCO to come back to him, as he felt they would have to do. But meanwhile, the matter of power in Quebec itself had become urgent. Development was no longer needed just to sell power to the Americans at a fat profit, but to save Quebec's industrial boom. The economists were predicting that without Churchill Falls Quebec would have to institute power rationing within a decade.

Meanwhile, Joey had gone to American power companies trying to get financing for the Anglo-Saxon Route, but he had been turned down. Power brought to New York that way would simply be too costly. The great days of atomic power stations were now dawning, and it was generally accepted that atomic power would be dirt cheap, not the expensive and dangerous luxury that it later proved to be.

In the end Lesage got a sweetheart deal that left Joey quietly fuming, and all Newfoundland governments since then convinced that they were royally screwed. The transmission line was built along a route heading straight for Quebec City. The power was sold to Hydro-Québec at the border at approximately 3.0 mills per kilowatt-hour, which was far less than the price of power anywhere else in the world. Then the surplus was resold at the American border at fantastic profits. By the 1970s Hydro-Québec was mopping up more than half a billion dollars annually, and the Newfoundland government, furious at the way it had been swindled, was threatening to turn off the power at Churchill Falls itself. The agreement was to run for forty years, but with an option to renew for another twenty-five years. So there was little hope that Newfoundland could sell the power at even one-tenth of its market value until well into the twenty-first century.

Smallwood had begun negotiating with the Rothschilds in 1952, and with the government of Quebec in 1962, but the deal was not signed until May 14, 1969. The agreement had been seventeen years in the making, and it was difficult in those years to foresee either double-digit inflation or the sky-rocketing cost of energy. In spite of that the accountants who vetted the deal for Newfoundland should at least have insisted that the agreement be hedged against inflation. They didn't, and it wasn't. So Newfoundland sold her most valuable single asset at bargain basement prices, and Quebec made an incredible killing, partly through the patience and cool negotiating skill of Jean Lesage, and partly through sheer luck.

The incredible deal that they finally signed provided that starting on September 1, 1976, Hydro-Québec would buy the power at just under 3.0 mills per kilowatt-hour, the price thence *declining* to just over 2.5 mills in the year 2001, and *declining again* to 2.0 mills in the year 2016.

After Smallwood's retirement, when Brian Peckford was minister of energy in the Moores government, he analysed the results of the Churchill Falls deal in detail, and concluded that by 1982 Hydro-Québec had benefited from the deal to the extent of $2 billion, and was then continuing to benefit to the tune of $810 million a year. Newfoundland's take, according to Peckford, amounted to little more than $100 million spread over ten years. The deal was equivalent, Peckford said, to purchasing oil at $1.80 a barrel for the first forty years of the deal, than at $1.20 a barrel for the next twenty-five years. According to those figures, Newfoundland will have given Quebec the equivalent of an $8.4 billion subsidy by the end of 1990.

The development cost $1.5 billion by the time the power was turned on (with Joey standing at the switch). Located in an artificial cave under a thousand feet of granite inside a mountain, it was the largest power development ever undertaken at a single site, on earth, the largest power house ever built. The power travelled to markets along the longest transmission ever constructed in the western hemisphere. Regardless of who got the benefit, it was one of the greatest engineering feats of its time.

Many of Smallwood's friends, including members of the Cabinet, made money out of the BRINCO deal. Joey also invested in the company, but failed to sell high when he should have, and did not benefit greatly. Today this would be called conflict of interest, and it would be material for a first-rate scandal, but at the time they were doing nothing illegal, and by the standards of the time, their actions may not even have been considered unethical. Throughout the seventeen years of negotiation and development, the project was a gamble, and no amount of inside information made a great deal of difference. Putting money into BRINCO looked more like an act of faith than like betting on a sure thing.

Winston Churchill was a minor shareholder in the company, and his reputation made a useful, but by no means crucial, contribution to BRINCO's success. But without the Rothschilds, and in particular Edmund de Rothschild's personal promotion, the corporation might never have floated. Robert Winters, a federal minister in the fifties who was in the running for the Liberal leadership in the sixties, became chairman of BRINCO and then of the Churchill Falls Power Corporation in 1963. He played a pivotal role in the negotiations with Quebec and the federal government. Pickersgill and Winters, between them, saw to it that Ottawa made all the needed tax concessions.

But even when you take all these efforts into account, the Churchill Falls power development remains Joey's personal achievement (or personal sellout, whichever way you view it). He believed in it and continued to promote it when everyone else had abandoned the idea. He lived with it daily for most of his career as premier of Newfoundland, and brought it to fulfillment against all odds.

It was an imaginative project that required new departures in engineering, so far beyond conventional experience that BRINCO, at one point, even investigated the possibility of wireless transmission. In the end, Churchill Falls proved that you could transmit power at very high voltage over thousands of miles safely and economically. Without this previous mega-project, the development of James Bay power might never have been considered, and Quebec might have begun to lock itself into atomic power, like Ontario. And if, in the end, it was Quebec that got most of the benefit, it was still Joey, and no one else, who did it. Like confederation itself, the development of Churchill Falls put the people of Canada permanently in his debt.

CHAPTER 12

# Out of the
# Frying Pan

JOEY HAD A GIFT FOR FORMING CLOSE PARTNERSHIPS WITH MEN WHOSE politics (if they had any at all) were far removed from his own. Alfred Valdmanis was only the first of a series of such connections that stretched the length of his public career. None of those partnerships was more unlikely, more enduring, or more sheer fun for Joey, than his long-lasting association with a flamboyant high-roller from Quebec, John C. Doyle. A gifted Irish-Canadian promoter, with a certain contempt for the rules laid down by bureaucrats, Doyle was a little out of place in the middle years of the twentieth century, but would have been right at home with the Guggenheims and the Rockefellers in the days before capital was yoked and bridled.

He was the son of a Canadian mining engineer, born in the United States, hence enjoying dual citizenship. He had worked in coal mining and marketing before buying a small foundry in Joliette, Quebec. Named Canadian Javelin Foundries and Machine Works, its principal product, at first, seems to have been iron frying pans. But not for long.

When the Newfoundland and Labrador Corporation shares went on sale in 1953—"un-crowning the corporation" as Joey called it— Doyle sensed an opportunity to get into the business he really dreamed about: mining promotion. Canadian Javelin began buying shares, and acquired 67,672 out of a total sale of 80,172. The takeover bid failed initially because Javelin itself was expelled from the Montreal and Toronto stock exchanges amidst charges of stock manipulation. The little corporation's shares had risen from $2.25 to $10.75 and then dropped to $5.75 for no apparent reason. The rise could hardly be justified by Javelin's bid to take over NALCO, a company with no record of earnings. The less dramatic fall was equally hard to explain in conventional terms. Somebody, it seemed, must be buying and then dumping the shares in order to push the price up and down for his own advantage. Doyle was later sued by members of his own company for doing this very thing, but none of this stopped him for a minute.

He flew to St. John's early in 1953 and called on Joey at Canada House. He explained his bid to take over NALCO and his wish to use the NALCO mining concessions in western Labrador to develop a massive iron-mining operation.

"If it's exploring ore fields that interests you," Joey told him, "I have just what you want."

They walked over to a wall map in his office, and he pointed to a place where the towns of Wabush and Labrador City would later be built. The Iron Ore Company of Canada had formerly owned the mining rights in this whole region, he explained, but under the terms of their lease they had been forced to drop a large slice of it. They had put their major effort into developing the huge iron mine at Knob Lake and had not explored the great deposits at Wabush Lake at all thoroughly. The ore in the area they had released seemed to be mostly low grade—about 35 percent iron—but if Doyle wanted to prospect the deposits there, he'd certainly get the concession. They talked a while longer, and Doyle made a proposal. He flew back to Montreal with Joey's blessing and a firm commitment to receive the concession to the Wabush deposits.

Canadian Javelin acquired not only thousands of square miles of mining rights in Labrador, but all the remaining NALCO concessions, as well. That happened some years later, when Javelin bought the government's remaining interest in NALCO and sold it to Wabush Iron Limited. Wabush sold it back to the government in 1963, as part of the deal to develop the Wabush iron mine, but the government sold it to Canadian Javelin for the second time in 1964. And there it has remained, for whatever it may now be worth.

Meanwhile, during all those years and those circular NALCO travels, Canadian Javelin grew from a frying-pan manufacturer into a massive multinational corporation, with headquarters still in its old home, Montreal. By the 1980s it owned ten subsidiary companies in

Canada, Panama, the Bahamas, Ethiopia, Bolivia, Uruguay, Honduras, and El Salvador, with affiliates in Panama, Bermuda, and Chile.

During this metamorphosis, Doyle had become enormously wealthy, had been charged in the United States with stock fraud, and had pleaded guilty to one charge of causing fifty unregistered shares to be sent through the mail. He had been sentenced to three months in jail, and had jumped bail, forfeiting a bond of US $100,000. Javelin shareholders had made a determined effort to get the company away from him, but he had cleverly managed to keep control of it.

All of this, however, was nothing compared with the adventures that Doyle and his friend Joey were having behind the scenes. First of all, Doyle demonstrated that one of the world's great iron mines could indeed be developed at Wabush. He spent $17 million there over the years. The concession proved to contain a billion tons of speculated hematite, iron ore in the form of coarse sand, with iron content of about 35 percent, and Doyle realized long before anyone else that this could be concentrated and pressed into pellets to produce an excellent grade of ore suitable for the largest steel plants in North America.

Having demonstrated that it could be done, he had to go about doing it, and this meant selling the ore in advance to steel companies, all of whom owned their own iron mines, and had no intention of admitting John C. Doyle to their international cartels. They tried every means to get Wabush away from him or to seal it off from the market. So he flew off to Germany, Britain, and Japan, inviting foreign steel companies to share his Labrador riches.

And that was the beginning of Joey's world-girdling trips in private aircraft. For by this time Doyle owned not any ordinary corporate plane, but a full-sized four-engined airliner, a DC-6, fitted out with carpet, glass chandeliers, a galley stocked with European wines, and a softly-lit dressing room complete with French perfumes. The seating was luxurious and classical music was piped into the cabin.

Obviously, John C. Doyle was no typical North American business lout. Like Valdmanis, he had an educated palate and was a fairly good amateur musician. He was also a gifted linguist: his French was faultless, his Italian more than adequate. It would be a mistake, however, to carry the parallels with Valdmanis too far. Doyle had a warm and joyful personality, not the chilly, hard, compulsion-ridden personality of the Latvian. He piled up personal wealth, but not in a compulsive manner. He was a large and enthusiastic spender.

Another quality that impressed Joey was Doyle's enormous energy and patience. When he went after something he did it single-mind-edly, and with bulldog determination. He'd simply never give up. Joey called it courage. Whatever it was, he needed a lot of it to compete in Labrador with the Iron Ore Company of Canada, which had the backing of some of the world's biggest steel companies, and which could hardly be expected to love Doyle for picking up a billion tons of ore that they had dropped by mistake—ore he had eventually shown to be more profitable than the massive deposit they had developed at Knob Lake.

Joey and Doyle flew in the mine developer's DC-6 to the capitals of Europe and Asia. They even stopped off at Doyle's ancestral home in Ireland, where the local press was shown, open-mouthed, through the airliner owned by the son of the poor Irishman who had left for Canada a generation ago. They rhapsodized about the "local boy" who had made good, and Doyle basked in the home-town glory.

On a whim one day, they took off from Monaco and flew to Isfahan, the fabled sacred city of Persia, with its silver-and-turquoise domes and its multitude of bridges in decorated stone. For Joey Isfahan was one of the high points of his travels, a marvel he never stopped describing to his friends.

One of Doyle's companies was in the tiny principality of Monaco. He did a multi-million-dollar business with the Swiss Bank. He took Joey to Liechtenstein, yet another tiny state that served as a shelter for underground money, where one or more of his shadow companies had its address. This indeed was wheeling and dealing on the grand scale. Joey watched with envious admiration. Valdmanis had never been such a big-timer as this.

But all the visits to the world's steel magnates were essentially a massive bluff. Joey and Doyle weren't really hoping to lure the Germans and the Japanese into western Labrador. They were actually aiming at Cleveland, by way of Tokyo. They had to convince the American steel companies that Wabush was going to be developed, with or without them, helped along by enormous government guaran-tees if the financing could not be arranged privately. To make it work, they had to carry their overseas negotiations right up to the verge of signing contracts.

This was one of the happiest periods of Joey's life. Perhaps he loved an election campaign above everything else, but his second great joy was travel, especially travel by air. He disliked ships and trains, but loved cars and aircraft. Landing in a new city a few hours out of

Gander or Torbay was unalloyed delight. Even after his retirement, he regretted that he had never visited the caravan city of Samarkand in the Soviet Union, though heaven knows he had seen most of the notable places of the world.

The Opposition in the House of Assembly harped continually on the theme that the premier was gadding about at government expense instead of attending to the business of the province at home. He did a good deal of gadding, it is true, but always in the course of some serious negotiations, and often at the expense of Canadian Javelin, rather than the government. Curtis often accompanied him to contribute sober second thoughts, and Power to share the delights of the journey.

"It's one of my regrets that I never did get to the Soviet Union, or the other countries of eastern Europe," Power says. "On one trip we did manage to get to East Germany, though. I was recounting this story to Joe, just the other day."

In Berlin, a city divided into occupation zones, like the country at large, they drove up to the gate of the Soviet sector in an official limousine, and were refused entry by the Russian officers. So Joey went to the British consul and asked if he could arrange a visit. He secured diplomatic passes for them, and Willie Brandt, then mayor of the city and later chancellor of West Germany, supplied them with a motorcycle escort.

Smallwood then enjoyed a great moment of triumph as the motorcade swept through the streets and soldiers, policemen, and civilians all came to attention and saluted. Joey, in the front seat, kept waving to spectators, while Power, in the back, complained, "You're not doing it right, Joe. Prince Philip wouldn't do it that way." When Joey had finally had enough of the heckling, he turned around and snapped, "And where did you learn to do it? In the cabbage patch at Placentia?" Power dissolved into laughter, and Joey, realizing he'd been had, joined in.

This time the Red Army bowed them through the gate, and took them on a tour of the city, including a visit to the underground bunker where Hitler, at the last minute, had married his mistress, spent his last day with her, and then shot himself as the tanks of the Red Army thundered overhead. Pointing to a large dark stain on the carpet, their guide, who spoke little English, explained in two words: "Hitler— blood."

On that trip they also visited a gas chamber where a hundred thousand Jews has been exterminated before being stuffed into the ovens of the crematorium. "They piled them in like cordwood, and threw the children in on top, until the vault was full, then sealed it and turned on the gas," Power recalls with a shudder. "Some of them scratched their names on the ceiling of the vault before they died, and you could still read the names when we were there."

It was the sort of experience that contributed to Smallwood's increasingly sombre view of humanity. State dinners in Germany and receptions given by General Franco did nothing to remove the cloud of doubt that gathered over the later years of his life. He began to wonder whether the social and economic reforms to which he had committed himself as a young man were really the answer to the human dilemma. He pondered the question in his old age as he pursued his second career in publishing, but he never did find an answer.

Joey kept telling the Opposition that he'd go to the back side of the moon, if he had to, to get development for Newfoundland. And indeed development did come out of it, though perhaps Doyle might have been able to bring it off on his own, while Joey tended to government affairs at St. John's. Most of the travel was certainly joy riding, but it did help bring the American steel companies to the bargaining table. They quite rightly regarded the Japanese and Germans as their toughest competitors, and they certainly did not want them on their doorstep. Doyle was shrewd enough to proceed right to the brink of a massive deal with the foreign steel companies, then hang fire just long enough to bring the Americans to southwestern Labrador.

He also managed to pile up wealth without ever producing very much. Nearly all of it came out of the money market, with Javelin and Doyle both getting their cuts of the investors' dollars. It was a procedure that failed to endear him to the financiers. Starting on a shoestring, he nevertheless managed to spend seventeen million dollars bringing one of the continent's largest iron mines to the verge of development, and to maintain a high standard of conspicuous consumption while he did it. The government of Newfoundland was pleased to see all this happening without risk to the solvency of the provincial treasury. Indeed, Doyle had opened negotiations back in 1953 by offering to pay a quarter of a million dollars for the concessions—the first time a developer had offered to pay them money, instead of asking for it.

Canadian Javelin, a small public company with many minor

stockholders and little production, invested five million of its own capital in the Wabush Lake iron field, a grave risk that could have ended in bankruptcy. However, the government still had to assume large risks. Joey had to go to the legislature with a request for a guarantee of $16.5 million for a Javelin bond issue. The Opposition screamed blue murder. This amounted to co-signing a Javelin note for that amount. If the development failed, then the Newfoundland government would have to pay $16.5 million to the bondholders—an amount almost equal to the total losses from all the earlier new industries. Joey was doubling his bets, a desperate and frightening gambling practice that he continued as long as he was in office. If the gamble succeeded, it would cost the government nothing. If it failed, well. . . .

Joey got his guarantee, backed by his docile Liberal majority (23 seats to 5), and the Opposition raged to no purpose. During the debate he made one of his rare errors of fact by stating that the Swiss Bank, obviously impressed by "the world's greatest iron discovery," had invested $4.8 million in the venture. The bank was forced to explain that the money was a purchase of Canadian Javelin stock by an anonymous investor. The anonymous investor was John C. Doyle.

Javelin needed the $16.5 million bond issue mainly to build a forty-mile railway from Wabush to a junction with the Quebec North Shore and Labrador Railway running from Knob Lake in Newfoundland Labrador to Sept Îles, on Quebec's gulf coast. This railway had been built by the steel companies that had developed Knob Lake, at a cost of hundreds of millions of dollars, but it was not controlled by those steel companies or by the Iron Ore Company of Canada. When the governments of Newfoundland and Quebec granted the land for the right of way, they had the foresight to insist that the railway be a common carrier. The idea that it might be the carrier for a second, competing iron mine, seemed very remote at the time.

The existing railway was a great windfall for Canadian Javelin. Doyle estimated the common carrier feature to be equivalent to an investment of $150 million—the amount he would have needed to build his own railway to the Gulf of St. Lawrence. It turned out that the $16.5 million bond issue didn't have to be floated, either. Following Doyle's lead, the Iron Ore Company of Canada began looking at its own property adjoining the Wabush Lake ore field, and discovered that a third enormous iron mine could be developed there. To work the deposits they would need to build a railway to within three miles of

Wabush, and a great squabble began over who would build and own this forty-mile line.

In the end, Joey resolved the quarrel himself by announcing that the government of Newfoundland would build and own the railway, and that it would be a common carrier, like the main line. Javelin and the Iron Ore Company accepted this, but it was the steel companies, not the government, who put up the actual cash for the development. In resolving the quarrel without having to find the money to build the branch line, Joey had masterminded a deal worthy of John C. Doyle himself. Only $2 million of the Javelin bond issue was floated before Doyle halted the sale.

In the early months of 1956 Doyle announced a firm agreement to sell Wabush ore to a syndicate of German steel producers, and also announced renewed negotiations with steel producers in Britain. The American steel companies finally decided that they had to buy the field from Doyle, and they formed a new corporation to develop it. Wabush Iron Limited was owned by some of the world's most powerful steel producers, led by Pickands Mather and Co. of Cleveland. Others involved were Pittsburgh Steel, Dominion Steel and Foundry, Stelco, and steel companies based in Germany and Italy.

The agreement between Wabush Iron and Canadian Javelin fulfilled all of Doyle's hopes. Wabush Iron agreed to a down payment of $2.5 million, with annual royalties beginning at $1.8 million and rising to $3.2 million at the end of five years. At one stroke, the small and speculative Canadian Javelin had become a large corporation with high guaranteed annual earnings. Doyle, with nothing but his own promotional ability and Joey's rhetoric, had pulled off perhaps the greatest *coup* of his generation in the mining industry.

Shortly after Wabush Iron began developing its deposit at Wabush Lake, the Iron Ore Company began developing the adjoining Carol Lake deposit. They named the mountain of rock that they began chewing down with some of the world's most massive machinery, the Smallwood Mine.

"When this one is exhausted we'll have to open Smallwood Mine Number Two," the manager told me, while showing me over the mine site. "And so on," he added with a grin. Joey himself had started the mine by pressing the lever to explode a hundred and fifty thousand pounds of dynamite buried in the rock beside the lake. Then he went off to inspect the operation.

To anyone who could be impressed by technology, the development was fascinating. Crushers that could digest cubic yards of rock at a single bite were operated by one man sitting in an electronic control room that looked liked the command capsule of a space ship. The railway ran entirely by itself, without human guidance. The trains slowed down and blew their whistles at crossings. If their electric eyes spotted an obstruction, they applied their brakes. They backed their cars into pits to be loaded, took them off to the nearby pelletizing plant, and hauled the pellets to tidewater, all according to the orders of electronic brains. We are accustomed, nowadays, to machines that can fly through the rings of distant planets and send brilliant pictures back to earth. But this was in the early 1960s. The developments at Carol Lake and Wabush were on the leading edge of the electronic technology of those years. To supply power for the mines and concentrators, BRINCO had brought on stream the first large power house in Labrador, a quarter-million-horsepower plant at Twin Falls on the Unknown River.

There was a good deal of rivalry between the Iron Ore Company of Canada and Wabush Iron, some of it expressed in petty ways. For example, Joey had suggested that the two companies ought to build a single townsite, with jointly owned shopping centres, schools, a town hall, and so on. The townsite was to be called Labrador City. But the companies refused. Instead, they built two towns three miles apart with duplicate services. The only services actually owned in common were provided by federal and provincial governments (the airport and the roads, for example). Between them, the two towns reached a population of 16,000 and were named Labrador City and the City of Wabush, respectively. Joey had at last achieved his ambition to create new population centres like those his Liberal predecessors had set up at Grand Falls and Corner Brook.

If you believe in industrial epics, then the Wabush development was an epic, and Canadian Javelin was a near-miracle of promotional skill. A few people "made" a lot of money in the process—in other words, they collected fortunes from risky stock trading. One of those people was Doyle himself. Among those who traded Canadian Javelin shares was Joey's son William, Member for Green Bay, who testified in 1967 that he then owned some $200,000 worth of BRINCO, Javelin and Julienne stock. (Julienne Mines was another Doyle promotion in Labrador.) Some of those who traded Javelin stock successfully were members of the Newfoundland government who made a very good thing out of inside information and the rapid rising and falling of Javelin shares. Les Curtis, for example, had started as a small-time lawyer, but, according to his own estimate, had a net worth of some $64 million by the time he retired. Not all of this came from riding on John C. Doyle's coat tails, of course. Curtis's law firm represented a whole spectrum of industries throughout the Smallwood era.

If members of the government didn't want the embarrassment of having shares registered in their own names, they found trustworthy friends to hold the stock for them. Others made no pretense about the matter. Jocy tended to brag about being part-owner of BRINCO, but he never discussed his dealing in Javelin stock, if he did any. BRINCO, of course, never did pull off a spectacular *coup* like Javelin's. In any case, the big winner in the Javelin game was Newfoundland.

The sale of Wabush Iron—later renamed Wabush Mines—was not the end of John C. Doyle's interest in Labrador or his last promotion of a Newfoundland development, and it was by no means the end of Canadian Javelin's rise to prominence. Long before the ore cars were rolling southward from Wabush, Doyle was tackling an equally massive ore body in Chile. He exchanged his grandiloquent airliner for a smaller, faster, less conspicuous executive jet, and in this machine he went on his swashbuckling way from strength to strength. There can be no doubt that he was one of the most successful milkers of the money market since the age of the great American "robber barons." As early as 1956 the United States Securities Commission estimated that his stock manipulations had cost American investors some $30 million—but that was just at the beginning of his career.

He was sued repeatedly, sometimes for amounts running into the millions. But all the early suits collapsed. Only the one conviction for sending fifty unregistered shares through the mail stood up in court. Edward Jaegerman, of the U.S. Securities Commission, once flew to St. John's for a meeting with Smallwood and the government on the subject of Doyle and Canadian Javelin. According to Smallwood, Jaegerman undertook at this meeting to drop all prosecutions against Doyle for earlier offences against U.S. security regulations. Jaegerman denied this, and Smallwood, in the legislature, called him "an unmitigated liar, an unadulterated scoundrel and liar." Six Newfoundland Cabinet ministers backed Smallwood's statement with affidavits.

On one occasion Joey flew to Washington, and saw Attorney-

General Robert Kennedy on Doyle's behalf. Kennedy was friendly, but of course refused to interfere. Doyle's legal troubles continued. He had to make a multi-million-dollar settlement, out of court, with Javelin shareholders who claimed he had defrauded them. The Canadian income tax assessors sent him a bill for $3.8 million in unpaid taxes. He also had to deal with a civil suit brought against him by Javelin's vice-president.

Doyle's rivals—those who had lost the struggle with him in the dog-eat-dog world of the stock exchanges, as well as his political enemies sitting opposite Joey in the legislature—loved to refer to him as "a fugitive from justice" and a "bail-jumper." The terms were technically correct. The question was whether any *moral* guilt attached to the offence of sending unregistered shares through the mail, or beating other gamblers at their own game. Joey insisted that it didn't. He added, "Never in the history of Newfoundland's industry was so much owed to the efforts of one man."

Doyle eventually resigned as Javelin's president, but remained a "consultant" at $50,000 a year, and became chairman of the board. Far more important, he continued to be Javelin's largest shareholder, with about 20 percent of its stock, and through his friends and supporters he still controlled something very close to a voting majority.

Following the successful promotion of the Wabush mine, and indirectly of the larger Carol Lake mine, Doyle turned his attention to a fourth Labrador iron field at Julienne Lake, about ten miles from Wabush, a deposit on which Canadian Javelin still held a lease. He built a road to it, and proved the existence of a large ore field. This time his negotiations with the Germans and the Japanese looked more serious than before. It was unlikely that he could get a third group of American steel companies interested in Labrador mining. But the negotiations dragged on for many years without conclusive results. At present the Julienne ore field is still sitting in the wilderness, awaiting development.

In the meantime, Doyle had teamed up with Joey on another project—the creation of the "third mill." From the days of Sir Richard Squires, who had won his second election with the promise to "put the gang on the Gander," Newfoundland had dreamed of having a third paper mill. The mills at Grand Falls and Corner Brook had created two centres of perennial prosperity in the island, supporting a population of some 50,000. By Joey's time paper had exceeded fish as Newfoundland's greatest money maker. The dream was that a third population centre could be created at Gander River or in Bay d'Espoir or some other likely site, exploiting what remained of Newfoundland's forest resources.

In fact, by 1950 there was little unused forest potential in Newfoundland itself. The Corner Brook operation had expanded eastward into the Gander watershed, adjoining the Grand Falls operations, and "boatwood" was being shipped to Corner Brook from places as distant as White Bay and Bay d'Espoir. Company after company came to the island at Joey's invitation, took careful note of what was available and went away disappointed. But in time the "boatwood" operation dwindled, leaving somewhat larger tracts of forest unharvested, but there was still not enough available for a third mill. I discussed the matter with Bowaters in the early 1960s, and they told me flatly, "A third paper mill in Newfoundland isn't possible. The wood just isn't there. If Newfoundland could support a third mill, we would build it."

Despite this, Joey wouldn't give up. He was never one to accept someone else's judgement that any of his dreams was impossible. He negotiated with the International Basic Economy Corporation of New York, hoping they would undertake the development. Instead, they agreed to do a survey at Newfoundland's expense. When it was complete, they sent the government a large, handsomely illustrated report which Joey refused to release to the public or to members of the legislature.

"Why?" I asked him privately.

"It shows—or I should say it *seems* to show—that a third mill is impossible," he told me.

Releasing it "would not be in the public interest," he informed members of the House who asked that it be tabled.

Actually, the IBEC report condemned the idea of a third mill *in Labrador*, which at that time was the main area of interest because Lake Melville and Sandwich Bay had millions of cords of unharvested black spruce of absolutely prime quality for paper making. The report did suggest that a mill might be barely possible at Bay d'Espoir, where there was adequate hydro power and quite a bit of softwood, mainly balsam fir, which would need to be supplemented by supplies of spruce shipped in from Labrador.

Kreuger Pulp and Paper of Quebec were briefly interested. (They eventually bought the Corner Brook mill after the Bowater companies had decided to cease operations in Newfoundland.) A royal commission on forestry reported that there was actually enough wood to support a third mill, even without tapping Labrador, if wood could be drawn from the existing reserves of the two operating paper companies. They recommended that the two companies undertake jointly to build and operate a third mill, but neither of the paper companies thought much of the idea.

The most promising prospect seemed to be Crown Zellerbach, the American multinational from the Pacific coast. They took options on forests in both Newfoundland and Labrador, carried out extensive surveys of their own, and for a time seemed about to sign an agreement with the government. But by 1959 they had dropped their options and gone home.

At last Joey turned to John C. Doyle, and Doyle came through once more. He was convinced that a mill could be built to produce a thousand tons daily—not of newsprint, perhaps, but of liner paper, the surfacing material for linerboard, otherwise known as corrugated cardboard and used by the packaging industry in vast quantities.

Doyle at first intended to build the mill somewhere on Lake Melville in Labrador, where the wood was plentiful, and could be cut right at tidewater, and along the valleys of great rivers where log drives would be simplicity itself, but he abandoned this plan after he learned that even with the help of icebreakers it would be impossible to ship paper out of Lake Melville in winter. Next he looked at Sandwich Bay. Then he considered a pipeline through which the pulp would be pumped over the mountains and through the forests to the Strait of Belle Isle. When all these alternatives proved economically hopeless, he turned to the idea of a mill on Newfoundland's west coast, using Labrador "boatwood."

Joey faced one of the greatest challenges of his life when he flew to Labrador to explain to a hostile audience of Labrador men and women why he was building the third mill at Stephenville in Newfoundland instead of in Labrador. He stood up to hisses and catcalls in a jam-packed auditorium. He stood there for three hours, expressing his disappointment, his sorrow, his confidence in Labrador's future, his regret that a mere logging operation was all he could manage for them as yet. It was a measure of his ability to sway crowds that he turned the hostility completely around. In the end they cheered him and gave him a standing ovation.

Stephenville got the mill for a number of reasons. It had a large airport and a good harbour, both built during the Second World War by the American forces, but now abandoned. There was a large seriously underemployed population. The entire infrastructure of a city was ready and waiting. Stephenville was a long distance from Lake Melville, but once cargo is on board a ship distance does not add greatly to cost—it is the cheapest of all methods of transport. Stephenville also happened to be near enough to Nova Scotia and New Brunswick to purchase pulpwood from woodlot operators there, should that prove necessary.

Financing for the third mill was arranged jointly by Canadian Javelin and the Newfoundland government. The total cost was more than $200 million. British banks loaned $41 million, guaranteed by the Newfoundland government and the British government through the Export Credits Department. German banks loaned $48 million on Newfoundland's guarantee, and a further loan of $2.25 million, raised in New York, was also guaranteed by Newfoundland. Javelin found $48 million beyond the government guarantees. That would have come close to the estimated cost, prior to construction, and it was a contingent liability of frightening proportions for Newfoundland. If the project flopped, the province could find itself with an increased debt of more than $90 million dollars.

But as with all major construction in Canada in the sixties and seventies, the final costs were much higher than the estimates, and the guarantees higher in proportion. One of the first things Joey's successors did, after he was defeated in the 1970s, was to nationalize the third mill, and look for a buyer, to get the government out of danger.

Joey had, in a sense, realized his lifelong ambition of building a third mill in Newfoundland, but the actual operation turned out to be rather different from the one that had been planned: it was a 400-ton newsprint mill, not a 1,000-ton linerboard mill. Although it helped to save Stephenville from depopulation, it did nothing to create a new population centre. It did not even boost Newfoundland's paper exports, but rather returned them to something less than the level reached in the 1960s. What it did do was help replace the production that had been lost at Corner Brook as the much larger mill there gradually cut back to a third of its maximum output. In this sense the third mill was an illusion.

The strange spectacle of a Tory government nationalizing a paper mill was merely a passing show. The government presumably never intended to run the mill as a crown enterprise. They sold it to Abitibi-Price, who were now the owners of the mill at Grand Falls. It did not get into production until 1981, ten years after the start of construction, but by that time, according to Abitibi-Price, it was a "world-class newsprint mill...one of the most modern in the world," with about half the capacity of their mill at Grand Falls.

Even after his defeat and his government's resignation, Joey continued to swear by John C. Doyle. None of his many close partnerships was happier or more productive than this one. High rollers like Doyle tend to end up either in the American Government, or in jail, sometimes in both. Doyle escaped prison, but only by becoming a permanent exile, an expatriate from the two countries of his citizenship and his principal enterprise, Canada and the United States.

Shortly after Smallwood's final fall from power in 1972 Doyle was arrested by the RCMP in Montreal, taken to St. John's, and there charged with fraud. The court set bail at $75,000. He jumped bail again, and fled to Panama. Stock fraud was not an extraditable offence in Panama, so the RCMP had to leave him where he was. But his legal troubles were far from ended.

Over the years the extent of the fraud charges increased, but nine years after he had fled to Panama Doyle was still collecting $209,000 a year as a consultant to Javelin International (as his company was now called). Moreover, the company was paying his personal income tax debt, now set at some $2 million. In August of 1982 the Restrictive Practices Commission began hearings on complaints from Javelin shareholders, and after fourteen months of investigation issued its report on October 11, 1983, upholding four of the five charges of fraud, and recommending that the company be put into the hands of trustees to dispose of its assets.

Doyle, still in Panama, was charged with defrauding Javelin shareholders of "some ten million." Smallwood was called as a witness before the Commission, pleaded immunity, and in an action before the Supreme Court of Canada was granted *relative* immunity in cases where a court decided that his testimony might harm the public interest of Newfoundland. Despite his intimate connection with the deals and with the investigation, there was no evidence that he had benefited personally from Doyle's many promotions, or that the government had ever abetted fraud.

On February 27, 1986, the Quebec Superior Court found that Doyle had defrauded Javelin between 1967 and 1972 of $4 million in a worthless timber concession in Labrador, $1.4 million in a "nonexistent" finder's fee, $.54 million in a fraudulent invoice scam, and about $5 million in consulting fees and fraudulent mining transactions.

The court ordered Doyle to pay $15.4 million indemnity to Javelin International for fraud, and ordered that he should be divested of the ownership of the 1,040,000 Javelin shares that he then held as majority shareholder. The court ordered the shares "frozen" until disposition was arranged. One request of the prosecutor was refused by the court: that Javelin International be placed in trusteeship and wound up.

Either by good luck or good judgment, Joey had managed to stay out of Doyle's financial entanglements. Skating successfully over the thinnest of ice, he had managed to reap for Newfoundland the fruits of Doyle's risky promotions, without falling, like Doyle, into the hands of the law.

By no means all of Joey's schemes of the 1950s and '60s were mediated by Doyle. For a while he had a close working relationship with the mining magnate James Boylen, an Ontario prospector who had promoted and developed four mining companies in various parts of Canada before he came to Newfoundland, at Joey's invitation, in 1955. Claude Howse, the deputy-minister of mines, suggested Boylen as the proper person to follow up air-magnetometer surveys of Newfoundland's northeast coast—surveys that had revealed magnetic anomalies that looked like mineral deposits of commercial value.

Boylen sent his prospectors to designated areas at Gull Pond (a large lake in central Newfoundland) to Tilt Cove, to Little Bay, and to the Baie Verte Peninsula. Eventually, he was responsible for opening mines in all those places: Gullbridge Mines at Gull Pond, First Maritime at Tilt Cove, Atlantic Coast Copper at Little Bay—all of them working low-grade copper deposits—and Advocate Mines at Baie Verte, extracting asbestos.

A fifth mine started by Boylen began producing copper in 1964, and was still producing in the 1980s. The asbestos mine and mill at Baie Verte, opened in 1963, were also still in production in the eighties. It employed about 550 people, and produced between 36,000 and 89,000 tons of asbestos fibre annually. The other Boylen mines produced for a while and then closed as market prices fell.

Boylen never achieved in Newfoundland anything as big and flashy as John C. Doyle pulled off in Labrador, but Joey cherished his modest achievements, and kept Boylen's signed photograph on his mantlepiece along with his photograph of Doyle.

# CHAPTER 13

# *Jack Be Nimble*

SMALLWOOD, THAT PRODUCT OF THE ROARING TWENTIES, FOUND HIS spiritual home in the Booming Fifties. That was the time when he and his world were most nearly in step. He never did adapt to the revolutionary changes of the sixties—and toward the end of the fifties he began to have nothing but trouble. In the years between 1958 and 1968 he suffered from labour unions, John Diefenbaker, chickens that laid silver-yolked eggs, and vipers that he nourished in his bosom.

Like populist politicians everywhere, he set out to reform the world in the image of his youth. That was okay for the 1950s when no fundamental social change had yet taken place. Affluence, ever-expanding economies, miraculous technology—they all seemed to be our birthright. Everyone in the western world was going to get richer and richer. "Science" would produce more and more marvels. Soon we'd all be cruising around in hover cars with cordless telephones while Belinda the Robot kept house for us.

Overnight, it all changed. Smallwood's generation of politicians never adjusted to the change, never understood a world in which people wanted freedom of choice more than they wanted hovercraft. And Joey had other limitations. One of the most serious was his failure to understand the nature and importance of social capital. Until his contractors finished building the Newfoundland link of the Trans-Canada Highway in 1965 he continued to think of roads—even trunk highways—as a kind of social service, almost a frill, like vacations with pay.

"I never realized," he told me, "that a major highway is equivalent to a great new industry. It creates *employment*; it creates a *lot* of employment. I mean a lot of *permanent* employment."

Even then he was thinking of social capital in terms of jobs. The movement toward individual initiative he simply never understood at all. When people began abandoning their jobs at "good cash wages" in Labrador City and voluntarily returning to the fishery, the whole thing struck him as perverse. The idea that catching fish or making pots on a wheel might be more important than manufacturing engine parts or mining asbestos he regarded as utterly bizarre. What the toiling masses wanted (or at any rate *needed*) was jobs at regular wages that would feed them adequately—not risk, not self-employment, not challenges and spiritual adventures, but jobs. His vision, in fact, never went beyond the First Industrial Revolution. He spent his whole career trying to drag Newfoundland kicking and screaming into the nineteenth century. His ambition for his province was to recreate, on a small scale, the American Industrial boom of the Gay Nineties—a rather extreme example of what Marshall McLuhan called "rearview-mirrorism," a disease endemic among politicians of his generation.

The great changes in Newfoundland began under Joey's administration not so much because he understood them as because he understood politics, including the political genius of that odd-looking little Humpty-Dumpty in Ottawa, John Whitney Pickersgill.

Pickersgill suffered none of Joey's limitations in education, economic knowledge, or experience with the mechanics of power. What he lacked was Joey's magic with the public—a gift that was forever beyond his reach, as he knew perfectly well. He was well aware of the importance of social capital and its effects on the economy. As soon as he had the chance he set about transforming Newfoundland in this way—the principal means by which an intimate knowledge of Ottawa and its functions could be put to use in the service of a have-not province.

He was a brilliant political operator with a first-class mind, handicapped by a rather squeaky voice and the appearance of a freshly boiled dumpling. Worse still, his face was remarkably like that of the famous ventriloquist's dummy, Charlie McCarthy. These handicaps had kept him in the back rooms and off the front benches of parliament.

He was conservative by inclination and by family tradition. Indeed, the middle name "Whitney" had been fastened upon him in honour of a long-gone Ontario Tory. He had no wish to reform the world, but he had a hunger to handle the levers of power and to be a force in moulding Canada's destiny. With these aims in view he attached himself to Mackenzie King as early as 1937.

Pickersgill rose among King's advisers until, by the end of the Second World War, he stood closest to the prime minister. To accomplish this he had made a special study of King's mind, and had accommodated himself to it—no mean feat, since King's mind was one of the most complex and irrational in the history of politics, at least in North America.

As for moulding Canada's destiny, he had done his part by helping to bring Newfoundland into Confederation. Aside from that, he seemed to be mainly the top-ranking servant of the Liberal Party. By the time Louis St. Laurent succeeded King as prime minister, Pickersgill was the one indispensable person in the prime minister's office, with an encyclopedic knowledge of just how each government department worked, and the routes by which it could be made to work in favour of the prime minister, the Liberal Party, or any other cause espoused by John Whitney Pickersgill.

Soon after Joey first appeared in Ottawa, Pickersgill had him tagged as a winner. He worked with him to bring Newfoundland into confederation, and to make confederation work for Newfoundland. The great roadblock in those first years was Gordon Bradley, Newfoundland's sole representative in the government. Because Bradley could not be persuaded to fight Newfoundland's battles inside the Cabinet, or to throw his weight around, as other ministers did, among senior civil servants, it was difficult for the premier, working through Pickersgill, to make Newfoundland much of a priority at the federal level.

In private, Joey often raged against Bradley, blaming him for letting down the side, for doing nothing just when Newfoundland needed a strong champion at the centre of power. Newfoundland was simply not getting its share of the federal pie. Very little money was being spent on public works in a province that obviously needed more than most. As for federal transfer payments (often assumed to be the very lifeblood of the Atlantic provinces) when you added them all up—

pensions, family allowances, unemployment insurance, subsidies—a strange fact came to light: Newfoundland received far less per capita than Ontario, British Columbia, or indeed *any other province except Quebec*. It was one of the ironies of confederation that the province with the greatest need for social subsidies was receiving next-to-the-least benefit in its relationship with Ottawa. After three years of it, Joey had made up his mind to ditch Bradley and find a new federal minister.

In January 1953 he flew to Ottawa to spend a day with Pickersgill, who had recently been appointed clerk of the Privy Council. Since the Privy Council was an honorary body that never met, the job was actually the nation's highest-ranking sinecure, permitting him to devote his energies to the service of the prime minister and the party. In the course of their day-long dialogue Joey convinced Pickersgill that he ought to resign his sinecure and run for election in Newfoundland. Bonavista-Twillingate, Bradley's riding, would elect absolutely anybody that Joey sent there, even such a green and funny-looking mainlander as Pickersgill. Nowhere else in Canada could Pickersgill expect to be elected. What to do with Bradley? Easy. Appoint him to the Senate.

No sooner said than done. By early summer Bradley had his Senate seat, and Joey was happily squiring Pickersgill, in oilskins and sou'wester, around Bonavista-Twillingate, introducing him as the father of family allowances and the next prime minister of Canada. Neither of the appelations was in any way correct. Pickersgill had, indeed, advised King that family allowances would be good for votes, but the real impetus had come from CCF members in Opposition—one of King's many successful thefts of major Opposition policies. And Joey must have known full well that Pickersgill had about as much chance of becoming prime minister as he had of becoming archbishop.

Anyway, it all went down nicely in Bonavista-Twillingate, where, if Joey had recited the Black Mass, the voters would have shouted "Amen!" After a triumphal tour in cars, ships, and trap boat, Pickersgill was elected, on August 10, 1953, by 10,072 votes to his opponent's 2,564.

After that nothing could stop him. He bought a house in the riding, where he and his family lived when parliament was not in session. He sent his son Alan to Memorial University in St. John's. His daughter Jane practised medicine in Gander. He bought an old schooner, the *Millie Ford*, and sailed around the riding in it. Cartoonists had great fun showing Pickersgill as a most unlikely fisherman.

They borrowed the refrain of the Newfoundland folksong, "Jack was every inch a sailor," and the nursery rhyme, "Jack be nimble, Jack be quick..." which was ready-made for satirists to apply to his manipulations in Ottawa. But Newfoundlanders, used to getting only the crumbs, were grateful for the sudden change he created in federal-provincial relations. Bonavista-Twillingate supported him with might and main, and they had good reason to do so. He ringed the coastline with public wharves and built neat new post offices in almost every village. No one in the history of Newfoundland politics could pamper a riding and keep the voters happy like Sailor Jack. After that first election Joey never needed to set foot in the riding again. Pickersgill won six elections in a row, always by margins of more than six thousand votes, and twice by margins of more than nine thousand. Looking at his record of vote gathering, Joey remarked that even he would hate to have to run against Pickersgill.

But showering Newfoundland with wharves and buildings was the least of his achievements. Against all odds he succeeded in having unemployment insurance extended to self-employed fishermen, a move that was totally contrary to the concepts on which unemployment insurance was based, and absolute anathema to the high-ranking civil servants in charge of the scheme. The revision came into effect in 1957.

It was the most important development in the Atlantic Coast fisheries after the building of the freezing plants. It saved the in-shore fishery of Newfoundland—the branch of the industry which provided the most employment and produced the greatest bulk of fish most cheaply—from dying on its feet. Within two years, seven thousand men had gone back to the fishing industry. Some of them sold off small businesses ashore to invest in boats and gear. Harbours that had been deserted were once again filled with boats swinging to their collars. There was a boom in small-boat building and the manufacture of cod traps. Soon the in-shore fishery was heading into the greatest era of prosperity it had enjoyed in three centuries.

Mainlanders typically failed to understand what was happening, even after the event. Richard Gwyn thought the return to the fishery was caused by despair, and quoted Parzival Copes, an imported economist at Memorial University, who called the outports "havens for the unemployed." The truth was that former fishermen returned to the outports at the first opportunity because that's where they wanted to be, in places where life was productive and had meaning.

At first they were "not fishing for fish, but fishing for stamps," as I described it in *The Evening Telegram* —working for a winter income in the form of transfer payments from Ottawa. Soon, though, they were building sixty-foot longliners at the rate of forty to fifty each year. Gradually, there was an improvement in fish prices, a union for fishermen, and diversification into new species: shrimp and crab became important, and there was even a sale for the roe from lumpfish and the formerly despised "whore's eggs" that mainlanders called sea urchins. One morning Newfoundland awakened to the fact that the fishermen were no longer poor. Some of them were paving their driveways and buying second cars. Almost every fisherman's home had a refrigerator and a TV set. The outports had been transformed by the greatest economic and social change in the history of the island. And with it came a new sense of self-respect. For the first time the fishermen began to realize that they, producing food—real wealth— literally by the *ton*, had at least as much right to a decent life as some economist pushing paper around his desk in a university, with the government paying his keep.

It was a development that Joey had not foreseen. Testifying before the Royal Commission on Economic Prospects a year or two earlier he had declared, "The cowboy looms larger than the fisherman in Newfoundland's future." Even as the fisheries boom was getting under way, he was trying to turn the Burin Peninsula, with its great stretches of heath land, into cattle country. Cattle brought from the Canadian West were turned loose at Goobies, and herded by cowboys a distance of ninety miles to Winterland on the Burin—with predictable results, one might add. To show his confidence in the scheme, Joey rode off at the head of one such cattle drive in person, wearing a ten-gallon hat. But Joey had brought the fisheries boom into being, without understanding what he was doing. Like Copes, he thought he was providing a kind of welfare, not the social capital needed for an economic revival. He did not understand it, but he did it just the same, with the help of that strange little man from Ottawa.

Unemployment insurance for fishermen affected not just Newfoundland, of course, but every community in coastal Canada. It was perhaps Pickersgill's greatest achievement, but only one of many. From being second-lowest on the totem pole, almost forgotten in the councils of central Canada, Newfoundland became Ottawa's pet province. Because we were greatly in need of roads, Pickersgill found ways to get them built with federal funds. Until he put his mind to work on the problem, roads had been almost exclusively a provincial responsibility. The one exception was the Trans-Canada Highway, for which Ottawa was paying half the cost. Pickersgill managed to increase that share to 90 percent, a move of great benefit to Newfoundland, where some six hundred miles of the road were yet to be completed. Under the new deal, road work rushed forward, and friends and supporters of Joey like the little Lundrigan firm of Corner Brook grew into massive corporations with fat road contracts. (The Lundrigans, starting with a small sawmill, eventually bought out Comstock, and became one of Canada's corporate giants, controlling companies in all ten provinces.)

But the one trunk road would not be enough. How to get the feds to build other highways? Hm-m-m-m ... access roads ... needed to link the main highway to whatever federal projects were being developed. Diefenbaker later invented the term "roads to resources," but he was following Pickersgill's lead. Even St. John's harbour eventually qualified, with a four-lane federal highway linking it to the federal Trans-Canada. Although it was built after Pickersgill retired, he had made it possible.

One of his imaginative projects was an overseas highway ("The Road to the Isles" tourist promoters liked to call it) starting at Notre Dame Junction and ending at Twillingate, a hundred miles to the north, skipping by bridge and causeway from island to island as it went past some of the most picturesque regions of the northeast coast. It skirted the farm once occupied by Sir William Coaker, and there a new provincial camping park was developed along the shore of Dildo Run.

Pickersgill also created the Atlantic Development Fund, endowed with $150 million of federal money. Designed with Newfoundland in mind, it proved of even greater benefit to the neighbouring Maritime provinces and was the foundation of all future schemes for federally financed regional development.

Joey and Pickersgill were never close personal friends, in the way that Joey and Doyle were. (Indeed, Pickersgill disliked Doyle intensely. He was almost Doyle's opposite—an intelligent, careful, conservative manipulator of the bureaucracy, not a high-flying gambler.) But they were close political allies, and they deeply admired each other's political skill. Joey was unquestionably the greatest Canadian of his time on a platform. Pickersgill was probably the greatest

Canadian of his time in a back room. They were perfect complements to each other and formed a remarkable partnership.

It was a shock to them both when the Liberal Party suffered utter disaster in the national election of 1957. Minister after minister who had been regarded as national treasures, as indispensable pillars of the state, went down to defeat in their own ridings. Even the monolithic C. D. Howe was beaten by an unknown school teacher. John Diefenbaker's victory was so completely unexpected by the political pundits that it caught the media unprepared. On election night all they could do was express their shock and incredulity. For nine months Canada had an uneasy minority government. Then Diefenbaker pulled off the landslide of 1958. Joey—and Newfoundland—would be in the wilderness for the next five years.

It is a measure of his political ability that Pickersgill increased his majority in that election, picking up two thousand over his majority of the year before, and winning 72 percent of the votes cast. It is a measure of Smallwood's ability that he managed to stem the Tory tide almost completely in Newfoundland, returning Liberals in five of the seven seats, and winning 55.44 percent of the popular vote—in complete opposition to the national trend. The only Newfoundland seats the Tories won were in St. John's, both of them by comfortable majorities.

In spite of their partisan differences, Joey had a natural liking for Diefenbaker. A few years earlier, when he and I had visited Ottawa together and sat in the visitors' gallery of the House of Commons, he had pointed out Diefenbaker as one of the real lights of the Opposition. He thought of Dief as a fellow populist, a campaigner for civil liberties, almost as a fellow "socialist" who had somehow got himself misplaced into the Tory ranks. He was more than ready to cooperate with the new prime minister, whom he also admired for his convincing, charismatic qualities.

Somehow, none of this ever got through to Dief. Soon after taking office he decided he was going to stamp on Joey, and less than a year after his landslide election, on the eve of Newfoundland's tenth anniversary as a province, he announced that financial aid to Newfoundland, under Term 29 of the Terms of Union, would be discontinued in another three years. The monies paid up to then would be a "final and irrevocable settlement." This was a clear violation of the spirit of the Terms of Union, and of the intention of

Term 29. The term reads as follows: "In view of the difficulty of predicting with sufficient accuracy the financial consequences to Newfoundland of becoming a Province of Canada, the Government of Canada will appoint a Royal Commission within eight years of the date of Union, to review the financial position of the Province of Newfoundland, and to recommend the form and scale of additional financial assistance, if any, that may be required by the Government of the Province of Newfoundland to enable it to continue the public services at the levels and standards reached subsequent to the date of Union, without resorting to taxation more burdensome, having regard to capacity to pay, than that obtaining generally in the region comprising the Maritime Provinces of Nova Scotia, New Brunswick, and Prince Edward Island."

The royal commission had been appointed by the Diefenbaker government in the autumn of 1957, and had reported in July 1958, recommending that $8 million a year be paid to Newfoundland annually, without time limit. This was $7 million less than Newfoundland had requested. The government's announced intention to cut off the grant altogether after three years struck Newfoundlanders as a monstrous injustice.

When Diefenbaker sat down after making his statement to the House of Commons announcing the end of Term 29, Lester Pearson, the leader of the Opposition, stood up and denounced it as completely unwarranted. Then Pickersgill left the Commons to issue a press statement calling it "an act of bad faith unequalled in the history of Canada."

The issue did not revolve around money. Eight million dollars here or there were no longer crucial to Newfoundland's survival—it was the principle of the government of Canada welshing on a contractual relationship with a province. No issue since confederation had cut across political lines the way this one did.

In St. John's Joey declared three days of official mourning, during which all flags on government buildings would fly at half-mast. The day after that he came out on the steps of Confederation Building to review a massive parade organized by the students of Memorial University. They were walking behind a black coffin, a band was playing a funeral march, and the leaders of the parade were dressed as undertakers, those following carrying placards demanding that Newfoundland secede from Confederation.

"Secession is not the answer!" Smallwood shouted to them.

"Canada hasn't betrayed us. John Diefenbaker has betrayed us. The rest of Canada is ready to rise up with us in rebellion against Mr. Diefenbaker for his cowardly attack on Newfoundland." The students went off to burn Diefenbaker in effigy.

The Tory Party of Newfoundland, which had enjoyed a great upsurge of popularity in the past two years, and was approaching 50 percent in the polls, was virtually destroyed by the Term 29 issue. Jim Higgins and Gus Duffy left the party and founded a new one, sitting in the legislature as members of the United Newfoundland Party. Joey, introducing a resolution to condemn Diefenbaker, asked for unanimous support of the House. Without unanimous support, he declared, he'd call an election. Two Tories, Malcolm Hollett and Rex Renouf, refused to vote with him, and the election was held August 29, 1959. The two Tories were both defeated. Smallwood himself ran against the Tory leader, Hollett, in St. John's West, and defeated him by almost two-to-one. The only seat where the PC candidate won an outright majority of the votes was in St. John's East, where they defeated the Liberal candidate by 147 votes. On Bell Island, they won by a slim plurality. In the two-seat district of Harbour Main they ran second to the leading Liberal, but beat his running mate by 351 votes. Joey had come within a hair's breadth of wiping them out altogether, but they had managed to pull three seats out of the debacle, and Jim Greene, a young lawyer from St. John's East, became the new Tory leader. In the popular vote the PCs dropped to 25 percent. In seven districts they ran third behind the NDP or an independent, and in four districts they failed to nominate candidates.

This was the PC Party's lowest point in the province. Hollett, however, received the reward of steadfastness and consistency. He had opposed Smallwood unrelentingly since 1946. In 1961 he received his appointment to the Senate.

It might not have been true, on March 27, 1959, that the rest of Canada was ready to "rise up with us in rebellion against Mr. Diefenbaker", but Joey set out to *make* it true. He descended on Ottawa five days later, primed for battle, and was met by a horde of reporters who quickly realized that he was just about the hottest copy in Canada. Here was David, with his verbal slingshot, taking on Goliath. When Diefenbaker tried to defend himself, he merely managed to sound like a bully, so for the most part he did the only safe thing and kept quiet, while Joey appeared on everyone's picture tube across the nation, appealing to Canada for "justice." Diefenbaker was inundated with letters from every province of Canada, but especially from the Maritimes, demanding that he stop picking on poor little Newfoundland. Before he was finished with his campaign, Joey even had three Tory premiers publicly on his side. Speaking to the staunch Tory Canadian Club in Ottawa, he pulled in the largest audience in the club's history, and brought them to their feet in a standing ovation.

Diefenbaker buckled. First he promised to "reconsider" Newfoundland's case, then he extended the cut-off period for the $8 million annual grant by five years. Joey knew he had the prime minister on the run, and ignored him. Term 29, he insisted, must remain (like an Indian treaty) "as long as the grass grows and the rivers run." Then he set out to make Diefenbaker look petty. He accused him of "pinching pennies." He said he was holding a grudge against Newfoundland because the Tenth Province was the only one that had failed to give him a majority of its seats in the 1958 election. Before Joey was finished with his speaking tour, Diefenbaker had dropped ten points in the polls.

The prime minister managed to get back at his attacker in a small and private way. He discovered that the government of Canada still owned Canada House at St. John's, the house that Smallwood had taken over and redecorated as his private residence, and in which he had his office and a personal collection of memorabilia. Dief decided to offer the house for sale, and sent Joey a notice to move out.

Joey was in no hurry to comply. He stalled for several months, not because he needed a place to live—he already owned a great estate forty miles from St. John's—but in the hope of embarrassing the prime minister even more than he was embarrassed already. "I hung on to the last moment," he said, "hoping he'd be misguided enough to have me evicted. I planned to have the photographers there to see my family and me sitting on the furniture on the sidewalk outside." But Diefenbaker had sense enough to avoid such a public spectacle. Joey moved out quietly late in 1960, and the house was sold. It was bought by Joseph D. Ashley, one of the group of young businessmen who had collected around Smallwood in 1949, and burgeoned into national prominence. By 1970 Ashley owned companies in St. John's and Halifax, and by 1978 also in Saint John and Calgary. But Ashley didn't keep the historic property. In the 1980s it was sold again, and converted into a duplex.

Joey retreated to his ranch on Roache's Line and began commuting daily by car, a government-owned Chrysler Imperial limousine that was part of the transportation pool of the Department of Health. According to Phil Forsey, it was "officially an ambulance." Joey often drove it at speeds of a hundred miles an hour or more, and according to his own boast, paid more than one speeding ticket. There is also a story of an RCMP patrolman who tried to catch the big black car on the road to Gander and failed, but overtook it at the airport, then, realizing whom he'd been chasing, stood smartly to attention and saluted as the little premier climbed grinning from the cockpit of the enormous machine. On one occasion I came close to having a head-on collision with him on Brigus Hill. We were both alone in our cars, travelling in opposite directions around a tight curve at speeds that would have assured our mutual destruction had we not managed to whisk past each other with a few inches' clearance. This may have been one of the experiences that finally induced him, after half a century behind the wheel, to place himself in the hands of a chauffeur.

The same year that he moved out of Canada House he moved into his new office at Confederation Building, a top-floor lookout with a private dining room, private elevator (to which Joey alone held a key), and private shower. Confederation Building was his first architectural monument, a $16 million box (original estimate, $11 million) that looked like an assembly plant for motor cars, with a tower sprouting disproportionately from its middle. One of Joey's dreams was to surround it with scores of ugly bronze statues of characters from Newfoundland's history. His friend Salazar, the Portuguese dictator, contributed a massive statue of Gaspar Corte-Real, who is supposed to have visited Newfoundland in 1500 A.D. in the course of a voyage during which he carried off the first Indian slaves from what is now Canada. Joey added, on his own, figures of John Cabot and Sir Wilfred Grenfell, and there, mercifully, the splurge of statue making stopped. Smallwood himself was sculpted, and his bronze bust erected in the foyer of the house on Roache's Line.

Joey's dream house was pure Hollywood, the first thing he had ever built for himself. A multilevelled, rambling glass-and-chrome creation which he financed partly on a mortgage, it was largely the gift of Liberal friends and supporters. Ashley Electric, for instance, had provided the wiring. The Crosbie companies had built the swimming pool. The Lundrigans loaned earth-moving machinery. And so on. Joey promised the house to the province, and did actually transfer the title late in his career, but continued to live there.

A basement library contained his Newfoundland collection, most of the volumes beautifully rebound in leather by Portuguese book-binders. It, too, was destined for public use—the nucleus of the Smallwood Centre for Newfoundland Studies at Memorial University.

By the late fifties his friendship with Salazar had reached the point where the Portuguese dictator was showering him with gifts. In the basement of the ranch house there was a secret panel that swung open to reveal a wine cellar, its shelves stocked with Portuguese wines, including jars of a fizzy pink brew that bore some resemblance to champagne.

In a corner of the sitting room Joey had his private nook, a kind of pocket-sized office in which he could work while reclining in a custom-built overstuffed chair, with its attached desk and unlisted telephone. More and more of his work was done while reclining there with his feet up, less and less in his office at Confederation Building. The telephone was his extension into the world. He would pick it up and dial Pickersgill or John C. Doyle or Robert Kennedy. He even dialed Diefenbaker—repeatedly. Indeed, he invited the Chief to come to St. John's for the official opening of the new university campus in 1961—an event at which he had persuaded Eleanor Roosevelt to preside.

"You just want to get me down there to make a fool of me," Diefenbaker growled.

"No! No indeed!" Joey assured him. "If you come I'll guarantee you a great, friendly reception. That's a promise." So Diefenbaker arrived, and had not a single rotten egg thrown his way. He and Joey met Mrs. Roosevelt at the airport, and they were all photographed together, smiling like old friends.

Outside the dream house there was a small lake, with acres and acres of lawn, which Joey trimmed himself, on a riding lawnmower. Behind it was a large greenhouse, where Clara Smallwood cultivated flowers. A few marble pillars from a demolished public building in St. John's provided a faint echo of Mackenzie King's famous ruins at Kingsmere.

But there the semblance of stateliness ended. Across the road was a restaurant and filling station owned by Joey's daughter, Clara Russell. On a bluff above the road stood a great black statue of a horse, looking just like the one on the label of Black Horse Ale. Many passersby assumed it was a gift from the well-known brewery, but in fact it had come from a defunct harness shop in St. John's. It stood there for several years until it blew down in a storm.

When Russwood Ranch was first carved out of the wilderness, the access to it was by way of a narrow dirt road called Roache's Line that left the Conception Bay shore not far from Port de Grave and wound painfully inland through valleys and past trout ponds until it lost itself among the blueberry bushes. Once the eastern link of the Trans-Canada Highway was completed from St. John's to Clarenville, Joey changed all this. The Trans-Canada nearly touched the borders of Russwood Ranch, and Roache's Line became the principal access road to the north side of Conception Bay, connected to the Trans-Canada by a cloverleaf. His hour-long commuting over the dangerous curves of the Brigus hills was now almost cut in half.

The ranch itself was a family affair, where his son-in-law, the ex-cowboy, ran cattle, his daughter indulged her love of horses, and Joey experimented with pigs, chickens, and even pheasants. Needless to say, none of his experiments paid their own way. His friend Nimshi Crewe, the accountant, commented wryly that any year the ranch lost less than a $100,000 was counted a great financial success.

Joey's chickens suffered psychotic attacks from overcrowding, and developed a fatal propensity for cannibalism. To cure this he consulted a mainland expert, and had them fitted with little plastic spectacles, attached to their beaks. The plastic, coloured red, was supposed to make it impossible for the chickens to see blood, and to indulge their unnatural appetites. Unfortunately the spectacles turned out to be just the right size to get caught in the meshes of the chicken wire that walled the cages. Every morning the ranch hands had to go through the chicken houses removing the corpses of the chickens that had hanged themselves the night before.

Then, to cap it all, there was an attack of silver yolks. The yolks of eggs are supposed to be golden yellow. Those from Russwood suddenly began to gleam like silver dollars. The puzzled expert called in for consultation went to see Greg Power, who had meanwhile established Newfoundland's largest chicken farm at St. John's.

"Do you know a cure for silver yolks?" the expert asked.

"No," said Greg, "but I know the cause."

"You do?"

"Yes. It's all that money that's been poured into those chickens."

Joey also tried sheep. To make the hills of Newfoundland white with sheep had been a recurrent dream of Newfoundland prime ministers since early in the nineteenth century. If sheep could thrive in the Outer Hebrides and on the Falkland Islands, there could be no reasonable doubt that, given half a chance, they'd thrive in Newfoundland. In pursuit of this dream, the Newfoundland wolf, a subspecies of the timber wolf, was exterminated by bounty hunters in the early twentieth century. Dogs, a much more serious problem than wolves, were usually allowed to roam at large by their owners, and were the subject, time and again, of anti-dog legislation. None of these measures had whitened the hills, but Joey was determined to have one more try on the vast semi-barren acreage that stretched beyond the horizon at Russwood.

He imported a ram of impeccable pedigree, transported it from St. John's to Russwood in the back seat of the limousine. He also imported a shepherd of superb credentials from the Highlands of Scotland. The shepherd took a look at the barrens above Russwood and reported that except for the lack of broom and heather, it seemed much like the sheep country at home. Joey sent off to the nearby outports, where people had been raising a few sheep, well protected by strong fences, for about four hundred years. He bought up their animals and collected them into a large flock. Far up on the wild barrens he built a cabin for the shepherd, and there he installed the sheep.

Things went swimmingly until one day when the fog rolled in from the distant ocean, too thick to see a hand before you. The fog sat there for weeks like rolls of carded wool while the shepherd, unable to venture more than a few steps without the danger of falling down a gulch into a bottomless tarn, sat in the cabin, consoling himself with a few sips of Scotland's favourite beverage. When the fog lifted and the sun come out the sheep were nowhere to be found. The best theory seemed to be that they had gone home to the outports where they were lambed.

And that's the way it went, year after year, one thing after another. Yet, somehow, Russwood weathered all the experiments, and was still supplying eggs, poultry, and pork to the Newfoundland supermarkets in the 1980s.

Joey's life at Russwood was filled with activity, but could not be called happy: it was dogged with tragedy. On May 12, 1957, while the ranch was in the early stages of development, a helicopter piloted by Gilbert Wass flew in, and offered Joey and his son Ramsay a low-level flight over their burgeoning domain. The small machine had room for the pilot and only two passengers, so at the last minute Joey gave up his seat to his daughter-in-law, Ramsay's wife. As the pilot revved the engine for takeoff, the co-pilot, standing in front, gestured to him, and pointed to the transmission line strung overhead. The pilot nodded, took off, and flew straight into the high tension wires. Somehow he had misunderstood the signal. The helicopter came crashing to the ground in flames.

Joey and others standing by rushed to pull the bodies from the wreck. The pilot was dead. Ramsay's wife was dead. Ramsay was terribly burned, but alive. Flown to Montreal, he received prolonged treatment and skin transplants, but was so disfigured by the accident that he shunned future appearances in public, and lived thenceforth in semi-retirement in his own house on Roache's Line.

Ten and a half years later, in October 1967, Joey's other son, William, a lawyer and the Liberal member for Green Bay, was involved in a custody battle with his estranged wife Marva, concerning their four children. Incredibly, the St. John's *Evening Telegram* decided to publish the court proceedings, something no Newfoundland paper had ever done before in the case of a custody dispute. The matter was eventually settled out of court, but as often happens in such cases, the accusations were shocking and damaging in the extreme.

Having his name dragged through the scandal columns of the daily press was certainly damaging to William Smallwood, who failed, at the nominating convention for the next election, to secure the nomination for Labrador South, losing to a previously unheard-of local man named Josiah Harvey. It was damaging and humiliating to Joey, too, who was required to give evidence, along with his wife, at the trial. One of the peculiarities of the press coverage was that *The Telegram* began reporting it only on the second day, after Smallwood's case against his wife had already been presented. On the basis of this one-sided reporting, Smallwood initiated a libel suit against *The Telegram*, but after the custody case was settled, the libel action was not pursued.

The third tragedy occurred in April 1973 when Edward J. Russell, married to Joey's daughter Clara, and the man principally responsible for the development of Russwood Ranch, shot himself while alone in a back field. He was found dead, hours later, by one of the ranch hands.

Joey found solace from such family disasters in his many grandchildren (and later great-grandchildren), whom he entertained in his home, and in whom he took increasing delight as the years passed.

They were the first children he had had around him to any extent. When his own children were young he had always been on the go, often in distant places, and as he expressed it himself, "they were raised almost exclusively by their mother."

The new generation of children not only had the run of the house, but he found time to play with them, read to them, and tell them stories as he had never managed to do with his own three. Among his descendants there was a Joey Smallwood II, and eventually a Joey Smallwood III. His granddaughter Dale Russell (later Dale Russell Fitzpatrick) eventually became his editor, the leading member of his publishing company, and finally the manager of the Joseph R. Smallwood Heritage Foundation.

Joey's feud with Diefenbaker lasted as long as the Tories remained in power. In 1962, at the end of the Chief's only full term in office, Joey campaigned vigorously in all Newfoundland ridings except Bonavista-Twillingate, and won six seats for the Liberals. Diefenbaker's government, reduced to a plurality, lasted only another six months. In 1963 Joey and Pickersgill brought all seven seats into the Liberal camp, the only close contest being in St. John's East, where Joe O'Keefe beat Jim McGrath by 857 votes. In a career that included nine federal elections, it was the only time McGrath was defeated.

Lester Pearson now became prime minister at the head of a minority government, with Pickersgill as Liberal house leader and minister of transport. One of their first acts was to repeal Diefenbaker's legislation on Term 29 and to make the $8 million payable in perpetuity as the term had clearly intended. The matter was not crucial anymore, however. Inflation and the increasing cost of government had by then reduced the Term 29 payment to less than 5 percent of the provincial budget.

The close partnership between Smallwood and Pickersgill, the success with which they used the federal system to help build a modern society in Newfoundland, continued throughout the Pearson years, and altered the entire pattern of federal-provincial relations in Canada. Not the least of the many disasters that overtook Joey in the late 1960s was the end of his partnership with Pickersgill. It, too, happened in 1967, which must be reckoned one of the worst years in his long career.

About twelve months after Joey's sweep in the 1966 election, Pickersgill told him that he was thinking of retiring from politics. After six years in power, Pearson was about to step down as party leader, and whole era of federal politics would pass away with him. The old-line politicians were going; the new managerial breed of political professionals was about to take over. Pickersgill was astute enough to perceive this process just as it was beginning to happen. At sixty-two he was not old, but he knew he belonged to the breed of politicians that included King, St. Laurent, and Pearson, and had no intention of becoming a political anachronism like John Diefenbaker. In no way could he expect to influence the affairs of state under the next prime minister, whoever he might be, as he had influenced them up to now. Finally, he had the opportunity to retire gracefully, with an appointment as head of the Canadian Transport Commission.

Joey was shocked. He had expected Pickersgill to go on for another ten or fifteen years as he intended to do himself. He argued, but Pickersgill was adamant. He suggested that Pickersgill might accept the post of Special Advisor to the Government of Newfoundland (in effect, Newfoundland's lobbyist in Ottawa) at nearly any salary he might like to name. But Pickersgill still said no. His retirement left a vacuum that was never filled.

When Joey went off to the Liberal Leadership Convention in April 1968 he was believed to be a supporter of Robert Winters, as were most of the Newfoundland delegates. He was one of those who had persuaded Winters to run, and had been closely associated with him, especially in the Churchill Falls development, for many years. But once Joey met Pierre Elliot Trudeau, he thought he had spotted a winner. He jumped on the Trudeau bandwagon, and took about three-quarters of the Newfoundland delegation with him. Winters never forgave the "betrayal." And Joey never again had any effective influence in Ottawa.

Unlike Pearson, who had treated Newfoundland as his favourite province, and had been rewarded with all seven seats in the 1965 federal election, Trudeau treated Newfoundland as just one more provincial counter in the political game. Although Don Jamieson became a power in Trudeau's governments from 1968 until 1979, at no time did he wield anything like Pickersgill's influence.

The road to political disaster became obvious when Joey lost six of the seven Newfoundland seats to the Tories in the federal election of June 1968.

# The Socialist and the Strikebreaker

THE LOGGERS' STRIKE THAT BEGAN ON JANUARY 2, 1959, WAS A watershed event in Joey's career. During this bitter strike by men at the very bottom of Newfoundland society he forsook the dreams of his youth—whatever remained of them by that time—and placed himself squarely in what the North American press would call the centre: no longer a "socialist," no longer leaning even a little bit to the left, but a typical North American bourgeois politician, supporting management against labour, and using police forces as strikebreakers.

Unions in the Newfoundland woods were nothing new in 1959. The loggers had been organized since the 1930s, when there were two unions competing for their loyalty. One was led by J. J. Thompson, who had started working in a logging camp at the age of twelve, earning $7 a month. He had organized the Newfoundland Lumbermen's Association in 1935 because the Fishermen's Protective Union, led by Ken Brown, was failing so badly to represent their interests— this in spite of the fact that "Brown's Union" by that time had little to do with the fishery, and concerned itself mainly with loggers. In 1936 Thompson succeeded in negotiating contracts with both paper companies, raising the price of wood from a range of $1 to $1.30 a cord to a range of $2 to $2.50 a cord, in effect doubling the loggers' earnings. As the chainsaw had not yet reached the Newfoundland woods, the men worked in pairs with crosscut saws or the slightly better bucksaws, producing an average of less than one cord of wood a day each. Out of their earnings they had to pay board to the camp owners, which were either paper companies or contractors.

Over the years both unions became less and less effective. By 1940 Thompson's union had split into three parts along regional lines, so that there were four competing unions of Newfoundland loggers. The Commission government then set up the Woods Labour Board to represent unions and management, with a government-appointed full-time secretary, Ray Gushue. Once a year it handed down contracts for the industry, and it also settled all grievances and disputes between contracts.

What was new in the late 1950s was not a loggers' union, but a union with professional leadership, wide experience in the industry, and a militant attitude not just about wage rates, but also about the utterly appalling living conditions in the logging camps. Those conditions were so bad that when Sir Eric Bowater once visited a camp unannounced he went back to Corner Brook and ordered the company to burn it down. The Bowater woods department then saw to it that one camp would be cleaned up and stocked with decent food especially for Sir Eric's visits.

Otherwise, the men were expected to live and eat like pigs in stinking hovels with four-foot walls. They slept on green boughs, thawed their clothes around a stove made from an oil drum, and washed, occasionally, in meltwater. Their main food was boiled navy beans, supplemented with white flour, rice, salt fish, salt beef, and black tea. This rough, cheap food was prepared by some of the world's worst cooks—common labourers with absolutely no training for their specialized jobs. Rats roamed the camps virtually unchecked by the cats brought in to fight them. Food was stored in special sheds built on posts with inverted metal buckets for collars. The sheds were also lined with metal mesh so that rats jumping from the trees would not be able to gnaw through the roof and walls.

By the 1950s, loggers were no longer commonly paid by the cord, but by the hour, and by 1958 the rate had risen to $1.05—a little lower, on the average, than the going rate across the province for unskilled labour, but not *much* lower. The real issue was not wages, but living conditions and the loggers' right to be represented by their own union, rather than having everything handed down from on high. The Woods Labour Board was anything but representative. It had always been a paternalistic bureaucracy

Into this situation stepped two powerful competitors: Joey and

H. Landon Ladd. Despite the poverty of his childhood, Joey had never really been a member of the working class. His family were farmers and small businessmen, not wage earners. It is true that he had worked as a printer's devil and reporter on St. John's newspapers, but only briefly, and only as a step toward writing and politics. His experience with unions was all from the outside: he had never been a rank-and-file member of any democratic organization, though he had served many of them in various capacities. To him the working class was the "ragged-arsed artillery" whose function was to elect crusading political leaders to make things better for them, not to take things into their own hands and create social change by economic pressure.

In 1959 Joey suddenly came up against the International Woodworkers of America, an industrial union that had broken away from the International Brotherhood of Carpenters and Joiners, whose interests as craftsmen were only vaguely related to the interests of the labouring loggers. It was a powerful, militant union, with headquarters in British Columbia, and its eastern director, Landon Ladd, had risen from the ranks of B.C. Loggers. A man of exceptional gifts, and a spellbinding speaker, Ladd also had a lot of appeal among the rank and file: he spoke their language; he was one of themselves.

He arrived in Newfoundland in 1956, seeking affiliation with Thompson's union, the Newfoundland Lumbermen's Association. When this failed, he turned to organizing the loggers directly, and won an instant response. He had two assistant organizers, Jeff Hall and Jack McCool, but Ladd was all over the operations himself, spending nearly all his time in Newfoundland. All three IWA organizers were democratic socialists, supporters of the CCF Party, exactly the kind of man Smallwood had once believed himself to be. Within six months of the start of organizing, the union applied for certification, but the application was rejected because it covered only a portion of the workforce. The union waited another six months, and tried again, supporting their claim with paid-up dues records of 87 percent of those working in the woods. Nothing comparable had happened in Newfoundland since the early days of Coaker.

Joey kept quiet, but was privately alarmed. He recognized in Landon Ladd the first opponent he had ever faced with his own brand of charisma, his own ability to appeal to the dispossessed. Ladd was talking openly about a social upheaval, a new economic deal for Newfoundland. Did he have the potential to sweep Joey out of power? It was a shocking thought. The man had the force and magnetism of a great evangelist: today the loggers, tomorrow the fisherman, next year the government? It was all too possible. What could Joey do about it? Nothing, at first, except wait, and watch carefully. Ladd undoubtedly underestimated his opponent—a fatal mistake.

Meanwhile, a serious worldwide recession had hit newsprint and was nearing its worst just as the Labour Relations Board announced the result of its supervised vote: IWA Local 545 was certified as bargaining agent for the loggers supplying the mill at Corner Brook; IWA Local 554 was certified for loggers supplying the mill at Grand Falls. Eighty-five percent of the men polled had voted for the IWA. The organizing drive had taken two years.

The Anglo-Newfoundland Development Company at Grand Falls bought some wood from contractors, but most of it by far came from its own logging camps, operated by its own woods department. Bowater Newfoundland Limited, at Corner Brook, bought most of its wood from contractors, who ran their own camps independently, usually on Bowater timber limits, under a Bowater franchise.

Albert Martin, general manager at Corner Brook, issued a statement to the press expressing "implacable opposition" to the IWA, but added that his company was nonetheless ready to open negotiations with the union (as indeed he was required to do by law). The negotiations never began. According to Martin, the union simply never got around to bargaining. It appeared that they had selected the AND Company as their first target for two reasons: first, the operation was less complex; second, AND was regarded as a "softer" company, less of a monolith than Sir Eric Bowater's far-flung empire.

This, as it happened, was a tactical error. The AND Company was as opposed as Bowater to the IWA, and it was actually in a stronger position, because it had the support of the public at Grand Falls, and even of the union locals working in its mill. At Corner Brook the situation was quite different. There the public, the mill unions, and the local press (as long as it was allowed) all supported the loggers, not only morally, but with large gifts of money. The choice of Grand Falls over Corner Brook could only have been made by someone quite unfamiliar with the sympathies of the unions and the climate of public opinion.

IWA strategy was to seek a first contract with terms that would be so easy on the company as to make refusal difficult. The tough bargaining would come later. They asked for a wage rate of $1.30 an hour, a work week reduced to fifty-four hours from sixty, and at least a token improvement in living conditions at the camps. The company met the union and offered absolutely nothing. The union then applied for a conciliation board. The board recommended the reduction in working hours requested by the union, improvement in camp conditions, and a wage increase to $1.22 an hour—17 cents more than the rate had been when the organizing drive began, but only 5 cents above the rate prevailing in December 1958. (In a bid to weaken the IWA drive, the paper companies had voluntarily increased loggers' pay by 12 cents an hour.) Willing to get a first contract at any price, the IWA accepted these recommendations, even though they represented a cut in take-home pay. Only a union with complete confidence in the support of its membership could have done so. Nevertheless, the company rejected the recommendations of the board and refused to make a counteroffer of any kind. Manager Ross Moore made a radio statement on December 18, 1958: "What we are actually faced with is a set of demands by the IWA that would cripple the entire AND operation."

Moore's contention requires some explanation. Obviously, he wasn't talking about five cents an hour. In fact, what both paper companies were worried about, though they could hardly admit it publicly, was that they would be forced, the following year or the year after, to bear the cost of building new logging camps with central heating, hot and cold running water, flush toilets, showers, and decent kitchen facilities. Company accountants were busy estimating the cost. Their estimates varied, but none was lower than $5 million.

When the IWA polled its members, 98 percent voted to strike. Ross Moore warned that a strike might cripple the economy and force the AND Company to shut down the Grand Falls mill permanently. Bowaters made a similar statement. They might be forced to move out of Newfoundland altogether, they said. This was a moth-eaten tactic of companies in American and Canadian mill towns, thoroughly familiar and thoroughly discredited, but in Newfoundland the threat was taken seriously—even, it would seem, by Joey Smallwood himself. By this time the issue was not whether the companies could bear this or that cost. It was a straightforward question of whether or not the loggers would be allowed to have the IWA as their bargaining agent. Asked to make any kind of compromise offer, the AND Company simply refused to budge. They had opted for the strike, believing that with government help they could break it. They had stockpiled a three-months supply of wood at the mill. The 1958 Christmas holiday was not yet over, and the camps were all but empty. On January 2 they began recruiting strikebreakers.

The union set up picket lines at the woods roads, and reportedly told any of its members who happened to be in the woods camps to stay there (to make it more difficult for strikebreakers to take them over). Strike committees were organized in each of the logging towns. With a clear perception of what was coming, Landon Ladd insisted that a majority of each committee must be women—they would be less likely to be hauled off to jail than the men. Soon women were manning the picket lines alongside their sons and husbands.

When the first truck was stopped on its way to the mill, the company appealed to the RCMP to "police the roads." In effect, this meant escorting strikebreakers through the picket lines in company vehicles. At first there was only an exchange of insults and cries of "scab." Soon there were roadblocks to stop independent operators from hauling loads of wood to the mill. Later, the strikers raided at least one camp, and turned strikebreakers out into the snow. Although the strike was peaceful at first, the company pumped a stream of propaganda to the press complaining of "lawlessness" by the strikers, and the press reported it uncritically, while giving little or no space to the union's viewpoint. The reporting in the *Western Star* was heavily slanted against the loggers by orders of the paper's management. It reached the point where the entire senior staff, including the managing editor, resigned in protest. From that point on, no paper in Newfoundland would publish the union's side of the story.

The daily press all over Newfoundland devoted its editorial pages to presenting the company's viewpoint. Day after day a stream of columns, editorials, and news stories painted the same picture—that of a violent, foreign union that had come to Newfoundland to take over the province's most important industry, threatening it with destruction. Soon the fundamentalist preachers were echoing the editorials from their pulpits. Joey would later claim that the IWA was opposed by the leaders of every religious body in the province. Perhaps so. At least some of the religious leaders were opposed, and said so in public. Gradually, an atmosphere of hysteria began to build, a kind of public madness that had not been seen in Newfoundland since the days of the religious riots more than half a century earlier.

At the end of five weeks the loggers seemed to be winning. The stockpile at the AND mill was shrinking visibly, and was not being replenished. Most of the strikebreakers had left the camps and gone home to the fishing outports. Soon, Ladd boasted, the spring runoff would be on, and the rivers would be empty of wood. Then the mill would have to shut down.

It was at this point, with the company virtually beaten, that Smallwood intervened. With no previous hint of his sympathies in the matter, he took to the radio on the night of February 12 to denounce the IWA as a vicious invasion force from the mainland, and the strike as "not a strike but a civil war."

"How dare these outsiders," said he, "come into this decent Christian province and by such desperate methods try to seize control of our province's main industry? How dare they come in here and spread their black poison of class hatred and bitter bigoted prejudice? How dare they come into this province amongst decent God-fearing people and let loose the dirt and filth and poison of the last four weeks?"

It was a declaration of war. Soon he was at Grand Falls, guest of the company, working full-time to break the strike. Organizers from militant mainland unions had predicted as long ago as 1950 that Smallwood would turn on the labour movement sooner or later, but Newfoundland union leaders, most of whom had taken his "leftism" seriously, were stunned. They had hoped he would intervene in the strike, forcing both sides to arbitration. They had never dreamed that he would line up with two foreign corporations to destroy an organization of Newfoundland workers.

Joey, once he came to the fight, came armed with every weapon; the power of his rhetoric, the strength of the police, the familiar old company union with a new twist—he offered the loggers a *government* union headed by one of his own Liberal members of the House of Assembly, C. Max Lane, a former magistrate who also happened to be general secretary of the nearly defunct Newfoundland Federation of Fishermen. The new union would not have to go through the tiresome process of winning the support of the loggers and applying to the Labour Relations Board for certification. Joey would certify it directly by passing a law. He predicted that the new union would have some 15,000 members, and would be gladly accepted by the Newfoundland Federation of Labour. In the days when logging was a part-time occupation for fishermen, a union of fishermen-loggers made sense. That was what Brown had tried to organize. But in 1959 it no longer made any sense at all. The loggers promptly named Joey's organization the "Fish and Chips Union" and otherwise ignored it, but the legislature tamely passed the bill he presented, creating and certifying the Newfoundland Brotherhood of Woods Workers without a dissenting vote. Contrary to his expectations, the Newfoundland Federation of Labour rejected the Brotherhood as a fake union organized for the purpose of strikebreaking.

As a matter of fact, even had it wanted to do so, the Newfoundland Federation of Labour could not have accepted the NBWW without the approval of the Canadian Labour Congress. But instead of taking a closer look at the structure of the labour movement, Joey simply turned on the Federation with tooth and claw. He discovered that Larry Daley, the federation's popular president, was chairman of a small St. John's local affiliated with the International Teamsters, whose American branch and its American president, James Hoffa, were then under investigation by Robert Kennedy for links to the criminal underworld. This was enough for Joey to paint the whole labour movement in Newfoundland as a conspiracy of gangsters, white slavers, dope pedlars, and embezzlers. In the legislature, he described Daley as "Hoffa's man" and connected the IWA with gangsterism and communism by inference.

Joey carried on this campaign of character assassination under cover of legislative immunity—he could not be sued for anything he said in the House of Assembly. Daley tried to get him to repeat his words outside the chamber, so he could sue for libel, but Joey discreetly confined his comments outside the House to dark hints.

In fact, there was absolutely no connection between the IWA and the underworld, or the IWA and any communist party, either in Canada or the United States. Neither was there any connection between the Newfoundland Federation of Labour and the leadership of the American Teamsters, as Joey very well knew.

On March 6 he had the House of Assembly pass two pieces of legislation that he described as emergency laws. The first decertified the two locals of the IWA in Newfoundland. The second gave the government power to dissolve any union if its officers had been "convicted of such heinous crimes as white slavery, dope peddling, manslaughter, embezzlement, such notorious crimes as these." This appears to have been the only occasion in Canada when a union was simply named and abolished by law. The constitutional question was a very nice one, but it was never examined properly. Joey had always had a curious attitude that the legislature was not subject to the rule of law, that, at least in theory, it could do absolutely anything. He stood in his place in the House and announced, "We are above *all* laws."

The second of the two "emergency laws" was never invoked. We can say in retrospect that it was never intended to be invoked. It was simply part of a smear campaign against the labour movement as a whole, because the labour movement supported the IWA—it had no other intended function.

Throughout Canada and the world the two laws aroused shock and indignation. Even John Diefenbaker's Conservative government was appalled, and it made a confidential overture to the lieutenant-governor to withold royal assent until the laws' constitutionality could be examined. It is a measure of the extent of the hysteria by then prevailing in Newfoundland that the lieutenant-governor did no such thing. He signed the two bills into law immediately.

The Canadian Labour Congress organized a campaign for funds to support the striking loggers, and workers across Canada responded by raising the largest strike fund in Canadian labour history up to that time: $865,000. The AFL–CIO wired its support, and the American branch of the IWA pledged "unlimited" funds. Dockworkers in both Great Britain and the United States refused to unload AND Company newsprint. Even most of the daily press across Canada supported the loggers and condemned Smallwood. Cartoonists for the first time portrayed him as a vicious little man with a crown and sceptre.

Meanwhile, Joey flew to central Newfoundland to "free the loggers from the tyranny of the foreign union," and spent a week as a union organizer to no avail. His meeting in the town hall at Grand Falls drew some 800 members of the general public—scarcely a logger among the lot of them. The same day Landon Ladd drew a meeting of more than 1,200, mostly loggers, in nearby Bishop's Falls.

Joey instructed welfare officers to issue welfare to any needy logger who produced a card issued by the NBWW. Any logger without such a card was to be refused. He not only issued such orders, but stated publicly that he had done it. In spite of it all, his organizing drive was a failure. No significant number of men deserted the IWA.

The little logging town of Badger, twenty miles west of Grand Falls, now became the centre of the strike. Roads from Badger led to the principal timber limits on the watershed of the Exploits River. The town was solid for the strike, men, women and children. The IWA massed 250 pickets in the town and blocked the roads leading up-country. The government responded to the pickets by sending in every RCMP constable who could possibly be spared from the whole of central Newfoundland. Joey ordered policemen from the Newfoundland Constabulary in St. John's to reinforce them. By March 10 there were seventy policemen in the village.

The position of the strikers was now hopeless. Even if they pushed the company into an agreement, it would have no legal force, and would not have to be honoured. All an outlawed union could do was go down fighting. And that's what they prepared for. A crowd of about 250 loggers and their families blocked the main road at Badger on the evening of March 10. The RCMP, supported by the Newfoundland Constabulary, decided first to clear the road, and then to disperse the loggers by charging into the picket line. The police riot that followed was witnessed by Ray Timson of the *Toronto Star*, reported in that paper on March 11, and subsequently carried across Canada by Canadian Press:

> Marching three abreast and carrying nightsticks, a column of 66 policemen waded into a throng of striking loggers last night, clubbed two of them unconscious, flattened dozens more while wives and children screamed for them to stop. I watched the attack on mainly defenceless men for about an hour. One Newfoundland policemen was hit with a two-foot-long piece of birch wood and is in hospital in Grand Falls in critical condition. One Mountie was punched in the face. Both blows were struck after the police started wielding billies. The police sticks were 18 inches long. I heard three sickening skull cracks. Nine of the loggers were arrested; most had been beaten to the ground, handcuffed and dragged to their feet. At the height of the club swinging, which occurred beside the Full Gospel church, children stood watching and began crying. Their mothers cried with them. One shouted, "the men can't do anything. There are too many police." At another point a logger standing in a backyard bordering the road watched the police escorting handcuffed, dazed loggers away. He shouted, "You sure have guts, haven't you?" An officer pointed to him and yelled, "Get that man. Get him now." The logger turned and fled and about 25 Mounties and policemen cleared the fence like jack rabbits and chased him down toward a row of houses. He was beaten to the ground and arrested.

What had happened, according to later testimony in court, was that RCMP Inspector Arthur Argent had sent the police column to clear the main road. The loggers had fallen back, leaving the road clear, but had then reformed at the junction of the woods road. Argent next halted the column, swung it about, and sent it charging into the crowd blocking the secondary road. At this point the police broke ranks and began indiscriminately clubbing the loggers. As the loggers fled from the scene, many of them lay beaten and handcuffed in the snow. Among the casualties was one policemen, a rookie from St. John's named William Moss.

The RCMP rushed him to Lady Northcliffe Hospital in Grand Falls. He had a fractured skull and brain haemorrhaging. He died a few hours later without regaining consciousness. The police said he had been killed by one of the loggers they had hauled away in handcuffs. They charged a man named Ronald Laing with murder.

Joey turned the death of Moss into a stage production. The coffin, draped in the Union Jack, was carried through the streets of Grand Falls to the railway station. In St. John's a state funeral was arranged, including a parade through the streets with an open hearse bearing the body, and a guard of honour at the graveside. The government announced a William Moss Memorial scholarship to be awarded annually to the son or daughter of a policeman.

But the real criminals, Joey declared, were not those who had been carted off to jail in handcuffs; they were the IWA organizers, Ladd, McCool, and Hall. "They are the real criminals. Up to now they have succeeded in evading arrest."

In Grand Falls there was further violence. Mobs of vigilantes roamed the streets looking for loggers. A crowd of them attacked and ransacked the IWA office at Bishop's Falls.

Even before the police riot, Joey had sent off a call to Ottawa for RCMP reinforcements to act as strikebreakers, and Commissioner Leonard Nicholson had replied that he was advised such reinforcements might not be necessary. Strictly speaking, under the contract by which the RCMP policed Newfoundland, they were obliged to provide extra policemen when the provincial government requested them. But the advice to stall the matter had come from Davie Fulton, the federal minister of justice. After Moss's death, Nicholson consulted Fulton again, and ordered fifty RCMP on their way to Newfoundland. At that point, the prime minister intervened. The supplementary force of federal police must be halted, he ordered, until Cabinet made a decision.

Diefenbaker was acutely aware of the RCMP's long record of strikebreaking, particularly in the west, the principal centre of his own political support. He cherished his own record as a champion of civil liberties, which he had won as a young Saskatchewan lawyer, and he was not willing to see a major strike smashed by RCMP intervention during his administration. He argued this before the Cabinet, and carried the majority with him. The extra policemen were recalled, and Nicholson resigned.

In the House of Commons Diefenbaker made a terse statement: "I feel impelled to say that the premier of Newfoundland has greatly aggravated the present situation in that province by intervening in a labour dispute in a way which apparently goes beyond the usual role of government."

The CCF Party had already registered its condemnation. Lester Pearson, leader of the Liberal Opposition, was strongly inclined to add his voice to the condemnation. He was dissuaded by Pickersgill, who threatened to resign from the party. Had it not been for that, Joey would probably have been censured unanimously by the three major parties in Canada.

In fact, the RCMP reinforcements were *not* needed, either as peacekeepers or as strikebreakers. The strike was already over. Two days after the police riot at Badger, the AND Company signed an agreement with Joey's union, setting wages at $1.22 an hour—the level recommended by the conciliation board—and on March 20 the IWA advised its members to take out cards in the fake union as the only means of getting their jobs back.

The aftermath was complex and long-lasting. The man who was said to have killed Moss was tried for murder at St. John's some two months after the riot. By then the public hysteria had died, and the danger of a judicial lynching was past. Laing was defended by Jim Higgins, Newfoundland's ablest criminal lawyer, and one of the members of the legislature who had tamely voted for Joey's bizarre labour laws. He had an easy time with the defence. The Crown was not even able to prove that Moss had been struck by a piece of wood wielded by a logger, as the *Toronto Star* story had suggested he might have been. It was quite possible that he had been killed in the darkness by a policeman's club. If, indeed, he had been struck by a logger, there was no doubt about the fact that it was in self-defence. The jury's verdict was swift and unanimous: "Not guilty."

Though the loggers lost their strike and their right to belong to the IWA, they won improved wages and living conditions. Eight thousand of them were herded into the Newfoundland Brotherhood of Woods Workers, but the organization lasted only two years and accomplished exactly nothing. Then a government-appointed commission found that in practice the loggers had no organization to represent them, and Joey replaced the NBWW by the International Brotherhood of Carpenters and Joiners, which was certified, on Joey's orders, without a vote.

That same commission found living conditions in the camps to be somewhat improved, but still disgracefully substandard. In fact, they reported, some camps were unfit for livestock, much less human beings. There was a rush to rebuild them to the very standards most feared by the paper companies before the strike started. Soon the contractors were installing hot and cold running water and central heating, or at least floor furnaces, in the logging camps. By the end of the decade the loggers' wages had doubled, and the workforce had been cut to an elite corps of five thousand—exactly what the IWA had advocated. And despite all this, the paper companies prospered as they had never prospered before. In the years following the loggers' strike their profits reached all-time record levels.

The loggers had won everything except self-determination. There was never the slightest doubt that in a free vote they would have brought the IWA back to represent them. They would still have done it ten years later.

The Newfoundland Federation of Labour suffered badly from the affray. Throughout the whole of it, Smallwood had continued to have his supporters, even among Federation officers, and when Larry Daley was forced to resign because of a dispute between his union and the CLC, a constitutional quirk brought one of Smallwood's supporters to the presidency. The year before the strike, membership in the federation stood at 73 unions with 22,328 members. Three years later, it was 61 unions with 12,476 members. That was the Federation's low point, followed by a slow and then more rapid recovery. By the end of the 1960s Newfoundland was once again the Canadian province with the best-organized workforce.

Joey was not so lucky. After the strike, he entered a long period of struggle with organized labour. Individual labour leaders might support him, but the rank and file of unionists never trusted him again. Knowing that he had supporters among Federation delegates, he was brash enough to attend the 1959 NFL convention as usual, only to sit there and be told to his face that he was a liar and a character assassin. When he called an election for August 29, the Federation organized its own political party, and ran seventeen candidates, ten of them placing second in the polls. Though hastily organized, the Newfoundland Democratic Party managed to show that the outports, at least those with significant numbers of loggers, were no longer safe Small-wood territory.

In the subsequent election of 1962 Smallwood lost Humber East to the Tories for the first time, and Ed Finn, the former managing editor of *The Western Star*, who had resigned in the midst of the strike and was now running for the NDP, came within 240 votes of unseating Joey's tame minister of labour, Charles Ballam. In that election, Smallwood also lost Grand Falls to the PCs, Labrador West to an independent, and won eight of his outport seats by less than 500 votes each. Eight members now sat in Opposition, but this was much less important than the change in the voting patterns: his solid hold on the outports had at last been broken.

Joey suffered more damage from the IWA strike than either the companies or the loggers. By taking the side of multinational corporations against outport Newfoundlanders and their union he had betrayed his own deepest convictions. The only time he ever discussed the matter willingly was in his long, rambling apologia, *I Chose Canada* (Macmillan, 1973). In this account he accused the loggers at Badger of launching an unprovoked attack on the peaceful column of police, using three- and four-foot clubs, bottles, and axes. This accusation was not only contrary to the eye-witness account of the one journalist who was on the scene, but also contrary to the evidence produced in court.

The betrayal of the loggers was Joey's one unforgiveable act. It left what his colleague and successor Ed Roberts calls "a deep psychic scar." What he did would not have been unexpected in Maurice Duplessis or Wacky Bennett, because decisions to break strikes were true to their natures. But Smallwood was not that kind of man. He destroyed the one effective union the loggers ever had, not because he regarded capital as sacred and organized labour as poor white trash, but because he lost his nerve. Having lost his nerve, he abandoned everything he had stood for. And he knew it. He fuelled the violence and hysteria that gripped Newfoundland as the strike progressed. Instead of statesmanship, he offered the people inflammatory rhetoric. And the public reaction that followed has bothered the consciences of Newfoundlanders ever since.

Apart from what all this may have done to Joey's self-respect, it had a disastrous effect, once sanity had returned, on his public image. Young voters, in particular, no longer looked up to him as a benevolent if sometimes mistaken father figure, but began to think of him as another Maurice Duplessis, another Huey Long, a demagogue whom it was dangerous to cross, sitting alone in the seat of power, opposed to democratic processes, opposed to the right of self-determination. It would take ten years to bring him down, but his decline was inexorable. From the moment he broke the strike, the forces that would destroy him were gathering, and gathering strength.

# CHAPTER 15

# The King of
# Cost-Plus

THE GREATEST BLOW JOEY SUFFERED IN THE WAKE OF THE LOGGERS'
strike was what he called the "defection" of Greg Power.

The only remaining member of the small band of idealists who had
formed the core of the Newfoundland Confederate Association,
Power had stuck by Smallwood without wavering for twelve years and
their personal friendship seemed indissoluble.

Power was executive assistant to the premier in 1949, the year he
ran and was defeated in the federal riding of St. John's West. He then
became chairman of the Board of Liquor Control, a position from
which he could strengthen and enrich the party. He won a decisive
victory in the provincial district of Placentia–St. Mary's (his ancestral
home) in 1951, taking 67 percent of the vote, and again in 1956, when
he won by 77 percent.

In Smallwood's second elected cabinet he was minister of finance,
and from 1952 to 1958 he accompanied Joey on many of his travels.
Indeed, Power was always Smallwood's number one man, and the
only minister besides the shrewd and clever attorney-general, Les
Curtis, who wielded real authority inside and outside the government.

Joey and Greg not only travelled together on government business, but took their holidays together, usually in Jamaica, where Power
had friends in the distilling business. (As Minister of Finance he still
had the Board of Liquor Control under his department.) It was on a
beach in Jamaica in 1953 that Smallwood and Power agreed together to

kick their drug habits. The evening before, Greg had been sampling the pale amber rum from the famous Lindo estate with what Joey thought was undue relish. Himself a near teetotaller, who limited his drinking to a glass of port or sherry, he had always regarded rum as outright poison.

"Greg," Joey said, noting what was perhaps a slight hangover, "if you don't quit drinking, you're going to kill yourself."

"Joe," Greg responded, "I'll quit drinking when you quit smoking."

"Done!" Joey said, jumping up. He grabbed Power's hand, and made him shake on it. A chain smoker who consumed a hundred cigarettes a day he knew perfectly well that tobacco imperilled his health, and he had been looking for just this trigger to fire his resolve.

He quit cold turkey. Rumour had it that he temporarily used some kind of prescription drug to reduce his craving for nicotine. Be that as it may, he threw away his filter cigarette holder and was never seen to smoke again. Power was equally self-disciplined about his drinking (which had never been excessive). He even became somewhat puritanical on the subject, and a few years later began scoffing at Joey for being a "wine-bibber."

Joey and Greg were received together by Pope Pius XII at Castle Gondolfo. They lugged into the papal presence a satchel full of cheap beads and crucifixes, and had the pope bless the trinkets, after which they flew back to St. John's, and had them distributed to Catholic voters in the districts of Ferryland and Placentia (where some of them are still kept as family treasures).

They went trout fishing together in the wilderness lakes near Placentia Junction where Power had fished as a boy. But one day when a cold northeast wind was blowing down their necks, with a drizzle of rain, and the fish weren't biting, Greg turned to his friend and said, "Look Joe, those little things have never done us any harm. Why don't we just leave them alone?"

"I agree absolutely," said Joey. They packed up their gear and headed back to their camper, and never went fishing again.

They had their disagreements, but Power was the one person who could differ with Smallwood and even privately heap scorn on his public pronouncements without making an enemy of him. Power, for instance, had always disliked Valdmanis, but managed to stick it out through Joey's three-year infatuation with the sinister little Latvian. On the subject of John C. Doyle they cheerfully agreed.

Doyle was not only an Irish romantic, like Power himself, but also the sort of swashbuckling wheeler-dealer that Power could admire. On Doyle's advice, he began buying corporate shares. Unlike many of his Cabinet colleagues, whose greed got the better of them, Power had the cool detachment to buy and sell at the right time, and made a modest killing on the stock market.

He also built the biggest poultry business in the province, and ran it with conspicuous success. For a while it was *de rigueur* for every public bar-room to have a gallon jug of "Gregseggs" on the counter top, to be sold as grogbits. A Gregsegg was a hardboiled egg, shelled and pickled at Power's establishment.

In the world of business, Power also had that indefinable quality known as luck. When he needed a separate place to raise pullets he bought Clovelly farm on the eastern border of St. John's, paying $20,000 for it, an amount his banker advised him was unreasonably high. By the time he sold it, at a fabulous profit, for the development of an expanding city, he estimated that the modest investment had returned a total of $860,000 to his company.

When he walked out of the government he was a millionaire. It had taken him just ten years to rise from the modest little farm at Dunville, Placentia Bay, that he had inherited from his father, to a secure place in the plutocracy of wealth. (At that point, incidentally, the income tax auditors descended on him, and billed him for a quarter of a million dollars, which he paid promptly.)

His personal expenditures were striking, but not flamboyant. At his new, comfortable, but modest-looking house, well hidden behind trees on Portugal Cove Road, St. John's, he had two swimming pools—one with a plexiglass roof to let the ultraviolet rays penetrate, the other in his basement, heated to therapeutic temperatures to help soak off some of the symptoms of arthritis. He had a tennis court for his children and grandchildren (who tended to adore him), and he travelled in a custom-built camper whose neat and functional design was the envy of all his friends, including Joey, who tried to copy it. His tastes were modest. He liked reading, and bought books, including rare books. He liked fishing. He liked to eat in Chinese restaurants.

Power was clever, witty, and cynical—a pose that Smallwood enjoyed. They both nourished a hidden sentimentalism. Power indulged a taste for Irish songs and nineteenth-century poetry, and produced some beautifully crafted lyrics himself, in a style reminiscent of Thomas Hardy. Perhaps that was why Joey could forgive him for being cynical, even at the expense of the ever-expanding Smallwood image. When Joey spouted a particularly nauseating bit of jingoistic propaganda, Greg would tell him so, without mincing words. On one occasion when my father, Andrew Horwood, had been received into The Presence as a contributor to Volume Four of *The Book of Newfoundland*, Joey made him listen to a speech that he had taped some weeks before, and asked what he thought of it.

"An extraordinary performance!" my father responded guardedly.

"Yes," Joey agreed, "and not a word of sense in the lot of it! Greg Power was absolutely right when he said he'd never heard such nonsense in his life."

By the end of his first decade as premier it was becoming difficult for close friends like Power and Nimshi Crewe to accept the personality changes brought about by Joey's apotheosis. He was becoming more smug and self-satisfied, and less prepared, even in private, to listen to constructive criticism. They rarely met him, nowadays, except on formal occasions.

Power, by contrast, changed hardly at all. He enjoyed being wealthy, but didn't worship money. In the late 1980s I could see little change in Power from when I'd first met him in 1945, and we'd gone tramping through the backwoods, looking for salmon and trout. But Joe, of course, had changed totally from the cocky little radical of Confederate Association days into the rather pompous Only Living Father of Confederation who so successfully destroyed the IWA, clipped the wings of the powerful Newfoundland Federation of Labour, and toured Spain at the personal invitation of the fascist dictator, General Francisco Franco.

When Power abruptly resigned from the government in 1959 it was widely believed that he and Smallwood had reached a fatal disagreement over the loggers' strike. Power, after all, was a former union leader, and had been notably absent when Smallwood rammed his antilabour legislation through the House. But in fact the estrangement had been growing between them before the loggers' strike began. Throughout 1958 Power had found it increasingly difficult to put up with Joey's pose as the Great Panjandrum, and had offered to resign before the end of the year. Joey, reluctant to sever this last tie with his days as confederate champion, had persuaded him to stay, and tried to win him with soft words. But Power stopped attending Cabinet meetings and meetings of the caucus, and even stayed away from his office. After three months during which Greg and Joe had scarcely seen each other, Joe wrote a letter saying he'd accept Power's resignation.

Through the middle years of the 1950s I had been Smallwood's principal critic as columnist, feature writer, and later editorial writer for *The Evening Telegram*. Whatever points were scored against Joey by the Opposition in the House had come first from my columns. But by 1958 I was tired of this, and resigned from the paper to take up freelance writing on nonpolitical topics. The voice of the critic had fallen silent. But not for long. Soon Greg Power had turned his vitriolic pen to exposing the faults, foibles, and pretentious weaknesses of his former friend and leader. Joey became "the King of Cost-Plus" in a series of lengthy and wickedly amusing letters-to-the-editor, in which Power carried the art of pamphleteering to heights that even Addison might have envied.

According to Greg, the government was paying as much as twice the normal bidding price for the spate of public buildings that were then flooding the Newfoundland landscape. Hospitals, nurses' residences, trade schools, arts and culture centres were all being built on cost-plus contracts, and cost-plus was the royal road to graft, according to Power.

This wasn't the first time Smallwood's government had been accused of graft. It had been a recurrent theme in my columns, fuelled by information secretly fed to me by high-ranking civil servants, including one of the top officials in the police department. I had even published a series explaining exactly how it worked, had written of "millions poured out in graft and corruption," and had invited a libel suit, which never materialized, by naming one Cabinet minister, and his brother, a merchant, as "this pair of grafters." Instead of firing the minister, Joey had moved him to a safer portfolio, where he'd have less responsibility for awarding contracts.

Smallwood denied Power's cost-plus charges, but this was really a matter of semantics. Technically speaking, the new buildings were not being constructed on a cost-plus basis, but on leaseback contracts, which were perhaps even worse. A contractor in government favour— one of the Lundrigan or Crosbie group, for instance—would submit both a plan and a price for a building. The government would accept or reject the proposal without calling tenders. The company would then go to the money market, raise the necessary funds, and lease building to the government under a hire-purchase agreement that might run for twenty years. Power called it cost-plus because everyone knew the term, it reflected reality, and as he put it, "the more cost, the more plus." In the 1960s the Newfoundland government spent some $200 million on leaseback contracts (most of it federal money).

Was the King of Cost-Plus enriching himself out of those massive building contracts? Power did not suggest that he was, and I had never suggested it in my columns about graft. In Joey's book graft was graft only if the money wound up in your private bank account. Manipulating government spending so as to divert funds into party treasuries was, in his view, almost a messianic activity. How could you reform the world, develop the country, lead your people into the promised land if you didn't get elected to do it? And how could you get elected without spending hundreds of thousands of dollars on a campaign? You needed almost limitless funds. And within the system then prevailing, the only way to get such funds was to sell privilege, to take kickbacks, to do exactly what Greg Power so loudly accused the King of Cost-Plus of doing.

Joey was baffled and deeply hurt by it all. Personal loyalty was important to him, and he was outraged by Power's behaviour. Instead of being angry, as he had been with earlier defectors, he was wounded and silent. He answered the charges about cost-plus contracts when questioned by reporters from the mainland press, assuring them that cost-plus contracts were *never* let by his government, but he did not turn on Power and try to destroy him the way he had turned on Ted Russell. Instead, he tried to say as little as possible about his former friend and companion.

At this period of his life, the early 1960s, Joey was increasingly alone. With the possible exceptions of Curtis and Keough, there was no one left in his Cabinet with whom he had any sense of personal friendship, and few for whom he had any great respect. Of the two Newfoundland politicians who were closest to him, Power had departed before 1960, and Ed Roberts did not arrive in his office until 1964.

At about the time of Power's "defection," Joey lost another of his early supporters in the person of Deputy-Minister of Agriculture Pat Murray. The Murrays were pioneer residents of Portugal Cove, where they still live, and where they have been farming for generations. Pat's brother Myles, a lawyer, had fought the good fight for Joey in such tough districts as Harbour Main (in 1949) and Ferryland. He won Ferryland after a recount and a by-election in 1952, and subsequently held it, along with a seat in the Cabinet, for thirteen years.

THE KING OF COST-PLUS 255

Pat, as deputy for agriculture, undoubtedly had a great deal to do with the creation of Russwood Ranch. Every possible government service was placed at the disposal of the Smallwood family, but perhaps not enough. The time came, as it came with all his associates, when Joey became disillusioned with Pat. Murray had not succeeded in turning Newfoundland into one of the major agricultural regions of Canada, and that (along with Russwood's failure to turn a profit) may have had something to do with the disillusionment. He demanded Murray's resignation.

After he had resigned Pat discovered, to his alarm, that his pension was at risk. It was not guaranteed by the Civil Service Act, but was at "executive pleasure." This meant that the government could pay him or not, as it wished, and after he had waited around for a couple of months, he realized that the government had little disposition to do so. He went to Power.

"I can't intervene directly, of course," Power told him, "but I can draft a letter that may help."

Power turned all his talents for fanciful composition to the creation of the letter. It was seven pages long. It explained that Murray's conscience was bothering him. The things he had been required to do as deputy-minister were in conflict with his religious convictions. He had been to see his friend and confessor, a Roman Catholic priest, who had advised him that in matters of conscience and morality the Official Secrets Act did not bind him. He was in a terrible dilemma, needing to make a clean breast of it all, and perhaps Joey, in turn, could help him resolve the matter . . . Pat sent the letter to the premier.

When Joey received it, he was appalled. It looked to him as if he might be dealing with a madman or at least with one teetering on the verge. He hastily sent for Murray, not to talk about the letter, but to talk about the pension—and not just the pension either. He assured Pat that he was going to keep him on full salary for the next three years, and full pension after that.

The rift with Power was perhaps the most emotionally distressing episode in Smallwood's career. Here was his closest colleague, his dearest friend for the past fifteen years, walking away and treating him with contempt. To Joey it was inexplicable—utterly baffling. He had done nothing to make Power hate him personally and could not get his mind around the fact that he himself had changed in ways that Power could never accept—that Power could no longer respect him. It is noteworthy that once Joey was properly out of politics, Power renewed his friendship with the former premier and indeed became the most devoted friend of Joey's declining years. Few important public figures enjoy the kind of disinterested, lifelong friendship that existed between Power and Smallwood.

According to Ed Roberts, who was Smallwood's closest working partner and most reliable political ally in the sixties and early seventies, it was a joy to work with him while he was at the peak of his power. By this time, it is true, the fun had gone out of him—politics was no longer the joyful game it had been in the 1940s—but he went at it with undiminished gusto, and "worked at least half as hard as he said he did." According to Roberts he was a physical dynamo but intellectually lazy. He didn't read a tenth of what he claimed to have read, but merely skimmed a book and put it aside. He rarely read government papers at all, and didn't bother much with his correspondence. Most of the time he would sign things unread and ask Roberts to fill him in orally, on the gist of any documents he needed to deal with in the House of Assembly.

One of the most amazing habits Joey had formed at this point was *signing blank income tax forms*.

"He'd just sign a blank form and hand it over to Al Vardy," Roberts recalls, "and would never lay eyes on it again." Vardy, by now, had reversed their early roles. He was almost contemptibly subservient to the premier—he was little better than a lackey. With the fine indifference to small matters that he always practised, Joey trusted Vardy to make out income tax returns that wouldn't land him in jail.

By now he had adopted a kind of Victorian formality. The early days of dashing around in shirt sleeves and tripping over the cat were buried somewhere back in the early fifties. He had developed a stiffness, an insistence on "manners" that doubtless stemmed from his upbringing as an unwashed brat on the underside of St. John's. He demanded "proper dress" from his colleagues—no one could come to a Cabinet meeting in a sports shirt. He might be "Joey" to the voters, but he was now always "Mr. Premier" in his office, both to staff and members of the government. Power was the last of his early associates, who usually called him "Joe." When talking to the lieutenant-governor, he invariably called him "Your Honour," and his secretaries were instructed to make sure the premier was the one to speak first whenever they consulted one another by phone.

Perhaps such symbolic respect, like the symbolic honours that he collected left and right, had become important to him because by the sixties very few people had much genuine respect for Smallwood. He was surrounded by an imperial guard of ministers, would-be ministers, and self-serving business associates and heirs apparent who flattered and cajoled him and pretended to be dazzled by the sheer luminosity of his presence, just as every tyrant has been surrounded throughout history. But with the notable exception of Roberts they were men of small talent and smaller principle, self-serving, biding their time, waiting for the main chance.

When Joey met able people from outside the sphere of politics, particularly someone distinguished in a field of endeavour he admired, he could be remarkably humble and almost pathetically eager to please, as he was when I took Farley Mowat to visit him at his Roache's Line ranch in 1966. He could also be unguardedly candid. During that visit he discussed at length his plans for free university education, and for paying allowances—salaries, he called them—to students on a rising scale as they progressed through college; a system that the Soviet Union had in place, and that he believed to be one of the principal foundations of Soviet progress. He had not yet announced those plans even to his colleagues.

The sixties was the great era of the silver shovel—a custom-made spade with a silver blade that Joey used for turning sods. In the early years of the decade he turned sods for hospitals at Grand Falls, Gander, and Baie Verte, among other places, then in the late sixties new hospitals were built in St. Anthony and St. John's. The teaching hospital on Memorial University campus was not actually opened until the 1970s, but Joey was there for that sod-turning, too.

Almost before the Confederation Building was completed, Joey was turning the sod for the College of Trades and Technology. He officiated at the opening of the Fisheries College in 1964, but could not turn a sod, because it was housed in the old Memorial University College building. Then, late in the decade, there were the government building at Corner Brook, and a rash of Arts and Culture centres, built mainly with federal money. The picture of Joey turning sods with his silver shovel, often assisted by a grandchild, became a familiar sight on the front pages of Newfoundland newspapers. He saw public buildings both as monuments and as symbols of progress.

Meanwhile, he did not neglect economic development, despite his early disappointments. The 1960s was the period of his great partnership with the American promoter John Shaheen. Unlike Doyle, who was essentially a mining promoter and not really comfortable with other forms of enterprise, Shaheen was interested in anything that might turn a dollar. He opened Newfoundland's first small oil refinery at Holyrood in 1961. Designed strictly for the local market, it ultimately had a capacity of 15,000 barrels a day. Known initially as Golden Eagle, it later became Ultramar, and was the foundation of an Ultramar empire that spread all over eastern Canada.

In April 1965 Shaheen took Joey to Finland on an entirely different mission. They went to interview pulp and paper manufacturers who might, with proper inducements, be persuaded to fulfill Joey's lifelong dream of building a third paper mill in Newfoundland.

Joey didn't get his mill just then, but he got something else—a trip to Moscow, and newspaper headlines all over North America. In Helsinki, he had barely checked into his hotel room when there was a knock on his door, and he opened it to find Richard Nixon, the former vice-president of the United States under Eisenhower, standing there.

"I'm John Shaheen's lawyer," Nixon told him as they shook hands. Between stages of his political career Nixon was once again practising law. He and Joey hit it off immediately—indeed, they became friends of long standing—and when they were finished with their business in Helsinki, Nixon suggested that they take a brief side trip to Russia.

Helsinki is one of the easiest places in the world to get a Soviet visa: busloads and trainloads of visitors shuttle back and forth between Helsinki and Leningrad every day of the year. Shaheen made the arrangements, and the next day the two politicians were on a train heading for Leningrad. Along the way, Nixon suggested that they go on to Moscow for at least a one-day visit, so they took the overnight train, and arrived in Moscow the next morning.

The Russians gave them cars, guides, tickets to the Bolshoi theatre, and a tour of the capital, including a visit to Moscow university. They were being treated as VIP tourists. But this didn't satisfy Nixon. He wanted to drop in for a private chat with his old friend and former debating opponent Nikita Khrushchev, who had made a great hit in the United States as general secretary of the Soviet Union and Russian spokesman at the United Nations, but who had since been retired as a nonperson to a Moscow apartment. Nixon kept dropping the word that he'd like to meet Khrushchev once more, but he was fairly sure his Russian hosts wouldn't allow it.

Someone mentioned Nixon's wish to David Levy, a journalist working in Moscow for the CBC. Levy, who spoke fluent Russian and knew his way around Moscow, sent word that he'd like to see Small-wood, and Nixon too, if possible, for a taped interview. This seemed natural enough, and Levy spirited the pair off to his apartment in a cab.

As it happened, Khrushchev lived only a block or two from the Canadian embassy. Levy offered to take the two visitors to the building and to act as their interpreter. They drove to the Canadian embassy, registered there, then walked to the apartment building, where Levy tried to talk the lobby attendants (a pair of middle-aged women) into taking "the important visitors from North America" to Khrushchev's apartment.

That was really the end of the business. They never even found out whether Khrushchev was actually in Moscow or at his country home, where he spent a good deal of his time working on his memoirs for publication in the West. Nixon left a note for him, they got a cab back to their hotel, and flew home the next day. But through Levy the story was picked up by the North American wire services, and the two of them were described by the newspapers as prowling about Moscow on their own at night, and knocking on Khrushchev's door, trying to get an interview.

They were equally unsuccessful in wooing the Finnish pulp magnates. Shaheen abandoned the idea of building a third mill in Newfoundland, and even for Joey the idea went into temporary cold storage.

CHAPTER 16

# More Stately Mansions

DURING THE 1960S, JOEY PAID MORE AND MORE ATTENTION TO THE mechanics of winning elections. In the early stages of his career winning had been all too easy for him: his own name and reputation were all that he ever required to pile up landslide majorities in 1949, 1951, 1956, and 1959. But now, with his reputation for infallability wearing thin, and with less to offer the voters, he began hiring public relations professionals to help him plan his campaigns. According to George Elliott, an advertising expert from Ontario, Joey didn't always take his advice, but at least he had the benefit of professional opinions during elections.

He also developed a new concern for picking the brightest available talent for his caucus. The days when he could have sent his dog Wolf to any outport district and had him elected by an 80 percent majority were gone for good. He would have to put on a consistently better show than the Tories, including a presentable slate of candidates.

Moreover, he began to feel that he must give some consideration to teamwork, and to proven political talent. So he started ransacking the town and city councils for men who had won seats by large majorities and looting the Opposition benches for their few superstars. Teamwork might still be a foreign word in Cabinet, but from now on it would be important on the hustings. Fifteen years after confederation,

Joey was facing a new generation of voters, who no longer planned to be buried with his picture over their hearts.

The glitter of power attracted to him some of Newfoundland's brightest and most ambitious young men. The day of the bright young women was yet to dawn. To this point, the only woman who had ever sat in a Newfoundland legislature was Helena Squires, who had won Lewisporte in a by-election in 1930, following the death of the FPU socialist, George Grimes.

Among the men Joey sought out was William Adams, deputy-mayor of St. John's. (The deputy-mayor was chosen by council, but by tradition it was the councillor who had headed the poll, so deputy-mayors were proven vote-getters.) Adams was the first Newfoundland politician to rely on professional image makers. He had learned that getting elected depended less on your own resources of brains and personality, than on the image you presented to the public, an image that could be shaped by public relations experts.

While remaining deputy-mayor, Adams won the provincial district of St. John's West for the Liberals in 1962. This was not the same district that Vardy and Spratt had contested successfully in 1949. Since then St. John's had been divided into four districts with one member each. Meanwhile, outport representation had increased from twenty-four to thirty-two. St. John's had a fifth of the population of the province, and if represented proportionally would have had seven seats, not four. When charged in the House with subdividing the province for his own political advantage, Joey blandly replied that outport voters deserved more representatives than city voters because they were more reliable people. He added that this tended to be true of rural voters everywhere. There was a further redistribution in 1962, increasing outport representation to thirty-seven, and city seats to five, thus maintaining the principle that an outport vote was worth about twice as much as a vote in the city.

The PCs won their first seats outside the Avalon Peninsula in 1962, and Labrador West elected an independent in the same year. On the other hand, Joey won seats that had once been Tory strongholds, including Bell Island and St. John's North, as well as St. John's West. On the surface, things still looked very one-sided, with the Liberals holding thirty-four seats to the Opposition's eight. But a shift in voting patterns was obvious. Max Lane, leader of Joey's "Fish and Chips Union," was defeated in St. Barbe South, once the very heart of

Smallwood territory. Grand Falls, which had always given Joey huge majorities, returned a PC. Humber East elected Dr. Noel Murphy, a St. Johnsman who had been a popular doctor in St. Barbe, then settled permanently in Corner Brook. He became leader of the Opposition, the first non-Liberal ever elected by a Humber constituency.

Joey would later recoup those losses, partly by absorbing the best political talent he could find, and this has led some writers to refer to the mid-sixties as the period when Joey was at "the height of his power and popularity." Such judgments, however, are in grave error. Power and popularity are not determined merely by adding and subtracting seats in a legislature. In the mid-sixties, despite appearances, Joey was on the skids.

Adams, Murphy, and a little later John Crosbie, all had rather strange political careers. Adams sat as MHA for St. John's West while serving as deputy-mayor. On the eve of the succeeding municipal election he resigned his seat in the House and ran successfully for Mayor of St. John's. While still wearing the chain of office he accepted an appointment to Smallwood's Cabinet as a minister without portfolio, and went as a parachute candidate to Twillingate, where he was elected in 1971. Meanwhile, he had been re-elected mayor of St. John's, and continued to hold that position while serving in the government and in the House of Assembly until Smallwood's resignation in 1972.

Electing the mayor of St. John's as MHA for Twillingate might have seemed odd to anyone except Twillingaters, on their ice-encircled island off Newfoundland's north coast. To them it seemed purely natural to vote the way Joey told them to. In his very, very last election he rewarded them by running in Twillingate himself, giving them the chance to mark their Xs, for the first time, after his very own name.

Noel Murphy was new to politics when he became leader of the Opposition in 1962. He lost his seat in 1966, then ran successfully for mayor of Corner Brook, held office for six years, was defeated in 1973, made a comeback in 1978, and finally retired in 1981. Meanwhile, Joey had also invited him to enter the Cabinet, and the former Opposition leader accepted, ran as a Smallwood Liberal, and was defeated by a wide margin in Humber West in the debacle of 1971.

In regions of chronic unemployment, roads have always been the best election bait, and Joey also used this ploy in the sixties to shore up his fortunes. The greatest boost of all was the Trans-Canada Highway. Newfoundlanders had dreamed of a road across their island from the days when the first motor traffic began pushing horses off the streets in the 1920s. The trouble was the distance. From St. John's to Port aux Basques by way of Grand Falls and Corner Brook was nearly six hundred miles, with not much on the way except rocks and forests and bogs. The province could not build a road along this route without incurring a crippling debt, and until the time of Pickersgill, federal road building had never been a Canadian tradition. When Terra Nova National Park was opened in Newfoundland in the early fifties it was considered a great achievement that the feds had built thirty miles of solid highway, with a paved surface, along a route that would later become part of the Trans-Canada. Meanwhile, Newfoundland struggled to get some kind of a road built to link the east and west coasts, using whatever existing roads there were and hooking up with all available local highways, including some that had been built on foundations of cordwood by the paper companies.

The first Trans-Canada Highway agreement required the provinces to pay half the cost of the highway, and many of them, including Newfoundland, felt they couldn't afford it. The long stretch between Montreal and Edmunston, New Brunswick, remained unbuilt, though a road of sorts existed there, and was responsible for an alarming toll of fatalities. By the late 1950s, Newfoundland had a more or less passable road along most of the route between St. John's and Port aux Basques, though there was one long remaining gap between Clarenville and Gander. It was bridged, temporarily, by a rail ferry that took motor traffic on flatcars a distance of some 150 miles each way. Later, when the road was open from Gander through Terra Nova National Park, but not to Clarenville, you could drive by local roads to Bunyan's Cove, then take a short ferry ride across Clode Sound to Charlottetown in the National Park, and drive on across Newfoundland. The last link was completed in the late fifties as a rough dirt road, and Joey was first across the island, accompanied by Greg Power, in a Land Rover with four-wheel drive.

In 1965 the road was completed and paved through an agreement that Pickersgill and Pearson had struggled successfully to get through the federal Cabinet: Ottawa was to bear 90 percent of the cost of building the remaining parts of the road. The final estimate was $120 million, with $92 million from the federal government, and $28 million from Newfoundland, but the figures were not exact, because long stretches of the road already existed, in one form or another, before the Trans-Canada Highway was even conceived.

Joey made a great occasion of the opening of the completed road. He led a motorcade from St. John's to Grand Falls, where he met a motorcade led by Prime Minister Pearson, driving from Port aux Basques. There, on an artificial mound a few miles west of the town, Pearson unveiled a stone pillar marking the mid-point of the road and commemorating his own part in its creation. Known as Pearson's Peak, it is a place where motorists often stop to eat a box lunch at the highway's halfway point. But the view is disappointing. It is one of the lowliest "peaks" in North America.

Joey then issued a decree—the next year, 1966, would be "Come Home Year"—and he launched a great advertising campaign to get former Newfoundlanders to return to the Old Rock for a visit and to experience the miracle of the new road. With Joey's usual luck, he happened to get a fine summer, and the campaign started a substantial annual influx of motor tourists.

The government provided an excellent string of camping parks, most of them along the main road, but soon they were overflowing, and tourists in campers and trailers, failing to find other spaces for their vehicles, were stopping in the gravel pits left by fifteen years of frantic road building. It was, indeed, the most rapid program of road expansion in the history of Canada. In 1950 a St. John's motorist could barely get beyond the Avalon Peninsula, on roads that were often little better than one-lane dirt tracks. By the late sixties Newfoundland had the best 500 miles of road in the Atlantic provinces, and the other provinces were rushing to catch up. By 1970 nearly every large settlement on the island had roads connecting it to the Trans-Canada. There were also roads in Labrador, at the mining centres in the west, along the Strait of Belle Isle in the east, and in the Goose Bay area.

It was scarcely surprising that Joey called an election in the autumn of Come Home Year. On September 8, 1966, he swept the province: thirty-nine seats to three for the Opposition. His faltering popularity in the early sixties seemed to have merely resulted from a few mistakes that had already been forgiven and forgotten. As it turned out, however, this was his Indian summer, not his second spring. A year later the arch-Tory Harold Collins, who had tried twice before to win the Gander seat, took it from the Liberals in a by-election. It was a portent of worse things to come, and Joey was shaken, though not yet dismayed.

A few months later, in the federal election of June 25, 1968, the PCs swept the province, taking all but one seat and winning the popular vote by a margin of nearly 16,000 over the Liberals. Since all federal elections in Newfoundland were for or against Joey, this represented a personal disaster, an upset unequalled even in the days of responsible government. It was all the more remarkable because it happened when Trudeaumania was at its height, when the voters of Canada (Joey included) had become a mob of groupies worshipping Pierre as their superstar. In the space of a year and nine months Joey's seemingly impregnable kingdom had virtually crumbled under his feet.

The only Liberal survivor from Newfoundland was Don Jamieson, Joey's former foe, and now his sole supporter in the nation's capital. A little later, when the question of the future leadership of the Newfoundland Liberals was being actively discussed and various potential successors to Smallwood were putting in their bids, I suggested to Jamieson that he might be the obvious man for the job, but he replied: "Having the leadership of the Liberal Party of Newfoundland just now would be like having an exclusive franchise on cancer."

Actually, a whole slew of future leaders and potential leaders had been elected in Joey's last great sweep—no fewer than six of them. Most remarkable, in many ways, was Edward (Scrappy) Roberts, a former whizz kid with an IQ that went off the charts. He had finished high school at the age of thirteen, then went to a private school until he was old enough to squeeze into university. He graduated from the University of Toronto at nineteen and finished his law degree at twenty-three. He led the University Liberals on campus, and worked for Pickersgill in the early sixties. Then he walked into Joey's office during the premier's absence in the summer of 1964, and at once began explaining to the staff how things should be run. Joey returned to find Roberts in charge and his files, for the first time, in order. He promptly adopted the young man as his executive assistant and heir apparent.

Roberts turned out to be not only a fine managerial politician of the new school (having grown up under the Bomb and the influence of Jack Kennedy, as he liked to say) but also a district politician with an unsurpassed gift for garnering votes. In his chosen district of White Bay North (later Strait of Belle Isle) he was undefeatable. Governments might come and go and leadership might change, but Scrappy Roberts kept right on getting elected in the same seat, always by overwhelming majorities. In a space of five years he was executive assistant, then parliamentary assistant to the premier, minister of welfare, and minister of health.

Another newcomer, later briefly party leader, was William N. Rowe, who was even younger than Roberts and had a Rhodes Scholarship and a law degree behind him. At twenty-six he was the youngest Newfoundlander ever to enter the Cabinet. Like Roberts, he had gone straight from law school into politics, and had married Penny Ayre, perhaps the most eligible young heiress in the province. Successively minister of housing and minister of community and social development, he lacked Roberts's almost uncanny political talents, but clearly had brains and ambition, and also good looks in a Little Lord Fauntleroy sort of way.

Rowe's father, Fred, a long-time Smallwood follower and Cabinet minister, was also a potential leader if a somewhat unlikely one, and for a while was Joey's choice as his successor—a safe enough candidate because at best the elder Rowe might become an interim leader, head of a caretaker government. He was only a little younger than Smallwood himself and carried his years not nearly so well. He lacked the popular appeal needed in a party leader, and it is unlikely he could have led the party to victory in any election, even with Smallwood's help.

Then there was Steve Neary, the Bell Island union leader and secretary of the Newfoundland Federation of Labour during the IWA strike who had jumped on the Smallwood bandwagon almost the moment the strike was over. Neary eventually led the party and the Liberal Opposition during some of their darkest days.

T. Alex Hickman, who had been a Young Liberal from the days of the first Smallwood government, and was now attorney-general, was also a potential leader. However, in one of those meandering careers so common among Newfoundland politicians, he instead became attorney-general in the Tory government of 1972, and finally chief justice of Newfoundland. For a brief time, in 1987 and 1988, Hickman was known to television viewers across Canada as he presided at Nova Scotia's Marshall inquiry—an investigation into why an innocent man had been convicted of murder, then left in jail for more than a decade despite proof of his innocence. The inquiry led to an investigation and exposure of rottenness in the entire system of justice.

Sixth, but by no means least in this lineup of leadership talent, was John C. Crosbie, also a lawyer, who had actually practised his profession for eight years before venturing into politics. Crosbie was thirty-

five when he entered the House of Assembly, and fresh from resounding victories in his first election campaigns (St. John's city council,
where he headed the poll, and St. John's West, which he won for Joey
by 4,054 votes to 2,980 for the PC candidate). Joey would later say of
Crosbie: "He wanted my job. That was the sole reason he went into
politics. He planned to seize my job at the first opportunity." But it is
difficult to see how this set him apart from the other leadership
hopefuls. Perhaps he was a little more ruthless and thorough.

The first Crosbie to make his mark in Newfoundland was John's
grandfather, also named John, who had founded Crosbie and Company in the early years of the twentieth century. Knighted for his
contributions to the war effort between 1914 and 1918, he held
portfolios of shipping, finance, and customs in various governments
under various political labels until his retirement in 1928. Like other
politicians of his time, he benefited greatly by doing business with the
governments of which he was a member.

Ches Crosbie, John's father, and Sir John's eldest son, was always
Smallwood's *bête noire*. Backer of some of Joey's enterprises, unsuccessful opponent in the confederation battle, unsuccessful candidate
for the Liberal nomination in Grand Falls, he was far more successful
in business than in his ventures into public life. He took the Crosbie
enterprises through enormous expansions—into transportation (air-
lines and international shipping), heavy and light construction,
engineering, and many other areas before dropping dead during his
second honeymoon at the age of fifty-seven.

Although many Crosbies were active in various branches of what
by now was the Crosbie empire, John, despite his relative youth,
clearly looked like number one when he entered the House of
Assembly in 1966. Joey had always yearned to have the number one
Crosbie serving under him in his government. This was a grave
mistake, as Greg Power had recognized back in 1949. But Power, out
of favour, out of politics, and sniping at Joey from the sidelines, was
not present to try to stop him from making the same mistake in 1966.

John had much more than his father's limited political ability. He
had brains, abundant good looks, charisma, charm, and stacks of
money. He had been in municipal politics for only eight months when
Joey grabbed him and made him minister of municipal affairs. John
held the portfolio for a year and two months, then accepted the
portfolio of health. A little less than eight months after that he had
resigned from the Cabinet and started his campaign to defeat the

premier, a campaign on which he spent a great deal of money, time, and effort over the next three years.

It is safe to say that there were no more than three or four people in his long public career whom Joey sincerely and deeply hated. One of those was John Crosbie, the viper whom he nourished so briefly in his bosom.

Come Home Year ended. Centennial Year began, the year of Expo 67, with the federal government scattering birthday money across the land like a Sunday school teacher distributing candy at a picnic. Playgrounds blossomed on the outskirts of villages (most of them unused, and many of them unequipped, except with a fence), and Joey grabbed the opportunity to build arts and culture centres from coast to coast. Half the money was to come from Ottawa and the other half, if he could arrange it, from industry, but the ideas were all to be Joey's, and the contracts were to be awarded to his favourite building companies.

He was greatly impressed by Expo, especially by the design and structure of some of the pavilions. Like the Emperor Hadrian, he was a builder and a lover of buildings, who would leave behind him a trail of architecture. He fell in love with the Czechoslovakian and Yugoslavian pavilions at first sight, and when Expo closed, he arranged to buy them lock, stock, and barrel. Then he had them taken to pieces and shipped to Newfoundland by freighter, to be reassembled into arts and culture centres at Grand Falls, Gander, and Grand Bank.

With federal money he also built large arts and culture centres at St. John's and Corner Brook. The one at Corner Brook included the unusual feature of an Olympic-size indoor swimming pool. The one at St. John's, adjoining the university campus, was a splendid building designed by the same architects who designed the National Arts and Culture Centre in Ottawa. It included a marine museum, two art galleries, two libraries, a small theatre for rehearsals and experimental work, and a large, beautifully designed theatre that quickly gained a high reputation among performing artists.

Even here, Joey couldn't keep his fingers out of the pie. He let the architects and builders have their way, but when it came to music, he knew what he wanted. His friend Salazar had taken him to see and hear a great electric organ in Lisbon. He had admired it enormously, and when the Arts and Culture Centre was built at St. John's, he ordered an exact copy to be built into the theatre. So of course it was done. It sounded magnificent when you played church music on it, or even the Prelude and Fugue in D Minor, or similar pieces written for the great church organs of Europe. Unfortunately, it wasn't a concert organ really suited to a modern theatre, but Joey didn't know the difference until long after he'd had it built and installed.

While he was building the arts and culture centres, he was also building the Sir Richard Squires tower at Corner Brook, to house government offices for western Newfoundland. In the lobby, rising to a height of four stories, he placed a crystal extravaganza from the Czechoslovakian pavilion. It looked like an enormous fountain, and Joey had a special spot in his heart for fountains, as he did for buildings. It must surely be the largest lobby ornament in Canada. Tier after tier, civil servants go tiptoeing around it daily while visitors stand in awe of this most curious of all the Smallwood monuments. He'd had other fountains installed in front of the Colonial Building at St. John's, and in the middle of a lake at Pippy Park. Neon-bright with pink and purple lights, they were described by his detractors as the result of penis-envy left over from his undersized childhood.

The Sir Richard Squires tower was originally billed as an eight-storey *skyscraper*, but added cubits to its stature on the day Joey arrived in Corner Brook to turn the first sod with his silver sod-turning shovel. He drove from St. John's that day at the wheel of his black government limousine, and Noel Murphy, Corner Brook's new mayor, who had been the city's first elected Tory, took the opportunity to twit the Premier with his eight-storey skyscraper. Knowing that Joey would be listening to his car radio as he drove westward, Murphy bought a series of spots, and had them filled with what he hoped would be embarrassing questions. One of them was, "Who ever heard of an eight-storey skyscraper?" Before Joey arrived he had listened to this question at least five times. He rose to speak to the assembled dignitaries:

"Right here, ladies and gentlemen," he announced, "we are going to build a *ten*-storey skyscraper, a magnificent building. . . . And over there" (pointing) "we are going to build another magnificent building, a great arts and culture centre. . . a three-way thing, with the great firm of Bowaters and the great firm of Lundrigans each contributing a third of the cost. . . ." It was the first anyone had heard of this, and the applause was deafening.

Final cost of the centre was approximately a million dollars. Bowaters gave $300,000, Lundrigans $200,000, and the federal government $500,000. As so often happened, Joey collected the credit without having to put up any of the cash, and got the benefits, into the bargain, of having it built by his friends the Lundrigans.

The 1960s were also the great decade of Newfoundland's Memorial University. For a while it came close to being a leader in certain fields. The University College of that name dated back to 1924. In 1949-50 Joey upgraded the institution from college to university, then provided a new and enormously expanded campus on what had formerly been farmland north of the city. In 1961 he held an official opening of the new campus with the biggest parade ever seen in the provincial capital. From England he brought Lord Taylor of Harlow to be its president—"the only live Lord in captivity on a Canadian campus!" he exclaimed proudly.

Taylor's great ambition was to add a medical school and teaching hospital to the university. He'd made his reputation as a doctor and a town planner, and rightly insisted that Newfoundland ought to be training her own doctors at St. John's. His principal achievement was to start the Health Sciences Complex, as it came to be called. He and Joey had both retired before it was completed, but it was their dream, and they who had pushed it towards fulfillment.

The old university campus now housed the College of Fisheries, teaching boat building, navigation, and skills related to radar, sonar, and electronics. A new building housed the College of Trades and Technology, which taught everything from cooking to industrial arts. It flanked the Confederation Building on the side opposite the university. The four-lane road that ran past Pippy Park, the university, Confederation Building and the trades college, now became a three-mile-long Smallwood memorial. The whole area was stamped with his vision and his personality and an eclectic lot of architectural styles that ranged from the beautiful to the banal.

A marine biology laboratory rose from the rocks of Logy Bay, near St. John's, specializing suitably in cold water research: the Labrador Current, lapping the rocks on which it was built, provided an unending supply of the cold wet stuff. The marine biology lab was one of Joey's true showpieces, attracting marine biologists from other provinces and countries.*

Still only in his sixties, Joey was now thinking and talking a lot

---

*Dr. Fred Aldrich, Director of Marine Biology, was a professor at Memorial University before moving to the laboratory at Logy Bay. He once set an exam question: "How would you set up a research program on the life history of the giant squid?" One bright young man wrote a four-word answer: "Show strong Liberal tendencies." Aldrich gave him full marks.

about retirement. He believed, at that point, that he had a genuine wish to leave politics and devote himself to writing, which he always considered to be his second major career. But of course he couldn't just let go, allowing things to take their own course. He would have to leave the government and the party in safe hands. What he meant by this he wasn't exactly sure himself, but it became obvious in time that what he really wanted was a successor whom he could direct and control, one who would rely on him constantly for advice. He wanted to be a sort of premier emeritus, living on the political campus without specific duties, but forever ready to intervene at destiny's crucial points.

From the time back in 1949 when Smallwood named me as his first heir apparent there had been a parade of heirs apparent (and presumptive) few of whom had lasted in the line of succession more than a year or so. In the early fifties there was Fred Rowe, who had inherited my old seat in Labrador, still young enough at that time to be seriously in the running. But Rowe fossilized at an early age and was soon a more obvious candidate for the Senate than for centre stage in an election. In the mid-fifties there was Jack Forsey, a brilliant if somewhat erratic young politician from Humber East. For a short while in the sixties there was Richard Cashin, latest rod out of the stem of the Ferryland Cashins who had produced Sir Michael and the redoubtable Peter. Rickie Cashin had first edged Bill Browne from the St. John's West seat, then made a bit of a name for himself in the House of Commons, and piled up comfortable leads in the elections of '63 and '65. Young Cashin was a tub-thumping rabble rouser like his Uncle Peter, and Smallwood went so far as to name him publicly as his chosen successor, but Greg Power insisted that he had done this only to pacify Catholic voters who were deeply offended by an interview that Joey gave in an unguarded moment to the United Church *Observer*. According to Power, Joey had hastily realized, after seeing himself quoted in print on the role of the Catholic Church in politics, that he'd better do something dramatic if he didn't want another feud with an archbishop. Hence, Rickie Cashin as premier-to-be. Anyway, Rickie was heir apparent for only a few months. When he was defeated in the succeeding federal election, he turned to union organizing with the radical priest Father Des McGrath, and together they built the first really effective fishermen's union in Newfoundland history.

Then there was the great company of heirs apparent that surfaced in the late sixties, several of whom actually did succeed to the leadership, though none (with the possible exception of young Rowe) did so with Smallwood's blessing. The first and longest-lasting of this crop of heirs was Ed Roberts, whom Joey was consciously grooming for the premiership until John Crosbie (and his brother Andrew, a little later) came on the scene.

With Roberts Smallwood always seemed to have a father-son relationship. Roberts was cautious, cool, distant, a very efficient manager, and he never made the slightest move to cross the aging leader. He just bided his time and did all the right things. With Crosbie things were different. He was arrogant, self-confident, and highly ambitious, as well as socially polished, the product of a private school. From the first he found it most difficult to hide his conviction that Joey was a has-been who ought to get out of the way of younger and brighter brains. He began making jokes at Joey's expense around the St. John's cocktail circuit.

That was how things stood when the critical stages of John Shaheen's Come-by-Chance refinery deal reached the round table of the Cabinet committee room. As usual, when he had gambled and lost, Joey had doubled his bets. He had lost the first round of economic development in the 1950s, and had gambled away tens of millions of dollars doing it. He had kept quiet for only a short time before he began gambling again, this time not with tens of millions, but with hundreds of millions. The biggest, and potentially the most disastrous, of such gambles was the Come-by-Chance oil refinery.

Shaheen had built his first small cracking plant for his fledgling Golden Eagle Refining Company at Holyrood, but it employed very few people. Joey dreamed of a vast refinery supplied by supertankers and associated with a petrochemical complex exporting plastics to the mainland, providing Newfoundlanders with thousands and *thousands* of jobs. He asked Shaheen if he thought it possible, and Shaheen, after thinking seriously about it for a while, said yes.

His plan was to create a *de facto* free port with a cracking plant where Arab oil could be refined for the international trade, then shipped off, tax free, to refuel airliners at such places as LaGuardia in New York. A Newfoundland crown corporation would have to own the refinery thus giving it tax-free status, with Shaheen holding a management lease and an option to buy. The only loser would be the federal government, which would fail to collect the excise tax on the refined oils—a few hundred million dollars a year, the exact amount depending on the refinery's output. The money saved would go to

Shaheen in management fees and to the Newfoundland government to pay off the mortgage on the plant. A neat kind of scam that in the right circumstances might have worked.

Joey had already succeeded with a similar deal when he had built a shipyard and large fish plant in Marystown. The difference in this case was the size of the project and the fact that he was horning into a field which at that time was the exclusive killing ground of giant American multinationals. Their lobbyists set about trying to stop the deal in Ottawa, and prevailed upon the federal government to pass a law against the tax shelter in cases where a private company from the beginning held an option to buy out a Crown corporation. It might still have been possible to get around that, of course, but once the American oil companies had shown their teeth and claws, it was fairly obvious that they'd manage to kill any tax-free oil refinery one way or another. The federal government would also have been required to make a large outlay as builder of a port in a place where nothing bigger than a fish stage had previously existed.

So the grand scheme collapsed, right there. But Joey forged ahead anyway. Where was the refinery to be built? He stuck a pin in a map. "Come-by-Chance," he announced. It was to be a new city, the latest New Jerusalem, with thousands of happy workers manning the petrochemical machines and building square miles of bungalows on thirty-year mortgages from the Central Mortgage and Housing Corporation. Joey was so proud of the vision that he arranged for a special lookout on a hill beside the Trans-Canada Highway where awed motorists could park their cars to admire the steel forest of refinery towers and (in years to come) the new city.

The government of Newfoundland, needless to say, would have to put up some of the initial capital, and take on the entire indebtedness of the plant as a contingent liability. According to the first projections, this would be in the order of $125 million. But of course everyone knew that this would turn into a quarter of a billion dollars before the plant got into operation. Such was the normal expectation of the time, such was the experience with massive construction projects across Canada—but especially in Newfoundland, where projects like this usually cost double the initial estimate. The scope of the debt was staggering. It amounted to $2,500 for *each family* in Newfoundland. Provincial bankruptcy was a clear possibility.

Set against this was the dream of a new Edmonton with Chemical Row spouting flames into the sky, and quarter-million-ton tankers threading their way past the one-hundred-odd sunken hazards between Cape Race and Come-by-Chance to fuel fires of the new city. Shaheen was already talking about raising production from 100,000 barrels a day to 600,000, making the refinery one of the largest on earth, and keeping a whole fleet of supertankers shuttling back and forth between the emirates of the Persian Gulf and the head of Newfoundland's Placentia Bay.

The idea was breathtaking, and irresponsible, and more than John Crosbie, for one, could swallow. Almost from the day he entered the House of Assembly he knew that a break with Smallwood would be inevitable. He didn't have to invent an issue or look for one. It would simply come of itself, and he would have no choice in the matter. There was no way the leading son of a great business house like the Crosbies could vote for a deal like Come-by-Chance and hope to live it down.

The first proposal was for an advance to Shaheen of $5 million, made necessary by the tax amendment passed at Ottawa. This would allow him to search out European companies that might take a mortgage on the plant in return for building it. Crosbie saw this unsecured loan as the first step in the bizarre and potentially disastrous process that it was, and refused to vote for it in Cabinet. The measure passed anyway, over his objections and those of Clyde Wells, for Joey by now had abandoned his early principle of deferring any decision that caused a serious disagreement inside the government. Crosbie then called a press conference to announce his resignation from Cabinet. At the press conference, held in the Newfoundland Press Club, he looked like an amateur tightrope walker about to take his first trembling step over Niagara Falls. He knew perfectly well that he was taking his political life in his hands.

Joey had appointed a committee of three lawyers to draft the complex Shaheen agreements. They were all Cabinet ministers: Crosbie, Attorney-General Hickman, and Clyde Wells, whom Joey had dragged out of his law office in Corner Brook to defeat Noel Murphy in Humber East. All three of them became "defectors," but Hickman remained, for the time, in the party and the Cabinet.

Crosbie and Wells explained that they wished to remain in the Liberal Party, even though they were leaving the government. But the day after their "defection" they arrived at the House to discover that their desks had been moved across the floor. They moved them away from the Tory Opposition and sat at them.

"Aha!" said Joey. "They've crossed the floor. They've left the Liberal Party. They can no longer attend party caucuses."

Crosbie then announced that he and Wells we sitting as Independent Liberals.

"He can forget that," Don Jamieson told me. "There's a federal election going on right now. At some other time he might be able to resign from the Cabinet, sit as an Independent Liberal, and later rejoin the party and have some kind of future in it. But the Liberal Party will never forgive him for bolting in the middle of an election and damaging the party's standing at the polls."

Crosbie did not understand this at the time, or for a year and a half afterwards. Throughout 1968 and 1969, while the Tories swept six of the seven federal seats, and Joey scrambled to pick up what pieces he could, John Crosbie was still determined to become the next Liberal premier of Newfoundland. I finally went to him myself and explained that his political future lay in only one possible place—with the Tories.

The federal election of 1968 was a great shock to Joey. He had never imagined that anything like it could happen. He went around talking about how many tons of anti-Trudeau smear literature had been spread across the province (as doubtless it had, but why was Newfoundland the only place that the smear literature had any effect?) and how he should have taken a more personal part in the campaign. But that was all for public consumption. In private he sang a different song. To Roberts it sounded like a swan song.

"It's a personal defeat on a massive scale," he admitted as they flew back together from Ottawa. "The only thing left for me to do is resign. I've been rejected by the Newfoundland people." The question that really bothered him just then, however, was the succession. Roberts was still deep in Joey's favour at that point, but in Joey's view, he was too young to inherit the premiership. He was twenty-eight on September 1 that year, and no one in Canada at that time had ever heard of a twenty-eight-year-old premier.

Roberts believes that Joey's decision to resign was genuine and deep. He was determined that he wouldn't be booted out of office by his own party, as he had seen Diefenbaker booted out—literally hooted and booed by a convention of federal Tories. But he was greatly bothered by the question of naming his successor. The idea of letting the party choose its own leader scarcely crossed his mind.

And then, Roberts says, something else happened. Between 1968 and 1970 he became desperate to hang on to power. Did he become aware, in those two years, that John C. Doyle, who was then trying to float the third mill, and making desperate deals in an effort to do so, was in danger of having his financial empire collapse around his ears? Was he trying to protect the flamboyant promoter with whom he had such a close relationship? It certainly seems possible.

Or did Vardy persuade him that they were all in the gravest danger if he left office? Those questions will probably never be answered. But it may be significant that both Vardy and Doyle became fugitives from Canadian justice shortly after Joey resigned.

# The Gathering of the Heirs-Apparent

By THE TIME JOEY GOT AROUND TO CALLING THE LIBERAL LEADERSHIP Convention of 1969, he seemed to have forgotten the convention twenty years earlier when some 1,500 delegates had elected him their leader, and had chosen candidates for all provincial districts. The Liberal Party of Newfoundland, he was now telling the world, had never really existed. It had just been himself. Now he was going to build it from the ground up, make it a great grass-roots movement, strong enough to stand on its own feet and make its own decisions, while he was sitting in his ranch house on Roache's Line writing the great volumes of Newfoundland history on which he planned to spend the rest of his working life. All this, of course, was before he had decided to "succeed himself."

In 1966 he was determined to end his career in a blaze of glory. In all likelihood, it was to be his last election, and he would do it up brown. Ad man George Elliott (the same who wrote *The Kissing Man*, including some of the eeriest stories in Canadian literature) gave the campaign professional pizazz, and Joey actually took some of his advice on strategy. He spent $300,000 on the flashiest campaign in Newfoundland history. He reshuffled his Cabinet, bringing to the council table such new faces as Aiden Maloney, who had the reputation of being an expert on the fisheries, and four young lawyers, including Roberts and Crosbie. He retired most of the old hands and sent out to the hustings the ablest young talent he could find. And his strategy clearly paid off. The election was a blaze of glory, right enough, and the party caucus was the strongest it had been since 1951, with talented politicians not only in the Cabinet, but on the back benches, as well.

If Joey was truly determined not to become another superannuated leader like John Diefenbaker, hanging on by his fingernails long after it was time for him to retire, now was his chance. He could safely leave the party in the hands of the caucus and allow the caucus to choose its own leader from the abundant talent in the House while he went off to the Senate or to Roache's Line to research and write his books after gracefully accepting whatever honours a grateful nation could find to bestow upon him in its centennial year.

Of all sad words of book or pen, the saddest are these, "It might have been." Joey waffled. And waffling, was lost. What if....

If John Crosbie had not been in such a great hurry to get rid of the sixty-six-year-old leader, if he had been willing to wait another four years, the Liberal Party of Newfoundland might well have dropped into his hands, as he was so desperately anxious that it should do. Even two or three years might have been enough. Instead his vocal criticisms of Smallwood pitted the premier against him. Within a few months Smallwood had conceived a rankling dislike for the flashy young Crosbie, who every day was looking more and more like his unchosen successor. Crosbie was already a power in the Cabinet. What if it turned out that Joey wasn't able to pass the succession to his own choice after all? What if Crosbie managed to worm his way into the leadership? What if the party, the government, the province fell into the wrong hands?

The 1968 federal election convinced Smallwood that he had become a liability to the Liberal Party of Canada (if not of Newfoundland) and he announced that a leadership convention would be held in 1969. The idea seemed safe enough at the time. John Crosbie was sitting in Opposition, even though he called himself an Independent Liberal, and so Joey assumed that he was safely out of the running. His plan was to step down himself, pass the leadership along to the aging Fred Rowe, and then work on the problem of a younger successor.

But if Rowe was expected to face a leadership convention and a general election, as tradition suggested that he should, within a few months of inheriting the premiership, then the whole thing was obvious nonsense, whether Joey realized it or not. He might take Rowe to the convention, already installed as Premier, and use all his authority to get him accepted as party leader. He might then shepherd him through the following election. This seemed possible from Joey's point of view; he had enormous confidence in his own persuasive powers, but from the point of view of the young Turks in the party it looked like an impossible agenda. They'd be united against Rowe at the convention, and they all had followers among potential delegates. If by some miracle Joey got the convention to accept Rowe there was still the problem of making the public vote for him. He could have won an election with Joey's backing in the early 1950s, but the 1970s would be a different story. Was Rowe set up as a stalking horse? Ed Roberts still wonders about it. Personally, I don't think so. I think Joey was sincere on this issue, as on so many others where his thinking was clearly off-base. In any case, once Joey had decided to run in an effort to succeed himself, he offered to pay Rowe's expenses out of his own campaign fund—and indeed did so.

The best-laid plans of mice and men . . . . A few months after Joey announced the convention, Crosbie announced his intention to run for the leadership. To say that Joey was shocked would be to put it mildly. He had assumed Crosbie was out of the running from the moment he had "crossed the floor," but he quickly discovered that it wasn't quite that simple. The way his bright new Liberal Party was set up, just about anybody could join it and run for the leadership.

The real founding of the bright new party had taken place at Grand Falls in September 1968, at the first general meeting of the Liberal Association of Newfoundland. Before the meeting was held, Crosbie, sitting across the floor of the House, announced his wish to attend. He also declared that he had never intended to leave the Liberal Party, and desired that he be moved to the government back benches, even though he disagreed with government policy.

Since he had not voted against the government in the House on division, Joey could find no valid excuse for keeping him in Opposition. If he wished to re-cross the floor and join the Liberal backbenchers, there seemed to be no legal way he could stop him. He did, however, demand a written pledge of allegiance to the party (something that was required of no one else). For Crosbie this was no problem. He moved his desk to the government side of the House and went to Grand Falls as one of the founding members of the Liberal Association of Newfoundland. Subsequently, the Liberal Association held general meetings at Clarenville and Corner Brook. Crosbie was present, and influential, at both. They were large-scale affairs, with well over a thousand delegates attending each gathering.

Despite the big meetings and the mass publicity, the Liberal Association of Newfoundland was in trouble from the moment of its birth. The delegates elected Richard Cashin, the former MP for St. John's West, as their president. This was contrary to Joey's clearly expressed wishes, but he swallowed his pride and allowed democracy to have its way.

He told the delegates that they should set a goal of 100,000 members for the Liberal Association, though he privately admitted that 30,000 might be more realistic. With membership at $5 a head, even 30,000 members would have made it possible to run an election without having to rely on kickbacks and influence peddling. Of course, there would always be contributions, even large ones, from the few big corporations who regarded themselves as Joey's special favourites. But he would have liked to see the whole system of patronage gradually phased out in favour of the kind of funding already being practised successfully by the NDP.

In fact, nothing of the kind happened. Membership in the Liberal Association never reached 100,000 or 30,000 or even 10,000, and no Liberal convention ever managed to pay its own way. Cashin also discovered quickly that "democracy" was intended for the media and the public, not for those personally involved. He resigned, declaring that the party was on a self-destructive course, and was replaced by a man much more to Joey's liking—John Mahoney, the junior member for Harbour Main, which was still a two-seat district. It was to Mahoney that Joey sent his letter of resignation as party leader, recommending that the party hold a leadership convention to choose his successor.

Fred Rowe, having consulted with Joey, declared his candidacy for the leadership. Apparently it was a profound shock to Joey when John Crosbie, just days later, did the same thing.

Once a successor is chosen, long-standing tradition in Canada requires the premier to go to the lieutenant-governor, tender his resignation, and advise the governor to invite the new leader to form a government. This might not be strictly required by the constitution, but Joey had too much respect for tradition to ignore it on such a basic issue. Normally, of course, the procedure was an innocuous formality, but with Crosbie in contention for the crown, Joey was in a dilemma. He couldn't see himself, now or at any time, voluntarily going to the lieutenant-governor and recommending that John Crosbie be invited to form a government. Rowe, yes; Crosbie, no!

Crosbie was the man he had publicly called a "rat" the year before, the man who had sat in Opposition just a few weeks ago! Surely the party wouldn't elect him as its new leader! But yes, the more he thought about it the more he was convinced that even he couldn't force Rowe on the party in competition with Crosbie.

He put out feelers among his followers. They confirmed his worst fears. There was no way he could keep control of the convention. It would go its own way and elect whomever it decided to elect. Those who had invested their five-dollar bills in democracy were determined to take it seriously.

Joey lay doggo, biding his time, trying to make up his own mind exactly what to do, while Crosbie set out to line up the delegates across the province and to make sure his own followers took out memberships and voted for the delegates of his choice. At first, it looked like a pushover for the popular young millionaire. His kid brother Andrew, leader of the rising generation of young businessmen in St. John's, became his campaign manager. Money was no object, and the Crosbies quickly learned how to put together an effective political organization.

Then Joey dropped his bombshell. He called a press conference and announced that because of massive demands from every corner of the province he was yielding to the popular will, and had consented to run for the leadership himself. He would become his own successor! It was the only certain way he could see to deny the succession to Crosbie. Rowe, lost somewhere back in the dust, withdrew his bid for the leadership, and announced that he was supporting Smallwood.

The convention was to be held in the St. John's Memorial Stadium during the last two days of October and the first day of November, 1969. The campaign leading up to it was frantic. Not the least amazing was the appearance of two additional candidates, who made it a four-way race. Randy Joyce, fresh from triumphs as a student union leader and a Young Liberal, made a passionate plea for the youth vote. Joyce was a fluent, if somewhat overpowering, speaker, both on the platform and on the tube. Alex Hickman, calm, reasonable, almost the opposite of Joyce, and perhaps having a naïve faith in the powers of common sense, offered himself as a "compromise candidate."

But it was Crosbie and Smallwood who put on the real battle. Crosbie's audited expenses ran to more than half a million dollars—

that is, he spent over a thousand dollars for every vote he received. Ed Roberts announced that he was waiting for the various candidates to "state their priorities," but everyone except Hickman ignored him. That was the beginning of his estrangement from Smallwood. Nothing but unquestioning loyalty to his leadership would do for Joey. The most visible element in the campaign was a well-organized "Crowds for Crosbie" movement, with placards, buttons, and demonstrations in the streets. Much more important, though, were the events going on behind closed doors.

Hickman, a gentle and affable man, professed to be appalled by the savagery with which the campaign was conducted. He called it "a campaign of fear and intimidation and threats and mudslinging the like of which would make Tammany Hall in New York look like a Sunday school picnic." He thus assured *his* own permanent estrangement from Smallwood.

*The Evening Telegram* agreed with Hickman, calling the campaign "a disgusting display of the callous and cynical use of every dirty trick known to the seamier side of politics." Specific examples were not named, but most of the dirty work consisted of promises of patronage, and threats of the loss of favour to people holding licences or doing business with the government at one level or another.

Smallwood's campaigners are believed to have outspent Crosbie's, bringing the expenses for herding the 1,800 delegates to the convention to a total of about $1.25 million. Though less flashy than the Crosbie campaign, Smallwood's tactics were more effective. Crosbie's campaign was run largely by professionals, Smallwood's by people steeped and seasoned in the art of Newfoundland politics, and most of them had personal axes on the grindstone. They knew their way around public platforms, and, perhaps more important, were at home on the backstairs.

The party's new constitution, adopted at its founding meeting the previous year, provided that each electoral district should hold a convention to elect delegates to the main convention in St. John's. All card-carrying Liberals were eligible to attend the district conventions, and there was no guarantee that they actually lived in the districts concerned. The delegates elected might or might not be committed to a particular candidate for the leadership, and, of course, were always at liberty to change their minds. These were obstacles to influencing the vote, but both principal candidates began packing the meetings with their supporters, just the same. At this game Crosbie and his managers were clearly at a disadvantage compared with the old pro who had been packing meetings of all kinds for half a century. By the time the date of the convention arrived, the results were no longer in doubt. The people in the streets may have been as enthusiastic in their support of Crosbie as the stage-managed demonstrations made it seem, but the committed delegates were Smallwood supporters by almost three to one.

At the convention there was an obvious generation gap. Except for Randy Joyce's handful of supporters, those under thirty were almost unanimously behind Crosbie. Those over forty-five—the vast majority—supported Joey or Hickman, and Hickman's support was small, except for delegates from his native corner of the province, the Burin Peninsula.

The convention lasted for three days, with all the hoopla, speeches, bands, balloons, cheerleaders, and other fanfare that could be borrowed from American political pow-wows. And when the time came for the vote, late on November 1, the delegates voted as they were already committed to do: Smallwood, 1,070; Crosbie, 440; Hickman, 187; Joyce, 13.

Smallwood's acceptance speech was drowned in the uproar, and he was hustled out of the auditorium by his supporters. Crosbie's backers remained, some of them screaming, some weeping, some ready to commit murder. The television cameras ground away, recording the hysterical scene for prime-time viewing across the province. Even during the confederation campaign there had not been such a wild demonstration of hatred against any one man.

While the Liberal Association of Newfoundland was busy tearing itself to shreds, the Progressive Conservatives had not been entirely idle. A new leader had emerged briefly in 1966 in the person of Gerald Ottenheimer, a *nouveau-riche* nouveau intellectual from the wealthy suburb of Waterford Bridge Road in St. John's West. His mother's father, Dan Ryan, had accumulated the money in the hurly-burly of Water Street during the first quarter of the century. Ryan's daughter had married her chauffeur and inherited her father's wealth. She was regarded as a wild eccentric, but had the foresight to give her son the best possible education at universities in London and Paris. Gerald not only knew law and economics, but could keep his private notes on his desk in classical Greek, which made them safe from prying eyes on either side of the House.

He was the most promising leader the Opposition had produced.

He mapped out new policy for the Progressive Conservative Party, toured the outports seeking advice on his party platform, and, like Joey, completed the full twenty miles of the first Oxfam walk in Newfoundland. Then, in 1970, disaster struck. Ottenheimer was set up in a Montreal hotel room with a call girl, hauled into police court, and fined. The story appeared next day in the St. John's papers. A little later Ottenheimer resigned as leader, and for a time was absent from the House of Assembly, and from the province.

Newfoundlanders in the 1970s no longer demanded puritanical hypocrisy in their politicians, but the political parties didn't realize this until some years after Ottenheimer's misfortune. Frank Moores, in fact, was elected premier while his wife was suing him for divorce. He could also laugh off the charge from the Liberal benches that he went skinny-dipping by moonlight in mixed company in the Gander River. Ottenheimer need not have resigned. In fact, he was re-elected the next year, held posts in the government, became Speaker of the House of Assembly, and was finally appointed to the Senate in 1987.

Meanwhile, Frank Moores had emerged to reap the benefits of Ottenheimer's work in the outports. The coolest cat in Newfoundland's political history, Moores was the son of a long line of fish merchants and plant owners in Harbour Grace. He first ran for election in 1968, and won the federal seat of Bonavista-Trinity-Conception by a comfortable majority. Next year he was elected president of the Progressive Conservative Association of Canada, succeeding Dalton Camp, the man who had engineered Diefenbaker's ouster. But Moores was not primarily interested in federal politics. Indeed, during his stay in the House of Commons he spent most of his time in Newfoundland, working to overthrow Smallwood, and was said to have set a record for non-attendance at Commons debates. What he really wanted was to be the giant killer who "got Joey."

When the PCs held a leadership convention in St. John's in 1970, following Ottenheimer's resignation, Moores won in a walk. Still holding his seat in the House of Commons, he immediately began to reorganize the provincial party. He made numerous TV and radio appearances, ending each of his messages with the ominous words, "It won't be long now, ladies and gentlemen."

The message, plainly, was that Newfoundland was suffering under the yoke of a tyrant, but that the tyrant would soon be forced to call an

Dictating correspondence at his home on Roache's Line. He showed up at the office every morning with tapes to be transcribed by his secretaries, and surrounded himself, day and night, with electronic equipment.

Working space at Roache's Line. The one corner that Ed Roberts was never allowed to organize, it remained in the clutter with which Joey's life had always been surrounded. He spent endless hours on the telephone, putting together political and economic deals.

An enthusiastic air traveller, the premier comes bouncing from the Lundrigan airplane at Torbay Airport, near St. John's. Corporation aircraft were his favourite means of travel. He visited almost every major country in the world, many of them in the sumptuously appointed airliner owned by mining promoter John C. Doyle.

A favourite recreation, in his later years as premier, was reading to his grandchildren. Dale Russell (later Fitzpatrick), who became his link with the world in the second half of the 1980s, here stands at his right. The others are Jane, Lorraine and Joey II.

Always good for a bit of clowning, Joey, dressed in oilskins, is baptized for the TV cameras by Colin Jamieson, younger brother of enemy-turned-supporter Don Jamieson. On TV Joey always tried too hard. A great hit on radio, he never mastered the offhand manner that made his arch-rival Frank Moores so successful on television.

Shocked and incredulous, Joey
listens to the count as he goes down
to defeat by Ed Roberts at the
leadership convention of 1973. It
was his first personal defeat in any
kind of election since 1932. Son
William, lawyer and politician,
stands at his shoulder.

Joey just after his final retirement.
He was happy enough, at first. Later
he was plagued by ill health and the
threat of bankruptcy.

election; then the people would cast him aside, and enter a new era of freedom. The pitch was far more damaging than reasoned argument. Indeed, reasoned argument was never one of Moores's strong points. He looked good on the box. He was friendly, offhand, and seemed totally candid. That was enough. He had studied hard under Marshall McLuhan, and knew how to use the picture tube to best advantage. The TV man had arrived. The day of the radio man was fast fading.

By the end of the sixties many of Joey's grandest schemes were stalled or turning sour. The second great round of economic development now looked as though it might well go the way of the first. Negotiations for the Come-by-Chance oil refinery were not concluded until 1970. Plans for the third paper mill had been dragging on for years and years and no mill was yet built; people were getting tired of hearing about it. The phosphorus plant at Long Harbour in Placentia Bay started production, but quickly turned into the ecological disaster that Joey's critics had predicted it would be. One of the reasons for choosing Long Harbour for that plant was its remoteness from population centres—supposedly remote enough that it could pollute its surroundings with impunity. This proved to be mere wishful thinking.

Phosphorus production, always an environmental hazard, looked like a strange activity for Newfoundland, but not quite so strange when you realized that what it required was a good buffer to absorb air pollution and an abundant supply of energy, its most expensive component because it relied on electric furnaces. Joey got the Electric Reduction Company of Canada (a wholly owned subsidiary of an American multinational) to build the plant by offering them a massive power subsidy. The operation increased Newfoundland's power demand by 16 percent. The power was sold to the company at 2.5 mills per kilowatt-hour (about a quarter of its market value) and the plant's demand required the building of a new fossil fuel plant at Holyrood to help supply St. John's. I estimated at the time that it would have been cheaper and far healthier for the government to have put all ERCO employees on a pension for life instead of supplying subsidized power to the company.

A few months after the plant opened at Long Harbour, the fish in Placentia Bay started to turn red. There were not just red herring.

There were red codfish, too. What's more, the lobsters were dying in the water, and even live ones were refused by the shippers. "Would *you* eat a lobster from Placentia Bay?" one plant owner demanded when interviewed by the press.

The fisherman accused the phosphorus operation of polluting the sea water; plant management denied the accusation. Nevertheless, after the federal Department of Fisheries began investigating, the plant closed down, and two days later the department closed the inner section of the bay to all fishing. Laboratory tests proved that the fish were, indeed, polluted with phosphorus, a substance formerly in wide use as a rat poison. The plant was also killing off the surrounding vegetation by fluorine emissions that turned to hydrofluoric acid in the atmosphere.

The plant remained closed for six months, while antipollution equipment was installed, and phosphorus-polluted mud was scooped from the bottom of the harbour. When it reopened, it appeared to be a relatively clean operation. At least, there were no more red fish in the bay. Within a short time Long Harbour was the world's largest producer of elemental phosphorus, and continued operating until 1989, when it closed its doors for the last time.

The fishermen, who had lost half their season before the fishery was reopened in late June, got together, and with federal assistance sued the company for damages. Represented in the case by Richard Cashin, they eventually won a settlement of $300,000.

Through all this the government of Newfoundland had not lifted a finger in the fishermen's defence. Joey, quite simply, had let them down, sincerely believing that a job in a factory, even in a phosphorus reduction plant, was much to be preferred to self-employment in a fishing boat. He thus lost the support of a substantial block of the fishermen, who were added to the loggers, the unionized workers, and the managerial class in the cities, whom he had already alienated. Frank Moores's slogan, "It won't be long now, ladies and gentlemen," looked more and more ominous.

At about this time there was a general exodus from the Liberal ranks. Wells had stayed in Opposition while Crosbie made his bid for the Liberal leadership. Val Earle, a Cabinet minister who had backed the wrong horse at the convention, was forced out of the Cabinet and crossed the floor to join the Tories. Earle was a heavyweight: a former president of the Newfoundland Board of Trade, Canadian observer at the United Nations, head of the Anglican school board of St. John's, and an executive member of the Diocesan Synod of Newfoundland. Hickman crossed the floor at the same time. So, eventually, did

THE GATHERING OF THE HEIRS-APPARENT 287

Crosbie. (He didn't actually join the Tory party until the election call.) Tom Burgess, a Liberal back-bencher from the mining district of Labrador, left the party to sit as an Independent. Two other Liberal back-benchers, Gerald Myrdon and Beaton Abbott, left to sit with Wells as Independent Liberals. This increased the combined Opposition to ten seats, from the mere three it had held in 1966.

At the same time, there were defections in the opposite direction. Not everybody believed that Joey's day was done. He had performed such political miracles in the past that they still expected him to pull at least one more election victory out of his hat. Hubert Kitchen, who had been president of the PC Association, and had run against Moores for the Tory leadership, was welcomed into Joey's cabinet. Noel Murphy, former leader of the Opposition, joined him at the council table. Newfoundland politics had become the familiar game of musical chairs that it had been back in the 1920s. All pretense that party loyalties meant anything were dropped; it was a question of picking winners and jockeying for position.

Joey still believed he could win an election—any election—if he threw himself into the campaign hard enough and hired the right experts to help with the planning. For the coming campaign he had the support of no less a person than the number two Crosbie, Andrew, soon to become the head of the Crosbie empire.

Andrew Crosbie, who lacked his brother's exceptional charm, but had better managerial skills, stuck with the Liberals when John gave up his dream of becoming Joey's successor and crossed the floor once again to support Frank Moores. Many of John's strongest supporters had already burned their Liberal Party membership cards. Although there was no chance that he could supplant Moores as Tory leader, he was beginning to see where his own political future lay. It would just take more time than he had originally hoped.

Everyone expected an election in the autumn of 1970, after the deal for the Come-by-Chance oil refinery was at last signed, and the sod turned. Joey looked good that year. The freebee book that he had sent to a hundred thousand households in advance of the leadership convention, *To You With Affection From Joey*, was still lying beside the Bibles and prayer books on the parlour tables of thousands of outport homes. The National Film Board released its flattering documentary, *A Little Fellow from Gambo*, in which Joey played himself, and received a "best actor" award from a jury in Toronto.

He had never pushed a term of office to its limit of five years. On the contrary, some of his general assemblies had lasted less than three. But this time he kept postponing the inevitable, hoping for an improvement in Newfoundland's economy, hoping the disaster at Long Harbour would gradually be forgotten, hoping for a resurgence of his own popularity, hoping for the conclusion of one more spectacular deal with the promise of thousands of jobs just around the corner. In particular, he hoped that he might be able to add his third paper mill to his list of accomplishments before going to the people in what he once more believed would be his last election. The hope for the third mill looked reasonable, despite the long series of delays in getting it started.

In December 1970 the provincial Department of Finance called a meeting at St. John's to outline to bankers and bond underwriters the government's capital needs for the coming year. John C. Doyle appeared at the conference, and gave the figure of $140 million as the estimated cost of bringing the third mill into production. Everything now seemed to be in place except for the underwriting of the various loans, and that was soon to follow. Financing had been promised not only in Newfoundland, but also in Britain and Germany. But as the summer of 1971 drew on, with the election constitutionally required that year, it became painfully obvious that the third mill was still dragging its feet. There was no real hope that the sod-turning ceremony could be held on the eve of the election.

The summer of 1971 also saw the first strike by the Fishermen, Food and Allied Workers Union, a branch of the Canadian Food and Allied Workers, now with seven thousand members in the Newfoundland outports. The union, organized by Cashin and Father Des McGrath, and backed by a powerful national organization, was the first effective fishermen's union since the time of Coaker, and had succeeded where Coaker had failed in uniting fishermen across all religious and geographical lines.

The strike was a small affair in a remote outport on Newfoundland's Southwest Coast. It involved only about two hundred workers at Burgeo Fish Industries, a plant managed by Spencer Lake. He was the son of H. B. Clyde Lake, the man who had made the unsuccessful deal with the Confederate Association for a senatorship. Spencer was married into another fish dynasty. His wife was the daughter of George J. Penney, the man who had collected the senatorship that

Lake had missed. The Lake-Penney family had a strong sense of hierarchy, ruling not only Burgeo and its satellite fishing settlements, but also the distant town of Gaultois, and the offshore island of Ramea.

The business at Burgeo was family-owned and paternalistic. Spencer Lake not only ran the plant, but most of the affairs of the town. And his views on employer-employee relationships scarcely belonged in the twentieth century. By law he was required to deal with the union, because the union had won a certification vote, but when it came to effective bargaining, he refused to recognize its existence.

The strike began on June 4, 1971. As with the IWA, the real issue was union recognition—not just at Burgeo, but across the province and throughout the industry. Burgeo was the union's test case. Lake hired strikebreakers almost as soon as the plant was closed. The strikers retaliated by smashing the plant windows with rocks. Did Joey call in the police? Did he send for RCMP reinforcements? Not on your life. Spencer Lake was expendable. And this was an election year, like it or not. Fishermen were fishermen, just about the last class of voters he could count on, provided he convinced them he was on their side. In the circumstances it is amazing that he showed almost no active support of the union. He contributed a token amount to the strike fund and went on the air to explain that Lake was making a serious mistake. Finally he even flew to Burgeo, and tried to get Lake to join him in talks with the union. Lake refused. Joey flew home, and continued to do nothing. The strike went on all summer, and was still going on when Joey was forced to call the overdue election in the autumn.

Meanwhile, the strike had become a *cause célèbre* in Newfoundland and across Canada. Bumper stickers with the slogan "It Started in Burgeo" blossomed across the province. They were seen not only on the cars of fishermen and trade unionists, but on those of lawyers, professors, civil servants, and Tory politicians. The thing that had started in Burgeo was not just a strike by a union; it was self-determination by the people of the outports.

Joey could easily have nationalized the Burgeo fish plant. (It was up to its eyebrows in debt to the government anyway.) He could then have put the plant workers and the trawlermen back to work at decent wages, and collected credit throughout the fishing outports of the whole province. Instead, he limited himself to empty rhetoric. As had happened when the fishermen of Placentia Bay fought the giant corporation that was poisoning their waters, he did nothing. Why? He gave his reasons, but only in private. He did not believe that the fishermen should be encouraged to endanger the industry by demanding too large a share of the product. By now he sincerely believed that unions, especially unions of primary producers, could damage or wreck the economy.

Eventually the fishermen won. Eventually Lake fled from Burgeo. Eventually the plant was nationalized by a Tory government. The Fishermen's Union went on from strength to strength. But this all happened after Joey had been defeated. His failure to support the fishermen at Burgeo and Long Harbour struck at the very heart of his constituency. The fishermen were his last and strongest supporters. When he failed them, what was left? The effects were to show up clearly in the voting that year. The Tories not only won Burgeo-LaPoile, but Port au Port, St. George's, St. Barbe South, St. Mary's, Lewisporte, and Ferryland—all of them fishing districts.

1971 was also a bad year for the Newfoundland economy. Fish landings dropped, and in some areas the fishery was a failure. The two paper mills, plagued by market troubles, went on short time. The American base at Argentia, which had been reducing its scope bit by bit since the end of the Second World War, abandoned another branch of its operations and laid off 700 employees.

To make Joey's troubles worse, a great grass-roots resurgence of the Tories was taking place at the same time. The Tories made no attempt to sell tens of thousand of party memberships, as the Liberals had done earlier with indifferent results. Instead, they invited all comers to attend their district conventions and help them elect party candidates. They estimated that more than twenty thousand people flocked into their meeting halls, and with few exceptions chose the candidates that the party organizers were promoting. They had managed, at least on a modest scale, to create the great democratic party machine that Joey had first proposed for the Liberals, and then wrecked with his own hands. On the breakwater of the fishing settlement of Hibbs's Hole, Conception Bay, in black letters six feet high a spray-painted sign proclaimed: "All PCs Welcome Here!"

In the face of this Tory activity Joey seemed to be suffering from paralysis. The Liberal Association that he had created with such fanfare three years earlier had simply confirmed his leadership and then melted away. His faction had gone home; Crosbie's faction had joined the Tories. There was nothing in place, by the end of the summer of 1971, to challenge the Tory organization that now extended into every district and virtually every village in the province—nothing, that is, except Joey himself, who was still the most powerful single force in Newfoundland. He had the assistance of whatever team of election workers Andrew Crosbie could throw together in the three or four weeks remaining before the legislature would have to be dissolved and the election announced. Crosbie, in fact, had the month of September to get ready, and the month of October to run the campaign. After that, if Joey won, there'd be another leadership convention, at which (perhaps) the old leader would hand the premiership to the number two Crosbie on a silver shovel.

Throughout the year, Joey had once again been talking of his retirement, and reminiscing about the "great moments" of his life—hardly the kind of self-indulgence a political leader should allow himself in an election year. Aside from such talk, however, there seemed to be few reasons why Joey should retire at seventy, few other marks of advancing age. He was now silver-haired and rather grim-featured, but not excessively fat, and not slowing down. He had passed over the wheel of the limousine to a chauffeur—one of his wife's relatives, Nelson Oates of Bay Roberts—and cat-napped during the fifty-minute drive from office to home, but he still worked until near midnight, rose before eight A.M., and made his own breakfast, which he ate alone. Mrs. Smallwood read books through most of the night, and slept in the mornings. Joey was in his office every day by 9:30 with tapes of his dictated correspondence ready for his stenographers.

He rarely received anyone now, except in his suite of offices in the tower of Confederation Building. There he was interviewed by the mainland press, pursued by political hopefuls who still expected him to boost them into the seats of the mighty, and plagued by ward heelers. There he held his luncheon meetings with a picked group of Cabinet ministers and whoever happened to be working with him on the latest miracle of economic development.

The main office was filled with equipment. Besides the two telephones (which he often used simultaneously), his desk was wired for tape recorders, intercoms, radio, and television. He thought of himself as the ultimate electronic man. But he never learned to use television with the easy familiarity he achieved on radio. On TV he tried too hard. He could be impressive, even magnetic, but his audiences tended to be overwhelmed; they came away with the feeling that they had been bludgeoned, rather than taken into his confidence, as they felt when Moores spoke so quietly and confidently. Even in 1971 Joey's "conversations with the premier," fifteen-minute slots on morning radio, were his most effective propaganda outlet.

At the end of the sixties Joey kept repeating that he really didn't understand this younger generation. It was true. When the university student paper mocked his chant of "Jobs, jobs, J-O-B-S" he was utterly baffled. If they didn't want jobs, what on earth *did* they want?

The answer was really quite simple, though nobody ever managed to get it through to Joey. They wanted social change. They wanted a climate in which they would have choices. They wanted a chance to control their own lives. That was what had started in Burgeo. If all you wanted was a job at the minimum wage, you could go to Toronto and work in a dog-food factory and come home for Christmas. Everybody knew somebody who did just that.

So Joey walked down the only path he knew, still dreaming in 1971 the dreams of Sir Richard Squires, heading for the bitterest experience of his life—the hour when the people of Newfoundland, and even the people of the outports, would cast him aside.

# CHAPTER 18

# *Joey and the Giant-Killer*

SMALLWOOD'S ABILITY AS A LEADER IS GENERALLY MISUNDERSTOOD. HE was such a resounding success as a politician that his excellence as a leader is taken for granted. In fact he had very little talent for leadership. He had great charisma, was a star performer on a platform or before a microphone, but knew nothing about teamwork. He ran a one-man show because that was the only kind of show he knew how to run.

Never was this more obvious than in the general election of 1971. There were two separate campaigns: the party campaign run by Andrew Crosbie and the Joey campaign run by Smallwood himself. Most of the time, each literally did not know what the other was doing. Andrew Crosbie put on a good show. He made some mistakes, and possibly one fatal mistake, but on the whole it was a sound, professional effort. Like all Crosbie campaigns, it was very expensive. The Liberal-come-latelys who were growing fat on government contracts coughed up about a million dollars to try to extend their term at the public feed trough by another five years. Needless to say, it was all spent.

Government departments like highways and public works were herded into the campaign. Hundreds of miles of election pavement began to spread, black and sticky, across the face of the land. Most of it would begin breaking up the next year; it had been laid right over the surface of the dirt roads, with no solid foundation below, but meanwhile it had served its purpose, making jobs for unemployed voters, and running a temporarily smooth road past their doors. It was rumoured that you might even get your driveway paved free of charge if you knew the right people.

The election machinery was already rolling in high gear and candidates for both sides were canvassing their districts long before Joey made his belated October 6 announcement that the election would be held October 28. He had always tried to catch his opponents unprepared and to make the actual campaigns as brief as legally possible. This time there was no surprise. He had left the election so late that there was even some question as to whether he was still legally in office.

The delay hadn't helped his cause in the least. It looked as if he might be afraid to face the voters, which was exactly the case. He had commissioned a poll by a mainland company, and the results were so bad that he didn't show it to anyone, even his closest friends and allies. He kept forgetting to bring it to his office.

He set off to try to change the trend by a direct, personal appeal to the people of the outports. Even if he lost all the seats in St. John's, Corner Brook, Grand Falls, and Gander, he could still come back with a comfortable majority. He might even lose such tricky seats as Labrador West, Ferryland, St. Mary's, Port-au-Port, and St. George's, and still win by a margin of eight seats—twenty-five to seventeen—provided only that the "real" outports held solid. The popular vote might go against him by as much as 20,000 without upsetting his government. His redistribution bills had seen to that. So he set out to make it happen by a long series of solo appearances on the streets of the outports—no Greg Power by his side this time, no Fred Rowe, just Joey and the people.

He toured in a mini-bus with a PA system and a microphone, a loudspeaker truck running ahead to announce his coming. The popular tune "All Around the Circle" became his theme song. It was a good choice, real outport music, and very upbeat. Liberal campaign headquarters in St. John's had nothing whatever to do with his tour. Most of the time they had no idea where he was or where he was going next. They turned out floods of election material, papered the province with pictures of Joey's bright new "team," and issued many hours of TV and radio propaganda expounding the achievements of the past two decades, the revolution that had taken place in Newfoundland since Smallwood's first term.

Andrew Crosbie knew by now how to run an election. But he made what may have been his most serious mistake with an expensive television film that was shown twice late in the campaign on all Newfoundland stations. Titled "The End of the Beginning," it showed Joey in full cry during the early stages of his public career, and it showed him walking out of the legislature into retirement, now that his career was over. It was an obvious play for sympathy for the retiring leader, but it was poor psychology. People usually prefer to believe they are voting for the future, not the past.

The Moores campaign, vigorously backed by John Crosbie's charm and caustic wit, was much better based. It made few promises, but drove home one clear message: "Get on the winning side. The time has come."

Joey's personal appeal on the mainstreets of the doubtful outports came within a whisker of winning him another term in office. Three or four hundred votes in close outport districts would have turned the trick. He discovered that the mothers and housewives of a hundred fishing villages still loved him, even when their sons and husbands were flocking after the pipes of Cashin and McGrath. Joey got so carried away by their friendly reception that he forgot his promise to retire—and Andrew Crosbie's campaign for the sympathy vote. If elected, he told his outport audiences, he'd remain in office for *the full five years* and that was a promise. By then he'd be seventy-five, a good age at which to begin a second career as author and historian.

The professionals kept him off live television as much as they possibly could. The faces they wanted the voters to see were those of the bright new team. But in the closing days of the campaign every talk show and phone-in radio show in the province invited Joey to appear as guest, and he accepted every one of them. He was vigorous, persuasive, as great a debater as ever, and it really looked as if he might squeak back into office.

Liberal and PC headquarters both claimed to have the election sewn up. Each said they'd win thirty seats out of forty-two. Translated into realistic terms, this meant fifteen seats each, with eleven seats that might go one way or the other, and one seat (Labrador West) a shoo-in for the New Labrador Party, a kind of separatist movement invented by the sitting member, Tom Burgess, who had first been elected as a Liberal five years before.

Joey had managed in a bare four weeks to turn things around. The polls and the mood across the province were strongly against him in the first week of October. By the end of the month the tide was running in his favour.

It was a beautiful autumn day—sunny, even warm for the time of year—and the voters flocked to the polls in record numbers. The turnout represented not only the absolute largest number of people ever to vote in a Newfoundland election; it represented the highest *proportion* of eligible voters to go to the polls since 1949. There was a feeling that this was a turning point, that it was going to be close, and that for once every vote might really matter.

The polls closed at 8:00 P.M. Before 8:30 the first counts were coming in, and before 9:00 the CBC election desk was awarding seats to both parties. John Crosbie was quickly confirmed in St. John's West and Ed Roberts in White Bay North. Moores was piling up a landslide in Humber West, and his running mate, Tom Farrell, was doing almost as well in Humber East. Gander was soon in the Tory column also. The St. John's seats quickly fell to the PCs by large majorities. Tom Burgess won Labrador West by an outright majority over both the Liberals and PCs.

But the outports were holding more strongly for Joey than the Moores team had thought possible. When the counting ceased for the night at 2:00 A.M. the major parties had elected eighteen members each, Burgess was elected in Labrador West, and five seats were undecided. Next morning three of the five seats went to the PCs and two to the Liberals, leaving the standings at twenty-one for the PCs, twenty for the Liberals, and one for the New Labrador Party.

It was all too much for Tom Burgess. He thought fate had landed him in the driver's seat. He announced that he was "holding the balance of power." Had he captured the two seats from coastal Labrador, this might have made more sense, but they both went to the Liberals. He was aware that a minority party can strongly influence public policy when neither of two major parties holds a majority. He didn't know that you cannot do this with just one vote, or that he was merely one of a number of small-time politicians ready to sit on either side of the House or in the middle, all depending.

Despite the even distribution of seats, the election was nothing less than a slaughter for the Liberals. Seven Cabinet ministers went down to defeat, including Joey's annointed successor Fred Rowe. The PCs won the popular vote by a majority of nearly 15,000. And in spite of the advance signs, the results were a shock to Newfoundlanders. Even his devoted enemies had scarcely dared to believe that Joey could really be defeated in a general election. He was such an institution that radio and TV announcers continued accidentally saying "Premier Smallwood" for a year or more after his defeat.

The situation was exceedingly tricky not because it was a virtual tie, and certainly not because Burgess had been elected, but because *seven members* had been elected with majorities of less than a hundred votes each. What's more, five of the seven were PCs. It was entirely possible that judicial recounts could alter the standings by two or three or more seats.

There were, of course, demands that Joey go at once to the lieutenant-governor and hand in his resignation. There was no precedent in the British Commonwealth for a defeated premier or prime minister continuing to hold power. Nevertheless, he lay low, saying absolutely nothing. He had decided to wait for the recounts and to see what the backstairs boys could do about wooing Tories with the bait of Cabinet posts. There were lots of those now, going begging. Burgess, as expected, was receiving flattering attention from both sides, and was playing hard to get. He announced that he had been offered a million dollars for his support, but that he had refused it with scorn.

Joey wouldn't talk to the press, but he taped a long interview with Geoff Stirling, his multimillionaire friend and sometime enemy who had published the *gaffe* about the voting nuns back in 1948. Stirling broadcast it over his station CJON-TV. It was the first thing the premier had said in public since election day. And it was a shocker.

He didn't intend to resign, he said, at least not until the recounts made it clear who had won the close seats, *and in any case the government was not constitutionally required to resign until it met the legislature and was defeated in the House*. The legislature, he pointed out, had not been called into session. Indeed, it did not have to be called into session until the end of March to vote supply, giving the government authority to spend money in the coming financial year. Actually, it would be interim supply, a stop-gap measure—a full supply bill could wait another month or two. So his government could remain in office for at least another five months should he choose. He wanted to make it clear that this wasn't an announcement of his intentions— just that he *could* do this if he wanted to.

There was public uproar. It looked so much like a negation of democracy that the PCs and the Newfoundland press both consulted experts on constitutional law, but received little enlightenment. The situation was unprecedented.

The next day John C. Doyle arrived from Labrador in his private jet, bringing Tom Burgess with him. Burgess smirked at the TV cameras and said he had both the Newfoundland parties exactly where he wanted them. Accordingly to the rumour mill, however, Smallwood had offered him a Cabinet post. He later said that Moores had offered him a Cabinet post as well—a statement that Moores denied. But in any case Burgess *did* meet with Moores, Crosbie, and Smallwood all on the same day, Sunday, October 31. Meanwhile, John C. Doyle was hobnobbing with various elected Tories. Was he trying to get them to bolt to the Liberals, reporters asked? Not at all, said Doyle. He was just being friendly. And perhaps he was, too, because he soon had them flying hither and yon with him. Soon they were making use of the Lundrigan airplane, too. No Tory had ever had it so good.

Next came a rash of opinions on Smallwood's declaration that he could remain in office for another five months, regardless of the results of the election. After the meeting with Joey, Don Jamieson told the press that the premier had assured him he would not remain in office if the judicial recounts made no changes in the distribution of seats. Then Senator Forsey, widely regarded as a constitutional expert, gave his opinion that the premier had the right to remain in office until the recounts were complete. Other constitutional experts disagreed with this, however, and Moores said he was considering legal action to evict Smallwood from the premiership.

But regardless of the constitutional question, Joey regarded himself as personally repudiated. On Thursday, November 11, he announced that there would be a leadership convention of the Liberal Party on February 4 and 5. This time he would not be a candidate. John Crosbie, too, was out of the running. And even Andrew Crosbie was no longer the heir apparent; Joey was anything but happy with the way he had run the election. Indeed, he was strongly inclined to blame the number two Crosbie for the Liberal defeat.

On Friday, November 12, Moores and Burgess held a joint press conference to announce that Burgess had thrown in his lot with the Tories. This gave Moores a clear majority of twenty-two seats to the Liberals' twenty. And as the results of the judicial recounts came in, the winning Conservatives were confirmed in their seats, one by one. The premiership was now hanging by a thread. Just one recount remained—St. Barbe South, which the Tories had won by a margin of eight votes.

On November 23 Supreme Court Judge Harold Puddester

dropped a bombshell. He had halted the recount in St. Barbe South, he announced, because 106 ballots from Sally's Cove had been burned on election night by Deputy Returning Officer Olive Payne, who apparently thought that once ballots were counted and the results phoned in, they were just waste paper.

The Liberals now filed suit to have the election in St. Barbe South set aside. This would reduce the Tory strength to twenty, not counting Burgess, whose party loyalties nobody took seriously. The PCs filed to have their elected member, Edward Maynard, confirmed in his seat. While the cases were being adjudicated, Joey would remain in office.

Throughout his career, Burgess belonged to more political parties than any other Newfoundlander on record. As an organizer for the International Steel Workers at Wabush and Labrador City, his first loyalty had been to the NDP, but he had joined the Liberals at the election call of 1966, crossed the floor to sit as an Independent, then formed his own New Labrador Party, and had now joined the PCs. There were no parties left for him to join unless he went on to organize yet another—and he actually talked about that: a new "left-of-centre alliance" that might indeed have materialized and become a power in the province had the potential leader not been such a political butterfly as Tom Burgess. Finally, he began fluttering back toward Joey, lured, one suspects, by Doyle and by the promise that he could become the newest and brightest heir apparent. Premier Tom Burgess! The prospect practically numbed his mind.

At this point both parties expected a by-election in St. Barbe South. Joey hoped he could persuade Richard Cashin to run there, and that he would be unbeatable. The bait to get Cashin was also a promise of the succession. If Cashin first won the by-election, Joey pointed out, the convention in February would be a pushover. The scenario looked reasonable, and Cashin was said to be thinking it over. If Joey could add both Burgess and Cashin to his followers, both believing they were to be his successor, both believing they could be simply *named* to the premiership without first having to win a general election, then he would have his twenty-two members, and could stay in office until the convention actually took place. After that, regardless of what else happened, he would be able to retire undefeated, to voluntarily resign the premiership without ever being booted out of office. It was convoluted thinking. But that's what was going on in his head.

Joey went off for the Christmas vacation to Florida, where he owned a condominium. While he was there, Burgess flew down and phoned him, and Joey drove to Tampa airport to meet him.

According to Joey's published account, this is what happened: Suppose he left the Tories and rejoined the Liberals, Burgess suggested, would Joey take him into the Cabinet?

Like a shot! Joey assured him. However ... hm-m-m ... yes. Burgess would first have to issue a categorical statement to the effect that his short stay with the Tories had thoroughly disillusioned him. He had discovered that the Tory party was, in fact, not fit to govern the province.

OK, said Burgess. And was it a fact that Joey intended to resign the leadership in February?

Oh, absolutely! There was no way he'd stay on!

Then, said Burgess, could he run for the leadership?

The question just about bowled Joey over, but he quickly recovered, and kept a straight face. Why sure, he said. If Burgess was a card-carrying Liberal, there was nothing whatever to stop his running for the leadership. And if he was already in the Cabinet, that would give him additional credibility. All he'd need would be members of the party to nominate him.

Well, Burgess persisted, would Joey support him for the leadership?

This, according to Joey's own account, was more than he was prepared to promise, but he explained that he would undoubtedly support his elected successor, whoever that happened to be.

Burgess went away to think this over. Then, at a second meeting two days later, he asked Joey to write a statement for him, explaining his decision to rejoin the Liberals after an absence of several years. Joey, always good at fiction, wrote the statement and read it to Burgess, who took it down in his own handwriting, because, as Joey explained, "I don't want it in mine!"

The statement said that Burgess had lost all faith in the Tories. They were split into warring factions and were not one party, but several. He had been elected originally as a Liberal in Labrador West, but had quarrelled with Smallwood, and then had sat on the opposite side of the House. Now, however, Smallwood had announced his intention to retire. So Burgess saw no reason not to return to the Liberal Party, his original political home.

Joey told Burgess he must issue this statement before the decision on the by-election in St. Barbe South was issued from the Supreme

Court. (It was expected within a few days.) Otherwise it would look too much as if he were climbing on a bandwagon. Burgess agreed, and departed with the statement in his pocket. But instead of flying home, as Joey did on January 4, he lingered in Florida, visiting his brother, an Irish priest who had a teaching job in that state.

The next Joey heard of him he was in Montreal. From there he phoned to explain that before he issued his statement he would have to go to Labrador City to confer with the leaders of his New Labrador Party.

"Then for heaven's sake go at once!" Joey urged. "The Supreme Court decision is due any day!"

Burgess phoned him again from Labrador City. There'd be a further slight delay, he explained. He had to go on to Goose Bay to consult with the executives of the two coastal districts, where there were also branches of the New Labrador Party.

The day after this last phone call, Moores made a blistering attack on Burgess, stating that he was about to join the Liberals and run for the Liberal leadership.

Some time after two o'clock the next morning Joey received a phone call from a reporter named Gerry Corbi, who worked for Radio Station VOCM in St. John's, where Joey broadcast his daily "Conversations with the Premier." He'd just been talking to Burgess, Corbi explained, and Burgess was denying Moores's allegations and reaffirming his loyalty to the Progressive Conservative Party. They had argued about it, because Burgess had earlier assured Corbi that he was rejoining the Liberals. Corbi had the phone conversation on tape, and played it back for Joey. Burgess had ended by asking Corbi for Moores's phone number.

Why this sudden change? Burgess, while in Labrador City, had heard a news report that the Supreme Court decision on St. Barbe was released. The decision, a surprise to Burgess and to everyone but the judges, confirmed the election of Edward Maynard, thus giving the Tories a one-seat advantage over the Liberals. The decision was well-reasoned, if unexpected. No irregularities had been found in the election itself; the ballots had been scrutinized and counted; the results of the election had to be regarded as valid unless irregularities were discovered, and could not be upset by someone's destruction of a batch of papers after the event.

If Burgess stayed put, Moores would now have the edge of twenty-two seats to the Liberals' twenty. If he rejoined the Liberals there'd be an even split at twenty-one. It was January 11, 1972. Everyone now confidently expected Joey's resignation. Jamieson even made another public statement calling on him to resign. But he continued to hesitate. He still suspected Burgess was ready to bolt to the Liberals even though he'd made no public statement as yet. And something else was going on behind the scenes without Jamieson's knowledge.

At least one elected PC was prepared to join the Liberals, and perhaps two. They had been in touch with Smallwood, inquiring about possible Cabinet posts. The myth of his invincibility, the belief that he could somehow pull it all together in spite of the electorate and confer the premiership on his chosen successor, died very hard.

Both sides seem to have had detailed information on what was supposedly happening in secret (probably supplied by members of the press) and Moores must have known that Burgess's party loyalties were in a very fluid state indeed. Nevertheless, he pretended to accept Burgess at face value, and issued a statement to the effect that he had been taken in by rumours: Burgess was, after all, loyal to the Progressive Conservative Party!

Joey might have delayed matters still further, had he chosen, and especially in view of the wavering Tories, but at this point he seems to have finally lost patience with the whole sorry mess. He had set a record for clinging to office after defeat, nearly three months, and there was no way he could stretch it beyond the leadership convention, now due in three weeks. He called a press conference, announced his resignation from office, and said he was committing himself to "the verdict of history."

But he still didn't resign. He waited for another five days while the trucks hauled load after load of papers, records, films, tapes, souvenirs, and plain junk from the premier's office in Confederation Building to his home on Roache's Line, where it was stored, bale on bale, in the basement. On January 18 he went to the lieutenant-governor, handed in his resignation, and recommended that Frank Moores be invited to form a government. Then he drove to the airport and flew to Florida for another vacation in the sun.

While he was away, the game of musical chairs continued as merrily as ever. Burgess announced that he was joining the Liberals anyway, and that he intended to contest the leadership at the impending convention. The only other candidate for the leadership was Roberts, who was running a very low-key campaign.

Then one of the St. John's members, Hugh Shea, who was the

only representative of a St. John's district who had not been invited into Moores's first Cabinet, made a public announcement that he was joining the Liberal Party. This left Moores with twenty seats—once again in a minority position, but at the moment it hardly mattered, because the House had not been called into session.

And then, as Joey delicately put it, "an extraordinary thing happened." Gus Oldford, the Liberal member for Fortune Bay, who had never sat in a legislature, resigned his seat. Oldford had edged out the Tory-come-lately H. V. R. Earle (formerly Joey's finance minister) by 251 votes. A few months earlier Joey had plucked Oldford out of the magistracy in Grand Falls and put him into the Cabinet. Now, faced with the dismal prospect of sitting on a back bench in Opposition, Oldford accepted the invitation of the new government to have his old job back. This came close to restoring the balance. The Liberals were back to twenty-one seats if you counted Burgess, but if the worse came to the worst, Moores could always invite Burgess into his Cabinet, then fire him immediately after the next election.

As it turned out, another strategy became possible; the by-election in Fortune Bay wasn't necessary, and Moores never did have to survive a vote in the legislature.

Joey returned to St. John's for the Liberal Leadership Convention of February 4 and 5. Though he wasn't running, he was once again the star of the show, "bowing out of public life" in a scene of unmitigated sentimentality.

Nearly a thousand delegates crowded the hall. They cheered, sang, wept, and pledged their undying love. Joey made an hour-long speech outlining the accomplishments of his twenty-three years in office. A little girl went up to the stage to present him with twenty-three red roses. The chairman of the Liberal Association handed him the keys of a new car, a farewell gift, now that he would no longer be travelling in the government limousine. The TV cameras ground away for hours, recording it all for the provincial networks, and the bands blared.

As the ceremonies on the stage drew to a close, people rushed forward to touch him. Among them was Joe Ashley, the electrical contractor who had been one of the brash young men who attached themselves to Joey the moment he came to power. No longer young, but grown inordinately rich and living in Canada House, Joey's former home, Ashley climbed up on the platform, his face streaming with tears, and hugged and kissed the departing leader. Joey mopped his own streaming eyes with an already sodden pocket handkerchief.

He cast his vote but didn't stay for the leadership "race" between Roberts and Burgess. Many others didn't stay either, and hundreds of delegates didn't even bother to vote. There was really no contest. Roberts won on the first ballot by 564 votes to 82. The only surprise was that Burgess collected as many votes as he did.

That was far from the end of Joey's public career, but it was very nearly the end of Burgess's, and of his New Labrador Party. In the succeeding election he ran for the Liberals in Labrador West and was soundly trounced by a Tory named Joe Rousseau. The New Labrador Party won a seat in Labrador South, ran second to the Liberals in Labrador North, and picked up to a token 438 votes in Labrador West. After that, like Burgess himself, it softly and silently vanished away. But radical protest in Labrador was by no means at an end. Though the Liberals and PCs split the territory between them for a while, no seat there was safe for any party, and when Newfoundland began electing NDP candidates in the late seventies and eighties, one of the first of them came from Labrador City.

Joey had planned to sit in the legislature as a quiet back-bencher, for he had been returned, personally, in Placentia East. He politely refused an invitation from Roberts to sit on a front bench at Roberts's right hand, and chose, instead, a desk next to the door. But all plans for a spring session of the House were adroitly short-circuited by Moores, who turned out to be a better backstairs politician than anyone had suspected.

He asked the lieutenant-governor to call the House into session on March 1. He now had only twenty members to the Opposition's twenty-one, so his government appeared to be at Roberts's mercy. But on the day the House opened one seat was vacant (Fortune Bay) and another was unoccupied, because the Liberal member for Bay de Verde, William Saunders, was not in his place. This evened matters out, but still left Moores short one vote in case of a division, since one of his supporters was in the Speaker's Chair. It all looked very touch-and-go, and the press gallery was crowded with reporters from main-land papers and wire services. What none of them knew was that Moores had Saunders's resignation from the House in his pocket.

Saunders had served in the House of Assembly for two terms. If he had served his third term he would have been eligible for a pension for life. Nevertheless, he chose not to serve that third term. If he had chosen to attend the new session, even for a single day, he would also have been eligible for the $10,000 sessional indemnity. This he also chose not to do. It is true that he was in a vulnerable position, having been elected by just twenty-one votes, and consequently facing nearly certain defeat if he stood for election again. According to Smallwood, he was also in financial difficulties. But none of this really explains his resignation.

The House met, and there was a brief Speech from the Throne, then formal speeches from government and Opposition—nothing that would justify a confidence motion. Then the House adjourned "until tomorrow." That evening, Moores went to Government House and asked for a dissolution, presenting Saunders's letter of resignation to the lieutenant-governor as he did so. Had Moores been in a minority position, the lieutenant-governor would normally have refused dissolution, and waited for a confidence motion, asking Roberts to form a government if Moores was unable to govern. But since the parties were now evenly divided, with twenty members each, there was no point in calling on Roberts. He granted dissolution, permitting Moores to "go to the electorate as premier"—supposedly a great advantage, and one for which leaders in tight positions have always jockeyed with great determination.

The next day Moores announced that the thirty-fifth general assembly was at an end. He was calling a new election for March 24, 1972. That would give him time to call the legislature into session after the election and present an interim supply bill so that the government would be able to issue cheques after the end of the financial year, March 31. A full budget, including a supply bill for the coming year, could wait another month or longer. It was all very neat timing. Moores had studied under Smallwood and learned his lessons well. The old pro could not have managed matters one whit better.

Joey decided to retire completely from public life and did not run in the election of March 24, 1972. The seat he had won in the previous year's election was taken by one of Moores's new boys, Finton Alyward. The election produced the inevitable landslide for Moores, but a few of Joey's bright young men survived. Roberts, as usual, won White Bay North by a thumping great majority. Bill Rowe (Fred Rowe's son) won a close contest in White Bay South. Steve Neary survived by 200 votes in Bell Island. Joey's old guard had been wiped out of existence. Only eight Liberals were returned, and all except Neary were in the far northern parts of the province. Moore's strategy had paid off, and his government settled down for a long stay in office. John Crosbie was sworn into the Moores Cabinet as minister of finance and minister of economic development on January 18. No one had previously carried the two heavy portfolios at the same time, but Crosbie was as famous for hard work as Moores was for taking it easy. His first action was to take a close look at the agreements for the building of the third mill at Stephenville. The agreements were bad ones, he decided, and there was a strong suspicion of dishonest dealings. He announced on January 26 that the mill would be taken over by the government unless John C. Doyle withdrew from the project or repaid the government $24 million of the amounts the government had guaranteed.

Before the Liberals left office, Crosbie explained, they had learned of a loan that Doyle had raised in West Germany, in the amount of $35 million, with the government guarantees as partial security. This money, he said, was now on deposit in a French bank, "awaiting transfer to Panama," where Doyle was resident. There was no guarantee that the money would be spent on the mill at Stephenville, and the government had intervened with the French bank to have the funds frozen, pending their final disposition.

Doyle did not respond to Crosbie's ultimatum, so the Newfoundland government proceeded to nationalize the project at Stephenville, and to complete it at government expense. Eventually they sold it to an established paper company.

Joey, meanwhile, had done just what he had said he would do when he retired. He was dashing off a daily column for the St. John's *Daily News* —writing as many as five or six of them at a sitting. He was also supposedly doing research for his two-volume *History of Newfoundland*, and compiling materials for his autobiography. Some of this work took him to England, and, he said, might also take him to Portugal, which had been involved in the Newfoundland fishery for at least 470 years, perhaps longer. Newfoundland politics could simply go its merry way without him.

The government of Canada offered him a seat in the Senate, and also suggested that a diplomatic appointment could be arranged for him if that was what he preferred. He declined both offers. He wanted to travel, he said, and though he had no accumulated wealth, he wasn't exactly in want. He had the usual Canada pensions, the full pension drawn by a former Newfoundland minister, and some income from investments. Among his investments were BRINCO shares and a string of service stations selling the products of his promoter-friend John Shaheen. (All these sources of income amounted to $28,012.32 a year according to Joey.)

The Tories suspected that he might have accumulated a bit too much in the way of property and securities. They learned that he or members of his family owned various bits of real estate in Newfoundland and elsewhere, including, they said, properties that had been rented to the government. They appointed a royal commission to investigate.

On July 5, 1972, Premier Moores told the House of Assembly that the commission had found the former premier to be a shareholder in a company that owned seven buildings and rented them to the government's Board of Liquor Control at what he called inflated rates: $73,192.00 a year, against what the commission had decided would be the fair rent of $37,545.80.

The buildings were rented from a firm named the "Bankers Trust Company," but they were owned by another firm named "Investment Developers Limited." Shares in this second company, Moores said, were "owned equally by Arthur Lundrigan of Corner Brook, Oliver L. Vardy of St. John's, and the Hon. J. R. Smallwood."

Three thousand shares of Investment Developers Limited, the Premier revealed, had been transferred to the Bank of Montreal as security for loans, and the loans in turn had been used to purchase shares in BRINCO. The loans totalled "between $1.5 and $1.6 million," and the bank had decided "not to press for interest." The Bank of Montreal, the Premier pointed out, was the banker for the Province of Newfoundland, as well as for Mr. Smallwood, the Lundrigan firm, and BRINCO.

Joey, who was then in London doing research for his memoirs, made a heated response to the press by telephone: "I deny and contradict and repudiate any suggestion or hint that I had anything whatsoever to do with these leases or the buildings or the company that owns them." And Oliver Vardy, also in Europe, denied by telephone that Smallwood was a shareholder in Investment Developers Limited.

When told that Moores intended to launch a civil suit for the collection of what the government regarded as overcharges on the leases, Joey (who had no connection with the leases) reacted in a truly typical fashion.

"I'm bankrupt," he said. Then he modified this a little. He was "financially secure on a day-to-day basis" he admitted, but he was heavily in debt: "If I were forced to liquidate my debts . . . well, it would be utterly impossible to do so, unless I'm given time to earn some extra income." He hoped to earn enough by his writing, he explained, to be out of debt by the age of seventy-five. (He wasn't. Apparently he had been deeply in debt all his life, and that was the way he remained.)

Later he admitted that he had indeed bought BRINCO shares with money borrowed from the Bank of Montreal. He was, he said, paying interest on this loan. He did not say how much interest he was paying, or when the payments had started.

Arthur Lundrigan also commented on Premier Moores's statement. Whether the rents were too high was a matter of opinion, he said.

And that seemed to be the end of the matter. The contradictions were never explained. It was, in any case, a rather trifling matter of a few thousand dollars, not the tens of millions that would be involved in later charges against Doyle.

But the government was still determined to "get Joey" if they possibly could. At 8:00 A.M. on December 15, 1972, eight RCMP officers arrived in cars and drove up to the doors of Joey's house on Roache's Line. They surrounded the building, so the occupants could not escape to the woods, and one of them knocked on the door. They had a search warrant, and they were looking for documents.

Joey was then at his condominium in Florida. His wife Clara, roused from sleep, brought the police into the house, where they were soon joined by Joey's son Ramsay, who lived nearby. His daughter, Clara Russell, lived just across the road.

Soon another eight policemen arrived and surrounded Mrs. Russell's house. Finally, two more arrived in a helicopter, bringing with them the RCMP's lock-picking expert. They had heard stories of secret compartments in the basement of the Russwood ranch house, where there was, in fact, an invisible door leading to the wine cellar.

According to Joey's account, they "ransacked" both his house and his daughter's house, and seized and carted off twenty boxes full of papers—documents, letters, road maps, photographs—nearly everything that he had taken from his office eleven months before and a good deal more that he had collected at his home. They didn't overlook his hundreds of tapes.

On the same day that they raided Joey's home, the RCMP raided Vardy's penthouse apartment in St. John's. Vardy wasn't at home either. Indeed, he wasn't in the province, and as far as they could learn, was not expected to return. They traced him to Panama, where he had apparently taken up permanent residence.

Moores passed along the job of explaining it all to Justice Minister T. Alex Hickman. The raids, Hickman said, were part of "a four-province investigation" by the fraud squad of the RCMP concerning "the disposition of funds relating to the linerboard mill" (the paper mill at Stephenville).

Vardy and Doyle were both later charged with fraud, but no charge was ever brought against Joey. He regarded the raid as persecution: "an effort to find something, anything, for which they could put me in jail." Vardy and Doyle didn't go to jail either. The government never managed to bring them to trial.

Nothing whatever happened as a result of the raid on Joey's archives. No charge was ever laid against him. No further revelations were made with respect to his private or public dealings. But he asked in vain to get his property back. The Tories—or the police, whoever were responsible—kept the materials for five years before returning them. Perhaps it took someone that long to leaf through them all.

CHAPTER 19

# *The Lion in Winter*

ONE OF JOEY'S MOST ASTONISHING CONTRADICTIONS CAME TO THE
surface after his defeat at the polls. He turned on the Liberal Party of
Newfoundland and wrecked it, leaving it in such a state of confusion
and strife that it took the party sixteen years to pull itself together to the
point where it could present a realistic challenge to the powerful ruling
Tories.

This didn't happen all at once, and it didn't happen because of his
defeat. It happened only after he discovered that the party was
determined to go its own way without him, and it was caused at least
partly by a personal feud that he conceived with Ed Roberts, the one
man who had survived a close association with him and had beaten off
all the other heirs apparent to become his successor.

Smallwood and Roberts had a relationship like that of master and
favoured apprentice almost from the day Roberts walked into the
premier's office and began putting order into the state of chaos that he
found there. Joey recognized brilliant political talent in the young
man, but there can be no doubt that he resented Roberts's superior
intellect and education, at least unconsciously. One of the limitations
often imposed by success is that its victims may glimpse their own
inadequacies, but never really confront them. So Joey went through
life remembering a baffling evening when he listened to Bertrand
Russell discussing symbolic logic, and never realized that some of the
men in his own Cabinets, or on his party's back benches, could have

followed Russell's arguments without difficulty. When he made contact with such a mind, Joey's subconscious impulse was to destroy it. This happened with Ted Russell, with Herb Pottle, and most notably and strikingly with the brilliant, humane young man who was for a while his anointed successor.

The first apparent rift in the relationship did not come until 1970, when the government of Canada offered Roberts the post of Newfoundland Regional director for the Department of Regional Economic Expansion. It was an important appointment, an opportunity to make a real difference to the future of the province. Roberts was still too young to consider the premiership seriously, he had a long political future ahead of him, and he was tempted by the offer. Smallwood apparently intervened to prevent the appointment; he wasn't going to have the feds looting his Cabinet for talent without his consent. What may have passed between Joey and Roberts at that time nobody ever said, but there was instant and obvious coolness in their dealings with each other. From that point Roberts was no longer heir apparent in Smallwood's own book, and he cast about on all sides for a substitute. With Roberts fallen from favour, he considered in turn John Crosbie, Andrew Crosbie, Don Jamieson, Richard Cashin, and when no one else seemed possible even Fred Rowe, despite his age.

But Roberts never had any doubts about his own fitness for the succession; he played it cool, made no hasty moves, and when the party was in dire straits in 1972, the leadership simply dropped into his lap, as he had always intended that it should.

What he inherited was a corporal's guard of seven colleagues, only one of whom, Bill Rowe, could be considered a true front-bencher. The Newfoundland Liberal Party had been decimated nearly completely. Such stalwarts as Ross Barbour and Harold Starkes—previously thought to be undefeatable in their pampered districts—had gone down to defeat in Bonavista South and Green Bay. Pat Canning, who had been elected in Placentia West for seven straight terms starting in 1949, was nosed out by a newcomer. Rupert Bartlett, a leading lawyer and a gifted debater, was defeated in Trinity South. Uriah Strickland, who had held one of the Trinity seats since the 1950s, was defeated in Trinity North.

Roberts faced a double task—to rebuild the party from the ground up, and to confront Moores successfully in the House of Assembly. Moores, as it happened, had the most powerful backing any Newfoundland premier had enjoyed in living memory: John Crosbie,

Gerald Ottenheimer, John Carter, Leo Barry, Thomas Farrell, Alex Hickman, Roy Cheesman, H. V. R. Earle, and Harold Collins (to mention a few) and the brash young newcomer, Brian Peckford. It is doubtful that any political leader had ever stood in the House of Assembly with such an array of talent behind him. And, as it turned out, he needed it; Moores was a better giant killer than a premier.

Roberts did well in difficult circumstances. His gifts for organization soon had the party not only functioning again, but champing at the bit, impatient for the next election. Joey, however, did not like Roberts's style in the House. He began to think that his former apprentice was a washout and perhaps even soft-on-Tories. Roberts launched none of the verbal thunderbolts that Joey himself would have hurled at Moores while the new premier busily nationalized the fish plant at Burgeo to bring the fishermen's strike to an end, nationalized the new paper mill at Stephenville, and got the Newfoundland government off the hook before the arrival of the impending disaster at the Come-by-Chance oil refinery. It was a strange spectacle indeed: Moores, the professed conservative and scion of merchants, nationalizing industries worth hundreds of millions of dollars. (Joey, the professed socialist, had never nationalized so much as a trucking service in his entire life.)

The salvaging of the Newfoundland treasury from the guarantees in the bankruptcy at Come-by-Chance must be regarded as Moores's (or perhaps Crosbie's) greatest contribution to Newfoundland. They saved the government millions by offering John Shaheen an even bigger deal than the one he had concluded with Joey. It was the kind of bait the American promoter couldn't refuse. The 100,000-barrel-a-day refinery just completed was all very well, but why stop there? Why not a second refinery, even bigger, to boost total production to 300,000 barrels a day?

Shaheen Natural Resources Inc. of New York was to do the building. The province agreed to lend Shaheen $78.5 million of the estimated cost of $308.5 million. Companies owned by Shaheen would invest $40 million, and $190 million would be borrowed, without government backing, through Britain's export credits. It looked so much like one of his own best deals that even Joey had to cheer. Moores was following in his footsteps as an economic developer. He issued a public statement congratulating the new premier and his colleagues for pressing forward with this great industrial development plan.

But there was a catch. As part of the deal (which, of course, soon collapsed), Shaheen's companies took over full responsibility for the financing of the first refinery. All government guarantees were withdrawn. And when the refinery went belly up in the biggest bankruptcy in the history of Canada up to that time, before it had even moved into full production, companies in Japan and Europe (its major creditors along with the Shaheen interests) were left holding the bag, not the Newfoundland treasury, as would certainly have happened had Joey won the election of 1971. The bankrupt refinery went into mothballs, and defied all efforts to get it going again for fifteen years. It finally resumed production on a modest scale under new owners in 1988, when it was sold to an American group for the sum of $1.

Meanwhile, Moores was in political trouble himself. It began to look suspiciously like another instance of a one-term Tory government (a common experience in both Newfoundland and Canada). Joey was now certain that he could defeat Moores in an election, given the chance, and he approached Roberts with a proposal. Roberts, he suggested, should resign the Liberal leadership and lead a "draught Joey" campaign. They would then go out and beat Moores in the election. Joey would become premier, and Roberts would become deputy-premier and attorney-general and Annointed Successor. A year or two after the election, when the political climate looked just right, Joey would resign in Roberts's favour, and Roberts would be able to go to the province as premier in the succeeding election. Roberts responded with an emphatic no. He wasn't having anything to do with a deal like that.

Joey then demanded a new leadership convention, in which the principal contenders would be himself and young Ed Roberts, and the party responded affirmatively. But, as it turned out, they were not the only contenders.

The convention was set for October 26, 1974, and turned into a vigorous contest between Roberts, who prepared his ground carefully, and Joey, who barged ahead with all his old flamboyance. When they addressed the seven-hundred-odd delegates in advance of the voting, both were confident of victory. The other two candidates, Steve Neary of Bell Island and Roger Simmons of Grand Falls, were scarcely in the race. On the first ballot the results of the vote were Roberts, 337; Smallwood, 298, Simmons, 57; and Neary, 24. Joey was still convinced he'd win by picking up all of Neary's and most of Simmons's votes. But the second ballot was decisive: Roberts, 403; Smallwood, 298; Simmons, 7. The old leader had been beaten by a wide margin.

Joey was flabbergasted by the result of the second vote. It had never occurred to him that he could lose. The defeat of his party in 1971 had left him in a fighting mood, determined to hang onto power by every conceivable trick. But the convention was an entirely different matter. This was only the second time in his life (the first was in 1932) that he had been personally defeated in any kind of election, and he took it very badly indeed. Although he professed to feel no resentment at being beaten by Roberts, his claim began to sound hollow a few weeks later when he set out to ruin Roberts's chances of winning the next election.

This was the point at which Roberts came fully of age. There was no question this time that the leadership had just dropped into his lap. And the Liberal Party, with a healthy instinct for survival, had done the politically sound thing by turning down Joey's bid for a comeback. The old man was attempting something at which no political leader had ever succeeded: not just a comeback from defeat (many others had managed that), but a comeback after defeat and resignation and replacement by a younger leader. Despite his charm, glamour and charisma, Joey was by now almost a museum piece, a man who had campaigned with Squires back in the days before the Great Depression, who thought of John Wesley as one of the founders of the modern world, and who thought of himself as a latter-day Wesley, leading his people to economic salvation. Joey had come out of the period of hot jazz, hot mammas, and hot politics. He looked upon the cool style of Roberts and Moores as pure incompetence, and was quite unable to understand that it appealed to the new generation that had "grown up under the Bomb, and the influence of Jack Kennedy."

Frank Moores was close to being the perfect "television man." A flop as an orator, stiff and awkward on a platform, he looked far better on the tube than he ever did in the flesh, and he discussed his policies in such an offhand way that he seemed to be thinking of something else. Indeed, he may have been, for if you were to believe his image, he was lazy by nature, a lover and a tippler who enjoyed a cocktail party far more than a party caucus. There was widespread speculation that he'd resign after his first term in office. In fact he didn't, possibly because Joey handed him such a tempting opportunity to run for a second term, but when he was still a political youngster of forty-eight, in office a mere seven years, he shucked off the party leadership like a winter coat at the coming of spring. He was the first Canadian premier to be divorced for infidelity while in office—indeed the suit was announced, though not actually tried, while he was running for election. To Joey's utter astonishment, the affair didn't seem to damage Moores's political image in the least.

Had the Liberal Party of Newfoundland believed that Joey could defeat Moores in the next election, they would have voted him back into the leadership, for the party machine was, above all, a machine for capturing and holding power and for sharing out the spoils of office. But they didn't believe it. They believed that Moores had to be challenged by a man of his own generation, who had learned something of the post-Kennedy style of politics.

But for a man of seventy-three, Joey was unbelievably young and vigorous. It was difficult for anyone who felt so young to accept the fact that his world had passed away with the Booming Fifties, that the world of Huey Long and Richard Squires was now ancient history. Joey never accepted that the change in society that took place in the sixties was fundamental. He fancied himself an economist, a social realist, who understood exactly what was going on in the world. But he understood it in terms of his own youth. He believed, for example, that he understood the Chinese Cultural Revolution, but he saw it from the standpoint of a Marxist of the 1920s. He believed that the wild-looking members of the New Left, waving their little red copies of the Sayings of Chairman Mao, were a bunch of lunatics—as perhaps they were, but lunatics of a breed far different from what Joey imagined.

Joey's bid to regain the leadership was perhaps the best thing that could have happened to Roberts. In terms of the Freudian myth of the Primal Horde, Roberts was now a leader who had "slain the father," head of the band of brothers, bigger than before, the only person who had ever beaten Smallwood face to face at a party convention. He seemed to be the unchallenged leader who was going to lead the anti-Moores forces into battle, and the Liberals back to the land of milk and honey.

And according to all the odds of the political game, Ed Roberts should have defeated the Moores government, and taken the premiership by 1976. He would have done it, except for just one thing: Joey Smallwood's opposition. It hadn't occurred to Roberts that Smallwood, rejected by the party, could still destroy him. But after his 1974 convention defeat, Joey apparently decided that if he did nothing else in life he was going to "get Roberts." If he had to tear the Liberal Party of Newfoundland to pieces in the process, well, too bad about it. The party, after all, had rejected him.

Rather than see Roberts do what he himself had failed to do, rather than watch the young pup go out and defeat that cool cat Moores, Joey decided to launch a new party, with the ancient and respectable name of the Liberal Reform Party (echoes of Squires!). His party would have little chance of capturing the government. But it would be sure to split the Liberal vote across the province badly enough to send Roberts down to defeat.

On Saturday, July 4, 1975, a group of 163 "dissident" Liberals met at the Knights of Columbus Hall in Gander to decide what they should do about the way the party was going under Roberts's leadership. The only member of the House of Assembly present was Steve Neary, but that old Smallwood supporter Joe Ashley was there, as was John Wiseman, a prominent labour leader and party officer, and several others who had been important Liberal supporters in the past.

When everything was ready, Joey came striding into the hall, took his place before the battery of microphones, and spoke for an hour and seven minutes, denouncing the party's "drift," and calling on his followers to "restore Liberalism to the Liberal Party." The dissidents applauded and cheered.

Then Wiseman presented a lengthy resolution, prepared in advance, professing no confidence in the party as now constituted, setting forth what he regarded as the principles of Liberalism, and pledging an all-out fight in the coming election, which Smallwood had predicted would come "very soon."

Finally, Wiseman nominated Joey Smallwood for leader of the new Liberal Reform Party, and he was elected by acclamation. The Liberal Reform Party pledged itself to run a full slate of candidates in the election. Political observers at the meeting were quoted in the newspapers as saying that if Moores had any sense he would call an election immediately, since the Liberal Reformers would have the effect of "giving the ruling Conservatives practically a free ride back into power." Joey realized this, of course, but he had still another trick up his sleeve. He wasn't especially interested in prolonging Moores's administration. What he wanted was to be premier once again.

By 1975 the Tories were in disarray. The economy was slumping. The brave new members of the Moores team had proved to be disappointing when it came to the art of district politics. Newfoundland was in the mood for yet another change of government. But

Moores's sense of timing was faultless, as it had been in 1972. He allowed the Liberal Reformers just enough time to get organized to the point where they would be certain to spoil Roberts's chances. Then he called the election for September 16, 1975. In fact, the Liberal Reformers did not run fifty-two candidates, as they had declared they would, but twenty-eight—enough to give them credibility, enough to form a majority government, had every one of them been returned. It was notable that they ran few candidates in safe Tory seats but a candidate in every district where they stood a chance of spoiling the vote for the official Liberal Party.

Then Joey played his last card. He once again sought out Roberts with a proposition: "Let's go to the country together," he suggested. "Let's not run against each other. We'll split the districts between us, and whoever comes back with the larger number of seats will be premier."

Again Roberts said no. "The plan, of course, was for Joey to pick the seats he wanted to contest," Roberts explains. "That way he'd get all the easy ones, and I'd be left with St. John's Centre and so on. I'd be fighting Moores wherever there was a tough fight, and there'd be no question about who'd end up with the government."

The New Democratic Party also ran 17 candidates in that election, but only in one or two St. John's districts did they attract enough votes to affect the outcome—notably in Pleasantville, where the PC candidate was elected by 46 percent of the votes cast, and the NDP ran second. In a subsequent by-election in St. John's West, which Crosbie vacated to enter federal politics, the Liberals nosed out the NDP by 41 votes, and the Tories ran third.

The Liberal Reform Party might not have been able to get off the ground at all except for the backing of expatriate John C. Doyle and the support of multimillionaire Geoff Stirling, Joey's old enemy from 1948 and now one of his closest friends and supporters. Stirling, a devotee of lost causes, spent money freely on any scheme that took his fancy. He built an enormous tree house in a banyan in India, for example, and took Joey there for a session of meditation. He embraced Yoga, not as a physical and mental discipline, but as a religion. He gave money to free schools and experimental music groups and many other enterprises. He took to Joey's new party with enthusiasm.

Stirling not only threw himself (and presumably his money) into the movement, but ran himself for election against Premier Moores in the district of Humber West. Moores won the seat by a little less than

50 percent of the votes cast, and Stirling collected slightly more than 28 percent. The Liberals and the New Democrats both made a poor showing.

The pictures published in the newspapers after the launching of the Liberal Reform Party show Joey looking just like the cat who has swallowed the canary. And the canary turned out to be Roberts. The Tories came back with thirty seats out of fifty-two—some of them by the slenderest of margins, and six of them by the grace of the Liberal Reformers. Smallwood's intervention had clearly cheated Roberts of his victory. Roberts took sixteen seats, the Liberal Reformers four. Steve Neary was elected as an Independent Liberal in LaPoile, where he had run for the party nomination, and lost it to a candidate whom he subsequently defeated by a vote of nearly three to one. In six districts the Liberal Reformers had split the party vote badly enough to elect Tories. Had they stayed out of it, Roberts would have returned twenty-seven members (including Neary) to the Tories' twenty-four, and might well have consolidated the party's position for another long stretch in office.

Following Roberts's defeat, the Liberals held yet another convention, and replaced Roberts with young William Rowe, a weaker leader, but one whom Joey could tolerate. The party was shattered, and remained in a state of chaos for more than a decade while the Tories romped through a series of successful elections, and Joey's descendants groped around for a leader who could help them find their way out of the wilderness.

Before long Rowe himself was replaced as party leader when it became obvious that he could not succeed against the resurgent Tories under their saucy new leader Brian Peckford, who—wouldn't you know it?—had started his political life as a Liberal in 1970.

Joey himself was returned for Twillingate in 1975, but said little in the House, and vacated his seat to make way for young Rowe, the last and briefest of his many heirs apparent. Joey's *real* heir turned out to be Brian Peckford, who scrambled into the Tory leadership with absolutely no help from the retiring Moores. Peckford was able to combine Smallwood's ambition and scrappiness with Moores's off-hand style, and to become, like Smallwood, an almost unbeatable political leader. But Peckford's best friends were the Liberals, who spent so much of their time at each other's throats that they practically shooed him into office one election after another.

As for Joey, this last venture into politics gave him one more chance to say farewell to public life in a blaze of publicity. On Wednesday, June 8, 1977, he sent a page to the Speaker of the House (his old enemy Gerald Ottenheimer) with his letter of resignation, and rose on a point of privilege to explain that he had spent twenty-five years in the House of Assembly and thought he had been "too long at the helm" to function well as an Opposition back-bencher. "I feel I'm just occupying the seat of someone who would be more useful," he said. He now intended to devote his full time to writing and editing the books that he had been promising to produce since his first "resignation" back in 1969.

But he wasn't *quite* through with public life. In the immediate future, before he got down to writing, he intended to campaign across the nation for national unity. He considered the future of Canada to be in peril and that "Newfoundland would suffer most grievously in consequence."

Frank Moores had been warned in advance of Joey's intentions, and he achieved in his tribute to the departing leader whom he had done so much to bring low one of his very few flights of oratory: Joey was "one of those rare individuals whose fires burn with the steady incandescence of a fixed and constant star." He noted that "the strongest lights cast the darkest shadows," so he expected there would remain those who still hated Mr. Smallwood, but "for just about a quarter of a century the people gave to Joe Smallwood their support, their affection, and their trust."

Opposition Leader Ed Roberts, who had the greatest reason of anyone in the House to resent Joey's final intrusion into public life, was more than magnanimous. He described Smallwood as "the greatest Newfoundlander of our time" and "the colossus of public life." "The history of our country in these last thirty years can be written in terms of his life alone," Roberts said. He denied that there had ever been any bitterness or malice between himself and Smallwood. "All of us in this House," he said, "will relate with pride that we served in the House of Assembly with him. Our boast will be that we knew him."

Many others, on both sides of the House, spoke in his praise. As Joey bowed to the Speaker and walked to the door they rose in their places to give him a standing ovation, thumping their desks as he walked away. It was his third and final resignation, the last, last, last hurrah. Once again he had done what he had set out to do. He had dislodged Roberts from the succession and was now vacating his seat in favour of William Rowe, his very last heir apparent.

CHAPTER 20

# *Music at the Close*

TRUE TO HIS PROMISE, JOEY CAMPAIGNED ACROSS CANADA IN 1977 AND 1978, trying to persuade English Canadians to accept French Canadians as equals and to accommodate Quebec's aspirations within the framework of Confederation. It was a time when it looked as if Quebec might try to secede from the union, and among fairly large numbers of English-speaking Canadians outside Ontario and Quebec, there was a feeling that we should "let them go and good riddance."

Joey set himself against this attitude. If Canada should ever break up, he told his audiences, the provinces that would suffer most would be those on the fringes, not just Ontario and Quebec, but the Atlantic Provinces and those in the West. According to his own reckoning, he spoke to meetings of one hundred and thirty-seven service clubs and other organizations in a tour that lasted twelve months. He also gave twenty-five press conferences, and appeared on thirty radio and television talk shows. His rambling book of memoirs, *I Chose Canada* ("written" mainly on a tape recorder and not always transcribed accurately by his stenographers) had appeared in 1973. This was his theme now: Canada was a country worth choosing, a country worthy of sacrifices, not an homogenous country, not a melting pot, but a union of many equals in which many national differences must be accommodated. And he should know. There was no greater "national difference" anywhere than in Newfoundland, the one province where

people still had to stop and think to remember that they were Canadians.

Everywhere he went he was acclaimed as "the only living father of
Confederation," whose mission now was to save the union. Did he
have any effect on the national unity debate? Who can say? Canada, at
any rate, didn't break up just then, and Joey went on to other things,
feeling that he had fulfilled his historic function as the last founding
father of his nation.

In his semi-retirement he spent part of his time, as he had planned,
in travel. The most ambitious of his trips was to China, a country he
had always hoped to visit, and one of the few he had failed to visit as
premier. All his life he had had a kind of unrequited love affair with
communism. It wasn't for the West, he had become convinced. But it
seemed to have done reasonably well in the Soviet Union, and he was
excited about the prospects of this new form of social and economic
organization in the Third World. He must go to China and then to
Cuba and see those experimental societies for himself.

As long ago as 1965, when he and Richard Nixon had been in
Moscow together, they had promised each other that the People's
Republic of China would be next on their list of countries to visit. But
it was some years before either of them got there.

Nixon returned to politics and became president of the United
States. The day after his inauguration, he invited Joey to breakfast in
the White House.

"I guess that trip to China is off now, isn't it?" Joey inquired when
they met. Nixon merely smiled enigmatically and talked about other
things. But some time later, watching TV in his Florida condominium, Joey saw news coverage of Nixon's departure from Washington
and his arrival in China to begin the *rapprochement* between the two
nations that had not been on speaking terms for a quarter of a century.
He at once began fishing around for a way of getting to China himself.

He discovered that a casual visit to Peking (as it was called in those
days) was not quite as simple as taking a side trip to Leningrad and
Moscow from Helsinki. He went off to London and got an introduction from the Canadian High Commissioner, Jake Warren, to the
Embassy of the People's Republic of China. Through Warren's
influence, he got his visa, which arrived by mail several weeks later.
Then he flew off to China, and sent a cable to Nixon in Washington:
"Greetings from Peking. You got here before me, but better late than
never. Your friend Joey Smallwood."

He was given the VIP tour by the Chinese: Canton, Hangchow, Shanghai, Nanking. He saw a confusing string of museums and art treasures. But that was not what interested him the most. In a chauffeur-driven limousine and with a translator, they visited three large communes, and Joey was impressed by the vast building projects that he saw going on. Some of them, he felt, were almost as impressive as the building of the pyramids, and, like the pyramids, were monuments to what could be accomplished by hand labour alone, for the Chinese still had little in the way of heavy machinery. He saw as many as 30,000 people working on a single project, and was told that others had employed as many as 50,000. The Chinese communes, he concluded, might well be the model for the future development of India, Southeast Asia, Africa, the West Indies, and Latin America.

He was astonished by the irrigation and flood control programmes that had been completed, and marvelled at vast public works undertaken by peasants without capital using picks and shovels. All that was needed to transform a backward society, it seemed, was the will to do it, limitless labour and enthusiasm, and skillful organization. He couldn't help contrasting the Chinese achievement with the hundreds of millions of dollars that had been poured into the modest public works of his own province.

He visited one of the numerous Children's Palaces where school kids spent their free time learning athletic skills, fine arts and crafts, chess, creative writing, and the performance of both traditional and western music. He was also impressed by the Chinese revival of such ancient skills as carving in ivory and jade, an almost-forgotten industry that now once again employed tens of thousands of young people producing hand-crafted art objects for export.

Joey travelled some five thousand miles in China, and was everywhere struck by the optimism and cheerfulness of the people—people he saw by the hundreds of thousands on the communes and in the squares of some of the world's largest cities. This was the way it ought to be in Third World countries! Talk of emerging societies! He was well-nigh overwhelmed by the communist genius for organization and social reform: "No unemployment, no crime, no prostitution, no drug addiction, no alcoholism!" he marvelled. He couldn't vouch for all this from personal experience, of course, but that's what he was told, and from what he saw he could well believe it.

On his return he was interviewed extensively by the press. The papers quoted him widely as saying that China was a "paradise." But this, he insisted, was a misunderstanding. He had indeed used the word "paradise," but had not applied it to the whole country, just to one commune where the people were obviously prosperous and happy in the midst of a vast production of foodstuffs, including apples, oranges, peaches, watermelons, wheat, corn, rice, and numerous other crops, on irrigated land that had once been regarded as worthless.

His one regret on his three-week China visit was that he failed to meet Chairman Mao. After his meeting with Churchill, he had become a "collector" of world leaders, listing seventeen of them, along with other celebrities, in his memoirs—and he was most anxious to add Mao Tse-tung to the list. But he had to be content with Mao's highly political wife Chiang Ching, and the charming Premier Chou En-lai, who was so widely liked among western politicians.

Joey was determined to repair this failure on his later visit to Cuba. Fidel Castro, after all, was famous for his accessibility. On one occasion Castro had even helped to push a stranger's car out of a snowbank in Gander, Newfoundland. So Joey flew off to Havana, accompanied by Geoff Stirling and filmmaker Michael Rubbo, with a promise that Castro would, indeed, receive them.

Sure enough, they got the full official treatment. They were housed in Protocol Residence Number Nine, identified as a house that had been owned by an American textile tycoon in the evil days when Cuba was an American economic colony. They visited all the official showplaces: schools, clinics, hospitals, housing projects. Here social-ism was doing all the things that Joey had imagined it should— providing people of the Third World with the needs of life and the opportunity for collective betterment. Now that he was no longer a bourgeois politician, he could afford to become a socialist once again, or a Third World socialist at any rate. No one had guessed, he lamented, how socialism could succeed in the Third World. Every theorist had assumed that you must first have a great accumulation of capital, the infrastructure that was called "the means of production." They should, he said, have gone back to Abraham Lincoln, who realized that labour itself was capital, a truth rediscovered by Chair-man Mao and his disciple Fidel.

But in the end, Cuba was a disappointment. Castro was busier than expected, his time pre-empted by a delegation from the German Democratic Republic. Instead of spending half a day with his Newfoundland visitors chatting about revolutionary accomplishments and answering the dozens of questions they had written down for him,

Fidel was only able to spare Joey a minute for a hug and a handshake at a diplomatic reception.

The one who did best out of the trip was the filmmaker Rubbo, who shot many hours of Cuban footage, and put the best of it together in a slyly humorous film, *Waiting for Fidel*. The film, which showed Stirling and Smallwood in a less than flattering light, nevertheless ran *in extenso* as a late-night special on Stirling's television stations.

Joey's major activity during the late years of his life was not so much writing as publishing. The writing that he did was hasty and careless, most of it, like the memoirs, not truly written at all, but recorded on tape and transcribed with little or no editing. The publishing company that he had founded back in 1967, at first mainly for propaganda purposes, turned out a string of books with such titles as *No Apology from Me*, *The Time Has Come to Tell*, and—most ambitious of the early titles—*The Face of Newfoundland*, a coffee-table book with no text, but hundreds of mug shots in colour, the one obvious omission from the gallery being John Crosbie.

At the age of eighty Joey was still working full-time as editor and publisher, and had eight employees working at his publishing house on Portugal Cove Road in St. John's. It was there that I saw him and talked with him for the last time, and though we had been political enemies for many years, he gave me almost a full day of his time, and talked with absolute candour about his successes and failures in public life.

Now that Joey was safely out of politics, Greg Power renewed his friendship with his former leader, and became perhaps the closest companion of Smallwood's old age. Power would drop into the office, and they would sometimes spend half a day together, reminiscing about the battles of the past, Power sometimes reading poetry while Joey sipped sherry.

The friendship continued after Joey's final retirement, when Power would make frequent visits to the former premier's home on Roache's Line to spend afternoons and evenings reminiscing about their travels together, and about the often ridiculous events of their years in politics. When Jesperson Press, in 1988, decided to publish a collection of Power's miscellaneous writings, mostly from *The Confederate*, and the St. John's daily press, Power agreed to eliminate from the corpus the pieces about the King of Cost-Plus, and the other anti-Smallwood satire that he had published in the sixties.

Joey had now abandoned the idea of writing a great Newfoundland history, and conceived an even grander plan: a five-volume *Encyclopedia of Newfoundland and Labrador*, running to some five thousand quarto pages. Newfoundland would be the first Canadian province with its own encyclopedia.

With the *Encyclopedia* Joey had returned to his first love—to glorifying Newfoundland, to making that small and wonderful nation better known to itself. It was *The Barrelman* on a far grander scale, a far more mature plan. As it turned out, it was a work he would never complete, a work that would have to be finished by others, but for him it was a kind of completion, just the same. There was a terrible purity in this last public action, in his willingness, at the end, not to accept the comforts of honours and adulation, but to expend himself to the limit, to sacrifice everything: not only his worldly wealth, of which he had accumulated a modest bit, but even his dignity, such as it was, to this all-important task. He was prepared to do anything, to turn himself into a door-to-door salesman, to act the clown, to play the fool in front of the TV cameras, in order to make the *Encyclopedia* succeed. And in the end the task was beyond him.

During a visit to India, Joey had been told by a Tibetan priest that he was going to live to be a hundred. He believed it, and acted on it, but his fortunate heredity didn't reach quite that far. He came from a long-lived family, but not a family of centenarians. The average lifespan of his long-lived ancestors was eighty-six, so Joey, with luck, might expect to remain in good health until he was eighty-five or ninety, but hardly longer. None of his direct ancestors had lived past the age of ninety-one. As it turned out, he made it to the age of eighty-three before his legendary good health broke down. And for a man whose only exercise was riding on a lawnmower that was remarkable enough.

Publishing the *Encyclopedia* all at once was out of the question: it would take at least five years, and cost perhaps a million dollars. The plan was to issue it one volume at a time, and sell it—from door to door if necessary—financing each succeeding volume out of the sales of the previous one.

Newfoundland Publishers (1967) Limited hired eighteen researchers and writers to carry out the monumental task, and invited contributions from some twenty other experts in such fields as science, medicine, and education. More than a thousand other people were given credit as consultants.

In addition to the text, each volume contained more than a

thousand line and half-tone cuts, coloured frontispieces and endpapers. The first volume appeared in 1981, financed in part by 115 pages of advertising, much of it from firms that had every reason to be grateful to the former premier: BRINCO, Canadian Javelin, Lundrigan's, Bowaters, The Iron Ore Company of Canada, the Electric Reduction Company, and scores of others.

From the start it was obvious that the *Encyclopedia* would be an important reference book for journalists, historians, biographers, teachers, and others in the information business, but it had little appeal to the general public, so there was a grave danger that it would be a financial disaster. To sell volume one, Joey, in his eighty-second year, took to the road with his trusty microphone and PA system and a vanfull of books. And once again he stood in front of the TV cameras to do a singing commercial. Anything at all to sell a few extra copies.

The year Joey enjoyed the triumph of seeing volume one of his *Encyclopedia* off the press, he was also the subject of the national stage hit *Joey*, written and produced by the Rising Tide Theatre of St. John's, with the help of a professional playwright. After a successful tour across Canada, a ninety-minute version of the production was shown on CBC television.

The play portrayed Joey as a half-comic, half-tragic figure—a tinpot dictator who destroyed all his friends as well as his enemies, a figure that might well have been played by Charlie Chaplin. Joey saw the play many times, and professed to enjoy it to the full. "It's fun," he commented, "but no history lesson," which was the strict truth. It did him far less than justice. One public man who saw the play with him in Toronto commented afterwards: "He must have a hide like a rhinoceros."

Interviewed on October 2, 1983, he revealed that the *Encyclopedia*, up to that point, had cost half a million dollars in salaries for research and editing. Volume two was now ready for the press, he said, but he didn't have the money to pay the printer.

On April 25, 1984, he announced that the Government of Canada had agreed to purchase 650 sets of the work for Newfoundland schools as an act to commemorate Newfoundland's confederation with Canada. Volumes one and two went to all the schools in the province. The value of the sale was $65,000, but it was anticipated that later volumes would be included, for a total of $162,500.

But the total sum was still not nearly enough. So he had to turn to wealthy friends, and the book contains acknowledgements to more than a dozen of them, including two patrons from mainland Canada. Even that funding was not enough. So he mailed a personal appeal to everyone who had purchased volume one, urging them to buy volume two in advance. Advance sales would be vital, he explained, to keep the project afloat. When the book appeared in 1984 he autographed all the presold copies and sent a letter with each shipped copy, stating that the book could not have been printed and bound without the help of the people who had bought copies in advance.

Still it wasn't enough. The *Encyclopedia* was deeply in debt. Nevertheless, production would probably have staggered forward to volume three by the autumn of 1987 had Joey's health and strength held out that long. Unfortunately, they didn't.

On September 24, 1984, he suffered a cerebral haemorrhage, a debilitating stroke that robbed him of his power of speech, and even of the power to read and write. He was rushed to the Health Sciences Complex at Memorial University, where he slowly regained some of his strength. He fought back, taking speech therapy, but the damage was irreparable. After his release from hospital he could take walks around the ranch and even go shopping, but five years later he was still unable to read, write, or make himself understood. He spent his days listening to the radio or watching TV.

A year and four months after the stroke he was hit by financial disaster. In January 1986 Cairn Capital Limited of Lindsay, Ontario, served him with a writ on behalf of John Deyell Company of the same town, printers and binders of the *Encyclopedia*, seeking $176,161 in unpaid publishing bills. Later that month his son, lawyer William Smallwood, used his house in St. John's as collateral to pay the company $90,000 in satisfaction of the debt.

Joey had made great efforts to keep the project afloat. He had not only signed over the copyright of the *Encyclopedia* itself to the printer as security for the printing bills, but had mortgaged the copyright of *everything he had ever written*.

But even that was not enough. To raise cash for the project he finally made an agonizing decision. He called a dealer in Montreal and offered to sell the most valuable items from his collection of Newfoundland books. The dealer flew down to St. John's, and they struck a bargain. Joey got $16,000 for his four rarest volumes, which included mint first editions of Vaughan's *Golden Fleece*, and Whitbourne's *Discourse and Discovery of the New Found Land*.

Ed Roberts, who didn't know that Smallwood had sold the books himself, bought just one book, Vaughan's *Golden Fleece*, from the dealer for $15,000. He recognized the binding as Smallwood's, and demanded an assurance that the book hadn't been stolen. The dealer gave him a signed statement to this effect, but didn't say how the books had come on the market.

Nothing that Joey could do himself was enough to save the *Encyclopedia*, but by 1988 the future of the project seemed to be virtually assured just the same. A new charitable institution, the Joseph R. Smallwood Heritage Foundation, had been organized to finance and publish the remaining volumes, and the money to do so was coming in.

The Foundation was managed by Dale Russell Fitzpatrick, Joey's capable granddaughter, under the patronage of the lieutenant-governor, with Gordon Pinsent as honorary chairman, Campbell Eaton as chairman, and a board of directors that included professional historians, members of the *nouveau riche* reputed to be in command of billions of dollars, and lawyers and chartered accountants thoroughly familiar with fund-raising.

The campaign was kicked off in September 1988 by entertainer Tommy Hunter, to start an effort by the Foundation to raise $2.5 million to complete the *Encyclopedia* and to help fund the Smallwood Institute of Newfoundland Studies at Memorial University. The Institute was also the beneficiary of Joey's enormous collection of Newfoundland books and documents, the most complete collection of its kind ever put together.

Tommy Hunter and Eddie Eastman were the stars at a benefit concert in the Arts and Culture Centre at St. John's, the proceeds going to the Foundation. Approximately a quarter of a million dollars had been collected or pledged by the time the fund was officially launched. The Foundation hoped to complete its funding in less than a year.

Meanwhile, though he continued to appear in public on special occasions such as the launching of the Foundation, Joey's health was in a precarious state. On January 6, 1985, he suffered the first of a number of bouts of pneumonia, and was hospitalized at the Medical Arts Centre. Apart from the stroke, two and a half months earlier, this was almost the first time in his life that he'd been sick. He had been in bed with influenza once or twice in his middle years, but just for two or three days. He had undergone one minor operation, for a detached retina of the eye, at Toronto on November 30, 1967. The pneumonia responded quickly to treatment. He was pronounced out of danger within two days, and was home by the end of the week. But he was now a frail old man, obviously no longer in health.

Friday, December 11, 1986. It was thirty-eight years to the day since Joey had signed the terms of union between Newfoundland and Canada. Only one other signatory to the terms was still living— Gordon Winter of St. John's. That day Winter was at Government House in St. John's with other invited guests to see Joey invested as a Companion of the Order of Canada by Lieutenant-Governor James McGrath, long-time Tory MP for St. John's East. The "little fellow from Gambo" was too frail to travel to Ottawa for the usual investiture by the governor general.

Four generations of Smallwoods watched the ceremony, including Joey's twelve-year-old great-grandson, Joey Smallwood III, decked out in white tie for the occasion.

Three weeks later, Joey went back to hospital with another bout of pneumonia. Again he bounced back, and was home within a few days. Life was wafer-thin, but Joey was hanging on there. Almost two years after this illness he was once again photographed at Government House for the launching of the fund-raising campaign by the Foundation. He still loved to relax and hear Power spin his yarns about the great days in the forties and fifties when they fought the good fight for Newfoundland and travelled the world together.

On March 31, 1989, he appeared at a banquet in his wife's home town, Carbonear, celebrating the fortieth anniversary of Newfoundland's entry into Confederation. Later that spring he went out to vote for the Liberals in their first successful election in Newfoundland since 1966.

Except for the last great adventure, Joey's travels were over. He would leave life the way he had left office—not in any sudden and dramatic fashion, but so slowly and reluctantly that you could hardly see when it happened.

# Appendix A

## Summary of election results

The first referendum, June 3, 1948:
Commission of Government . . . . . . . . . . . . . . . . . . . . . . . . . . . . . 22,311 (14.322%)
Confederation with Canada . . . . . . . . . . . . . . . . . . . . . . . . . 64,066 (41.127%)
Responsible Government . . . . . . . . . . . . . . . . . . . . . . . . . . . . . 69,400 (44.551%)

The second referendum, July 22, 1948:
Confederation with Canada . . . . . . . . . . . . . . . . . . . . . . . . . . . 78,323 (52.335%)
Responsible Government . . . . . . . . . . . . . . . . . . . . . . . . . . . . . 71,334(47.665%)

General Election, May 27, 1949:
Liberal . . . . . . . . . . . . . . . . . . . . . . . . . . . . . . . . . . . . . . . . . . . . . 22
Progressive Conservative . . . . . . . . . . . . . . . . . . . . . . . . . . . . . . . 5
Independent . . . . . . . . . . . . . . . . . . . . . . . . . . . . . . . . . . . . . . . . . 1

General Election, November 26, 1951:
Liberal . . . . . . . . . . . . . . . . . . . . . . . . . . . . . . . . . . . . . . . . . . . . 23
Progressive Conservative . . . . . . . . . . . . . . . . . . . . . . . . . . . . . . . 5

General Election, October 2, 1956:
Liberal . . . . . . . . . . . . . . . . . . . . . . . . . . . . . . . . . . . . . . . . . . . . 32
Progressive Conservative . . . . . . . . . . . . . . . . . . . . . . . . . . . . . . . 4

General Election, August 29, 1959:
Liberal . . . . . . . . . . . . . . . . . . . . . . . . . . . . . . . . . . . . . . . . . . . . 31
Progressive Conservative . . . . . . . . . . . . . . . . . . . . . . . . . . . . . . . 3
United Newfoundland Party . . . . . . . . . . . . . . . . . . . . . . . . . . . . . 2

General Election, November 19, 1962:
Liberal . . . . . . . . . . . . . . . . . . . . . . . . . . . . . . . . . . . . . . . . . . . . 34
Progressive Conservative . . . . . . . . . . . . . . . . . . . . . . . . . . . . . . . 7
Independent . . . . . . . . . . . . . . . . . . . . . . . . . . . . . . . . . . . . . . . . . 1

General Election, September 8, 1966:
Liberal . . . . . . . . . . . . . . . . . . . . . . . . . . . . . . . . . . . . . . . . . . . . . . .39
Progressive Conservative . . . . . . . . . . . . . . . . . . . . . . . . . . . . . . . . . .3

General Election, October 28, 1971:
Progressive Conservative . . . . . . . . . . . . . . . . . . . . . . . . . . . . . . . . . .21
Liberal . . . . . . . . . . . . . . . . . . . . . . . . . . . . . . . . . . . . . . . . . . . . . . . . .20
New Labrador Party . . . . . . . . . . . . . . . . . . . . . . . . . . . . . . . . . . . . . .1

General Election, March 24, 1972:
Progressive Conservative . . . . . . . . . . . . . . . . . . . . . . . . . . . . . . . . . .33
Liberal . . . . . . . . . . . . . . . . . . . . . . . . . . . . . . . . . . . . . . . . . . . . . . . . .8
New Labrador Party . . . . . . . . . . . . . . . . . . . . . . . . . . . . . . . . . . . . . .1

General Election, September 16, 1975:
Progressive Conservative . . . . . . . . . . . . . . . . . . . . . . . . . . . . . . . . . .30
Liberal . . . . . . . . . . . . . . . . . . . . . . . . . . . . . . . . . . . . . . . . . . . . . . . . .16
Independent Liberal . . . . . . . . . . . . . . . . . . . . . . . . . . . . . . . . . . . . . .1
Liberal Reform . . . . . . . . . . . . . . . . . . . . . . . . . . . . . . . . . . . . . . . . . .4

# Appendix B

## Members of the National Convention, 1946-48

Wilfrid Dawe, Bay Roberts
D.I. Jackman, Bell Island
J.R. Smallwood, Bonavista Centre*
F. Gordon Bradley, Bonavista East*
Samuel Vincent, Bonavista North*
Ken Brown, Bonavista South
Percy Figary, Burgeo*
E.P. Reddy, Burin East
Daniel Hillier, Burin West*
Albert Penney, Carbonear
Albert Goodridge, Ferryland
Alfred Watton, Fogo
William J. Banfield, Fortune Bay*
Malcolm Hollett, Grand Falls
Malcolm McDonald, Grand Falls*
Roland Starkes, Green Bay*
Colin Jones, Harbour Grace
Thomas Kennedy, Harbour Main
J.A. Hannon, Harbour Main
John T. Spencer, Hermitage*
Pierce Fudge, Humber
Charles Ballam, Humber*
Lester Burry, Labrador*
Archibald Northcott, Lewisporte
Leonard Miller, Placentia East
Dennis Ryan, Placentia West
Michael McCarthy, Port au Port*
Joseph Fowler, Port de Grave

Edgar Roberts, St. Barbe*
W.J. Keough, St. George's*
Gordon Higgins, St. John's East
Edgar Hickman, St. John's East
R.B. Job, St. John's East
Frank Fogwill, St. John's East Extern
Ches Crosbie, St. John's West
Peter J. Cashin, St. John's West
Michael Harrington, St. John's West
Bert Butt, St. John's West Extern
John J. MacCormack, St. Mary's
E.C. Crawford, Trinity Centre
Reuben Vardy, Trinity North
Charles Bailey, Trinity South
T.G.W. Ashbourne, Twillingate*
Isaac Newell, White Bay*

---

*These voted to have confederation with Canada placed on the ballot paper in the referendum.

333

# Appendix C

## Members of the House of Assembly from Smallwood's first election in 1949 until his defeat in 1971

Party affiliations: L—Liberal; IL—Independent Liberal; PC—Progressive Conservative; CCF—Co-operative Commonwealth Federation; UNP—United Newfoundland Party; NLP—New Labrador Party; I—Independent.

Joseph R. Smallwood L
Edward Russell L, CCF
Herman W. Quinton L
Philip S. Forsey L
Herbert L. Pottle L
Peter J. Cashin I, PC
Gordon Janes L
John R. Courage L
Edward Spencer L
A. Baxter Morgan L
James R. Chalker L
D.I. Jackman PC
R.J. Fahey PC
Charles Ballam L
Harold Horwood L
Leonard J. Miller PC
Patrick J. Canning L
George T. Makinson L
Reginald Sparkes L
W.J. Keough L
John G. Higgins PC
Frank Fogwill PC

Oliver L. Vardy L
James J. Spratt L
C. Max Button L
Leslie R. Curtis L
Samuel Drover L, CCF
Clyde Brown L
George M. Norman L
Augustine M. Duffy PC, UNP
Philip J. Lewis L
Frederick W. Rowe L
Gregory J. Power L
Isaac Mercer L
James D. Higgins PC, UNP
Myles Murray L
Joseph P. O'Driscoll L
Uriah F. Strickland L
John T. Cheeseman L
Eric S. Jones L
George W. Clark L
Beaton J. Abbott L, IL
William R. Smallwood L
Claude A. Sheppard L

Matthew P. Whalen L
John A. Forsey L
Earl W. Winsor L
George Sellars L
Stephen K. Smith L
Llewellyn Strange L
George M. Nightingale L
William J. Browne PC
James M. McGrath L
Malcolm M. Hollett PC
Arthur S. Mifflin L
Richard J. Greene PC
Ross Barbour L
Raymond W. Guy L
Albert E. Fury PC
G. Alain Frecker L
James J. Greene PC
John R. O'Dea, UNP
William P. Saunders L
Stephen A. Neary L, IL
Walter H. Hodder L
H.V.R. Earle L, PC
Ambrose Peddle PC
Clifton W. Joy L
Noel Murphy PC, L
Gerald Hill L
Charles S. Devine I
Harold Starkes L
Eric N. Dawe L
William Smith PC
Anthony J. Murphy PC
Geoffrey C. Carnell L
G. Rex Renouf PC
William G. Adams L
Walter Carter L
T. Alexander Hickman L, PC
Aiden J. Maloney L
Charles H. Granger L
Alexander D. Moores L
John W. Mahoney L
Abel C. Wornell L
Clyde Wells, L, IL
Thomas W. Burgess L, I, NLP, PC, L
William R. Callahan L
Gerald Myrdon L, IL
Anthony J. Murphy PC

Gerald Ottenheimer PC
Thomas V. Hickey PC
Nathaniel S. Noel L
John A. Nolan L
John C. Crosbie L, IL, PC
C. Maxwell Lane L
Edward Roberts L
William N. Rowe L
Harold A. Collins PC
William Marshall PC
Paul S. Thoms L
Allan Evans PC
Augustus T. Rowe PC
Augustus Oldford L
Aubrey Senior PC
Hubert Kitchen L
Gordon Dawe PC
William Doody PC
Harold Piercy L
Thomas C. Farrell PC
Frank Moores PC
Melvin Woodward L
Josiah Harvey L
M. James Russell PC
Frederick R. Stagg PC
James R. Hussey L
Edward Maynard PC
Alexander Dunphy PC
John Carter PC
Hugh Shea PC, L
Rupert Bartlett L

# Selected Bibliography

Ammon, Charles George. *Newfoundland, the Forgotten Island*. London: Victor Gollancz, 1944.

Baker, Melvin; Cuff, Robert, and Gillespie, Bill. *Workingmen's St. John's*. St. John's: Cuff, 1982.

Campbell, Colin. *Canadian Political Facts, 1945-1976*. Toronto: Methuen, 1977

Cashin, Peter. *My Life and Times*. St. John's: Breakwater, 1976.

Chadwick, St. John. *Newfoundland—Island into Province*. Cambridge University Press, 1967

Coaker, W.F. (editor) *Twenty Years of the Fishermen's Protective Union of Newfoundland*. St. John's: Creative Printers and Publishers, 1984.

Gillespie, Bill. *A Class Act. An Illustrated History of the Labour Movement in Newfoundland and Labrador*. St. John's: The Newfoundland and Labrador Federation of Labour, 1986.

Gwyn, Richard. *Smallwood, the Unlikely Revolutionary*. Toronto: McClelland and Stewart, 1968, 1974.

Harrington, Michael. *The Prime Ministers of Newfoundland*. St. John's: The Evening Telegram, 1962.

Hibbs, R. *Who's Who in and from Newfoundland*. St. John: Dicks and Co., 1927, 1930, 1937.

Hillier, James K., and Neary, Peter. (editors) *Newfoundland in the Nineteenth and Twentieth Centuries; Essays in Interpretation*. University of Toronto Press, 1980.

Horwood, Harold. *Newfoundland*. Toronto: Macmillan, 1969, 1977.

————. *Bartlett, the Great Explorer*. Toronto: Doubleday, 1977, 1978.

————. *Corner Brook, The Social History of a Paper Town*. St. John's: Breakwater, 1986.

————. *A History of the Newfoundland Ranger Force*. St. John's: Breakwater, 1986.

Iverson, N. and Matthews, R. *Communities in Decline*. St. John's: Memorial University of Newfoundland, 1968.

Lodge, Thomas. *Dictatorship in Newfoundland*. London: Cassell, 1939.

McAllister, R.I. (editor) *The First Fifteen Years of Confederation*. St. John's: Dicks and Co., 1965.

McDonald, Gordon. *Newfoundland at the Crossroads*. Toronto: Ryerson, 1949.

MacKay, R.A. (editor) *Newfoundland: economic, diplomatic and strategic studies*. Toronto: Oxford University Press, 1946.

O'Neill, Paul. *The Oldest City*. Erin, Ont.: Presse Porcépic, 1975.

————. *A Seaport Legacy*. Erin, Ont.: Presse Porcépic, 1976.

Parsons, Bill, with Bowman, Bill. *The Challenge of the Atlantic*. St. John's: Robinson-Blackmore, 1983.

Pearson, L.B. *Mike: The Memoirs of the Right Honourable Lester B. Pearson*. 3 vols. Toronto University Press, 1971-75.

Peckford, A. Brian. *The Past in the Present*. St. John's: Cuff, 1983.

Perlin, A.B. *The Story of Newfoundland*. St. John's: private publication, 1959.

Pickersgill, J.W. *My Years with Louis St. Laurent*. University of Toronto Press, 1975.

Pickersgill, J. W., and D.M. Forster. *The Mackenzie King Record*. 4 vols. Toronto, 1960-70.

Pottle, Herbert L. *Newfoundland Dawn Without Light*. St. John's: Breakwater, 1979.

Prowse, D.W. *A History of Newfoundland*. London, Macmillan, 1895.

Rawlyk, G.A. (editor) *The Atlantic Provinces and the Problems of Confederation*. St. John's: Breakwater, 1979.

Reeves, John. *Report and Documents Relating to Union of Newfoundland with Canada*. Ottawa: Department of External Affairs, 1949.

Rowe, Frederick W. *A History of Newfoundland and Labrador*. Toronto: McGraw-Hill Ryerson, 1980.

———. *The Smallwood Era*. Toronto: McGraw-Hill Ryerson, 1985.

Simeon, Richard. *Federal-Provincial Diplomacy*. University of Toronto Press, 1972.

Smallwood, Joseph R. *Coaker of Newfoundland*. London: Labour Publishing Co., 1927.

———. *The New Newfoundland*. New York: Macmillan, 1931.

———. *Surrogate Robert Carter*. St. John's: privately published, 1936.

———. (ed.) *The Book of Newfoundland*. 6 vols. St. John's: Newfoundland Book Publishers, 1937, 1967, 1975.

———. *Newfoundland Handbook and Gazetteer, 1940 and 1941*. St. John's: Long Bros., 1941.

———. *To You With Affection From Joey*. St. John's: privately published, 1969.

———. *I Chose Canada*. Toronto: Macmillan, 1973.

———. *Newfoundland Miscellany*. St. John's: Newfoundland Book Publishers, 1978.

———. *Dr. William Carson*. St. John's: Newfoundland Book Publishers, 1978.

———. *No Apology from Me*. St. John's: Newfoundland Book Publishers, 1979.

———. *The Time Has Come To Tell*. St. John's: Newfoundland Book Publishers, 1980.

———. (ed.) *The Encyclopedia of Newfoundland and Labrador*. 2 vols. (3 vols. as yet unpublished.) St. John's: Newfoundland Book Publishers, 1981, 1984.

Smith, Philip. *Brinco. The Story of Churchill Falls*. Toronto: McClelland and Stewart, 1975.

Thoms, James R. *Newfoundland and Labrador Who's Who*. St. John's: Boone Advertising, 1968.

———. *Who's Who Silver Anniversary Edition*. St. John's: Public Relations Consultants Limited, 1975.

Walsh, Bren. *More Than A Poor Majority*. St. John's: Breakwater, 1985.

Wilson, Harold F. *The Newfoundland Fishery Dispute*. St. John's: S.E. Garland, 1904.

# Index